Jurists: Profiles in Legal Theory

General Editor:
William Twining

'The field of evidence is no other than the field of knowledge.'

Bentham, *An Introductory View*, chapter 1

'Evidence is the basis of justice: exclude evidence, you exclude justice.'

Bentham, *Rationale of Judicial Evidence*, Part III, chapter 1

' "Have you ever given any attention to the Science of Evidence?" said Mr Grodman.

"How do you mean?" asked the Home Secretary, rather puzzled, but with a melancholy smile. "I should hardly speak of it as a science; I look at it as a question of common sense."

"Pardon me, sir. It is the most subtle and difficult of all the sciences. It is indeed rather the science of the sciences. What is the whole of inductive logic, as laid down (say) by Bacon and Mill, but an attempt to appraise the value of evidence, the said evidence being the trails left by the Creator, so to speak? The Creator has (I say it in all reverence) drawn a myriad red herrings across the track. But the true scientist refuses to be baffled by superficial appearances in detecting the secrets of Nature".'

Israel Zangwill, *The Big Bow Mystery*
(cited by Wigmore as the frontispiece of
The Principles of Judicial Proof)

THEORIES OF EVIDENCE: BENTHAM AND WIGMORE

William Twining
Quain Professor of Jurisprudence,
University College, London

WEIDENFELD & NICOLSON
LONDON

To Karen

© 1985 William Twining
All rights reserved. No part of this
publication may be reproduced, stored in
a retrieval system, or transmitted, in
any form or by any means, electronic,
mechanical, photocopying, recording or
otherwise, without the prior permission
of the Copyright owner.

George Weidenfeld and Nicolson
91 Clapham High Street, London SW4 7TA

ISBN 0 297 78668 7 cased
ISBN 0 297 78669 5 paperback

Typeset by Deltatype, Ellesmere Port
Printed by Butler & Tanner Ltd
Frome and London

Contents

Introduction	vii
1 The Rationalist Tradition of evidence scholarship	1

2 Bentham on evidence
(i)	Introduction	19
(ii)	An outline of the *Rationale of Judicial Evidence*	27
(iii)	Selected themes in Bentham's theory of evidence	
	(a) The natural system	47
	(b) Evaluation of evidence	52
	(c) The anti-nomian thesis	66
	(d) The causes of the technical system	75
	(e) Rectitude of decision as a value	88
(iv)	Aftermath: *The Edinburgh Review*	100

3 Wigmore on proof
(i)	Old Northwestern	109
(ii)	Bentham and Wigmore	114
(iii)	The genesis and conception of *The Principles of Judicial Proof*	119
(iv)	Analytical dimensions of proof	125
(v)	Psychology and forensic science	135
(vi)	General experience	142
(vii)	The Science of Proof and the Rules of Evidence	151
(viii)	The lead balloon	164

4 The contemporary significance of Bentham and Wigmore	167
Appendix Wigmore's method: a personal evaluation	179
Acknowledgements	187
Notes	188
Abbreviations	188
Biographical Note	189
Bibliography	244
Index	257

Introduction

Jurisprudence is the theoretical part of law as a discipline. It addresses diverse questions at different levels. It is hardly surprising that jurisprudence and jurists should normally be perceived as being concerned with the most fundamental questions about law as a whole, such as questions about the nature of law and state, connections between law and morals, and the problem of justice. These questions are important, but they represent only one sector of the whole range of theoretical issues underlying the study of law. This book deals with a different sector: theories of evidence and proof in adjudication and litigation. This is a rich and complex area, which also addresses a wide range of questions at a variety of levels such as: what is involved in 'proving' the truth of allegations of fact? to what extent is adjudication primarily concerned with the discovery of truth? what kinds of institutions and procedures are best designed to promote such discoveries? how far can and do rules of evidence further this or other ends? is the Anglo-American approach to fact-finding rational? what kinds of reasoning and rationality are involved? what is meant by 'truth' and 'rationality' in this context?

This particular study grew out of somewhat broader concerns. Within the discipline of law there is one approach which is sometimes expressed in terms of an aspiration 'to broaden the study of law from within', that is to say to redefine the scope and methods of academic law, as the discipline mainly located in schools and faculties of law. While there has been some preliminary theorizing about this approach at a general level, most of the work has been done in relation to particular areas of legal study: sometimes this has involved developing a broader approach to an already established field (for example the work of Eekelaar on Law and the Family), sometimes it has required the adoption of a new organizing category (for example, Atiyah's substitution of Compensation for Accidents for the traditional category of Torts). The connecting theme is a concern to develop a broader and more socially-oriented conception of legal scholarship as an activity which can be appropriately carried out by scholars whose primary discipline is law. The relative failure of attempts to displace narrower 'expository' or 'black-letter' approaches is in part

viii *Introduction*

due to a failure to develop coherent alternatives within particular fields of law. This, too, is a task for theorists.

It has long seemed to me that the subject of evidence was ripe for this kind of rethinking. The central problem may be summarized as follows: traditional evidence scholarship in the Anglo-American tradition has concentrated almost entirely on the *rules* of evidence, especially the exclusionary rules. Within that tradition, work on other aspects of evidence, proof and fact-finding has been, at best, fragmented and spasmodic. Ironically, orthodox study of the Law of Evidence has been one of the least empirically-oriented branches of legal scholarship. Work in such fields as forensic science, witness psychology, the logic of proof, probability theory, and the systematic study of fact-finding institutions and processes has proceeded largely independently not only of the others but also of the study of evidence doctrine. All these lines of enquiry – and many others – seem to be related, but the exact nature of the relationships is puzzling and obscure. From the point of view of a broadened conception of legal scholarship it is worth asking: is it possible to develop a coherent framework for the study of evidence, proof and related matters within the discipline of law?

In tackling this question a natural first step was to enquire whether any such enterprise had been attempted before. Preliminary enquiries revealed that theorizing about evidence and proof has a rich and complex history that stretches back at least as far as classical rhetoric. They also showed that, partly because of the special importance of the law of evidence in the common law tradition, some of the most ambitious attempts to develop broad theoretical approaches to the subject had been made by English and American lawyers. Two features of the Anglo-American heritage of writing about evidence are particularly striking. First, nearly all specialist writers on the subject share very similar assumptions. They belong to a single, remarkably homogeneous intellectual tradition – here characterized as optimistic rationalism – that bears many of the hallmarks of eighteenth-century post-enlightenment thought. It is a tradition that is remarkable for its continuity, especially in respect of commitment to some central ideas, characterized by essentially shared conceptions of truth, reason and justice under the law. In recent years this kind of perspective has been confronted by a series of challenges, especially from sceptical writers on judicial processes.

Secondly, within this tradition two individuals stand out as major figures: Jeremy Bentham (1748–1832)[1] and John Henry Wigmore (1863–1943).[2] Bentham's theory of judicial evidence received its fullest treatment in his *Rationale of Judicial Evidence* (1827); Wigmore is best known for his multi-volume *Treatise on the Anglo-American System of Evidence in Trials at Common Law* (first edn 1904–8), but his theoretical views on his chosen field were stated more fully and clearly in his *The Principles of Judicial Proof* (1913, 1931) which was later renamed *The*

Science of Judicial Proof (1937). Bentham's and Wigmore's perspectives and ideas present many contrasts. For example, Bentham was an eighteenth-century radical reformer; Wigmore was a twentieth-century conservative who was aptly called 'the last Mid-Victorian'. Bentham was against all rules of evidence, especially judge-made rules; Wigmore saw at least some of the rules of admissibility as being wise products of judicial experience. Bentham's theory of evidence is an integral part of his grand design for an ideal system of laws in a utilitarian polity; Wigmore's 'science of proof' was the most general part of the ideas of a specialist in the law of evidence. Despite these and other differences, two important factors link Bentham's *Rationale* and Wigmore's *Principles*. Both belong to the mainstream of the Rationalist Tradition of evidence scholarship. They share almost identical basic assumptions about the nature of proof and similar, but not identical, views on the nature and purposes of adjudication. Each tried to develop a broad general theory of evidence and proof; yet both failed to gain acceptance as providing a coherent foundation for broad approaches to the study of the field. As we shall see, Bentham's recommendations for reform achieved a partial success, but his overall perspective and radical approach did not gain general acceptance. In the twentieth century, the *Rationale* has been largely ignored by evidence scholars, and to a lesser extent even by Benthamists. Similarly, while Wigmore's *Treatise* has dominated the field since its first publication, it has been perceived more as a great work of reference for practitioners and scholars than as a contribution to theory. *The Principles* was not taken very seriously during his lifetime and has been almost entirely forgotten since his death.

The main purpose of the present work is to provide an introduction to Bentham's *Rationale* and Wigmore's *Principles*, set in the context of an overview of the dominant tradition of Anglo-American writing about evidence. I hope to show that these two relatively neglected works deserve the attention of legal theorists, philosophers and others besides specialists in evidence and Bentham scholars. The treatment is more expository than critical because both works range very widely over difficult and, for many, unfamiliar territory.

The book will proceed as follows: the first chapter will present a broad historical survey of the development of the Rationalist Tradition of Evidence scholarship, of which Bentham and Wigmore are the two leading figures. There follows a lengthy essay on Bentham on Evidence, which seeks to expound the basic ideas of the *Rationale of Judicial Evidence* and some of its more important themes in the context of his thought as a whole and of contemporary debates. This essay should be of as much interest to students of Bentham as to specialists on evidence and to legal theorists.

The next essay will concentrate on a relatively little-known work of Wigmore's – his *Principles* (later *Science*) *of Judicial Proof* – because this x *Introduction*

represents the fullest and most coherent statement of the general ideas underlying his general approach to evidence. The introduction will present two images of Wigmore: the Master of the Law of Evidence and the energetic, intellectual dilettante with a penchant for detective stories, travelogues, bad verse and Heath Robinson gadgets. It will pose the question: which Wigmore was author of the *Principles*? The academic world, put off by his use of symbols and accounts of *causes célèbres*, seems to have decided that this was another example of the intellectual gimmickry of Colonel Wigmore, the intellectual tourist. I shall argue that there was only one Wigmore and that the *Principles* provides the key to his general approach and to the most developed twentieth-century theory of evidence and proof.

As this book is part of a larger enterprise, it would not be appropriate to use it as a vehicle for developing a new approach to a traditional field. However, intellectual history has its uses, one of which is to provide a basis for taking stock of a received heritage of doctrines and ideas. In the final chapter, an attempt will be made to compare and contrast the two theories and to assess their current significance at a time when there is a considerable resurgence of interest in the subject, exemplified by burgeoning interest in forensic psychology and by recent debates on reform and codification of the Law of Evidence and about probabilities and proof. I shall suggest that by and large they typify the strengths and limitations of the Rationalist Tradition as a whole, that is to say that it represents a rich heritage of specific concepts and ideas, but that it tends to be rather narrowly focused and to make rather simplistic assumptions about that complex form of social process known as litigation.

1

The Rationalist Tradition of evidence scholarship[1]

The history of the law of evidence is the history of a series of largely isolated responses to particular problems at different times.[2] Some rules, such as the conclusiveness of documents under seal, emerged relatively early; restrictions on the competency of witnesses were established in the sixteenth century; the privilege against self-incrimination, the hearsay rule and its exceptions, and the presumption of innocence have their own stories, not all of which have yet been traced definitively.[3] Even less well-documented is the continuing history of piecemeal legislative interventions and attempts at codification from the middle of the nineteenth century until the present day.[4] The intellectual history of the study of evidence is similarly complex – it reaches back at least as far as classical rhetoric and has fascinating ramifications for the philosophy of knowledge, debates about proof of the existence of God, the emergence of theories of probability and the development of modern psychology, forensic science and several other fields. The immediate context of this study is the development of specialized secondary writings on judicial evidence.

Despite the richness and variety of this heritage, the general outlines of the story can be sketched quite simply. Until the late eighteenth century, evidence doctrine consisted almost entirely of a disconnected pot pourri of scattered precedents. Commentators and practising lawyers perceived the law of evidence as little more than a few general maxims that could all be subsumed under a single principle, 'the best evidence rule'. Thus Buller's *Nisi Prius* restated the law of evidence first in nine and later in twelve propositions.[5] At the trial of Warren Hastings in 1794, Edmund Burke is reported to have said that he knew a parrot who could learn the rules of evidence in a half-hour and repeat them in five minutes.[6]

Two developments between 1750 and 1800 were of critical import-ance. It was in this period that the first specialized works on evidence appeared. The very first was the most important. This was the *Law of Evidence* by Lord Chief Baron Gilbert, written in the 1720s but not published until 1754.[7] Gilbert was a disciple of Locke and an amateur mathematician. In this work, he attempted to advance a coherent theory of the rules of evidence, based explicitly on Locke's philosophy and centred on the notion that 'there can be no Demonstration of a Fact

2 Theories of Evidence

without the best Evidence that the Nature of the Thing is capable of' – a very general and rather rigid version of 'the best evidence rule'.[8] Gilbert influenced the more practical treatises of Bathurst (1761), Buller (1772) and Peake (1801), that represented the first wave of specialized practitioners' works on evidence in England. Another important development was the expansion of law reporting, especially of Nisi Prius cases. Wigmore suggests that the number of rulings on evidence at Nisi Prius in the period 1790–1815 was more than in all the previous reports of the preceding two centuries.[9]

Thus when Bentham came to write about evidence, largely in the first decade of the nineteenth century, he was confronting a body of law that had the following characteristics; it was judge-made; most of it was either relatively new or was newly perceived as having the force of law; and it was highly fragmented, full of exceptions, distinctions and obscure technicalities developed *ad hoc* in response to particular situations in different contexts. The works of Gilbert, Buller and Peake attempted to impose some sort of order on this emergent body of law and to provide coherent rationales for some strange and diverse doctrines. In making the law of evidence more visible and in trying to rationalize and to systematize some highly unpromising bits and pieces, they provided targets that were at once convenient and vulnerable. Bentham used the works of Gilbert and Peake as the focus for his savage assault on all rules of evidence and on the professionals who, he claimed, had made and defended them to advance their own sinister interests.

We shall look at Bentham's particular concerns in more detail later. Here it is pertinent to note that he wrote at a relatively early stage in the development both of a separate body of judge-made rules and of specialized literature about those rules. It is also worth remarking that the technicalities of procedure and evidence were the subject of a good deal of criticism and controversy during the early years of the nineteenth century, not only outside the legal profession. Bentham wrote about evidence mainly between 1803 and 1812, but his principal works were not published until the 1820s. By then, some other notable contributions to the subject had begun to appear. In particular, William David Evans dealt with the law of evidence at some length in his two-volume study of Lord Mansfield's decisions in civil law cases, published in 1803.[10] This work was largely ignored, but Evans returned to the subject more systematically and at even greater length in his very influential translation of Pothier's *Traité des Obligations*, published in 1806.[11] Apart from several mundane practitioners' compendiums, the period 1800–30 saw the publication of two major scholarly treatises by Phillipps (first edition 1814) and Starkie (first edition 1824) that dominated the market for many years. Almost contemporaneously with Bentham, but, so far as one can tell, quite independently of him, a Scottish lawyer, William Glassford, published an elaborate theory of judicial proof that was based

The Rationalist Tradition of evidence scholarship 3

on the work of Scottish common-sense philosophers such as Reid and Stewart, who were opposed to Lockean empiricism.[12] Glassford advanced a holistic, as opposed to atomistic, approach to the evaluation of evidence. This seems to have made very little impact during the nineteenth century, even in Scotland, but his theory contains the seeds of a possible modern alternative to the view that evidence can be 'weighed' by considering the probative force of individual items of evidence on their own or in combination according to one or other standard theory of probability. This alternative, as we shall see, may provide a significantly different approach to the evaluation of evidence from that accepted by nearly all Anglo-American writers on evidence.

When Bentham's *Treatise* and *Rationale* were published in the 1820s they did not appear in a literary vacuum.[13] Bentham claimed he was writing on a *tabula rasa*, but his readers had the opportunity to contrast what he said not only with mundane practitioners' works of reference, such as *Buller* and *Peake*, but also with the reflective and principled contributions of Gilbert, Evans, Phillipps, Starkie and others. The contrasts were sharp. The standard works were written by lawyers for lawyers. Writers like Gilbert and Evans attempted to systematize the law on the basis of principle; most advocated piecemeal reform of particular doctrines, but by and large they accepted the practical value of the technical rules developed pragmatically, if messily, by the courts on the basis of experience. Bentham, on the other hand, advocated the abolition of all formal rules and a return to a 'natural' system of free proof, based on everyday experience and common-sense reasoning. He linked his radical critique of all artificial technicalities to a wholesale condemnation of the legal profession and of judge-made law. It is hardly surprising that his writings on evidence received a mixed reception. Even his closest disciple, Dumont, had reservations. Other admirers, such as Denman, Brougham and later Best, were highly selective in accepting his conclusions and arguments. Conversely even his sharpest critics, such as William Empson, acknowledged the profound importance of his work on evidence.[14]

Bentham's radical critique provoked ambivalent reactions and inspired cautious, piecemeal reforms. It is a further irony that these reforms were largely promoted by members of the profession that he had so viciously attacked – Denman, Brougham, Appleton and others. Yet, I shall argue, Bentham's victory was a good deal more far-reaching than has generally been recognized: nearly all changes since his time have been in the direction that he charted, and, perhaps more important, the number of evidentiary questions that are covered by binding rules is much smaller than one might suspect from reading the orthodox texts. Evidence as a subject is at least as interesting in respect of what is *not* governed by rules, as of the diminishing scope of the practical operation of such rules. During the period 1830–70 Bentham's ideas were kept

4 Theories of Evidence

alive by practical reformers, such as Denman and Brougham, and by writers such as Best and Appleton.[15] Over time his visibility waned and even his disciples cited him selectively. References to his writing steadily diminished but selective enactment of some of his proposals, especially in respect of competency of witnesses, helped to draw his sting. By 1876 Fitzjames Stephen could write:

> During the last generation or more Bentham's influence has to some extent declined, partly because some of his books are like exploded shells, buried under the ruins which they have made, and partly because, under the influence of some of the most distinguished of living authors, great attention has been directed to legal history and in particular to the study of Roman Law.[16]

Perhaps even more important was the steady erosion of support for unqualified intellectual utilitarianism, which was the basis of Bentham's *Rationale* as of all his other works. John Austin, himself a committed utilitarian, helped to focus attention on scientific analysis of the law as it is, and, perhaps inadvertently, to divert attention away from censorial jurisprudence. John Stuart Mill tried to develop a modified softer brand of utilitarianism. Denman, as we shall see, mixed non-utilitarian with utilitarian arguments in defending technical safeguards for the accused. In late-nineteenth-century English legal thought, as exemplified by men like Stephen and Pollock, pragmatic appeals to common sense and practical experience ('it works') represented, at best, a debased form of utilitarianism which bore only tenuous connections with Bentham's use of utility as a tool of principled, highly articulate analysis.[17] Similarly, there are few, if any, out and out utilitarians to be found among American reformers and writers about evidence in the second half of the nineteenth century.[18]

This partial rejection of Benthamism is apparent in the work of the last important English theorist of Evidence, Sir James Fitzjames Stephen (1829–94).[19] He agreed with Bentham that English law was unduly complex and technical; he favoured particular reforms; and he was committed to both systematization and simplification. However, unlike Bentham, he found the judge-made law of evidence to be 'full of sagacity and practical experience'.[20] He saw a role for formal rules in excluding prejudicial material, in requiring the production of the best available evidence and, above all, in ensuring the exclusion of all that is irrelevant.

Stephen was the chief draftsman of the influential Indian Evidence Act 1872, on which he published a lengthy introduction and commentary.[21] On his return to England, he tried to have an Evidence Bill introduced in Parliament, but when this failed, he embodied the substance of his ideas in *A Digest of the Law of Evidence*, which became extraordinarily influential throughout the common law world. Like Gilbert, Stephen sought to subsume the whole of the law of evidence under a single

The Rationalist Tradition of evidence scholarship   5

principle. John Stuart Mill's logic replaced Locke's epistemology as the explicit philosophical foundation and for 'the best evidence rule' he substituted the doctrine of relevancy as the underlying principle: 'exceptions excepted, all [judge-made] rules are reducible to the principle that facts in issue or relevant to the issue, and no others, may be proved'.[22]

During the nineteenth century, the centre of gravity of evidence scholarship began to shift to the United States. Simon Greenleaf's *A Treatise on the Law of Evidence* became the first home-grown work to dominate the American market; it also made an impact in England through *Taylor on Evidence* (first edition 1848), a highly successful practitioners' treatise that was so close to *Greenleaf* as to invite charges of plagiarism.[23] Greenleaf was one of the great series of treatise writers associated with Harvard. The first edition of his *Treatise* was published in 1842. It was originally planned as a student text, but from the start the author 'was naturally led to endeavor to render the work acceptable to the profession as well as useful to the student'. Up to that time the field in the United States had been dominated by two English works, *Phillipps* and *Starkie*, supplemented by notes on American cases. These had become increasingly inconvenient to use and less and less satisfactory as the rules of evidence in England and the various American jurisdictions diverged through both legislation and judicial activity.

Greenleaf's aim was 'to state those doctrines and rules of the Law of Evidence which are common to all the United States', without trying to note all local variations. In later editions recent decisions in England and Ireland, as well as the United States and Canada, were included. The first volume dealt with theoretical matters and general principles, but the second (and latterly subsequent volumes) dealt with details of the evidence requisite in certain particular actions and issues at common law, matters of great value to the practitioner, but belonging more to substantive law and procedure than to the law of evidence. Thus *Greenleaf on Evidence* was a hybrid: it dealt not with the law of any one jurisdiction, but rather with the principles of the Anglo-American law of evidence; it was designed to meet the needs of both students and practitioners – two rather different audiences, especially after the rise of teaching by the case method. It soon became established as the leading practitioners' treatise on the subject. The fact that it went through sixteen editions in less than sixty years is a measure both of its success and of the pace of change in this branch of the law during the period.

Wigmore began his career as a writer on evidence by editing the first volume of the sixteenth edition of *Greenleaf* in 1899, only to displace it soon afterwards by his own *Treatise*.

Even more important than *Greenleaf* was the work of James B. Thayer (1831–1902) who, in the eyes of some, was the greatest of all evidence scholars.[24] After a period in practice, Thayer came to the Harvard Law

6 Theories of Evidence

School in 1874 as Royall Professor of Law. Soon after he arrived he resolved to write a major treatise on evidence: during the remaining twenty-eight years of his life and beyond he exerted tremendous influence through his teaching, his casebooks on evidence and constitutional law, and his superb volume of historical and analytical essays entitled *A Preliminary Treatise on Evidence at the Common Law* (1898).

Thayer is important in the present context for several reasons. He is one of the most important theorists of evidence in his own right: his considered views represent as clearly as anyone's the partial acceptance and partial rejection of the path advocated by Bentham; Wigmore was his disciple and, in a sense, completed Thayer's work by producing a systematic treatise based on a coherent theory of judicial proof. In this view, Thayer paved the way and Wigmore completed the task.

Thayer was an historian who had none of Bentham's aversion to judge-made law. Like Bentham, he was highly critical of the law of evidence as he found it in the case law and the secondary literature based on the cases:

> The chief defects in this body of law, as it now stands, are [the] motley and undiscriminated character of its contents . . . the ambiguity of its terminology; the multiplicity and rigor of its rules and exceptions to rules; the difficulty of grasping these and perceiving their true place and relation in the system, and of determining, in the decision of new questions, whether to give scope and extension to the rational principles that lie at the bottom of all modern theories of evidence, or to those checks and qualifications of these principles which have grown out of the machinery through which our system is applied, namely, the jury.[25]

Thayer admired Fitzjames Stephen for his brave attempt to cut through the jungle of detail and confusion to establish a systematic foundation for the subject on the basis of principle. But Stephen's chosen principle, his doctrine of relevancy, failed to perform the task. It was, as Pollock called it, 'a splendid mistake'.[26] Thayer told his pupils that 'a more excellent way' was still needed.[27] As a preliminary to writing a practical treatise he embarked on detailed historical research which took him further and further away from his original project. The result was one of the classic works of legal history, but no systematic treatise.

Some of Thayer's main theses are familiar: he linked the origin and continuance of the exclusionary rules of evidence to the survival of the jury, a view adopted by Wigmore, but challenged by Edmund Morgan.[28] More firmly and clearly than his predecessors he emphasized the narrowness of the scope of the common law of evidence:[29] it was a mistake to treat presumptions and the burden of proof as rules of evidence; the most common grounds for exclusion of evidence were materiality – a matter of substantive law – and relevance, which was a

The Rationalist Tradition of evidence scholarship 7

matter of logic, not law. Stephen's basic error was to treat the logical presuppositions of a rational system of evidence as formal rules of evidence. Bentham's *Rationale* was not a law book.[30]

Thayer's main approach was not anti-nomian but he did favour an extension of judicial discretion and a radical simplification of the law of evidence. Rather he was concerned to clarify, both historically and analytically, the differences between rules of evidence, on the one hand, and rules of substantive law and precepts of logic on the other. In this view the core of the law of evidence was an essentially negative 'set of regulative and excluding precepts' based on policy,[31] which set certain artificial constraints on what witnesses and what classes of probative facts may be presented to a jury and how certain types of fact may or must be proved. For Thayer the modern system of proof is essentially rational, but 'the law has no mandamus to the logical faculty'.[32] Some legitimate constraints are placed on the operation of natural reason by substantive law, by the exigencies of litigation, by extrinsic policy and, above all, by the institution of the jury. But the scope and functions of the law of evidence are quite limited and could be reduced to a simple system, based on two principles: '(1) that nothing is to be received which is not logically probative of some matter requiring to be proved; and (2) that everything which is thus probative should come in, unless a clear ground of policy of law excludes it.'[33]

Thayer is mainly remembered today for his *Preliminary Treatise*, but his influence may have been at least as great, if not greater, through his teaching. His academic career coincided with the era of the blossoming of the Harvard law school as the home both of the Langdellian system of legal education and of the inspired and varied scholarship of Holmes, Langdell, Ames, Gray, Williston and Thayer himself. Three of the leading evidence scholars of the next generation – Charles Chamberlayne, John McKelvey and John Henry Wigmore – were his pupils. Several more, including Edmund Morgan, John Maguire and Zechariah Chafee, narrowly missed being taught by him, but lived in the shadow of his influence, modified perhaps by the more down-to-earth approach of the great John Chipman Gray, who reluctantly took over teaching evidence after Thayer's death. Perhaps the main medium of Thayer's continuing influence was his *Select Cases on Evidence at the Common Law*, first published in 1892. It was revised by Thayer in 1900, shortly before his death, and in this form it became the leading casebook on evidence in American law schools for a quarter of a century. In 1925 Maguire produced a revised edition, by arrangement with the Thayer family.[34] Then in 1934 it was transformed, under the direction of Morgan, into what was in most respects a new book, but with an acknowledged and legitimated parentage. Morgan and Maguire's *Cases on Evidence* lasted through successive editions until 1965, when it was succeeded by the Foundation Press casebook, *Cases and Materials on Evidence*, the latest

8 Theories of Evidence

edition of which appeared in the names of Maguire, Weinstein, Chadbourn and Mansfield in 1973.[35] This explicitly claims to trace its lineage directly back to Thayer's *Cases*. It is still one of the leading casebooks used in American law schools.

Thayer never got round to expounding the simple system of evidence doctrine that he advocated. Whether he was too fastidious or otherwise temperamentally unsuited to the task, or whether it was a contingent fact that he died before completing it, is uncertain.[36] It was left to three of his pupils, Wigmore, Chamberlayne and McKelvey, to continue the search for 'a more excellent way'. He inspired each of them to do this in strikingly different fashions.

McKelvey produced a successful and provocative black letter text which was widely used as a companion to Thayer's casebook, but which made no visible impact on the development of the law of evidence nor on legal scholarhip.[37]

Chamberlayne, an interesting and underrated figure, set out to establish a new system based on 'the principle of administration', which on inspection turns out to be Bentham's anti-nomian thesis: 'In connection with the law of evidence, the nerve of the octopus can readily be cut. It is the theory that judicial administration must be regulated by rigid rules.'[38] Chamberlayne's *magnum opus* was *A Treatise on the Modern Law of Evidence*, published in five volumes between 1911 and 1916. It was a work on the grand scale, comparable in size and basic conception to Wigmore's *Treatise*. It was conspicuously ignored by other writers, no doubt partly because it was overshadowed by Wigmore's great work, partly because the last two volumes were shoddily edited and produced after Chamberlayne's death, but perhaps also because Chamberlayne presented a polemical, and to some extreme, argument *de lege ferenda* in the shape of an encyclopedic practitioners' treatise. Its failure is a minor tragedy of intellectual history.

Thayer's failure to produce his promised treatise and the absence of serious competitors provided Wigmore with his opportunity. He took it with such conspicuous success that he earned more praise than his mentor and overshadowed all other writers on evidence for the next fifty years. It is, of course, quite misleading to depict Wigmore merely as a disciple of Thayer. Wigmore explicitly adopted Thayer's general theory of the law of evidence and drew heavily on his historical researches; both belong to the central tradition of Evidence scholarship and share most of its basic assumptions, but the resemblance ends here. Thayer was a subtle intensive thinker; his forte lay in the penetrating analysis of sharply focused questions; he was a lawyer who became obsessed by a rather narrow kind of history. Wigmore's talents were more extensive and systematic: he had broad legal interests and he was insatiably curious about other disciplines and other countries; he was an efficient and well-organized scholar with a great capacity for synthesis and simplification.

The Rationalist Tradition of evidence scholarship 9

Their contributions to the theory of Evidence are correspondingly different: Thayer provided the prevailing rationale for the *law* of Evidence; Wigmore adopted Thayer's theory as one part of a much broader inter-disciplinary 'Science' of Evidence and Proof.[39] The nature and quality of Wigmore's achievements will be explored later. Here it is worth noting one negative impact of his success. The next generation of specialists in evidence in the United States contained some men of outstanding ability: Morgan, Chafee, McCormick and several others. They worked in the shadow of the master. Only one of them, McCormick, attempted to write a systematic treatise and this was quite modest in its aims and fairly pedestrian in execution. Whether Wigmore's dominance was the sole or even the primary cause, the first fifty years of the twentieth century represent a relatively fallow period, marked by much excellent and sophisticated work on particular topics, but more remarkable for the absence of attempts to develop general theories or to write systematic treatises as alternatives to Wigmore's.

There are of course, some exceptions to these broad generalizations. Two deserve mention here. First, in this period a great deal of the energy of leading American evidence scholars, of whom Morgan was the most prominent, was channelled into drafting and debating proposed codes of evidence. The products of this long and complicated process were a series of consolidations and codes, notably the Model Code of Evidence (1942), the Uniform Rules of Evidence (1953), the California Evidence Code (first implemented 1965–7), the Federal Rules of Evidence (enacted 1975) and legislation based on one or other of these.[40] Although this movement towards codification represents the general trend in the direction of simplification and further narrowing of the scope of the formal rules of evidence, these codes represent achievements of pragmatic, incremental change based on compromise rather than a clear victory for Thayerism, let alone Benthamism.

One theorist who wrote in this period was Jerome Michael of Columbia, who for many years explored the theoretical foundations of evidence and civil procedure, including the logical and psychological dimensions of proof.[41] Much of the work was never completed, but a tentative edition of an ambitious theoretical book, written in collaboration with a philosopher, Mortimer Adler, was privately printed in 1931, as *The Nature of Judicial Proof: an Inquiry into the Logical, Legal, and Empirical Aspects of the Law of Evidence.*[42] Of this Wigmore wrote somewhat harshly:

> [it] is a metaphysical analysis of the elements of probative reasoning; but its remarkable subtleties seem to have no more service for the practitioner than do the mathematical and physical formulas on which the physicist constructs his practicable microscope.[43]

The period 1900–60 was also a fallow period for English evidence

10 Theories of Evidence

scholarship and theorizing.[44] The most notable contribution was the first edition of *Cross on Evidence*, which soon became recognized by practitioners and academics alike as the leading English work in the field.[45] Its success was in part indicative of a need: it helped to fill a vacuum. Its limitations are equally revealing of the state of the subject at the time. Cross was pragmatic in respect of both form and substance: he set out to cater for two rather different markets, students and practitioners, simultaneously.[46] He sought to go beyond simple exposition to provide 'an up-to-date account of the theory of the subject'. But his notion of theory stopped at giving purported explanations for particular doctrines. Cross was a good expositor, clear and concise and with an excellent command of the case law. He also had a good sense of what issues practitioners thought important. But he set himself rather modest aims, he concentrated almost exclusively on the rules of evidence, and he exhibited little interest in the broader dimensions of the underlying theory of the subject or in its logical, psychological and empirical aspects. The first edition of *Cross* contains no references either to Bentham or to Wigmore's Science.[47] His robust no-nonsense approach was typified by his remark, made in my presence: 'I am working for the day that my subject is abolished.'

Since 1960 there has been a slow, but steady, revival of interest in the study of evidence.[48] In England a series of reports by the Law Reform Committee culminated in the Civil Evidence Acts of 1968 and 1972 which significantly reduced the scope and practical importance of the Law of Evidence in civil cases. On the criminal side, the Eleventh Report of the Criminal Law Revision Committee (C.L.R.C., 1972) and the Report of the Royal Commission on Criminal Procedure (Philips, 1981) both invoked Benthamite utilitarianism in rather dubious ways and stimulated public debates with strong echoes of the 1830s without producing significant legislative changes.[49] During this period some notable contributions have been made by Commonwealth scholars and law reformers, but without producing any radical breaks with the predominant tradition.

In selecting only a few highlights from a vast mass of material I have no wish to slight either the learning or sophistication of much of the case law and secondary writings, especially in the periodicals, that appeared in the years between the establishment of Wigmore's supremacy and the late 1960s. Evidence has tended to attract some of the finest minds among legal scholars and, in the United States in particular, there has been great strength in depth. But most of the learning has been particularistic and much of it has proved to be relatively ephemeral. The enactment of the Federal Rules and other quasi-codes of evidence has also created some hitherto unresolved problems for teachers of the subject. By simplifying the old law they have made some of the old learning obsolete, yet the new codes may not provide such a satisfactory basis for teaching skills of

The Rationalist Tradition of evidence scholarship   11

statutory interpretation as the Uniform Commercial Code or the Internal Revenue Code.[50] Writing in 1977, shortly after the enactment of the Federal Rules, two leading commentators remarked:

> . . . the field of evidence can use a bit of shaking up; it has become stagnant since the defeat of the last generation of reformers. It would be only a slight exaggeration to say that there has not been one significant contribution to the field in the last twenty-five years.[51]

From the perspective of 1984, this does seem to be a bit of an exaggeration. One of the reasons for this relative stagnation is that in England, the United States and other parts of the common law world, teaching, writing and thinking about evidence have centred on the *law* of evidence. The scholars have tended to follow the rules. These have diminished in scope and declined in importance over the years; they have also tended to become simpler. A number of recent developments promise to take the subject out of the doldrums. Significantly each of these is concerned with aspects of evidence and proof that are largely independent of the technical rules.

First in time was the development of 'the new rhetoric' by Chaim Perelman and his associates.[52] This has helped to remind us of the close historical connection of questions of proof with classical and medieval rhetoric, which itself originally developed in large part in the forensic arena. It has also shown that questions of fact pose as interesting and important problems of 'lawyers' reasonings' as questions of law.

A second, connected development has been a series of debates about the nature of probabilistic reasoning in forensic contexts. It is a commonplace of evidence discourse that triers of fact are concerned with 'probabilities, not certainties'. For many years almost no attention was given by lawyers to the nature of the probabilities that were involved, despite enormous interest in probability theory in several adjacent disciplines. Then, stimulated in part by some elementary statistical errors in the California case of *People* v. *Collins*, a lively debate developed in the United States about the potential uses and abuses of mathematics in litigation.[53] To begin with the main participants took it for granted that all reasoning about probabilities is in principle mathematical; they disagreed about the correct way of applying the calculus of probability to particular situations and about the feasibility and desirability, as a matter of policy, of explicit resort to mathematical arguments in the courtroom. In the late 1970s whole books began to appear devoted to the application of statistics and mathematical probability to law.[54] In 1977 a British philosopher, Jonathan Cohen, advanced the thesis that not all reasoning about probabilities is in principle mathematical (Pascalian) and that some judgements of probability can be appropriately justified and criticized on the basis of objective, non-mathematical (Baconian) criteria.[55] He further argued that most, but not all, arguments about

12 Theories of Evidence

probabilities in forensic contexts fitted his Baconian theory of induction better than any of the standard versions of mathematical probability and that most leading theorists of evidence, including Bentham and possibly Wigmore, were probably Baconians. Cohen's thesis stimulated lively debates in several disciplines, including law.[56] These debates have not yet run their course.

A third, largely independent development has been a revival of interest in law and psychology including, but not confined to, witness psychology. Between about 1890 and 1920 there was considerable interest in this field, especially in Germany and the United States. Then, for rather obscure reasons, interest almost completely died out for nearly fifty years. It began to revive in the 1960s, partly through the work of Lionel Haward, James Marshall, Arne Trankell and others. To begin with, much of the research was narrowly empirical and highly particularistic; but over time more critical and analytical approaches began to develop.[57] Theory was becoming respectable again.

The Rationalist Tradition

This brief survey of some of the highlights of the intellectual history of the specialized study of evidence in England and the United States should at least be enough to suggest that the story is by no means a straightforward case study of the development of a specialized branch of expository scholarship. From an early stage there was a continuing uneasiness about whether there were or should be any formal rules of evidence, what precisely might be the status of such rules (and, in particular, of judicial rulings on points of evidence) and about the scope of evidence as a subject. There were recurrent tensions between authors' concerns and the demands of the market, so that there was often an uneasy fit between substantive content and literary form. Most writers could hardly fail to be aware of the artificiality of isolating the study of evidence from the study of procedure, of substantive law and of 'non-legal' dimensions, especially the logical, epistemological and psychological aspects. Yet the desire to systematize, to simplify and, in some instances, to codify generated equally strong pressures to draw the boundaries of evidence doctrine precisely and narrowly. The systematic exposition of the law of evidence on the basis of principle was a primary concern of Gilbert and most of his successors. For some, like Bentham and Chamberlayne, the fundamental principle was some version of free proof. Gilbert, Peake and several leading nineteenth-century writers each tried to subsume the rules of evidence under different versions of 'the best evidence rule'. Stephen purported to find a single unifying principle in the notion of 'relevance'. All of these efforts failed and, since Thayer, the modern tendency has been to see the law of evidence largely as a collection of disparate constraints on freedom of proof and free evaluation of evidence.[58]

Evidence scholarship has also been a forum for a series of protracted controversies. Some of these belong fairly specifically to the study of evidence – conceptual disagreements, the debates about presumptions, hearsay and the best evidence rule, for example. Others represent particular applications of standard legal or juristic controversies, such as debates about the pros and cons of the jury or the adversary system or judge-made law or codification. Some, such as disagreements between utilitarians and deontologists, between civil libertarians and proponents of 'law and order', between Pascalians and Baconians, reflect wider differences. There is a remarkable degree of continuity about some of these controversies: for example, a reader of the *Edinburgh Review* in the 1820s and 1830s would have found a great deal that was familiar in recent debates in England about the reform of criminal evidence and procedure.

Despite these strains and disagreements there is a truly remarkable homogeneity about the basic assumptions of almost all specialist writings on evidence from Gilbert through Bentham, Thayer and Wigmore to Cross and McCormick. Almost without exception, Anglo-American writers about evidence show very similar assumptions, either explicitly or implicitly, about the nature and ends of adjudication, about knowledge or belief about past events and about what is involved in reasoning about disputed questions of fact in forensic contexts. They differ about such matters as the scope of and the need for rules of evidence, about the role and rationale of the law of evidence in general, about the details of particular rules and about many other things. But these disagreements have by and large taken place within a shared framework of basic assumptions and concepts.

It is convenient to present the main epistemological and logical assumptions in the form of model or ideal type, consisting of a series of propositions. One possible formulation is as follows:

1. Epistemological assumptions

(a) Events and states of affairs occur and have an existence independently of human observation; true statements are statements which correspond with facts, i.e. real events and states of affairs in the external world.

(b) Present knowledge about past events is in principle possible; in this context, 'knowledge' means warranted beliefs that satisfy specified standards of proof relating to the truth of statements about facts in the real world.

(c) Present knowledge about past events is typically based upon incomplete evidence; it follows from this that establishing the truth about alleged past events is typically a matter of probabilities or likelihoods falling short of complete certainty.

14 Theories of Evidence

(d) Judgements about the probable truth of allegations about past events must, generally speaking, be based on the available 'stock of knowledge' about the common course of events in the external world. In any given society at a particular time, the 'stock of knowledge' includes, in a descending scale of probability, generalizations accepted by the scientific community as established, the opinions of experts and 'common-sense' generalizations based on the experience of members of society.

2. Assumptions about fact-finding in adjudication

(a) It is a necessary condition for implementation of substantive laws that the truth of allegations about particular past events, 'the facts in issue' in a case, be established on the basis of *relevant* evidence presented to the decider.

(b) The implementation of substantive laws by the determination of the truth about allegations of fact on the basis of evidence is a necessary condition of achieving expletive justice, i.e. justice under the law.

(c) Given that decisions about the truth of allegations of fact typically take place in conditions of uncertainty (see 1c. above) justice under the law has to be satisfied with standards of proof falling short of absolute certainty.

(d) Rectitude of decision (i.e. the correct application of valid substantive laws to facts established as true) is an important social value. There is room for disagreement about the priority that should be accorded to rectitude of decision when there is a potential conflict with other values such as the security of the state, the protection of family relationships, procedural fairness, and so on. How far particular institutions, rules, procedures, techniques and practices are estimated to maximize accuracy in fact-determination is one important criterion for evaluating them: but other criteria of evaluation are also applicable, such as speed, cheapness, procedural fairness, humaneness, public confidence and the avoidance of vexation to participants. The relevant priorities to be given to these various criteria are also a matter of contention.

3. Reasoning in adjudication

(a) A method of adjudicative fact-finding is 'rational' if, and only if, judgements about the probable truth of allegations about the facts in issue are based on inferences from relevant evidence presented to the decision-maker.

(b) The validity of inferences from evidence is governed by the principles of logic, the characteristic mode of reasoning appropriate to forming and justifying judgements of probability about alleged facts is induction, with deduction playing a secondary role. It is a matter of contention whether all reasoning about probabilities is in principle

The Rationalist Tradition of evidence scholarship   15

mathematical or whether some probability judgements in forensic contexts are in principle non-mathematical (Baconian).

(c) The application of the principles of induction to present evidence makes it possible to assign a probable truth value to a present proposition about a past event.

If such propositions represent standard elements in rationalist theories of evidence, it should be clear that it is artificial to make a sharp distinction between theories of evidence and theories of adjudication: generally speaking, the former presuppose or form part of the latter. However, it is necessary to proceed with caution partly because by no means all evidence scholars articulated clear and developed statements of their views about adjudication and partly because there appears to be less of a consensus in the relevant literature about the ends and the achievements of the Anglo-American system of adjudication than about the logic and epistemology of proof. It is, however, possible to postulate a rationalist model of adjudication as an ideal type which both fits a rationalist theory of evidence and is recognizable as a reasonably sophisticated version of a widely-held, if controversial, view. What follows is a modified version of a Benthamite model of adjudication, presented in a way which suggests a number of possible points of departure or disagreement. Although by no means all leading evidence scholars have been legal positivists and utilitarians, a Rationalist Theory of Evidence necessarily presupposes a theory of adjudication that postulates something like Bentham's 'rectitude of decision' as the main objective. There is scope for divergence on a number of points of detail, but not from what might be called 'the rational core'.[59]

A rationalist model of adjudication

A. Prescriptive
1. The direct end
2. of adjective law
3. is rectitude of decision through correct application
4. of valid substantive laws
5. deemed to be consonant with utility (or otherwise good)
6. and through accurate determination
7. of the true past facts
8. material to
9. precisely specified allegations expressed in categories defined in advance by law, i.e. facts in issue,
10. proved to specified standards of probability or likelihood
11. on the basis of the careful
12. and rational
13. weighing of

16 Theories of Evidence

14. evidence
15. which is both relevant
16. and reliable
17. presented (in a form designed to bring out truth and discover untruth)
18. to a supposedly competent
19. and impartial
20. decision-maker
21. with adequate safeguards against corruption
22. and mistake
23. and adequate provision for review and appeal.

B. Descriptive

24. Generally speaking this objective is largely achieved
25. in a consistent
26. fair
27. and predictable manner.[60]

It is reasonable, and sufficient for present purposes, to assert that by and large the leading Anglo-American scholars and theorists of evidence from Gilbert to Wigmore (and, for the most part, until the present) have either implicitly or explicitly accepted such notions as these, although not in this particular formulation. Central to this model are two ideas: first that the Anglo-American system has adopted a 'rational' mode of determining issues of fact in contrast with older 'irrational' modes of proof. As Thayer put it: 'What was formerly "tried" by the method of force or the mechanical following of form is now tried by the method of reason.'[61] Secondly, a particular view of 'rationality' was adopted or taken for granted. This found its classic expression in English empirical philosophy in the writings of Bacon, Locke and John Stuart Mill. But for the ungainliness of the term it would be appropriate to refer to this 'intellectual mainstream' as the Classical Rationalist Tradition of Evidence Scholarship, in order to emphasize 'rational proof' as its central idea and a particular view of rationality as one of its basic assumptions.

The characteristic assumptions of discourse about evidence within the Rationalist Tradition can be succinctly restated as follows: epistemology is cognitivist rather than sceptical; a correspondence theory of truth is generally preferred to a coherence theory of truth; the mode of decision-making is seen as 'rational' contrasted with 'irrational' modes such as battle, compurgation, or ordeal; the characteristic mode of reasoning is induction; the pursuit of truth as a *means* to justice under the law commands a high, but not necessarily an overriding, priority as a social value.

The claim that the modern system of adjudication is 'rational' is a statement of what is considered to be a feasible *aspiration* of the system; it does not necessarily involve commitment to the view that this aspiration

The Rationalist Tradition of evidence scholarship   17

is always, generally, or even sometimes, realized in practice. It is commonplace within the Rationalist Tradition to criticize existing practices, procedures, rules and institutions in terms of their failure to satisfy the standards of this aspirational model. Part A of the model is prescriptive: it states an aspiration and a standard by which to judge actual rules, institutions, procedures and practices. Acceptance of such standards involves no necessary commitment to the view that a particular system, or some aspect of it, at a particular time satisfies these standards either in its design or its actual operation. Part B of the model is intended to represent typical claims or judgements of the kind 'on the whole the system works well'. None of the leading theorists in the Rationalist Tradition were perfectionists who expected one hundred per cent conformity with the ideal. Some were highly critical of existing arrangements and practices. Indeed Bentham, whose *Rationale of Judicial Evidence* is the main source of the model, made his theory of adjudication the basis for a radical and far-ranging critique of English (and, to a lesser extent, Scottish and continental) procedure, practice and rules of evidence in his day. It is, of course, possible to explore how far any individual writers have been complacent, either generally or in particular respects, about the design or practical operation of their own system; but this kind of judgement involves an additional step – moving from prescribing general standards to applying them to particular examples.

Thus it is important to distinguish clearly between *aspirational* and *complacent rationalism* in respect of adjudication. It is also useful to differentiate a third category, which might be referred to as *optimistic rationalism*. For in invoking prescriptive standards one often makes some judgement about the prospects for attaining or approximating to such standards in practice in a given context: in the case of many writers on evidence and judicial process who accepted some variant of Part A of the rationalist model, it is reasonable to attribute to them the view that its standards represent a feasible aspiration rather than a remote or unattainable Utopian ideal. Even virulently critical writers such as Bentham and Frank can be shown to have believed that their own favoured recommendations would in practice lead to significant increases in the level of rationality in adjudication. They were optimistic rationalists. Nearly all of the literature on evidence that has been discussed in this chapter is generally optimistic in this sense. In brief: almost all the leading writers in the mainstream of Anglo-American evidence scholarship were aspirational rationalists, most were optimistic rationalists most of the time and many, but by no means all, were fairly complacent about the general operation of the adversary system in their own jurisdiction in their day.

In emphasizing the continuity of the Rationalist Tradition one must be careful to avoid anachronism. The worlds of Bentham, Wigmore and

18 *Theories of Evidence*

modern evidence scholars are in many important respects radically different from each other. To take but two examples: Bentham wrote before the creation of a regular police force; 'Wigmore was already an old man when Bonnie and Clyde got their first machine gun';[62] today's evidence scholars are, *inter alia*, struggling with the implications of the computer revolution. Again, Bentham's psychology – in some respects original and ahead of its time – did not go much beyond the psychological theory of association of David Hartley and his disciples; Wigmore, even in 1937, drew heavily on James Sully's *The Human Mind*, published in 1892; he wrote as if Freud and Jung had not yet appeared and as if there was a widespread consensus among 'scientific' psychologists. In 1981, there were reported to be several hundred articles devoted to psychology and law published in a single year.[63] Yet the continuity of the central ideas in evidence scholarship is truly remarkable. Several factors may help to explain this. First, writers on evidence have been said to feed off each other without re-examining their basic assumptions.[64] During the nineteenth century and beyond this both encouraged and was supported by the increasing isolation of writing and teaching about the subject. The search for principle and the desire to codify the rules of evidence provided a strong motive for making sharp distinctions between rules of evidence and rules of substantive law and procedure. This tendency, carried to an extreme by Stephen and Thayer, laid the foundations for the extraordinary isolation of the study of evidence from intellectual developments in other fields during the twentieth century. The study of evidence was equated with the study of the rules of evidence and the scope of these rules was interpreted narrowly. These tendencies also made it natural for Anglo–American evidence scholarship to be rooted in a single philosophical tradition – English empiricism, as represented by Locke, Bentham, J. S. Mill, Sidgwick and modern analytical philosophers such as A. J. Ayer. Bentham and Wigmore differ from most contemporary specialists on evidence in taking a broad view of their subject; that is one reason for their continuing significance. But, subject to a few *caveats*, they belong to the mainstream of a single relatively homogeneous tradition that still has deep roots in eighteenth-century thought. This, I shall seek to show, contains the key to understanding both the strengths and the limitations not only of the theories of Bentham and Wigmore, but of most contemporary thought about judicial evidence.

2

Bentham on evidence

(i) Introduction

It may seem strange to introduce a theory of evidence with anecdotes about ghosts, the Thirty Nine Articles and the experiences of a reformed courtesan. Yet three of Bentham's childhood experiences provide a clue to some lifelong obsessions that underlay his voluminous writings on adjective law. Such anecdotes help to set the context. Neither their historical accuracy nor their possible psychological implications need unduly concern us; they are significant here for the light that they cast on some of Bentham's central concerns when he wrote about adjective law: the relationship between the world of fact, the world of fiction and our modes of apprehending both; the institution of the oath as an instrument and as a symbol of both coercion and abuse of power by the forces of unreason; and the defects of English legal procedure.

Bentham himself is responsible for the idea that his views on the nature of the real world, of belief and of language – brought together in his theory of fictions – grew directly out of his childhood fear of ghosts and phantoms. In an autobiographical fragment he tells us:

> My grandmother's mother was a matron, I was told, of high respectability and corresponding piety; well-informed and strong-minded. She was distinguished, however; for, while other matrons of her age and quality had seen many a ghost, she had seen but *one*. She was, in this particular, on a level with the learned lecturer, afterwards judge, the commentator Blackstone. But she was heretical, and her belief bordered on Unitarianism. And, by the way, this subject of ghosts has been among the torments of my life. Even now, when sixty or seventy years have passed over my head since my boyhood received the impression which my grandmother gave it, though my judgment is wholly free, my imagination is not wholly so.[1]

In time these childhood terrors became transformed into a metaphysic and a theory of language.[2] In coming to terms with phantoms, suggests C. K. Ogden, Bentham developed a crucial distinction between real and fictitious entities.[3] This formed the basis for his theory of fictions, which contains his ideas about the nature of the real world and how we

20 Theories of Evidence

construct our knowledge of it largely by means of language. These ideas underlie his theory of evidence: we form judgements about the truth of statements about the real world on the basis of evidence which we evaluate in terms of general experience; experience is the basis of all knowledge; language is the instrument, at once misleading and necessary, by which all experience is apprehended and ordered. This aspect of his thought was so much ahead of its time that its significance was not fully appreciated, even by some of his closest disciples, until the centenary of his death, when C. K. Ogden established Bentham as an important forerunner of much that is central in modern English analytical philosophy. Bentham's theory of fictions is the main philosophical basis of his theory of evidence. It is not a coincidence that the main period of work on evidence (1803–12) immediately precedes that of the most complete works on metaphysics and language.[4]

The second anecdote concerns swearing. When Bentham went up to Oxford at the age of twelve he found that he was exempted by reason of his age from having to take the normal range of university oaths. He was relieved, for, it is reported, he *already* disapproved of oaths.[5] However, he was asked to sign a declaration that he subscribed to the Thirty Nine Articles of the Church of England. It has been doubted whether Bentham was 'really a lawyer';[6] on this occasion the precocious boy exhibited some standard lawyerlike qualities: he asked to see the text, he read the small print carefully and he reflected on the consequences of signing. He found some of the articles meaningless and others to have 'no meaning but one which, in my eyes, was but too plainly irreconcileable either to reason or scripture'.[7] He found that some of his contemporaries shared his doubts: they raised the matter with a fellow of the College whose office it was 'to remove all such scruples'. They were told that it was not for uninformed youth to set their 'private judgements against a public one, formed by some of the holiest as well as best and wisest men that ever lived'.[8] Bentham signed reluctantly, but he bitterly resented it. He reports it as a formative experience. His subsequent rationalization of his resentment is revealing: first, belief was being treated as a matter of authority rather than individual judgement; secondly, to be forced to sign what you did not believe was perjury, an offence backed by religious, moral and legal sanctions; thirdly, the church and the university authorities, both part of one powerful establishment, were abusing their power by coercing him to commit perjury against his conscience. The oath was thus made an instrument of tyranny. Fourthly, those who refused to take the oath were excluded – in the university from membership, in the courts of law from giving testimony. Conversely, the law, by restricting punishment for perjury to statements made under oath, gave a 'mendacity-license' to all other statements.[9] Each of these reasons became central notions in his theory of evidence: the capacity of the individual to make up his own mind rationally about the truth; the use and abuse of sanctions to encourage or to deter mendacity; the importance of the factor of power, and of its potential abuse, in the gathering and presentation of evidence; and the artificial exclusion of witnesses and of evidence on grounds that had little or nothing to do with either their importance or their reliability.

The third incident has a more direct connection with the law. Bentham's highly critical view of the administration of justice, especially of the technicalities of procedure, was formed at an early stage. In 1759, aged eleven or twelve, he came across a recently published bestseller entitled *An Apology for the Conduct of Mrs T. C. Phillips*.[10] It made an immediate impression on him. This 'ghosted', picaresque autobiography detailed over three volumes the story of Teresa Constantia Phillips who was rescued from prostitution by marriage to a young Dutch merchant only to be ruined through attempts to vindicate her rights in the courts after the marriage had been annulled:

> Dingdong went the tocsin of the law. Tossed from pillar to post was the fair penitent – from Courts Temporal to Courts Spiritual, by Blackstone called Courts Christian . . . while reading and musing, the Daemon of Chicane appeared to me in all his hideousness. What followed? I abjured his empire. I vowed war against him.[11]

We need not take this fragment of autobiography too seriously, for other factors also affected Bentham's views on procedure. But the sad tale of Mrs Phillips contained many of the ingredients that he was later to attack in the technical system of procedure: interminable delays; multiple jurisdictions; obfuscating technicalities; exclusion of relevant evidence; exclusion of parties (and others) as witnesses; the tolerance of chicanery and perjury; abuse of religion and, above all, appalling expense arising from the financial interests of lawyers and officials who were responsible for prolonging and complicating legal proceedings.[12]

In 1800, adjective law in England hardly deserved to be called a 'system': it was the confused and confusing product of largely *ad hoc* and often arbitrary growth, developed very largely by lawyers and judges with little regard for principle or consistency.[13] Civil litigation was at once over-centralized and unduly complex. Criminal procedure was a mass of technicalities. Some technical rules, such as the forms of indictment, were absurd hangovers from the past; because of the severities of the criminal law – by 1820 over 200 crimes were capital offences – juries were reluctant to convict, the judges interpreted the law in a legalistic fashion and had developed a series of doctrines that, in Bentham's view, protected the guilty even more than the innocent; clemency was exercised in a hit-and-miss fashion. Bentham wished to substitute strict enforcement of less stringent laws for lenient administration of harsh ones.[14] The law of evidence provided what today may seem some obvious targets for attack, especially in respect of competency

22   *Theories of Evidence*

of witnesses: the evidence of the accused, of parties to litigation, of spouses and of almost anyone with any interest in the matter was excluded; Quakers and others who, for reasons of conscience, refused to take the oath in its prescribed form were also unable to testify; provisions for proof of births, marriages and deaths were rudimentary and ill-suited to their purposes; and the law of hearsay was a tangle of rules, exceptions and rationalizations.

The technicality of the law provided opportunities for quibbling and other abuses which helped to generate a more general unease. Keeton and Marshall put the matter admirably:

> If we sum up the Law of Evidence as it existed at the beginning of the nineteenth century, we can say that it was practically entirely judge-made law, the product of the decisions of the courts in the first century after the Restoration. Not all its rules were clearly understood, the origins of a number of them were obscure, and the application of others was uncertain. There were, moreover, wide variations between the rules of evidence applied in Common Law Courts and those enforced in Courts of Equity. Some parts of the law of evidence – for example, that which relates to documentary evidence, and especially to public documents – was still primitive and unsystematic. Finally, the rules had grown up in isolation. They were the product of our own peculiar legal history, and they had few points of contact with continental legal thinking on similar topics. By far the most important of Bentham's contributions to the law of evidence was that, for the first time in English legal history, he undertook to test the rules of evidence by reference to general philosophy and logic, and in the light of his knowledge of the rules of continental systems.[15]

It seemed to Bentham that these defects would be almost self-evident to anyone who was not a lawyer. But they were by-and-large hidden from the view of non-lawyers by a screen of technicalities and bogus rationalizations; and lawyers, by virtue of self-interest and inertia, either did not see them or pretended not to. During his relatively brief period in practice at the Bar, Bentham had a number of experiences that 'added . . . fuel to the flame which Constantia had lighted up'.[16] He was quick to realize his incompatibility with legal practice:

> My optics were to such a degree distorted, that, to my eyes, the imperfections of the phantom rule of action seemed only errors calling for an easy remedy. I had not learned how far they served as sources of wealth, power and factitious dignity. I had contracted – oh, horrible! that unnatural, and, at that time, almost unexampled appetite – the love of innovation.[17]

Judicial evidence is often considered to be a dry, technical and specialized subject. By contrast Bentham's writings are notable for their

Bentham on evidence 23

passion, their sincerity, and their obsessiveness, as well as for their extent.[18] These autobiographical fragments vividly depict the spirit and the flavour of his approach to adjective law; they provide a revealing link with some of his more general lifelong concerns and obsessions. By themselves they do not explain why he devoted so much attention to this subject at a particular time and they are, in one important respect, misleading: English civil procedure was the subject of criticism from within the legal profession as well as from outside it.[19] It may be that one reason for concentrating on the reform of adjective law was that it provided a vulnerable, and potentially popular, point on which to attack 'the establishment'.[20]

An early manuscript sketches the outline of a project on Evidence and Procedure and the topic is touched on in several of his early writings;[21] but Bentham did not settle down to work out the details until fairly late. Then for a decade, between about 1803 and 1812, this was his main preoccupation. The result was a mass of manuscript, only about half of which has ever been published.[22] Why did he turn his attention to the subject at this particular time? And why did he think it deserved so much attention?

There are several possible answers to these questions.[23] First, Bentham was acutely conscious of the importance of procedure in politics, as well as law. Perhaps more clearly than anyone before him he perceived the importance of parliamentary procedure; he saw equally clearly that the most perfect system of substantive law would be useless without the support of adequate machinery for its application and enforcement. For him, the direct end of procedure must always be vindication of rights and enforcement of law.[24] This concern with implementation and process – commonplace for a lawyer, but unusual for a theorist – is one crucial link between theory and practice in Bentham's Science of Legislation; the idea permeates all his major writings. His theory of evidence represents one of his attempts to work out the details of the basic insight systematically and comprehensively.

The French Revolution provided a direct stimulus to the development of his ideas.[25] *An Essay on Political Tactics*, written in 1789, urged the French to model the procedure of their National Assembly on a systematized version of English parliamentary practice. *Judicial Establishment in France* anticipates views on judicial organization and administration that were to be developed more fully in *Scotch Reform*, *Court of Lords Delegates*, various smaller works, and ultimately in the *Constitutional Code*. There is a clear progression from these working papers for the French written mainly between 1788 and 1790, through the writings on evidence and judicial organization of the first decade or so of the nineteenth century, to the grand design, more comprehensive and more Utopian, of the later works, notably the *Constitutional Code* and the *Principles of Judicial Procedure*. The suggestion is plausible that each of

24 Theories of Evidence

these works represents the working out in detail of a programme that had been sketched at an early stage of his life.[26]

Thirdly, there may be a contingent, political reason for the timing and form of Bentham's main work on evidence. During the 1790s he had concentrated on political economy and issues of social policy, such as the poor law and the National Charity Company. In particular he had invested a great deal of time and emotion in promoting his plans for a model penitentiary, the Panopticon.[27] It became a lost cause in March 1801 when the Treasury, after many delays, decided to adopt a more modest scheme that was quite unacceptable to Bentham.[28] He made strenuous efforts to have the decision reversed but it was not until 1803 that he admitted defeat. He was bitterly disappointed and his resentment was kept fresh by a protracted dispute over compensation for the cancellation of his contract. The collapse of the venture freed him to direct his attention to other matters; it also led him to re-examine his fundamental ideas and the form of government requisite for their implementation. It is significant that the *Rationale of Judicial Evidence* and cognate writings are the product of the period immediately following the collapse of the Panopticon scheme: the subject may seem technical, but Bentham's motives were in part political. This is probably the period of his transition to political radicalism. As a practical reformer he was on the look out for ways of winning political support for his ideas; there is also a strong suggestion of a desire for revenge.[29]

Dr Hume has suggested that:

> . . . despite the undeniable differences in subject-matter and overt political stance in his works written before and after 1808, it is possible to see nearly all that he wrote between 1802 and 1822 as parts of a single intellectual enterprise, the development of a campaign against misrule in all its forms.[30]

In this view, Bentham, having failed to move part of the establishment to adopt one particular project for reform, deliberately switched his attention to an area where he might have a better chance of success: for there were many aspects of judicial procedure and administration that were patently in need of reform; the confusing complexities of litigation and the attendant cumulation of vexation, expense and delay were the subject of popular concern; lawyers are rarely, if ever, popular as a class. From a political point of view, it made good tactical sense to choose such an unpopular target for attack.

On the constructive side, Bentham also saw the subjects of evidence, procedure and judicial administration as having great constitutional significance. It was consistently a part of his design that the will of the supreme legislator should be paramount, that the power of the Executive, of the Church and of other aristocratic elements should be curtailed and controlled, and that the judiciary should be so established as to perform its proper role as co-operative servants and agents of the legislature. The primary duty of judges was to implement the law in accordance with utility, but not to make it.[31] Some of Bentham's most important writings on judicial administration, notably *Scotch Reform*, *Court of Lords Delegates*, and *Elements of the Act of Packing*, were written during the same period as his main work on evidence.[32] All of these are informed by his vision of the ideal utilitarian polity and they all in turn contributed to the development of his theory of Government and the *Constitutional Code*, which occupied much of his attention from 1822 onwards. Whether or not Bentham was 'converted' to democracy in 1808 or earlier – a question which is still debated among Bentham scholars – he seems to have consistently held the view that a theory of evidence represented an important part of a theory of adjudication which in turn is a sub-theory of a general theory of government. Bentham's theory of evidence is remarkable for the consistency of its standpoint: the whole work is addressed to the legislator; even the very detailed consideration of the problem of assessing the probative force of different kinds of evidence takes the form of advice to the legislator on what instructions to give to triers of fact. It is as clear an example of a design theory as one can find.

Bentham's interest in constitutional reform and the remedy of specific abuses are important ingredients of his approach to evidence, but other concerns are also relevant. We have seen that his ideas on evidence are intimately related to his theory of fictions and that some of his attitudes to religion, to morality and to the abuse of power by authority come together in his treatment of oaths. We shall see that the related themes of fallacies, jargon and mystification feature prominently here as in other writings; his somewhat mechanistic psychology, which is at present best known through his account of motives in *An Introduction to the Principles of Morals and Legislation*, receives what is in certain respects its fullest development in Books I and II of the *Rationale of Judicial Evidence*; *The Table of the Springs of Action* (1805-15) also belongs to the same period. Most important of all, the theory of evidence represents a clear and relatively straightforward application of the principle of utility. All of this confirms the view that Bentham was an extraordinarily consistent thinker: his theory of evidence flowed from and fed into his ideas on many other subjects. The *Rationale of Judicial Evidence* and its satellites need to be seen in the context of his ideas as a whole; they also provide one illuminating route towards an understanding of England's most remarkable jurist.[33]

Sources

'In the map of science, the department of evidence remains to this hour a perfect blank. Power has hitherto kept it in a state of wilderness: reason

26   Theories of Evidence

has never visited it.'[34] Bentham gives the impression that he wrote largely from his head. There is some support for this view in both the published writings and the manuscripts. There are very few references or footnotes and even fewer direct quotations; he was disdainful of case law and less than half-a-dozen cases – mostly trials, such as the *Donnellan* and *Calas* cases – are used again and again;[35] the organization and much of the substance can, indeed, be claimed as original. He was also acutely aware of the difficulties of presenting a systematic account of common sense without appearing to belabour the obvious.

Bentham's unbookish approach might not commend itself to those lawyers who see scholarship as the accumulation and synthesis of authorities. However, it is misleading to suggest that he wrote on a *tabula rasa*. There was a substantial, if diverse, body of literature in existence and he was familiar with it. Apart from general works on law and procedure, the three leading specialized treatises on evidence provided him with a starting-point: he relied on *Peake* for the exposition of the law as it was and even commended it;[36] he launched a lengthy and detailed attack on *Gilbert*[37] and made some critical comments on *Buller*.[38] There is no explicit reference to Evans' translation of Pothier, which was published in 1806, but it would be very surprising indeed if he were unacquainted with a work which attracted a great deal of attention and was edited, with extensive commentary, by a fellow disciple of Lord Mansfield.[39] Bacon, Hartley, Locke, Paley and Hume at the very least provide the starting-point of Bentham's epistemology[40] and psychology, and there is plenty of evidence that he was intimate with the writings of Beccaria, Montesquieu and Voltaire; to some extent he reacted against them.[41] He had studied classical rhetoric. Although his knowledge of Roman Law may not have been very profound, he was familiar with the writings of Heineccius, Justinian, Gaius, and others.[42] Unlike most English lawyers, he took an active interest in the law of other jurisdictions, and, in respect of evidence, makes quite extensive reference to particular laws of Belgium, Denmark, Germany, France and Scotland, among others.[43]

Apart from direct sources, the *Rationale* bears the marks of eighteenth-century thought. The emphasis on reason, on the substitution of individual judgement for authority, and on experience are all characteristic of post-enlightenment thought. During the eighteenth century, interest in evidence and probability had been stimulated by attempts to place belief in the existence of God on the basis of evidence and reason rather than revelation – Gilbert and Hale were among those who had participated in debates in the Royal Society on this and related topics.[44] This is also the period of significant progress in the development of probability theory. It is not just a coincidence that three important theorists of evidence – Bentham, Evans and Glassford – raised similar questions, but advanced rather different answers, apparently largely independently of each other, although further research is needed to establish what, if any, were the connections between them.[45] Civil procedure and the rules of evidence were popular targets for criticism and Bentham was by no means alone in blaming the self-interest and traditionalism of the legal profession for the resulting vexations. Even if Bentham wrote largely from his head, many of the issues and ideas were 'in the air' at the time.

Halévy suggests that his emphasis on simplicity echoes Cartwright,[46] that many of his views on judicial organization and procedure were directly inspired by de Lolme[47] and that '[b]y a curious detour . . . Bentham's radicalism, in the sphere of judicial procedure and organization, involved a restoration of the patriarchal system advocated by Sir Robert Filmer, the defender of absolute monarchy'.[48] It is difficult to judge how far to attribute such similarities of view to influence or to affinity; what is important to bear in mind is that Bentham's originality lies not so much in the substance of his views on a number of philosophical and political issues; rather no one before or since has presented so comprehensive, systematic or radical an analysis of the foundations of judicial evidence and procedure. Nor has anyone taken such an uncompromising stance against all types of rigid formality and regulation in adjudication.

(ii) An Outline of the *Rationale of Judicial Evidence*

The purpose of this section is to present an analytical précis of the *Rationale of Judicial Evidence*.[1] While no secondary account can be a substitute for the original, it is hoped that this will provide a sufficiently detailed guide to relieve all but the specialist from the burden of reading through the whole of this enormous work. Unlike some great books, not much is gained from trying to read it through as a whole: the central argument is quite easily grasped; the detail on many topics can be studied selectively and much that is outdated, repetitious or trivial can be skipped judiciously.[2] This outline will also serve as a stepping-stone for considering selected themes in Bentham's theory of evidence in more detail.

The central thesis of the *Rationale* can be succinctly stated in the form of a catechism:

Q. What are the ends of procedure?
A. The direct end is rectitude of decision, that is the correct application of substantive law to true facts. The subordinate end is avoidance of vexation, expense or delay. Conflicts between the direct and subordinate ends are to be resolved by reference to the principle of utility.

28 *Theories of Evidence*

Q. What system of procedure is best calculated to further the ends of procedure?

A. The Natural System, that is a system characterized by the absence of the artificial rules and technical devices of the Technical System of Procedure.

Q. When should evidence be excluded from consideration by the trier of fact?

A. Hear everyone, admit everything unless the evidence is (a) irrelevant or (b) superfluous or (c) its production would involve preponderant vexation, expense or delay.

Q. By what means can the legislator provide for the completeness and the accuracy of testimony?

A. By prescribing sanctions for 'forthcomingness' of witnesses and of evidence and against mendacity; by providing admonitory instructions addressed to the understanding of the judge, concerning the value and weight of different kinds of evidence. To eschew all artificial binding rules addressed to the will rather than the understanding.

Q. What are the causes of the creation and survival of the Technical System?

A. The sinister interests of the legal profession and the judiciary (Judge and Co.).

Q. By what means can the causes of the Technical System be opposed?

A. By adoption of the Natural System; by paying judges a salary rather than fees; by placing responsibility for decisions squarely on the single judge; and by subjecting these decisions to the security of publicity and other securities.

This, in a nutshell, is the gist of Bentham's thesis. It is, as it were, the 'plot' of the *Rationale*. On its own it conveys very little of the flavour or the underlying reasons for the argument. Yet, unlike the plots of novels and operas, this précis does represent the core of Bentham's theory. For the *Rationale* is in essence the lengthy elaboration of a quite simple argument against artificial technicality in the administration of justice.[3]

The *Rationale* begins with a brief statement of objectives: there is one theorem to be proved and two problems to be solved.[4] The theorem is the non-exclusion principle: that, with a view to rectitude of decision, no evidence should be excluded unless its production would involve preponderant vexation, expense or delay.[5] The first problem concerns the means of implementing this principle; the solution takes the form of advice addressed to the legislator, 'the species of legislator who as yet remains to be formed',[6] on how to establish a system that maximizes rectitude of decision in adjudication. As we shall see, the advice is mainly negative. The weighing of evidence is not susceptible to regulation by rules;[7] the main tasks of the legislator are to replace the technical system with the natural system of procedure and to give general instructions on judging the truth of evidence. The form and content of these instructions are the subject of the second problem. In short, the *Rationale* consists almost entirely of advice by Bentham to the ideal legislator on what needs to be done about evidence in an ideal system of adjudication and what instructions to give to judges in weighing evidence. Other aspects of adjudication belong to the subject of procedure.[8]

Bentham's general conclusions, baldly stated at the start, are not fully elaborated until the last two books.[9] In between are over 2,500 pages of 'rationale' – a patient, labyrinthine exploration of a wide range of issues which all bear directly or indirectly on the central conclusions. Book I is entitled 'Theoretic Grounds'. The early sections deal with basic concepts and general considerations – the nature of evidence in general and in the context of adjudication, facts in general and different species of facts and of evidence.[10] For Bentham 'facts' were events or states of things; in the judicial context the main concern is with 'those facts, and those only, concerning the existence or non-existence of which, at a certain point of time or place, a persuasion may be formed by a judge, for the purpose of grounding a decision thereupon'.[11] The main distinction in this context is between principal facts (the fact to be proved or *factum probandum*) and evidentiary facts (the probative fact or *factum probans*).[12] Evidence is a word of relation, referring to 'any matter of fact, the effect, tendency, or design of which, when presented to the mind, is to produce a persuasion concerning the existence of some other matter of fact: a persuasion either affirmative or disaffirmative of its existence'.[13] Although Bentham does not explicitly use the term in this context, the relation between the *factum probans* and *factum probandum* is normally referred to as 'relevance'; because he defined evidence in terms of 'the tendency . . . to produce a persuasion'[14] he has been criticized for introducing a subjective, psychological element into a concept that is best treated as being concerned with objective, logical relations.[15]

Bentham next considers the notions of probative force and persuasion, their relationship to each other and how (and whether) they can be measured, a topic which provoked an exchange between his editors, Dumont and John Stuart Mill.[16] These sections lay the groundwork for the later discussion of probability, improbability and impossibility in Book V. Chapter VII explores the cause of belief in testimony and, in general, takes the side of Hume and Locke in rejecting intuitionist notions of innate ideas (and other 'nonsense pisteutics' of the Scottish common-sense school)[17] and in defending the position that 'experience is the foundation of all our knowledge'.[18] Chapter VIII analyses the different modes of incorrectness or falsehood in testimony as a prelude to a lengthy consideration of the psychological, intellectual and moral causes of correctness and completeness in testimony and their opposites. These chapters are notable for a compact exposition of Bentham's

30 *Theories of Evidence*

psychology and for a direct and explicit application of the theory of motives and sanctions that had been expounded in *An Introduction to the Principles of Morals and Legislation* and the *Table of the Springs of Action*.[19] Bentham's main thesis, that any motive may operate as a cause either of verity, veracity or mendacity,[20] is one of the main springboards for his attack on the technical system and on the very idea of rules of evidence. Chapter XII pauses to consider and reject the suggestion that a decision taken without evidence from external sources can be well grounded.

Having surveyed the causes of trustworthiness and untrustworthiness in testimony, Bentham turns in the second book to a double question: by what means, within the power of the legislator, can trustworthiness be maximized and the danger of deception be minimized? The analysis is systematic. The main dangers (incorrectness, mendacity, incompleteness, indistinctness), the main stations to be guarded (deponents, including the parties, and the judge), and the main objects (detection, correction, prevention) are identified and distinguished as a preliminary to the detailed consideration of internal and external securities of trustworthiness. Bentham's argument, which fills nearly 450 pages, may be roughly summarized as follows: the primary qualities of trustworthiness, correctness and completeness, are backed by eight secondary qualities with correspond to internal securities. It is desirable that evidence should be particular; sufficiently recollected; unpremeditated; assisted by suggestion; not assisted by false suggestion; extracted and tested by interrogation; expressed distinctly and in permanent form. Sometimes those qualities conflict: for example, testimony cannot simultaneously be recollected and unpremeditated; suggestion may frustrate as well as further correctness. A key problem for the legislator is to reconcile these conflicts or to decide which to sacrifice if they are irreconcilable.[21] A number of external securities present themselves as possible means for securing desirable qualities in a mass of testimony. These can be grouped into five general categories. First, securities which may reduce the temptation to falsehood, notably punishment, oath, shame. Secondly, securities which reduce the power or the opportunity of a witness to give in to temptation, especially means for reducing premeditation and access to mendacity-serving information. Thirdly, powers conferred on officials to procure evidence, such as the power to compel answers, to compel production of evidence and to investigate. Fourthly, publicity, which is for Bentham the key instrument 'to give power and efficiency to all those other instruments'.[22] Fifthly, writing, 'that handmaid of all the other arts and sciences'.[23] Finally, and predictably, exclusion of relevant testimony is declared to be a false security for trustworthiness.

The major part of Book II consists of a systematic account of the uses and limitations of each of the external securities. The alleged basis is 'the experience and applause of ages'[24] and common sense. We will not attempt to summarize these chapters, which encompass a rich variety of topics, including Bentham's views on the limited value of oaths;[25] a pungent critique of the English law of perjury[26] and some interesting observations on inquisitorial and adversary proceedings,[27] on privacy,[28] and on the use and abuse of writing.[29] With regard to trustworthiness, Bentham emphasizes above all the value of cross-examination and of publicity, the two saving graces of the English system of procedure.[30]

Book III deals with the extraction of testimonial evidence. It consists for the most part of a long examination of the potentialities and limitations of five different modes of interrogation and a critique of English and Roman law in the light of this analysis. Bentham's main conclusions are clear and forthright: 'there is but one perfectly good and fit mode of collecting testimony'[31] – oral interrogation before the judge in public; it is of paramount importance to commit oral testimony to writing 'in proportion as it issues from the lips of the person deposing or examined'.[32] All other methods of extraction of evidence are inferior and should be resorted to only if using 'the perfect mode' would involve preponderant vexation, expense or delay. To England belongs the glory of developing the mode of oral interrogation and counter-interrogation,[33] but it is not used as extensively as it should be; instead spurious reasons are advanced for many unjustified departures from this practice and, through a confusion by association, it is trial by jury that is held up as the glory of the English system rather than trial by oral examination.[34]

Book IV is devoted to 'Preappointed Evidence', that is, evidence created or preserved with a view to being used as evidence at some future time.[35] 'The sort of facts which such evidence is employed to prove, are mostly facts constitutive or evidentiary of *right*.'[36] Preappointed evidence may be original, for example registers of births and deaths, or 'transcriptitious', such as copies of official documents or records. This book is one of the most original and the most influential in the whole *Rationale*. The subject, claims Bentham, is 'new in denomination . . . and even in idea'.[37] It encompasses the use and dangers of formalities in contracts and wills, publication and evidence of laws, official evidence, registration of legally-operative facts at large, and of genealogical facts (deaths, births and marriages in particular) – the latter providing a springboard for an irreverent attack on the registration of religious *ceremonies*, of funerals, baptisms and weddings instead of the basic facts of death, birth and marriage. Because of this absurd example of the pernicious influence of priestcraft, whenever a ceremony has not taken place there is no legal evidence of the crucial fact. If the government were to take the place of the church in keeping records not only would a more efficient system of proving such facts be established, but such registers could also form a valuable source of statistical information for the legislator. Bentham summarized his conclusions on preappointed

32 *Theories of Evidence*

evidence as follows:

> In the book having for its subject *preappointed* evidence – in bringing to
> view the *uses* or *advantages* derivable from that kind of evidence,
> considered as applied to instruments expressive of contracts, taken in
> the largest sense; prevention of spurious or falsified instruments, i.e.
> spurious in the whole or in part, was stated as being of the number of
> those uses.
>
> The function then considered as belonging to the legislator was, so
> to order matters, that, in so far as contracts have been entered into,
> genuine instruments expressive of them shall be in existence; and that
> spurious instruments, instruments expressive of discourses that were
> never uttered by the persons by whom they purport, or by some one
> are pretended, to have been uttered, may not be in existence.[38]

At the time Bentham wrote, English law lagged far behind continental
systems in its provisions for official 'preappointed' evidence and for
perpetuating testimony. During the nineteenth century a number of
statutes were directed to remedying this situation; Bentham was given
some of the credit for these reforms,[39] even though this piecemeal
approach produced results that were less comprehensive, cheap and
expeditious than his own recommendations.

Although he used his knowledge of other systems to good effect, his
treatment of the subject is comprehensive, penetrating and in some
respects highly original. Bentham's analysis points in two different
directions: on the one hand, having perceived the value of creating and
preserving evidence of a very wide range of kinds of events, transactions
and proceedings, he argued for a substantial extension of record-
keeping; on the other hand he was acutely aware of the danger of treating
official records as sacrosanct by giving them special evidentiary value
through formal rules of weight: Gilbert's hierarchy of rules was based on
the fallacy of confusing authenticity and verity of documents.[40] Bentham
advised the legislator to facilitate the creation and preservation of
evidence through writing, but to leave it to the trier of fact to assess the
credibility of the contents in each case.

Book V, 'Of Circumstantial Evidence', might well have been placed a
good deal earlier in the *Rationale*, for much of it extends and elaborates
the theoretical analysis in Book I. The early chapters introduce some
additional basic concepts: direct and circumstantial evidence, *factum
probans* and *factum probandum*, relevance, probability, probabilizing,
disprobabilizing and infirmative facts, and real evidence.[41] Chapters 4–
13 deal systematically with different modes of circumstantial evidence,
including silence, confessorial evidence and various examples of what
Wigmore was later to term prospectant, concomitant, and retrospectant
evidence, that is circumstances taking place before, concurrently with or
after the fact in issue – a topic dealt with in chapter 14. There follows a

Bentham on evidence 33

general discussion of the probative force of circumstantial evidence and then 126 pages on improbability and impossibility. The book ends with a brief consideration of how far the atrocity of an alleged offence is a ground for incredibility.

Book v thus contains some of the most important theoretical passages in the *Rationale*. The complex topic of probabilities will be considered in detail below.[42] We cannot attempt here to do justice to Bentham's conceptual scheme, much of which was assimilated into the mainstream of evidence discourse, but it is worth giving a brief account of his distinction between direct and circumstantial evidence, the central argument of Book v and the discussion of impossibility.

For Bentham all evidence is either direct or circumstantial; real evidence is a species of the latter:

> The evidence afforded by any given mass of testimony is either direct or circumstantial, according to the relation it bears to the fact to which it is considered as applying. It is direct, in respect of any and every fact expressly narrated by it; and, in particular, every fact of which the witness represents himself as having been a percipient witness. It is circumstantial, in respect of any and every fact not thus expressly narrated by it: in particular, every fact of which the witness does *not* represent himself as having been a percipient witness, and the existence of which, therefore, is a matter of inference, being left to be concluded from its supposed connexion with the facts spoken to by the testimony in its character of direct evidence.[43]

The main significance of the distinction relates to the nature of the logical processes involved: Where all the evidence is direct 'the case is such as affords not room for any *special* inference: for any other inference than that general one, by which, from the discourse of which the existence of this or that fact is asserted, the existence of that fact is inferred, and credited'.[44] With circumstantial evidence an additional (special) inference is always involved. To put it very simply, with direct evidence the form of inference is: 'From W's statement "Y exists" we infer that Y exists' – $(W^1 \to Y)$. With circumstantial evidence there is at least one additional step: 'From W's statement "X exists", we infer that X exists; from the proposition "X exists" we infer that Y exists' – $(W^1 \to X \to Y)$. There is thus a 'chain of facts', with at least two inferences involved. In the case of direct evidence there is a direct inference from an evidentiary fact (*factum probans*) to an ultimate principal fact (*factum probandum*), but 'the evidentiary fact is throughout of an uniform description'[45] – a statement by a witness that the principal fact exists 'on the ground of its having, in some way or other, come within the cognizance of his perceptive faculties'.[46] The probative force of direct evidence depends on our general grounds for belief in testimony and the credibility of this particular witness in the circumstances. Circumstantial

34 Theories of Evidence

evidence embraces many different kinds of facts. As it is put in the *Treatise*:

> Circumstantial evidence is that deduced from the existence of a fact, or a group of facts, which, being directly applicable to the principal fact, lead to the conclusion that the latter exists. This conclusion is an operation of judgment. The distinction between *fact* and *circumstance* regards only a given case. Every fact may be called a circumstance in relation to another. That it thundered or hailed on the day a murder was committed, is an event extremely independent of the principal fact, but it may be a circumstance worthy of being remarked, and may lead to evidence. Circumstances, then, are facts placed round some other fact; each fact may be considered as a centre, and all others as ranged round it.
>
> Circumstances comprehend the state of things and the conduct of persons. Things furnish what is called *real evidence*; but whether we argue from things, or from the conduct of persons, this species of evidence is always the same, always founded on analogy, on the connection between cause and effect; therefore it was, that we said (Book I, chapter 3.), that all real evidence is circumstantial.[47]

Because additional, special inferences are involved and because of the variety of circumstantial evidentiary facts, the assessment of the probative force of circumstantial evidence is more complex and more problematic than in the case of direct evidence. Bentham is clear that it does not follow from this that one type of evidence is generally superior to the other. He attacks both the fallacy that 'circumstances cannot lie'[48] and the notion that direct evidence should *ipso facto* be treated as superior to circumstantial.[49]

Book V centres on the three main questions: what can be done by way of rules to ensure that circumstantial evidence is given due weight? What instructions of a general nature can be given by the legislator to the judge? What is the probative force of circumstantial evidence? Bentham's response to all three follows a consistent theme: the subject is hardly susceptible of generalization. As he put it in the *Treatise*:

> To find infallible rules for evidence, rules which insure a just decision is, from the nature of things, absolutely impossible; but the human mind is too apt to establish rules which only increase the probabilities of a bad decision. All the service that an impartial investigator of the truth can perform in this respect is, to put legislators and judges on their guard against such hasty rules.[50]

In answer to the first question he unequivocally maintains that the legislator should lay down no binding rules about the admissibility or the weight to be attached to particular kinds of circumstantial evidence. In response to the second question he is merely prepared to give a few

Bentham on evidence 35

warnings to prevent undervaluation or overvaluation of evidence, for example, 'Reject no article of circumstantial evidence on the score of weakness'; 'set down no article, nor any aggregate mass, of circumstantial evidence, as even provisionally conclusive in *all* cases'.[51] The advice is only slightly more concrete than the general recommendation to consider all relevant evidence, give it due weight, be careful not to overlook possible invalidating facts and, wherever practicable, to use interrogation to clarify the situation.[52]

Bentham is wary of generalization about the probative force of circumstantial evidence. He classifies it as a species of 'inferior' evidence, because an additional step in the process of persuasion is involved:[53] direct evidence relates directly to the fact in issue; with circumstantial evidence the judge (or jury) has first to be persuaded of the existence of the circumstance (the *factum probans*) and then to make an inference which may be more or less doubtful from this to the existence of the fact in issue (*factum probandum*). The inference is never a necessary one, because there is always the possibility of some infirmative fact that will negative it. Often more than one inference has to be made, there is then an evidentiary chain,[54] each link of which is liable to have its 'infirmative counter-probabilities', so that the probative force of the evidentiary fact is diminished. To designate circumstantial evidence as 'inferior' might suggest that circumstantial evidence is of less probative value than direct evidence. However, this is misleading (indeed, Dumont may have been misled).[55] Bentham explicitly rejected the view that circumstantial evidence, 'considered in the lump',[56] is either inferior or superior to direct evidence in respect of probative force. Each type has certain characteristics which may tend to make it more or less trustworthy in different ways, but strong generalization is dangerous because of the (almost) infinite diversity of facts to be proved and of potential evidentiary facts. In short, Bentham's message is: 'It all depends on the circumstances.'

Bentham's lengthy exploration of the topics of improbability and impossibility will be considered below.[57] So far as the central argument of the *Rationale* is concerned the main point is that the notion of 'impossibility' does not properly belong to the theory of evidence. 'Impossibility' either means logically impossible, which falls outside the scope of the subject, or it means incredibility. Credibility is a matter of evidence; but no fact is universally recognized to be incredible and disagreements about particular facts are best expressed in terms of probabilities which, as we shall see, Bentham defines in terms of persuasion and links to his theory of belief. Improbability and impossibility are resolvable into judgements about disconformity to the established course of nature, but since knowledge of nature is constantly changing, such judgements are only relative:

36   Theories of Evidence

In truth, the degree of incredibility that can with propriety be the subject of consideration for any purpose of judicature, is merely relative and comparative. The object of comparison is the probative force of the evidence by which the existence of the fact considered as improbable is indicated: and the question is, which of the two forces ought to be deemed the greater? – the probative force of the testimony by which the existence of the fact in question is indicated? or the disprobative force designated or pointed to by the word *incredibility*, as employed to express an attribute of the fact? Let the disprobative force of the incredibility be but ever so little greater than the probative force of the testimony by which the existence of the fact is maintained, it is sufficient for the purpose of judicature: the question concerning any superior degree, is purely speculative, not applicable to judicial practice, and, as such, irrelevant to the business of judicature, to the question (whatever it be) before the court.[58]

Bentham's treatment of circumstantial evidence is one of the theoretical highlights of the *Rationale*. His terminology, his account of the process of reasoning involved, his rejection of a number of fallacies and, above all, his thesis that judgements about the probative force of circumstantial evidence are not susceptible to governance by binding rules have all exercised a profound influence on subsequent writings on the subject.[59] The discussion ranges widely and throws some interesting light on his ideas on the nature of science, on the state of psychological knowledge and on a number of specific topics, such as witches, ghosts, alibis, punishment for beliefs and free will. Later we shall consider in detail the relationship between his treatment of probabilities and his general ontology and epistemology. Here it may help to prepare the way by giving a brief account of his very lengthy exploration of the topics of improbability and impossibility.

Improbability and impossibility are names not for any qualities of facts themselves, but for our persuasion of their non-existence. Impossible facts need to be distinguished from (a) contradictions in terms and (b) inconceivable facts, e.g. 'that two right lines should of themselves enclose a space'. No facts are universally recognized to be incredible, for incredibility has only one cause, that is disconformity to nature. There are three modes of disconformity to nature: (1) disconformity *in toto*, for example, that a body is at the same time in different places; (2) disconformity in degree, for example a man sixty feet high; (3) disconformity *in specie*, that is 'facts altogether different from any which have ever been observed, but which, if true, would not be violations of any generally recognized law of nature, e.g. the unicorn.'[60]

The improbability of a fact, relative to a particular individual, depends upon the degree of his acquaintance with the course of nature. Locke recounted, and Bentham several times refers to, the story of the King of

Siam, who laughed scornfully at Dutchmen when they told him of winter scenes in which water was hardened sufficiently to bear men and waggons like dry land. Improbability is a particular case of counter-evidence, that is evidence which is infirmative, but not destructive. But it may be objected that some facts are intrinsically impossible – that impossibility may be a property of the fact itself. Not so, says Bentham; I am as firmly convinced as any person that belief in witches flying on broomsticks is absurd. But the basis for my belief is not the intrinsic impossibility of such a phenomenon; it is the circumstantial evidence of two physical laws – the law of gravity and the law that no body ever changes its place without some specific cause of motion. However, my belief in these laws is based on a mass of circumstantial evidence; the laws may be subject to revision in the light of direct evidence of their violation: 'Think not that, because their existence is not to be believed without evidence, therefore their existence can be reasonably disbelieved against evidence'.[60A] There are good grounds for disbelieving facts that are disconformable to the course of nature. In the case of anti-physical or supernatural facts – such as ghosts, apparitions and witches – the evidence typically presented in support of such claims is untrustworthy: supernatural facts are never supported by the best evidence; they are rarely presented to several persons at the same time; they tend to be presented to persons suffering from a mental or physical indisposition; the reported facts are always of the evanescent kind; they are never corroborated by real evidence. Why then is there a propensity to believe in anti-physical facts? One reason is precedent: if one instance of witchcraft is accepted as true, this opens the door to belief in other instances. Furthermore, there are strong motives for believing or affirming certain kinds of fact disconformable to nature, such as facts promising wealth or the cure of diseases (real or supposed), or facts promising happiness or threatening unhappiness, both in the extreme. Judgement, opinion and persuasion are, to a very considerable degree, under the dominion of the will; discourse and declared opinion are altogether under the dominion of the will. Not only is the propensity to give credence to false facts supported by ordinary hope of pleasure or fear of pain, but also by acceptance of authority instead of evidence; the situation is all too well understood by men in power, who proceed more effectively by ascribing merit to belief and crushing open expressions of offending opinions than by trying to make war upon opinion by direct application of factitious political sanctions.

Arguments appealing to impossibility or incredibility are capable of being presented on two occasions. First, when in response to a fact deposed by a witness, for example a fact pretended to have taken place through witchcraft, the defence avers that it is impossible; secondly, when a fact deposed by a witness is met by a fact which is incompatible with it, as in the case of alibi evidence. Where alibi evidence is true, it is

38   Theories of Evidence

indeed highly persuasive because it is contrary to the course of nature for the same person to be in two different places at the same time. However, such evidence is particularly suspect in practice, because there may be uncertainty that the point of time was exactly the same and because of its susceptibility to abuse. Bentham called the first type of case impossibility *per se*, the second impossibility *si alia*; however, his editor inserted a passage in the text pointing out that in both cases the nature of the impossibility is exactly the same: the argument is that the allegation is in disconformity to the established course of nature. The difference is rather that in the first case the alleged fact, taken by itself, cannot be true; in the second, the alleged facts may be true, but both together cannot.

Bentham ends with a brief discussion of impossibility in relation to psychological facts. He suggests that, although the science of psychology has not progressed as far as the physical sciences, nevertheless there is a basis for making judgements about the probability or improbability of alleged psychological facts in terms of their conformity or disconformity to the established course of nature. Because such facts are not so open to direct observation as physical facts and because of '[t]he sort of internal perception or consciousness we all feel of what is called the freedom of our will',[61] we are less inclined to talk of *impossibility* in regard to pyschological facts.

Such caution is all to the good. Bentham puts in a powerful plea for the importance of psychological studies in connection with judicial evidence. 'To weigh evidence against evidence, to weigh particular evidence against general probability, requires a proportionable skill in the science of psychology.' Alleged improbabilities are far more frequent in relation to alleged acts or states of mind than in relation to physical facts. Irrational modes of proof existed because of deficiencies in 'this useful science'. Their disappearance, he implies, is attributable to advances in psychology. Yet many of the surviving defects of procedure even among the most enlightened nations are attributable to the same cause. 'To investigate these defects, step by step, is the direct object of the present work.'[62]

Book VI is devoted to Makeshift Evidence, that is, evidence which is to a greater or lesser degree inferior by virtue of the absence of one or more of the securities applying to ordinary evidence.[63] The task of the legislator is to identify the different species of makeshift evidence, to examine the reasons for their infirmity and either to give securities against these infirmities or to facilitate the availability of better evidence. The two main classes of makeshift evidence are extra-judicially written evidence, which includes all 'casually written' documents and unoriginal evidence, which includes hearsay, unoriginal written evidence (such as copies), and reported real evidence. All kinds of makeshift evidence share certain properties: because typically they are not subject to the securities of cross-examination and the law of perjury, they are open to a

Bentham on evidence 39

characteristic fraud, viz. the fabrication and utterance of pretended information;[64] deception apart, they are also lacking in normal securities against incorrectness and incompleteness. The main general safeguard against these infirmities is the creation of preappointed evidence. Exclusion of makeshift evidence is never a good security against misdecision, unless the information can be conveyed by other evidence in a superior form – e.g. by producing the original rather than a copy.[65]

The traditional justification for excluding some kinds of makeshift, for example hearsay, is based on a confusion between falsity and deception. There is a risk of falsity, but the dangers of deception can be lessened by precautionary instructions (not rules) addressed to the judge, by taking steps to lessen the dangers of each species of makeshift evidence – for example to cross-examine the exhibitant of a document about it on oath – and by using makeshift as indicative evidence, that is as evidence of other, often superior, evidence which can then be sought. The remedy of exclusion is worse than the disease, for absence of information is worse than potentially unreliable information.[66]

Most of Book VI is devoted to a systematic analysis of the dangers attaching to each species and sub-species of makeshift evidence and to laying down admonitory instructions to the judge in respect of them. Thus a chapter is devoted to each of the following: supposed oral evidence transmitted through oral (hearsay);[67] supposed written evidence, transmitted through oral (memoriter);[68] supposed oral evidence, transmitted through written (minuted);[69] supposed written evidence, transmitted through written (transcriptitious);[70] reported real evidence[71] and evidence transmitted through an indefinite number of media.[72]

The manuscript basis of this book was somewhat fragmentary in parts and the editor had to make good some gaps. Parts of it give the impression of being less carefully thought out and less tightly drafted than most of the *Rationale*. This includes the final chapter on Aberrations of English Law in regard to makeshift evidence. Bentham only produced a fragmentary discussion of some examples, rather than a systematic critique, and his young editor, with only a rudimentary legal background, after struggling with sixty pages of intricate technical detail on 'adscititious evidence' (i.e. evidence borrowed from another cause, in particular the doctrine of *res inter alios acta*),[73] takes refuge in rhetorical generalities and asks: 'To what purpose weary the reader with the dull detail of the cases in which casually-written or *exparte* preappointed evidence are excluded, with the equally long and equally dull list of the cases in which, though exclusion would be just as reasonable (if it were reasonable at all), admission, and not exclusion, is the rule?'[74] It is enough to know that the established system is radically wrong, because it is based on wrong principles. If one knows that a system is rotten to the core, to explore in detail which parts are less bad than others is 'as

40 Theories of Evidence

destitute of instruction, as it always and necessarily must be of amusement'.[75]

Perhaps the most interesting part of Book VI for the modern reader, or at least for lawyers, is the discussion of hearsay and the comparison of it with other types of unoriginal evidence.[76] Hearsay is one species of makeshift evidence, similar in most respects to 'casually-written evidence', such as private letters, notes, journals and memoranda. Both are inferior because they lack two of the main securities against incorrectness and incompleteness, viz. fear of punishment for falsehood and the possibility of interrogation and counter-interrogation.[77] Bentham lays down some rules which at first sight look like rules of exclusion:

Rule 1. Except in the cases excepted in the next rule, admit it not. . . .
Rule 2. . . . in the following cases admit it.[78]

But the first rule only applies in the situation when 'the person whose discourse it purports to be [is] forthcoming and interrogable'.[79] In this case no information is excluded by the refusal to admit. But if the witness is dead or otherwise unavailable, or if the hearsay is to be used to invalidate or confirm the evidence of the witness or if the original narrator is a party to the cause, the evidence is to be admitted. What this amounts to is an admonition to make every effort to secure the forthcomingness of the original narrator in order that he may be subject to the securities of sanctions and interrogation. Whether or not Rule 1 deserves to be classified as a 'rule of exclusion', as Chadbourn suggests, or merely as an application of the principle that one ground for excluding evidence is that it is superfluous is of little consequence.[80] The crucial point is that Bentham was prepared to admit hearsay whenever the original narrator was not forthcoming, even in the case of 'hearsay passing through an indefinite number of intermediate persons'.[81] For the rest he makes the various kinds of danger attributable to each category of hearsay and other kinds of makeshift evidence the basis for admonitory instructions rather than formal rules.[82]

Book VII deals with authentication of evidence. The object of pre-appointed evidence is to prevent the fabrication of spurious instruments by providing genuine ones; this is a matter for regulation.[83] The topic of authentication is concerned with how to ensure that genuine instruments are recognized as genuine, and spurious as spurious. This is a matter for instruction. The methods of authentication differ for real, personal, oral and written evidence. Most of the difficulties arise in relation to the last category, especially when the author or other witness of the making of the document is not forthcoming or to summon them would involve preponderant vexation, expense or delay. Much of the book is taken up with a somewhat dry listing of different modes of authenticating and deauthenticating private contracts, official and casually written documents. Bentham's main argument is that the many formalities required

Bentham on evidence 41

by English law on the whole promote trustworthiness, but ignore the collateral ends of procedure and, in particular, involve a great deal of unnecessary expense. The cause of these technicalities is the sinister interest of Judge and Co.; the main rationale advanced is that such formalities are a protection against forgery. But this is based on the fallacious assumption that forgery is the norm: 'Thus it happens, that, for one grain of mischief produced, or that would or could be produced, by fraud in the shape of *forgery*, a thousand, ten thousand, are produced by fraud in the shape of *chicane*.'[84]

Bentham's solution, in addition to providing admonitory instructions, is to suggest a distinction between provisional and definitive authentication.[85] Although he does not use the term, he is suggesting that there should be a presumption in favour of authenticity; normally it should suffice for one party to produce the document and for the other party either to admit its authenticity or to declare his intention to contest it, with the risk of paying costs if he fails. Thus 'definitive' authentication becomes an extraordinary measure, only to be used when fabrication is alleged.

Up to this point the *Rationale* has been concerned with surveying in a fairly general way the main theoretical topics which might form the basis for a prescriptive theory of evidence, addressed directly to the legislator and through him to judges operating under the Natural System of Procedure. So far Bentham has been charting the foothills. There have been some polemical passages and some pungent remarks, but these are only preliminary skirmishes. Books VIII and IX, the two longest books in the *Rationale*, contain the main assault on the exclusionary rules of evidence as part of the Technical System of Procedure. The tone is more polemical, the subject is more specific and the argument is more tightly integrated – a sustained attack on a particular target. If the *Rationale* is considered to be primarily as a radical critique of the technical rules of evidence in Bentham's day, then these two books constitute its core. We will examine the main strands of the argument in detail below,[86] so it will suffice at this stage to give a very brief outline of their organization and contents.

Book VIII, 'Of the Cause of Exclusion of Evidence, The Technical System of Procedure', has been interpreted as an *ad hominem* argument on a grand scale – a polemic against the legal establishment. But it is more an attack on a system of structuring interests than on lawyers as individuals. The exclusionary rules are part and parcel of the technical or fee-gathering system of procedure, which is to be explained almost exclusively in terms of the sinister interests of judges and lawyers.[87] The fundamental evil of the system is that it is set up to further the financial and other interests of a small professional class rather than the greatest happiness of the greatest number.[88] The ends of established judicature are in constant opposition to the ends of justice.[89] Most of the book is

42 Theories of Evidence

taken up with a systematic exposé of twenty devices employed to further those sinister ends. In chapter 27, the main remedies are sketched: the substitution of salaries for fees in all judicial offices; the substitution of the natural for the technical system 'throughout the whole field of procedure';[90] the transformation of all substantive law from juris-prudential (i.e. case law) to pure statutory law; and to set up a system for 'the preservation and amelioration of the fabric of the laws',[91] including provision for monitoring the actual operation of all laws. Bentham's proposals are negative, for the chief characteristic of the Natural System is the absence of technical rules and devices, and many of his specific proposals go beyond the topic of evidence and belong to the fields of judicial organization and procedure.

In Book IX he returns specifically to the theme of the Exclusion of Evidence. After looking at the Exclusionary System in General (Part I), he re-examines the cases in which exclusion of evidence is proper: apart from the special case of confessions to a Catholic priest, his conclusions almost without exception can be subsumed under the general principle that no evidence should be excluded unless it is irrelevant or superfluous or its production would involve preponderant vexation, expense or delay.[92] Part II ends with a survey of remedies 'succadenous' to (i.e. substitutes for) the exclusion of evidence, such as tribunals within reach, uninterrupted sittings, meetings of the parties in the presence of the judge, and various devices for reducing expense and delay. Next Bentham turns to a detailed systematic critique of cases in which evidence has been improperly excluded on the grounds of deception (Part III), of vexation (Part IV), on the double account of vexation and deception (Part V), and finally of disguised exclusion, especially rules regulating the minimum and maximum number of witnesses in various situations, and of negative exclusions.

Although the critique of the exclusionary system extends over nearly 800 pages, most of the argument is at a fairly general level and consists largely of the reiteration and application of a limited number of themes, for example, that deliberately false testimony is exceptional, because lying is a difficult art requiring both skill and effort;[93] that there is almost always less risk of misdecision from false evidence than from absence of evidence; that falsehood does not necessarily lead to deception and that false testimony and silence themselves have value as evidence; that the weighing of evidence is a matter for instruction rather than for regulation by strict rules. Bentham makes no attempt to give a comprehensive account and critique of the morass of contemporary technical rules of evidence. Rather, he took selected examples of particular doctrines to show that in so far as they were ascertainable, they were based on false assumptions (backed by sinister interest) and that, almost without exception, the reasons given to justify particular exceptions undermined the general rules and that they inevitably bred inconsistency. Among his principal specific targets are the doctrine that interest (of parties or extraneous witnesses) is a ground for exclusion,[94] the maxim *nemo tenetur seipsum accusare* (which covers both the privilege against self-incrimination and at least parts of the modern right to silence)[95] and the existing rules relating to privilege, incompetency and corroboration. Some of these will be explored in detail below.

There is much that is of interest in the details of Bentham's argument, but what is striking is the sustained, indeed relentless, application of a few simple ideas to demolish one by one the whole complex structure of the technical system. Although many of his arguments have lost their force by virtue of their own success,[96] and others may seem misconceived or overstated or unfair, taken as a whole Books VIII and IX can still be read with enjoyment and profit as a polemical *tour de force*.

Book x is entitled 'Instructions, to be delivered from the Legislator to the Judge, for the Estimation of the Probative Force of Evidence'. If this leads the reader to expect a succinct restatement of the conclusions of the *Rationale* in the form of a clear set of principles or guidelines, he will be disappointed. For the final book contains a discursive and, in places, fragmentary treatment of a number of topics to do with the weighing of *testimonial* evidence, but it does not attempt to bring together the various instructions scattered throughout the *Rationale* and it barely touches on circumstantial evidence. By this stage, it seems, both author and editor were flagging. Rather more convenient collections of instructions are to be found in the *Introductory View* and *The Treatise*, but even these are not as systematic as Bentham's general theory deserves.[97]

The first chapter returns to the theme of the need for instructions rather than rules in respect of evidence. Exclusionary rules, addressed to the will, are 'so many insults offered by the author of each rule to the understanding of those whose hands are expected to be tied by it';[98] instruction, 'the rival remedy',[99] is a 'gentle and rational substitute'.[100] Most of the instructions that Bentham proposes are obvious and, he suggests, might seem superfluous, except as a reminder to the judge when, in dealing with a complex case, for want of a simultaneous view, one may have been forgotten.[101] He purports only to offer a sample: 'The more plainly true it may happen to them to be, the less extraordinary they will appear, and the less free from all pretension to be taken for any thing beyond the obvious dictates of simple common sense.'[102]

However, the art of the English lawyer is 'the art of knowing that which has no existence, and the art of not knowing what is known to every body else'.[103] English law deals solely with the question of admissibility and gives no guidance on probative force. Judges, inhibited by the rules themselves and by the absurdities which would be shown up if they tried to give overt guidance to juries on credibility of evidence, stay silent. If evidence has been excluded on grounds of its untrustworthiness, warnings to be suspicious of that which has been admitted

44 Theories of Evidence

would look incongruous. Thus 'against calculation, comparison, ratiocination, the door is shut by a kind of instinct'.[104]

The object of the instructions is:

> . . . to point out to the notice of the judge the several circumstances, which, by the influence they exert on the will of the witness, or the indications they afford of his disposition and character, moral and intellectual, present themselves as having the effect of demonstrating the trustworthiness of his evidence – the probability of its being at once correct and complete[105] . . . or, of diminishing the degree of its probative or persuasive force.

The next five chapters deal with various grounds of untrustworthiness: interest in general; pecuniary interest; social connections (particularly the relations of subordinates and superiors); sexual connections; the station of the witness in the cause or suit and improbity. Any interest can promote either mendacity or veracity. Five kinds of interest in particular, each backed by a corresponding sanction, tend to restrain mendacity and falsity: love of ease, fear of shame, fear of legal punishment, fear of supernatural punishment, and regret.[106] The testimony of every man is at all times exposed to the operation of these interests as restraints on falsehood; the same interests may also promote mendacity, but only irregularly as a matter of accident.[107] It is the task of the judge (subject to the constraints of vexation, expense and delay) to bring to light all the interests operating on each piece of testimony and to try to assess in what way they may affect the trustworthiness of the testimony in fact.[108] Here all generalization is dangerous. Bentham was particularly concerned to attack some fallacies of English law based on oversimple notions of the operation of interests and of character on trustworthiness;[109] for example, the supposition that there is any man whose testimony is all true or all untrue; the assumption that any one kind of interest or any number of interests can be *sure* to overpower the force of the tutelary interests;[110] or the assumption that because testimony is false in respect of one fact, it is certain to be false in respect of another. Such spurious reasons provide the purported basis for some exclusions, including one of his main targets: the rules of competency.

In advocating an empirical, as opposed to an *a priori* approach, Bentham struggles uneasily with the dual task of emphasizing the complexity of the subject and trying to give general guidance on how to calculate the effect of different interests and other factors on the trustworthiness of particular pieces of evidence. In the event his instructions do not add up to much more than advice to take nothing for granted, to weigh all factors, and to subject all testimony to the test of consistency, 'the grand instrument' for detecting falsehood.[111]

Chapter VIII is an aberration. It deals briefly, and quite inadequately, with the important question of how to decide in situations of uncertainty.

Bentham on evidence 45

Bentham might have undertaken a thorough-going examination of the problems of standards and burdens of proof and the relative evils of different kinds of misdecision. Instead, this chapter deals quite cursorily with some of the mischiefs of misdecision based on either a party's mendacious self-serving testimony, or that of an extraneous witness, or of mendacious self-disserving testimony. No distinction is made between civil and criminal cases, a narrow range of elementary examples is considered and the mischiefs are ranked solely on the basis of the likelihood of recurrence of this kind of situation. Both *An Introductory View* and the *Treatise* contain clearer treatments of these topics;[112] however, John Stuart Mill should not take the whole blame for the lapse, for Bentham's treatment of standards and burdens of proof is one of the weakest parts of his theory of evidence.[113]

The last three chapters of the *Rationale* are also something of an anticlimax. In chapter IX, in order to reassure those fearful of reform, he briefly discusses some ulterior safeguards against inconveniences which might arise, or be thought to arise from the abolition of all exclusionary rules. Bentham concentrates on allaying two fears – the fear of deception through an increase in mendacious testimony and the fear of increased vexation. False testimony, he argues, can generally be detected by cross-examination and its lack of consistency with other evidence. Admittedly there is a danger in admitting self-serving testimony, but the dangers of exclusion are greater. He also proposes a new ulterior safeguard, a 'system of judicial book-keeping' in which the species and nature of each item of evidence is registered under apposite heads, with the dual aim of minimizing misdecision and making a systematic accounting of the expense, vexation and delay.[114] The second aspect is set out more fully in *Scotch Reform* in elaborate 'Delay and Complication Tables'.[115] The idea of tabulating the evidence in a complex case may be a simple and undeveloped forerunner of Wigmore's chart method of analysing a mixed mass of evidence.[116]

Throughout the *Rationale*, Bentham has maintained that preponderant vexation, expense or delay takes priority over rectitude of decision judged by the standard of utility. Here he contents himself with a purple passage:

> For the avoidance of unnecessary vexation, an important maxim remains to be brought to view.
> I suppose the ends of justice substituted to the ends of judicature. I suppose hypocrisy unmasked. I suppose honest eyes opened; imbecility in honest guidance. I suppose the door thrown wide open, not only to all willing testimony, but to all lights that are to be elicited from interrogatories administered to unwilling testimony: to unwilling testimony, whatsoever be the now terrible, the now tremendous, fruits of it: lights collected without reserve from unwilling witnesses,

46 Theories of Evidence

although the result should be the diminishing the multitude of misdeeds of all kinds, and diminishing (if English lawyers and their dupes endure to see it diminished) the barbarity, as well as imbecility, of their penal code.[117]

Chapter x, 'Recapitulation', lists seven errors against which a judge should be on his guard and then wanders off, somewhat inconsequentially, into a critique of existing sources of guidance, the law reports and practitioners' works. Research into such documents is merely of use for illustration and amusement: 'To engage in any such research, in the hope of any instruction . . . would be at the best like the reading over and studying the Bibliotheca of Alchemy, in the expectation of meeting with instruction applicable to the advancement of modern chemistry.'[118]

The *Rationale* ends with a brief 'Conclusion'. Given that the existing system of procedure is framed in pursuit of private sinister ends, a new system is required directed to the attainment of the ends of justice. Neither foreign models nor Utopian ideas are needed; every man's family, the Saxon county courts and the sheriff's courts and borough courts in Scotland provide adequate models for 'a perfect system'.[119] All that is necessary is for the lawful legislator to act:

5. Nothing more is required, than the extending, in all causes and cases, to rich and poor, without distinction, that relief which in certain causes and cases, and in certain districts, has been afforded to the poor: torn (by the appointed guardians and friends of the people) from the rapacity, or abandoned by the negligence, of their natural enemies.
6. It requires, indeed, the establishment of local judicatures: but even this is not innovation, (not that even innovation, where necessary, should ever be declined,) not innovation, but restoration and extension. *Restoration* of powers once in existence,[120] before they were swallowed up by the framers of the existing system of abuse, under favour of their own resistless power, working by their own frauds, covered by their own disguises, in pursuit of their own sinister ends. *Extension*, the restoring, though with some increase of amplitude, to one half of the island, the fountains of justice so happily retained by the other.[121]

Bentham is at pains to point out that, by advocating a return to the pre-Norman system of justice, he is not committing the fallacy of 'the Chinese Argument', that is supposing 'men in the savage state endued with perfect wisdom, but growing less and less wise as experience accumulates, and progress is made in the track of civilization'.[122] The natural system of procedure accords with the dictates of reason and utility. 'I give it for good, not *because* it is old, but *although* it happens to be so':[123]

In the case at present on the carpet, the supposed wisdom of the maxim may find an apparent confirmation. By doing away the work of five or six hundred years, and throwing back the system of procedure, as to the most fundamental parts, into the state in which it was at the time of Edward I and much earlier, a mountain of abuse might be removed, and even a near approach to perfection made. Why? Because in principle there is but one mode of searching out the truth: and (bating the corruptions introduced by superstition, or fraud, or folly, under the mask of science) this mode, in so far as truth has been searched out and brought to light, is, and ever has been, and ever will be, the same, in all times, and in all places; in all cottages, and in all palaces: in every family, and in every court of justice. Be the dispute what it may, – see every thing that is to be seen; hear every body who is likely to know any thing about the matter: hear every body, but most attentively of all, and first of all, those who are likely to know most about it, the parties.[124]

(iii) Selected themes in Bentham's theory of evidence

It would take a substantial monograph to do justice to the complex arguments that support the central thesis of the *Rationale* and to the many particular topics with which it deals. This essay has more modest objectives. Having sketched a résumé of his longest, but by no means his only, work specifically on evidence, I shall examine five general themes: the place of the Natural System of Procedure in Bentham's theory of adjudication; his treatment of fictions and probabilities; the anti-nomian thesis; his analysis of the causes of the Technical System; and rectitude of decision as a social value. Taken together, these sections may help to clarify the general nature of Bentham's theory of evidence and its relationship to other aspects of his thought and to some central themes in the Anglo-American tradition of evidence scholarship. This in turn may help to clarify an apparent paradox: how the most expansive and radical of our theorists of evidence belongs to the mainstream of an intellectual tradition that is characterized by a narrow focus and an optimism bordering on complacency about the rationality of judicial processes.

(a) The natural system

As we have seen, the *Rationale* has three main objectives: to establish the principle of non-exclusion; to advise the legislator on means for securing the forthcomingness and the trustworthiness of evidence; and to provide guidance for the judge in assessing the weight of evidence. The general theory of evidence presupposes a general theory of adjudication, which is outlined in the *Rationale*, but developed in more detail in other writings.[1] The core of this theory of adjudication is simply stated: the

48 Theories of Evidence

direct end of procedure is rectitude of decision, that is the correct application of substantive law to reliably determined facts. The system of procedure which is calculated to maximize rectitude of decision is the Natural System, the main principles of which can be restated in a few general precepts: admit all relevant evidence; minimize vexation, expense and delay; hear all parties and witnesses *viva voce* in public; subject them to counter-interrogation; weigh evidence solely on the merits of the individual case without reference to rigid rules; place the sole responsibility for the design of the system and for changes in it in the hands of the legislator; place responsibility for rectitude of decision in individual cases squarely on the single judge; rely on publicity, underwritten by simplicity, as the main security against misdecision and non-decision; above all, seek truth unremittingly, subject only to preponderant vexation, expense or delay.[2]

The main characteristics of the Natural System are negative; Bentham presents and defines it largely in terms of *absence of devices* that characterize the Technical System.[3] This does not mean that the main import of Bentham's theory is negative in the sense of being critical without being constructive. Rather it is a plea for a return to simplicity, common sense and reason – the ordinary reason of everyday practical life. As Bentham is well aware, it is difficult to present a systematic account of common sense without appearing to belabour the obvious.[4]

One way of looking at the notions of the Natural and Technical Systems is as two contrasting models (or 'ideal types' in the Weberian sense). In *Scotch Reform* they are presented in just such a way. Although it involves some repetition, it may be helpful to set out, in abbreviated form, the model as Bentham presented it in *Scotch Reform*:

Chart of the Natural and Technical Systems of Procedure[5]

Natural Procedure Arrangements	Technical Procedure Corresponding Devices
1. Parties heard, in the character of witnesses as well as parties, *face to face*.	1. Parties excluded from first to last as effectually as possible from the presence of the judge.
2. No writing, except in the character of *evidence*, in the shape of minutes taken of *viva voce* testimony, as *supplement* or justified *succadeneum* (i.e. substitute) to *viva voce* testimony.	2. Abuse of writing.
3. Testimony received in none but the best *shape*, viz. *viva voce* testification subject to counter-interrogation, *ex adverso* and *per judicem*.	3. Testimony received, in some cases, in inferior shapes, e.g. 1. Epistolatory answers; 2. Depositions; 3. Affidavit evidence.

Bentham on evidence   49

4. Tribunals *within reach*, consequently distributed over the country.

4. Tribunals *out of reach*, immoderate centralization in the metropolis.

5. Suits usually terminated at first meeting; times for subsequent meetings settled with regard to the convenience of the court and all parties.

5. *Blind fixation of times* by general rules; sinister use and objects of the fixation.

6. Sittings *uninterrupted* or at short and equal intervals.

6. Sittings at *long intervals*.

7. The cause heard from beginning to end by the same judge; division of jurisdiction performed purely on the *geographical* principle.

7. *Bandying* the cause from court to court.

8. No decision, but upon the joint *consideration* of the law and of the evidence.

8. Decision *without thought* and upon *mechanical principles* (because of blind fixation of times); parties penalized for failure to comply with impossible or pretended requirements; indigence penalized; imprisonment for *debt, on mesne process*, before judgment; party abroad, consignable to ruin, for non-compliance with a demand of which it has been rendered impossible for him to be apprised.

9. No decision, but *upon the merits*, as above.

9. Principle of *nullification*; decision on grounds avowedly foreign to the merits; e.g. suitor punished for failure, real or imaginary, of his lawyer; making two causes out of one.

10. Not a syllable ever received from any person without a *security for veracity*, equivalent to that attached to the oath.

10. *Mendacity Licence* e.g. no security for veracity in respect of pleadings.

11. The general nature of the plaintiff's demand, the grounds for the demand, and the precise details of allegations clearly consigned to *printed forms*, bearing reference to corresponding articles of substantive law; and so in regard to the defence.

11. Abuse of pleadings, especially *special* pleadings at common law, excessively abridged, uninformative, unintelligible, misleading; under favour of the mendacity-licence, the principal ingredients, falsehood, nonsense and surplusage.

50 *Theories of Evidence*

12. Means of securing *forthcomingness* of persons and things provided on a uniform and comprehensive plan, adapted to the advances made by the age and country in the arts of life.

12. Means of securing forthcomingness diversified; often oppressive; in the aggregate scanty and inadequate.

13. A plan of intercourse settled by judge and parties to be carried on in the promptest, least expensive, and most certain mode. Especially in regard to notice, the sole question *received or not received*?

13. Modes of conveying notice ineffectual, diversified and subject to chicaneries.

14. Neither *time* nor *place* exempt from the remedial power of justice, subject only to preponderant vexation.

14. Diverse asylums, local and chronological.

15. No *incidental application* to the judge but by the party himself, where possible *viva voce*.

15. *Motion business* – business made by and for Judge and Co., by the exclusion of parties from the presence of the judge, subject to requirements almost peculiar to English practice.

16. *Language* of the instruments composed, as far as possible, of words in ordinary use.

16. Use of jargon; principle and practice of jargonization, to produce 1. on the part of the law uncertainty, incognoscibility; 2. on the part of the non-lawyer, ignorance; hence dependence on lawyers; 3. on the part of the legislator, ignorance or misconception or disgust or awe, propensity to regard reform as hopeless or undesirable; 4. In favour of the professional lawyer, monopoly of the faculty of succeeding to judicial offices.

17. *Truth* unremittingly and exclusively sought for: truth, the whole truth and nothing but the truth.

17. Use of *fictions*.

18. Magnification of jurisprudential law, i.e. judge-made law, sham law.

> 19. Contempt manifested towards real law, i.e. law made by the legislator.
>
> 20. *Double-fountain* principle.

Without attempting an extensive commentary on this chart, it is worth making a few general observations. First, although the tendency of the Natural Model is to move away from the artificial complexities of the Technical System, not all the elements are negative. For example, the Natural System requires the establishment of a decentralized system of courts, unrestricted justiciability, increased powers to secure forth-comingness of witnesses and of evidence (including discovery) and provision for cross-examination face to face. Bentham was aware that simplicity and order require a good bureaucratic organization; the Natural Model is not a prescription for disorganized muddling through.

Bentham did not claim that the English system in his day corres-ponded exactly to the Technical Model.[6] It is true that many of the specific elements refer directly to actual devices that he was criticizing; but some of these features were restricted to particular courts. Indeed, one of his general criticisms is that there is a lack of system and consistency in existing provisions.[7] Moreover, he explicitly wished to preserve and extend some features of the common law adversary process – especially the orality of proceedings, cross-examination, and publicity. Thus the Technical System is not co-extensive with the actual situation in England at the beginning of the nineteenth century; rather it is an 'ideal type' to which actual institutions in different jurisdictions approximated in different degrees and in different respects.[8] English adjective law was open to criticism in so far as it exhibited these features to a very large extent; but it was also to be criticized on the grounds that it was an arbitrary and confusing jumble that did not deserve to be called a 'system' at all.[9]

At first sight, Bentham's espousal of 'the natural system' is a little surprising. Is not the idealized picture of the wise father adjudicating in the bosom of the family uncharacteristically sentimental? Does not his praise of the Saxon system of informal local justice smack of the Chinese Argument – the romantic fallacy of appealing to the wisdom of our ancestors?[10] Does his use of the word 'natural' imply an acceptance of some universal natural laws of adjudication?

There are passages where Bentham does seem to have been carried away by his own rhetoric – and he may also have been appealing to some popular prejudices – but it is quite easy to rescue him from serious charges of inconsistency. For his central thesis is not based on an appeal to history: rather it rests on the idea that evidence in law turns on the same principles as evidence in all fields of human activity. Questions in

52 Theories of Evidence

natural philosophy, natural history, technology, medicine, mathematics, and 'the first question in natural religion'[11] – belief in the existence of a higher being – are all questions of evidence.[12] So too is tracking a deer or cooking a leg of mutton:

> [Q]uestions of evidence are continually presenting themselves to every human being, every day, and almost every waking hour, of his life . . . Whether the leg of mutton now on the spit be roasted enough, is a question of evidence . . . which the cook decides upon in the cook's way, as if by instinct; deciding upon evidence, as Monsieur Jourdan talked prose, without having ever heard of any such word, perhaps, in the whole course of her life.[13]

Bentham's theory of evidence is based on common sense. It is the common-sense empiricism of Locke, based on '*observation*, *experience* and *experiment*'.[14] It is close to the unsophisticated common sense of ordinary people conducting their practical affairs; it postulates both a general cognitive competence and a widespread cognitive consensus on the part of ordinary adult members of society.[15] But the responsibility is to rest primarily with officials whose task is to apply *informed utilitarian* common sense – a sort of utilitarian version of Karl Llewellyn's 'horse sense'.[16]

'Natural' in this context means 'the original and irremedial work of nature' as contrasted with 'factitious – the work of human agency or omission, of human artifice or imbecility'.[17] The natural system is not so much a method of fact-finding *prescribed* by Nature, but rather the best that can be hoped for given the human conditions in which our only means to knowledge is through the data presented by our senses, as opposed to the metaphysical theory of innate ideas.[18] 'Experience is the foundation of all our knowledge, and of all our reasoning: the sole guide of our conduct, the sole basis of our security.'[19]

Bentham's view appears to be that, in the field of evidence, almost all attempts to improve on common sense and ordinary experience are not only doomed to failure, they are also typically the product of sinister interests or of folly. This view is directly linked both to the epistemology of the theory of fictions and the apparently extreme form of rule-scepticism that underlies the anti-nomian thesis. These topics will be considered in the following two sections.

(b) Evaluation of evidence

Bentham believed that the direct end of adjudication is to maximize the correctness of judgements about the truth of allegations of fact. Such judgements are decisions which should be based on the persuasion[1] of the trier of fact after considering the law and all the available evidence relevant to the facts in issue – what he called the 'ultimate principal facts'.[2] The task of the judge is to assess the probative force of the relevant evidence in terms of the degree of persuasion that it produces in his mind; like other writers on evidence, Bentham accepts that in practice one has typically to be satisfied with judgements of probability – that, is something less than certainty.[3] Thus decisions on questions of fact in adjudication should typically take the form 'I am persuaded that this allegation is probably true' (or untrue).

What is meant by 'probability' and 'probative force' in this context? How are degrees of probative force best expressed? Is the basis for judgements of probability subjective or objective? If the latter, by what criteria are such judgements to be reached, justified and appraised? Such questions are central to any theory of evidence that accepts the premises of the Rationalist Tradition that judgements about the truth of allegations of fact are central features of adjudicative decisions and should so far as possible be based on rational assessment of the weight or cogency or probative force of the evidence. Bentham addressed each of these issues directly and at some length.[4] His account needs to be approached with caution, for it is important to bear in mind that he was writing at a time when theories of probability were only beginning to emerge.[5] In the light of modern writings in such fields as statistics, decision theory and inductive logic his views may seem unsophisticated and rather crude.[6] In some respects his ideas were ahead of their time, but we must be wary of reading too much into what is best seen as a penetrating, but not very developed, pioneering effort.

To explicate Bentham's views on evaluation of evidence it is necessary to consider in turn his general theory of belief; the epistemological basis for that theory, as developed in his theory of fictions; his proposal for a 'moral thermometer'; and the method of infirmative suppositions. This involves exploring some of the most difficult and least familiar aspects of Bentham's theory. It may be helpful to start by looking at the method of infirmative suppositions and by reconstructing in simple terms the guidance he gives to a judge within the natural system on how to go about evaluating evidence in a particular case.

Suppose that a witness (W^1) testifies to proposition T, where T is an ultimate fact (i.e. a fact in issue). Suppose further that W^1 states that he is very confident that his testimony is correct – for example, on a scale of zero to plus ten, his degree of persuasion is eight. What credence or weight is the judge (or other trier of fact) to give to such testimony? Other things being equal, suggests Bentham, the probative force of this testimony corresponds with the degree of persuasion of the witness, and the degree of persuasion of the judge will, and should, also correspond with the degree of persuasion of the witness.[7]

But how is one to be assured that other things are equal? Under the Natural System there are a number of internal and external securities for ensuring the trustworthiness, the completeness and the accuracy of

54 Theories of Evidence

testimony.[8] These, both generally and in the particular case, should help to prevent, detect and correct the dangers of incorrectness, mendacity, incompleteness and indistinctness of testimony. Similarly the Natural System is designed to secure against similar threats to misdecision on the part of the judge. These safeguards against the dangers of mendacity, incompleteness and inaccuracy on the part of witnesses and of misdecision on the part of the judge help to bolster the general tendency of the bulk of human testimony to be true.[9] Nevertheless, even under the Natural System, Bentham warns against the supposition that the testimony of any man is true 'to the purpose of warranting the judge to treat it as conclusive, i.e. exclusive of all counter-evidence'.[10] Thus the probative force of the testimony of W^1 must be considered in the context of all other available general and special evidence.[11] In this context it must be subjected to a series of tests.[12]

First, does the fact deposed to (T) conform 'to the established course of nature' as understood by the judge?[13] If T is a commonplace event, such as that 'X entered Y's house', then general experience does not diminish the probability of T. If, however, T is an event which is highly unusual or which runs counter to what the judge believes to be the established course of nature, then this 'general testimony' operates as a mode of infirmative circumstantial evidence to reduce the degree of persuasion in the bosom of the judge.[14] The degree of distrust will depend upon the judge's confidence in his knowledge of the laws of nature (in respect of physical facts) or of human nature in respect of 'moral improbabilities'.[15] Thus, if T is the allegation that X flew away on a broomstick, even Bentham would accept that this is so contrary to his view of the established course of nature that no amount of testimonial evidence would alter his disbelief in T.[16] If, however, T is the allegation that W's garden was damaged 'by the fall of the first inhabited air balloon that ever rose' then, if he has any doubt, the judge will have recourse to scientific evidence of experts.[17]

Secondly, are there grounds of suspicion of the trustworthiness of the testimony on grounds of interest or for other reasons? If so, such grounds also operate as disprobabilizing factors.[18]

Thirdly, are there any other infirmative suppositions in the testimony or in any other particular evidence, testimonial or circumstantial, that run counter to T?[19] For example, does W^1's testimony, tested under cross-examination, reveal any internal inconsistencies? Is there any other evidence that makes it less probable, i.e. weakens its probative force? If there are no such 'disprobabilizing' or infirmative suppositions, then W^1's testimony is conclusive, for the purposes of this case, for T – that is the degree of persuasion of the judge should correspond to the degree of persuasion of W^1. If, however, there is counter-evidence, the degree of persuasion of the judge should correspond to the probative force of T minus the probative force of the other general and particular infirmative suppositions. Similarly, if other evidence, whether testimonial or circumstantial, supports T the degree of persuasion of the judge is correspondingly enhanced above that of W^1.[20] In theory the degrees of persuasion and of disbelief are infinite; in practice, a single item or a mass of evidence is conclusive if it produces moral certainty. In practical affairs where there is conflicting evidence many decisions have to be taken on the basis of a degree of persuasion less than moral certainty.[21]

To sum up: each piece of testimony (T) is subject to a number of tests. First, how confident is the witness (W) of the truth of T? Second, how conformable to general experience is T? Third, are there any grounds for suspicion of the trustworthiness of W? Fourth, is T supported or doubted by any other special or particular evidence? Where there is a mass of evidence, each item of evidence is to be subjected to these tests. This involves considering each item in relation to the rest. The degree of persuasion of the judge about the case as a whole is a function of the probative force of all the positive evidence minus the probative force of all the infirmative suppositions (including the doubts of each of the witnesses).[22] Arriving at such conclusions may involve a complicated exercise of judgement, which cannot be governed by strict mathematical or logical axioms. Moreover, the assessment of probabilities is relative to each judge's individual beliefs about the general course of nature. Accordingly, even if this procedure has been followed by honest and competent judges, it is possible that individual judges will arrive at different degrees of persuasion in respect of the same body of evidence.

This reconstruction of Bentham's guidance to judges in evaluating evidence raises a number of questions. Is he advancing a subjectivist theory of probability and, if so, how can that be reconciled with his rejection of intuitionism and other forms of 'nonsense pisteutics'?[23] The method of infirmative suppositions looks remarkably like a Baconian (i.e. non-mathematical) theory of probability; moreover, Bentham explicitly rejects the possibility of applying mathematics to the evaluation of evidence. Yet he seriously proposes that degrees of probative force and of persuasion can usefully be expressed in numerical terms and that degrees of belief of judges as well as witnesses should be added instead of merely counting the 'number of voices'.[24] Is that not a crude form of 'misplaced mathematization'[25]? Finally, he indicates that judgements of probability are relative to the general beliefs and 'knowledge' of the person making the assessment. Can one reconcile this apparent relativism with his espousal of an empirical epistemology?

Not surprisingly, Bentham's views in this area have been subjected to a variety of interpretations and criticisms, especially in relation to the question of whether he was advancing a 'subjectivist' or 'objectivist' theory of proof or an incoherent mixture of the two. Montrose, for example, criticizes him for introducing subjective, psychological factors into his concepts of evidence and relevance[26]; the French jurist, Bonnier,

56 Theories of Evidence

and other continental writers sympathetic to Bentham, scornfully dismissed his proposal for expressing degrees of persuasion in numerical terms on the grounds that judicial evidence is not a suitable field for mathematical calculation[27]; Gulson criticized Bentham for basing what purports to be a theory dealing with the objective cogency of evidence on the basis of a subjective theory of belief and persuasion.[28] Jonathan Cohen sees Bentham as vacillating between a subjectivist theory (which can legitimately be converted into numerical terms on the analogy of wagering, as has been done by modern subjectivists) and an implicit Baconian theory which assumes that judgements of probability can be justified on the basis of objective principles of induction.[29] Recently Gerald Postema has attempted to rescue Bentham from charges of extreme irrationalism and of inconsistency by suggesting that he advanced a form of modified subjectivism, which allows an important but limited place for objective standards of rational criticism.[30] Following Postema, I shall suggest that Bentham's theory, like Gilbert's, gave a place to subjective judgements and objective standards, but that his views were not as fully worked out nor as coherent as Postema suggests. Nevertheless, like Gilbert, he attempted to accommodate both subjective psychological factors and objective standards of rationality within this theory – as, indeed, any rounded theory of evidence must do. Before considering Postema's argument, it is first necessary to look at Bentham's discussion of the problem of expressing and grading degrees of persuasion and probative force.

The thermometer of persuasion The strength of persuasion of a witness, the probative force of testimonial or circumstantial evidence, and the strength of persuasion of the judge as to a given fact or as to the case as a whole are all matters of degree. How can these degrees be measured and expressed? Bentham's solution – his 'thermometer of persuasion' as it came to be called[31] – attracted more fire than almost any other part of his theory of evidence. Yet there are grounds for saying that much of this criticism is misplaced.

In Bentham's view, there are good practical reasons for having a reasonably precise way of measuring, expressing and grading degrees of persuasion and of probative force. The judge needs to gauge the strength of persuasion of each witness about his own testimony. There are also occasions when it is useful to know the degree of persuasion of an individual judge as to a given fact or case; for example,[32] where there are several judges and their number is equally divided; on appeal; in the exercise of pardon; when the same question is 'moved elsewhere in another judicatory and in another cause';[33] where punishment or satisfaction is to be administered *pro modo probationum* (e.g. where different standards of proof apply to the same fact for different purposes);[34] where the judge or other functionary gives scientific evidence. In all these cases there is a need for an 'instrument of accurate judicature'.[35]

Bentham considers and rejects existing modes of expression. Ordinary language has too few gradations (I know – I believe) and is too imprecise.[36] He scornfully dismisses Roman and French variants of the numerical system on the grounds that they only apply to aggregate masses of evidence (rather than to the persuasion of individuals), that they involve artificial and nonsensical rules of enumeration (for instance, the evidence of one witness alone counts for zero).[37] Similarly, English distinctions between positive proof, violent presumption, probable presumption, and light or rash presumption is a scale 'considered without distinction made as to the quantity and composition of the evidence to which the probative force is considered to belong'.[38] Thus existing scales either have too few gradations or do not measure degrees of persuasion.

Bentham turns to mathematics for assistance.[39] Here his treatment is brief and rather cryptic, but it is of potential significance in the light of later developments in probability theory. Among the various kinds of theory – or, to be more precise, criteria of correctness of judgements of probability – at least four main types are commonly distinguished: (a) *a priori* theories or the doctrine of chances; (b) statistical or actuarial theories, based on judgements or estimates of actual frequency; (c) subjective theories; and (d) non-mathematical theories, such as Jonathan Cohen's Baconian theory of inductive probability.[40] Although some of these theories have only been developed to any degree of sophistication quite recently, it is illuminating to consider Bentham's flirtation with mathematics in the light of these distinctions.

Bentham expressly rejects the doctrine of chances (*a priori* probability) as being inapplicable: 'the language of mathematicians will be seen to afford two different modes or principles. One is perfectly correct: it is the mode of expression used in speaking of the doctrine of chances. But unfortunately it will be found not applicable to the present purpose'.[41] He gives no explicit reason in the present context, but it is not difficult to infer one. The calculus of chances only applies to closed, finite, classes, such as an unmarked pack of 52 cards or a 'fair' dice, that by definition has six sides.[42] Problems of judicial proof typically arise in contexts where the conditions for the application of the calculus are not satisfied. Like most theorists of evidence, Bentham treats the subject of judicial evidence as belonging to a sphere of discourse in which the possibilities are open-ended. Similarly the degrees of probative force, of persuasion and of probability are in theory infinite:[43] there is no end to the number of witnesses or the amount of evidence that could in principle be adduced in support of the existence of a single fact. One of his objections to Gilbert[44] (and, in an analogous context, to Descartes[45]) is that he considered them to have drawn a false analogy between the axioms of

58   Theories of Evidence

closed systems of *a priori* reasoning and probability judgements about facts in the real world.[46] In this sense, the whole thrust of Bentham's theory is anti-axiomatic.

Bentham does not seem to have considered the possibility of translating notions of probability and probative force into estimates of statistical frequency, as some modern frequentists do,[47] but he does explicitly treat the problem of expressing degrees of persuasion and probative force as analogous to wagering and insurance.[48] The passage which attracted the most criticism, including from Dumont himself, appeared in *the Treatise*:

> Another fact, equally notorious, is, that these various degrees, of which belief is susceptible, have a very strong influence on our conduct; it would be more correct to say that all our determinations depend upon them. We have an obvious application of them in wagers. He who wagers, stakes one against one, one against two, or three or ten, according to the different apparent probabilities. Insurances, which are a sort of wager, are made at a higher or lower rate, according as the event in question is more or less probable. If different degrees of conjectual strength in wagers and insurances can be expressed, why should it not be possible to express likewise the different degrees of proving power in testimony? And if it can be done, is it not desirable that it should be done?[49]

This suggestion was criticized by Dumont on the ground that 'Testimony turns on past events; wagers turn on future events: as a witness, I know, I believe, or I doubt; as a wagerer, I know nothing, but I conjecture, I calculate probabilities, my rashness can injure nobody but myself . . .'[50] As Postema points out, the difference between wagering and judicial judgements of probabilities does not turn on the distinction between past and future events, but on the distinction between wagers with determinable outcomes and wagers 'on matters which are in principle unsettlable'.[51] Perhaps implicit in Dumont's criticism, and that of some other commentators, is a suggestion that judging is a matter of chance and speculation, like wagering – compare, for example, the notion of 'the forensic lottery' and Rabelais' Judge Bridlegoose's method of deciding cases by casting dice.[52] But this misses the point of Bentham's analogy. Acute as ever, he has perceived the possibility that wagering and insurance can be based on rational assessments of probabilities.[53] But at this point, he is only using the analogy in connection with finding a *terminology* for expressing degrees of persuasion; he does not follow the path that leads some subjectivists to use the analogy with wagering as a basis for a procedure for decision – for that, Bentham advances the method of infirmative suppositions which was outlined above.[54] There is a difference between the mode of expressing the strength of one's belief and what constitutes a rational mode of arriving at or justifying a belief. Thus his use of the wagering analogy does not commit Bentham to a subjectivist theory of probability along the lines of modern decision theory.

The only true scale of measurement of persuasion and probative force is an infinite one,[55] but that is inapplicable for practical reasons, not least that it would lead to the hearing of a great deal of superfluous evidence.[56] In theory, the testimony of the two thousand and first witness should add something to the total sum of persuasion; in practice there would be rapidly diminishing returns and some undesirable side effects, apart from the expense, vexation and delay involved. On the other hand, mathematics offers a mode of measurement which is incorrect in principle, but 'its incorrectness will not be found attended with any practical inconvenience'.[57] This is to assume that the greatest possible quantity is a finite quantity and then to divide it into parts – as a circle is divided into 360 degrees, or a thermometer is divided into degrees above and below zero, as if there is a maximum and minimum grade.[58] On the analogy of the French *decigrade* thermometer, Bentham suggests a scale of 0–10 for affirmative persuasion and 0–10 for negative persuasion or disbelief, with zero 'denoting the absence of all belief either for or against the fact in question'.[59] Each witness could then be asked to express the strength of his persuasion regarding a particular fact in terms of the scale. If the witness is trustworthy and there is no contrary evidence, the judge's degree of persuasion should correspond to that of the witness. If there are several trustworthy witnesses all testifying to the same fact, but with different degrees of confidence, the persuasive force of their testimony can be added; if they contradict each other, it can be subtracted. Similarly, the single judge can be aided in clarifying the strength of his persuasion in the light of a mass of evidence by means of such a scale. So also where there is a bench of judges, the 'real strength of testimony' may be more accurately measured by computing the degree of persuasion of each, than merely by counting their votes, for 'the united amount of the degrees of belief of three judges may be less than that of two others'.[60]

Bentham's proposal received a torrid reception at the hands of almost all commentators.[61] One of the editors of *Best on Evidence*, J. M. Lely, went so far as to cut out Best's critique on the grounds that this 'fantastic suggestion' was 'one of the few follies of a very wise man'.[62] So dismissive are some writers that their grounds for dismissal are not always clear.[63] More interestingly, some of them cancel each other out. Thus, on one view, the proposal represents a plunge into pure subjectivism and on another it introduces precise mathematical calculations into an area that is not susceptible to this kind of (presumably objective) analysis.[64] Dumont, whose criticisms were adopted by several commentators (despite Mill's attempted rebuttal), was careful to base his objections on grounds of feasibility rather than principle.[65] Apart from his rejection of

60   *Theories of Evidence*

the wagering analogy, mentioned above, he doubted whether accuracy and comparability would be feasible in practice and he argued that the authority of the testimony would often be inversely proportional to the wisdom of the witnesses, for the reserved would understate the strength of their belief, while passionate men would overstate it.[66]

We need not here concern ourselves unduly with the arguments about practical feasibility, which in any case depend on context. Like Mill one may doubt whether it will be of much positive help, without rejecting it on the basis of principle or because it will do positive harm.[67] Bentham anticipated such objections by stipulating that the device should only be used when it would be helpful[68] and, more important, by recognizing that he was putting forward a mode of expression as a *convention* which would have to be learned through familiarity and general instruction.[69] It is closely analogous to numerical schemes of marking examinations and other scales which are widely used in practice as admittedly rough conventional ways of expressing gradations of judgement and aiding complex or collective decisions involving a multiplicity of more or less subjective judgements. Bentham acknowledged that such a device was not precise and that it was a matter of convenience whether there were 5, 10, 100 or 1000 points on the scale.[70] He no doubt realized, but failed to make clear, that the same result in respect of expression, as opposed to calculation,[71] could have been achieved by other means than numbers – for example, by coining new terms or by using letters (as in an alphabetical scheme of marking). There is no magic in numbers. As is shown on the probability table (p. 61), ten different gradations of probability can be expressed in a variety of ways.[72] Some of the modes of expression may suggest that a particular scale indicates 'subjective' or 'objective' judgements, but the notion that degrees of probative force and of persuasion can be usefully differentiated on a scale of roughly equal gradations is neutral as to whether these judgements are reached on a wholly objective or wholly subjective basis or something in between. In so far as the moral thermometer is a proposal for expressing gradations of subjective belief or persuasion, as Bentham probably intended,[73] the proposal does not commit him to a subjectivist theory of probability. What precisely was his position on that issue remains to be discussed.

Was Bentham a subjectivist?   In an important recent paper, Professor Gerald Postema has attempted to rescue Bentham from charges of extreme subjectivism and of inconsistency. Bentham was a subjectivist, Postema suggests, 'but a subjectivist with a difference'.[74] If one interprets his theory of evidence in the light of his theory of fictions, then it appears that he consistently combined a Lockean empiricism, and an admittedly rudimentary 'Baconian' (objective) theory of probabilities, with an optimistically rational theory of evidence.

While it is not possible here to do full justice to Postema's argument, it

A PROBABILITY TABLE

Chance	Frequency	Wager	Belief (subjective)	Strength of support (objective)	Marks
1	100%	No Contest	I know	Beyond peradventure	A+
.9	90%	9–1	I am positive	Overwhelming	A
.8	80%	8–2/4–1	I am sure	Cogent	A–
.7	70%	7–3	I am confident	Strong	B+
.6	60%	6–4/3–2	I think	More likely than not	B
.5	50%	Evens/1–1	I wonder whether	Evenly balanced	B–
.4	40%	4–6/2–3	I suspect	Not very likely	C+
.3	30%	3–7	I surmise	Unlikely	C
.2	20%	2–8/1–4	I doubt that	Weak	C–
.1	10%	1–9	I very much doubt that	Minimal	D+
0	0	0	I disbelieve	Nil	D/F

62 Theories of Evidence

is worth trying to restate it briefly. Bentham's theory of fictions is concerned with the relationship between language, the real world, and human beliefs. A central difficulty for human beings is that we are dependent on language to construct, to analyse and to communicate our beliefs about the real world; yet language is not merely an imperfect instrument for such a purpose – rather it is systematically misleading. In particular, it commits us to think and talk in terms of non-existing entities, as if they exist. Language is an indispensable distorting mirror for apprehending reality.

Bentham distinguished between real and fictitious entities. Real entities are of two kinds: concrete material substances and mental entities (impressions and ideas). Concrete material objects and events (that is, such objects in motion) exist independently of our apprehension of them, quite apart from language and mind. To put the matter very simply, Bentham's ontological position is that there is a real world of material objects that exists in nature: mental entities also exist in reality. All other entities are fictions, that is they do not exist in nature. Rather they are mental constructions; their 'existence' is dependent on the active powers of the mind operating through language. Fictions 'reside' around real entities at different removes: first-order fictions include motion, matter, space and time; at one further remove are second-order fictions, such as qualities and aggregations; beyond that are even more abstract fictions such as rights, duties, liberty, and justice.

All knowledge of real entities is derived from experience; all ideas are derived from sense impressions; we also apprehend concrete material objects through impressions, but in a highly complex way:

> No portion of matter ever presents itself to *sense*, without presenting, at one and the same time, a multitude of *simple* ideas, of all which taken together, the *concrete* one, in a state more or less correct and complete, is composed. At the same time, though naturally all these ideas present themselves together, the mind has it in its power to detach . . . any one or more of them from the rest, and either keep it in view in this detached state, or make it up into a compound with other simple ideas, detached in like manner from other sources. But, for the making of this separation – this abstraction, as it is called – more *trouble*, a stronger force of *attention*, is necessary, than for the taking them up, in a promiscuous bundle, as it were; in the bundle in which they have been tied together by the hand of Nature: that is, than for the consideration of the object in its *concrete* state.[75]

Fictitious entities are produced by 'decomposing' or analysing a concrete object.[76] By focusing on one part of the composite impression produced by an object a new idea of its shape or colour or relation to another object; from this further, even more abstract, ideas are constructed, such as the 'abstract' idea of shape or relation independ-

Bentham on evidence   63

ently of any particular object. These ideas are constructs, the product of active mental operations. In order to express such ideas we need language, but language requires us to talk as if they are entities which exist in reality. We know that such fictions do not exist, but we have to talk as if they do. For language is necessary to thought and fictions are necessary to language.

The main link between Bentham's theory of fictions and his theory of evidence is that the latter is dependent on fictions of a special kind, viz. 'ontological fictions' such as probability, possibility, and necessity. These are fictions concerned with existence. They are special because they are 'fictitious qualities', which are doubly fictitious because qualities are themselves fictitious entities and because these qualities are falsely ascribed, in ordinary parlance, to facts or events rather than to modifications of belief. Probability is a matter of degree; we talk of 'events' and 'facts' being probable, but facts and events either exist or they do not. Judgements of probability are modifications of degrees of persuasion about the existence or non-existence of facts in the real world. Postema puts the matter as follows:

Bentham's argument for this subjectivist interpretation of probability should now be clear. Noting correctly that probability was not an ordinary natural property of events, he was forced by his lean ontology to regard probability language as expressive of certain ideas without direct reference to real entities. His theory of language surely encouraged this move and suggested to him the most plausible alternative analysis. One implication of his distinction between the immediate and ulterior subjects of discourse is his doctrine of elliptical expression, a doctrine which leads naturally to regarding probability language as expressive of degrees of persuasion. In his view, my utterance 'Eurybiades struck Themistocles' must be regarded as elliptical, since the expression inside the quotation marks does not capture and display all that is conveyed by my utterance. In particular, it leaves out the fact that I *expressed* my belief in the event's having taken place. Thus, says Bentham, if the matter were fully to be expressed, the representation of my utterance should read: 'It is my belief that Eurybiades struck Themistocles.' Now, accepting this doctrine for the time being, consider the utterance 'Eurybiades probably struck Themistocles'. How should this be understood? One might try: 'It is my belief that E probably struck T.' But that would locate the probability as a property of the event and that has already been ruled out. A more natural analysis would be: 'I am reasonably confident that E struck T.' For we say, for example, 'I know E struck T', or 'I think E struck T'; and in each case the qualifier modifies the opinion, not the fact. To say, 'I know that E struck T' is, among other things, to say quite emphatically 'E struck T'. And to do so in no way

64 Theories of Evidence

changes the event referred to. Rather, it qualifies the speaker's relationship to the statement referring to that event. The use of 'probably' and its kin most naturally fits this pattern.[77]

It follows from this that Bentham held a subjectivist view of probability, in that it refers to degrees of persuasion of the mind rather than to the events or facts. But, if this is so, how can it be claimed that Bentham was a rationalist in the sense that he accepted that judgements of probability are susceptible to rational justification, criticism and argument? A short answer is that to define probability in terms of subjective persuasion does not necessarily lead to a denial that persuasion can and should be based on argument. Because the statement 'E probably struck T' means 'I am fairly confident that E struck T', this does not preclude rational appraisal of the grounds for such confidence.[78] Such judgements can be produced more or less by the exercise of a person's rational faculties and these are subject to critical assessment. Bentham expressly rejected Hume's subjectivism as an example of 'nonsense pisteutics',[79] that is, an epistemology that accounts for belief in terms of an alleged propensity to give credit to testimony rather than in terms of correct beliefs being formed on the basis of reason, experience and utility. Such subjectivism is analogous to the 'principles of sympathy and antipathy' in ethics, which he associated, *inter alia*, with irrationalist theories of the moral sense.[80] Bentham's deals with both the psychological *causes* of belief and with *justification* for particular judgements.

Degrees of persuasion and probative force   At the start of *The Law of Evidence*, Gilbert, following Locke, had distinguished between Degrees of Evidence – ranging from Demonstration to Impossibility – and Degrees of Assent, ranging 'from full Assurance and Confidence, quite down to Conjecture, Doubt, Distrust and Disbelief'.[81] The Degrees of Assent are 'proportioned' to the Degrees of Evidence. Gilbert thus neatly suggested two parallel scales for expressing strength of belief (subjective) and probative force (objective) and gave a place to both in his theory of evidence.

Postema suggests that, according to Bentham, the probative force of rewarding P *just is* the intensity of one's persuasion of P given E.[82] This I believe is misleading. Postema is correct in pointing out that Bentham's position was that facts either exist or they do not, whereas notions of probability, probative force and degrees of persuasion all admit of degrees. Accordingly there is no such thing as a probable fact and there is a close connection between the notions of probability, probative force and persuasion.[83] However, Bentham explicitly differentiates between probative force and degrees of persuasion and he conceives of situations where they do not coincide. For example, in the *Introductory View*, chapter VI is headed: 'Degrees of persuasion – thence of Probative Force

Bentham on evidence 65

– how expressible.'[84] The degree of persuasion of the witness is not the same as the probative force of his testimony, for the latter depends also on other probabilizing and disprobabilizing factors, such as the trustworthiness of the witness, the presence of counter-evidence and so on.[85] The degree of persuasion of a witness and the probative force of his testimony may coincide, if the witness is trustworthy and there is no counter-evidence.[86] Furthermore, 'probative force' is a term applicable to circumstantial as well as to direct evidence.[87]

From the standpoint of the judge, his degree of persuasion and the probative force of a given item or mass of evidence does normally and should coincide.[88] In some places, Bentham does seem to imply that they are the same. One passage, in particular, requires explication:

> Between the *degree of probative force* on the part of the evidence (the whole mass of evidence being taken together) and *intensity of persuasion* on the part of the judge, the coincidence seems to be complete: and this, whether the question be concerning what *is*, or concerning what *ought to be*. To say that the probative force of the evidence *is* at such or such a degree, is to say that, in the bosom of the judge, intensity of persuasion *is* at that degree: to say that such a degree of probative force is *properly belonging* to the mass of evidence in question, is to say that, upon the receipt of that same mass of evidence, the same degree of intensity of persuasion is the degree which is *fit and proper* to have place in the bosom of the judge.[89]

At first sight this statement is indeed puzzling. For not only does it suggest that 'probative force' is to be viewed as a matter of subjective persuasion or belief, but it also states that the actual persuasive effect on the mind of the judge is always the 'fit and proper' one. This seems to exclude objective criteria of probative force and to conflate actual psychological influence with prescriptions about the fit and proper way to evaluate evidence. This in turn suggests that Bentham's terminology excludes the possibility of irrational means of persuasion or of such notions as 'prejudicial evidence' or misjudgement of probative force.[90] If the probative force of evidence *just* is and should be the actual effect of evidence on the mind of the judge, then Bentham is surely committed to an extreme subjectivist and irrationalist view.

While Bentham, in this and a number of other passages, can be convicted of lack of clarity, it is possible to rescue him from charges of inconsistency and irrationalism in respect of this passage. In the first place, his terminology implicitly suggests a distinction between the concepts of 'probative force' and 'degrees of persuasion': both are matters of degree, both are expressible in terms of the same scale and they often coincide. But that coincidence is not complete: as we have seen, the degree of persuasion of a witness as to T does not necessarily coincide with the probative force of T from the point of view of the judge.

66   Theories of Evidence

Moreover, under the Technical System, Bentham argues that judges do give too little or too much weight to different kinds of evidence – thus the probative force of evidence and the degree of persuasion of judges do not always coincide.

The context of the present passage is a prescriptive theory of evidence under the Natural System of procedure. 'The judge' in this context can be interpreted to mean the model judge within that system: trustworthy, competent, and rational.[91] Thus the context is essentially normative. Viewed thus, the passage can be interpreted to mean that, if Bentham's prescriptions for rational adjudication are satisfied, then the probative force of the evidence will produce the appropriate degree of persuasion in the bosom of the judge.

(c) The anti-nomian thesis

The *Rationale* is, in nearly all respects, a strikingly unsceptical work: it is based on a cognitivist epistemology and a deep commitment to a utilitarian theory of value; it accepts that rational argument is both possible and desirable in weighing evidence, even when the conditions for formal deductive reasoning or for mathematical calculation are not satisfied. Yet the central thesis of the work can be interpreted as a more radical form of rule-scepticism than is attributable to any American Realist. For Bentham not only attacked all existing rules of evidence; he even doubted the possibility of subjecting the weighing of evidence to the governance of rules. For example, in his chapter 'On the Probative Force of Circumstantial Evidence' he states:

> *What ought to be done, and what avoided, in estimating the probative force of circumstantial evidence?*
>
> On this as on every other part of the field of evidence, rules capable of rendering right decisions secure, are *what the nature of things denies* [italics supplied]. To the establishment of rules by which misdecision is rendered more probable than it would otherwise be, the nature of man is prone. To put the legislator and the judge upon their guard against such rashness, is all that the industry of the free inquirer can do in favour of the ends of justice.[1]

This is not an isolated passage. It is part of a general theme repeated throughout his writings on evidence.[2] It is an argument against the desirability, the feasibility and even the possibility of making artificial, binding rules of evidence which will result in better decisions.

The *Rationale* begins with a forthright statement that is worth quoting in full:

> The results may be comprised in three propositions: the one, a theorem to be proved; the other two, problems to be solved.

Bentham on evidence 67

The theorem is this: that, merely with a view to rectitude of decision, to the avoidance of the mischiefs attached to undue decision, no species of evidence whatsoever, willing or unwilling, ought to be excluded: for that although in certain cases it may be right that this or that lot of evidence, though tendered, should not be admitted, yet in these cases, the reason for the exclusion rests on the other grounds: viz. avoidance of vexation, expense, and delay. The proof of this theorem constitutes the first of the three main results.

To give instructions, pointing out the means by which what can be done may be done towards securing the truth of evidence: this is one of the two main problems, the solution of which is here attempted . . .

To give instructions serving to assist the mind of the judge in forming its estimate of the probability of truth, in the instance of the evidence presented to it; in a word, in judging of the weight of evidence: this is the other of the two main problems which are here attempted to be solved.[3]

Bentham's 'theorem', which he referred to as 'the non-exclusion' principle, is in fact only one aspect of a wider thesis – an attack on the idea that adjudicative decisions on questions of fact are susceptible to regulation by binding rules. The exclusionary rules of evidence – especially the rules of competency – were the main, but not the only, target of attack. Bentham was concerned to destroy all technical rules of procedure, all rigid formalities, and all mandatory rules of evidence. A decentralized, informal system of judicature based on 'The Natural System' was to replace the centralized, lawyer-dominated, technical system. Bentham's theory takes the form of advice to the legislator about the design of the system and about weighing evidence. He gives instructions to the legislator who in turn is to give instructions to judge. Bentham's advice is simple: abolish all formal rules. His choice of words is deliberate and precise. Rules are addressed to the will; instructions address the understanding.

The anti-nomian thesis is much wider than the 'non-exclusion' principle. The main thrust of the argument in the *Rationale* is directed against rules of exclusion, rules of weight and, to a lesser extent, rules of quantum, but there are passages which support the view that Bentham was opposed to the formal regulation of all aspects of evidence, including rules governing standards of proof, burdens and presumptions. Moreover, the thesis is not restricted to rules of evidence: there is at least one passage that suggests that it covers procedure as well.[4] The proposition that Bentham was opposed to all rules of evidence needs to be read subject to four caveats; two are minor, two are central to understanding his theory. First, in one passage he qualifies the suggestion that it is not in principle possible to maximize rectitude of decision by means of formal regulation: 'To take the business out of the hands of instinct, to subject it

68   *Theories of Evidence*

to rules, is a task which, if it lies within the reach of human faculties, must at any rate be reserved, I think, for the improved powers of some maturer age.'[5]

It is not clear how much significance to attach to this caveat. There is a difference between a thesis that some form of decision-making is not in principle susceptible to formal regulation in advance and a claim that all man-made rules have hitherto been counter-productive and that the time is not yet ripe to try to take on this kind of task. Much of the language of the *Rationale* supports the first interpretation; but it may be possible to build a case from other sources to support the second, more pragmatic view. Bentham seems to have left the question open.

Another minor caveat need not detain us: in a number of passages Bentham concedes that his case against peremptory exclusion of classes of evidence is subject to 'a very few exceptions'.[6] This hardly undermines either the strength or the comprehensiveness of the anti-nomian thesis.

There are, however, two points which make the thesis (at least in respect of evidence) less extreme and controversial than might at first sight appear: Bentham was not opposed to the exclusion of any evidence; his argument is directed against peremptory general rules excluding *classes* of evidence and of witnesses. Evidence may, indeed should, be excluded if any of three conditions is satisfied: (a) it is irrelevant; or (b) it is superfluous; or (c) its production would involve preponderant vexation, expense or delay in the individual case, judged by the standard of utility.[7] None of these, in his view, are suitable matters for formal regulation. A *factum probans* is relevant if it tends to 'probabilize' or 'disprobabilize' a *factum probandum*; the test of relevance is logic and general experience rather than official rules. Superfluity can only be judged according to the circumstances of the particular case. Similarly the third ground requires the direct application of the principle of utility to the particular situation, without the interposition of any fixed rules.

Even more important is the narrow sense in which the word 'rule' is used in this context. The anti-nomian thesis is only directed against man-made (artificial, technical) regulations which are 'peremptory', 'inflexible', 'rigid' or 'unbending' – that is formal, binding rules addressed to the will of the judge.[8] It is appropriate for the legislator to provide 'cautionary instructions', 'guiding principles', 'admonitory maxims' addressed in first instance to the understanding of the judge and indirectly to all concerned persons. Such instructions can include guidance on the appropriate logical 'rules' or 'standards' or 'strategies', but these are neither man-made nor peremptory: they are as Postema suggests, pragmatic 'strategies for the direction of the mind'.[9] In judicial evidence, formal reasoning has almost no place; that, for Bentham, is a central characteristic of practical decision-making. In several passages Bentham uses the term 'rule' loosely to refer to such admonitory instructions.

Bentham is consistent here, except in his usage of the word 'rule', but these caveats considerably narrow the potential area of controversy. For example, it is the predominant, if not the universal, Anglo-American view, that 'the law furnishes no test of relevancy'.[10] Similarly, the exclusion of superfluous evidence is normally left to the discretion of the judge. The effect of many of Bentham's cautionary instructions, in respect of both testimonial and circumstantial evidence, is to recommend that little or no or even a negative weight should be attached to particular examples of suspect evidence. Several leading writers on evidence have explicitly favoured the idea of making all rules of evidence merely guidelines.[11] Even Wigmore, in debating the Model Code of Evidence, went so far as to suggest that its rules should be 'directory, not mandatory'.[12]

Viewed in this light, Bentham's anti-nomian thesis has some distinguished allies. Furthermore, the general tendency of legal change since his day has been in the direction of reducing the scope of the exclusionary rules, of admitting more evidence and of leaving a wider range of questions of admissibility to the discretion of the judge. In so far as the trend in the common law world has generally been to forego rules of weight, to retain only a few relatively unimportant quantitative and preferential rules and to reduce the scope of rules of admissibility, there has been a convergence between the law of evidence and Bentham's uncompromising thesis. Indeed, his ideas – whether or not as a result of his 'influence' – have gained a good deal more support than has generally been acknowledged.

Nevertheless there are important theoretical and practical differences between making provision for exclusion (on the basis of rules or of judicial discretion) and admitting all evidence, subject to Bentham's three criteria, thereby leaving all matters of credibility to the judgement of the decider. To take but one example: in many common law jurisdictions, some rigid rules of exclusion have been replaced by a requirement that the judge should use his discretion to exclude evidence on the basis that 'its probative value is substantially outweighed by its prejudicial effect'.[13] At first sight this looks like a Benthamic-weighing criterion; and, indeed, such rules typically give little or no guidance on how probative value is to be assessed; but Bentham would not have approved of such provisions. He did not accept the notion of 'prejudicial effect' and his basic principle was to admit everything and then to give guidance to the trier of fact on how much weight to give to the particular evidence before him.[14]

The reasons for the anti-nomian thesis   It is not possible here to explore the details of Bentham's arguments against other particular rules of evidence. But the more general arguments against exclusion are relevant to the broader thesis.[15] The reasons he advances are at different levels of

70 *Theories of Evidence*

generality and of different kinds. Scattered throughout the *Rationale* and other works are detailed critiques of particular rules: in some instances he shows them to be contradictory, or counter-productive or unnecessary or based on false pretext or arbitrary or irrational for other reasons or a combination of these. At both general and particular levels he explains their existence and survival in terms of the sinister interests of 'Judge and Co.' and the delusions of ideology (religious, political and professional).

The most general argument against all exclusionary rules might be summarized as follows: 'Evidence is the basis of justice: exclude evidence you exclude justice.'[16] Thus exclusion of any evidence needs justification. Most testimony is true; rigid exclusionary rules tend to exclude much information that is reliable; even false or unreliable evidence is better than no evidence: the former may be useful – for example, in identifying inconsistencies or as indicative evidence leading to other, better evidence.[17] Exclusion is almost always a false security against misdecision. There are other, better, safeguards for securing the completeness and accuracy of testimony (and of other evidence). Thus the exclusion of relevant evidence is unnecessary as a safeguard against deception and is likely to lead to the loss of useful information.

The complexity of Bentham's argument is reflected in the variety of the grounds on which it has been attacked. For example, some exclusionary rules have been – and are still – defended primarily by appeal to non-utilitarian arguments about due process and procedural rights. Such arguments Bentham explicitly rejected as fallacies of sentimental liberalism ('the fox-hunter's argument'; 'the old women's argument'; 'noscitur a sociis').[18]

A second strategic line of attack has been that Bentham overvalued rectitude of decision and underestimated the evils of certain kinds of misdecision, notably conviction of the innocent.[19] In terms of utility, he miscalculated. This provides one basis for retaining some heads of privilege and for excluding certain classes of prejudicial evidence (e.g. evidence of previous convictions).

A third general line of criticism is that Bentham was prepared to place too much faith in officials – especially the single judge exercising discretion unfettered by rules – and in publicity as a safeguard against official abuse.[20] Some arguments for artificial or technical safeguards against abuse are sometimes rooted in 'the politics of mistrust' – here Bentham is accused of a different kind of miscalculation.[21]

A fourth general ground for challenging Bentham's view is that some rules of evidence have stood the test of experience. This is, for example, Wigmore's main ground for retaining some exclusionary rules. The disinterested experience of trial lawyers and judges suggests that misdecision is reduced by some artificial rules. Here the tables are turned: Bentham is accused of being too distrustful of the legal profession; his attacks on the sinister interests of 'Judge and Co.' are treated as a cranky, *ad hominem* argument, which is at best overstated, and he is accused of being blind to the lessons of practical experience.[22]

Concern for procedural fairness, giving a higher priority to other social values than the pursuit of truth in adjudication, minimizing official abuse of power and giving credence to what the legal profession claims to be the lessons of experience are the main, but by no means the only, kinds of reason that are typically advanced to justify the retention of some formal rules of exclusion. They have variable application to the question whether any rules of weight or quantum will tend to reduce misdecision. The first two kinds of argument are not directly relevant, in that they deal with what priority to give to rectitude of decision; the last two are more directly concerned with *how* best to achieve it.

There is one important link between Bentham's reasons for the non-exclusion principle and for the more general anti-nomian thesis. Bentham's attack on the technical system and on all formality can be seen as a rejection of artificial complexity, a plea for simplicity in man-made institutions.[23] However, one of his main arguments for the anti-nomian thesis in general and for the non-exclusion principle is that 'hasty rules' over-generalize – they do not take account of the complexities of the real world. This point is the main ground in his otherwise rather skimpy argument against rules of weight. His case can perhaps be briefly restated in four propositions:

(1) There is scarcely an imaginable fact that is not capable of being the subject of judicial inquiry;[24]
(2) Evidentiary facts can be combined in innumerable ways in particular cases;[25]
(3) Judgements of probability are matters of degree on a theoretically infinite scale of gradations (continuous variation);[26]
(4) Experience has shown that attempts by judges to translate the lessons of experience into rules for the assistance of jurors have been over-generalized when made in good faith and have also been susceptible of abuse.[27]

The first three points are arguments against over-simplification and in favour of leaving judgements about the probative value of all kinds of evidence in particular cases to the discretion of the decider of fact, guided only by cautionary instructions and the rules of logic. These seem to be powerful general arguments for a presumption in favour of free proof,[28] but they are by no means dispositive as an argument against some particular rules of weight. For, if it is shown by empirical research or by more impressionistic experience that certain kinds of evidence (e.g. eye-witness identification evidence, or evidence of previous convictions) tend regularly to be overvalued or undervalued despite cautionary instructions and if, as a result, the chances of misdecision are increased, the presumption is rebutted. The test is empirical: the best experience we

72   *Theories of Evidence*

can muster. And some of our surviving rules of exclusion, corroboration, presumptions and so on are regularly justified on precisely this ground. In this view, Bentham's anti-nomian thesis is itself over-generalized.

What we have here called Bentham's 'anti-nomian thesis' is central to an understanding of his theory of evidence. In interpreting that thesis it is important to bear in mind that his main concerns, when writing about evidence, were more legal and political than philosophical. To be sure there are many passages of potential philosophical interest, but it is not surprising that the basic epistemology is not as fully developed in the writings on evidence as elsewhere. It is perhaps also not surprising, but it is regrettable, that Bentham's ideas on probabilities and his reasons for being opposed to rules of weight are not developed more fully. This makes it difficult to decide how seriously to take the anti-nomian thesis as an attack on the *possibility* of having any formal rules that will tend to maximize rectitude of decision. The author's view is that Bentham meant what he said about exclusion, but overstated his case. In respect of rules of weight, the general thesis that it is beyond the wit of man to devise some formal rules of weighing evidence which would improve on ordinary common-sense practical reasoning seems less strange, but the reasons Bentham gives for this are neither fully worked out nor are they, on their own, entirely convincing.

In respect of substantive law, Bentham is generally thought of as the main advocate of the ideal of a complete and internally consistent body of laws. Gaps, vagueness, ambiguity, and delegation to judges of discretion to make law are all contrary to the principles of legislation. Bentham is seen as the most optimistic of all jurists about the feasibility of achieving this aspiration.[29] Yet, in respect of adjective law, the tendency of his thought appears to point in the opposite direction. He was not merely opposed to having any exclusionary rules of evidence; he was generally against rigid rules of procedure, inflexible rules for the weighing of evidence, and formal requirements for validity of contracts and like documents. Does this not suggest a fundamental inconsistency between his approaches to substantive and adjective law?

Bentham does not address this question directly, but it is possible to reconstruct more than one possible reply to the charge. First, there are fundamental differences between substantive and adjective law. All rights and duties are the creatures of substantive law; the sole function of adjective law is to provide for the efficient implementation of these rights and duties.[30] There is no place for a doctrine of procedural rights in Bentham's theory. Moreover, substantive law generally looks to the future; the main task of a system of procedure is to facilitate the discovery of the truth about past events. One of Bentham's objections to judicial law-making is that it operates retrospectively. Bentham, it is true, has much to say about pre-appointed evidence, that is to say registers, records and documents prepared in advance as evidence that a particular

Bentham on evidence 73

event or transaction, such as a birth or a contract, has taken place. But he is consistent in treating this as just one type of evidence, albeit important, which should only exceptionally be made a necessary condition for the existence of a right.[31] Generally speaking, the existence of rights and duties should be susceptible to proof by whatever is the best means available.

This line of reasoning is not likely to satisfy the sceptic. If the legislator is not competent to make rules based on experience for weighing evidence, why should he be any more competent to make general laws affecting all future contingencies? Do not the factors which militate against regulating proof – the extent of the subject-matter, the potential complexity, the possibility of continuous variation – also affect the making of substantive laws? Is discovering the past more difficult than controlling the future? Is retroactivity always objectionable? If the legislator can delegate discretion in respect of one function, why not in respect of another?

A more radical explanation of the anti-nomian thesis has been suggested by Professor Gerald Postema, but has yet to be fully argued in print.[32] The suggestion is that Bentham was an anti-nomian in respect of substantive as well as adjective law. On this interpretation, Bentham was a consistent act-utilitarian concerned to design a system in which all decisions of judges as well as legislators should be directly governed by the principle of utility. A comprehensive system of codes would serve a number of functions, the most important being the creation of a basis for settled expectations. The most important principle subordinate to utility, the principle of security, puts a very high value on the securing and 'non-disappointment' of expectations. Accordingly, only in exceptional cases would utility be in conflict with the substantive law. In a particular case, in weighing the utilities the judge would have to take account *inter alia* of the consequences of deviating from the code. Only very exceptionally would deviation be justified. However, in case of conflict, '[t]he fundamental allegiance of the judge is not to the existing substantive law but to the Principle of Utility'.[33]

It would be premature to comment on this thesis in detail before it has been fully argued. It is likely to occasion controversy among Bentham scholars. Although it does, on the surface, seem rather difficult to reconcile with many passages in Bentham and with the idea of 'rectitude of decision' as set out in the writings on evidence, it has the attraction of coherence. Even if it is not possible to reconcile it with all the texts, it provides an attractive rational reconstruction of what Bentham might have said, if he had worked out an internally consistent act-utilitarian theory. In this view, the basis for the anti-nomian thesis would not so much be the kinds of reasons explored above as the principle of utility itself. The anti-nomian thesis in respect of evidence would thus be seen to be part of a much more general thesis about the proper role of rules

74   *Theories of Evidence*

within a utilitarian philosophy.

One implication of doing away with rules for excluding and for weighing evidence is that considerable power and discretion are thereby given to the judge. But can this be reconciled with Bentham's distrust of Judge and Co. and his opposition to judicial discretion in dealing with questions of law? Bentham was careful to acknowledge the general probity of judges as individuals and to blame the existence of their sinister interest on the fee-gathering system.[34] When the Natural System is introduced lawyers and judges would have to unlearn a great deal, but Bentham was confident that they would not be incurably tainted. The remedy is to pay judges a salary to ensure that they have an interest in a reputation for impartiality, and to provide adequate safeguards for trustworthiness of testimony and against misdecision.[35] He gives a long and systematic account of securities for trustworthiness in testimony.[36] Judges should be given adequate powers to ensure 'forthcomingness' of testimony, including powers to investigate, to summon witnesses and to compel them to answer questions. Opportunities for falsehood should be reduced by the use of writing, interrogation and counter-interrogation and by notation, that is by keeping a record of what is said. Punishment, a modified form of oath, and shame, should be used together to counteract any temptation to falsehood; for these, rather than exclusionary rules, are the best securities for completeness and accuracy of testimony.

As for the judge, Bentham acknowledged that he was given considerable power under the Natural System, and that this was susceptible to abuse. To guard against such abuse it is desirable to make individual judges take full responsibility for their decisions – Bentham's equivalent to 'the buck stops here'.[37] 'A *board*, my Lord, is a *screen*', he wrote in *Scotch Reform*.[38] The single judge must take responsibility, he should give reasons and, above all, he should be subject to the check of publicity. For this is the ultimate and crucial check against all kinds of misrule. The fact that publicity predominates over secrecy in English judicature is one of the main factors making it 'perhaps the least bad extant' system,[39] instead of being among the worst.

> Upon his moral faculties [publicity] acts as a check, restraining him from active partiality and improbity in every shape; upon his intellectual faculties it acts as a spur, urging him to that habit of unremitting exertion, without which his attention can never be kept up to the pitch of his duty. Without any addition to the mass of delay and vexation and expense, it keeps the judge himself, while trying, under trial . . . Without publicity all other checks are insufficient: in comparison of publicity, all other checks are of small account.[40]

Is Bentham inconsistent in opposing all forms of judicial law-making, yet freeing judges from regulation in respect of proof? He did not think

Bentham on evidence 75

so. Laws *create* rights and duties and look to the future; judge-made law is objectionable because it is retrospective and because the judges have usurped this power. Fact-finding, on the other hand, is by its nature retrospective; it is a necessary part of the *enforcement* of existing rights and duties; it is a power that should be given to them by law.

(d) The causes of the technical system

Why did the technical system come into existence and, if it is consistently opposed to the ends of justice, why is it not changed?[1] Much of Bentham's analysis could, with a few adjustments of terminology and emphasis, be adopted by a modern Marxist:[2] the characteristics of the technical system are directly attributable to the material interests of a powerful class, interests which by and large conflict with those of the rest of society; the system is conserved through a combination of falsehood, mystification and self-deception and is cemented by an underlying liberal ideology. The system is so rotten that it requires complete restructuring, including a radical change in the attitudes of its functionaries. An important preliminary to such a change is exposing its defects by means of a systematic radical critique.

Bentham's central argument is indeed systematic and closely integrated. It is based on two central ideas; an identity of the sinister interests of the legal fraternity and of *mala fide* suitors, that is litigants who know that their cause is unjust;[3] and the cumulation of devices which serve these sinister interests and mask the true nature of the technical system from the legislator, the public and, to a lesser extent, from the lawyers themselves.

The technical system is judge-made; it is contrary to human nature for men to act against their own interests. Because judges are remunerated, not by salaries financed by the community at large, but by the fees paid by litigants, they have a direct financial interest in the number of suits and the way they are conducted.[4] Because it is easier to increase the number of occasions on which fees are extracted than to add to the quantum of each fee, they have a direct interest in increasing the number of separate transactions, documents and meetings, thereby increasing delay and vexation, as well as expense, for the parties. The technical system is the fee-gathering system of judicature; its direct end is profit, its collateral ends the increase in vexation, expense and delay. Thus the ends of judicature are in direct and constant opposition to the ends of justice.[5]

The primary economic interest is supported by other motives, notably indolence ('love of ease')[6] and an interest in mystery.[7] It is natural for judges to wish to make as much money as possible with a minimum of effort: accordingly it is in their interest to deter or dismiss suits in which the litigants are unable or unwilling to pay fees; to reduce the amount of

76   Theories of Evidence

work by excluding evidence and witnesses; and to make their tasks easier by relying on mechanical rules of evidence instead of having to weigh each item of evidence on the merits.[8] There is also an interest in mystification: the more abstruse and irrational the system, the greater the admiration for the 'learning' of its priests and the less vulnerable it is to criticism from non-experts:[9] 'Out of the den of iniquity and nonsense dealt out blindfold, and in return for such dispensations, not wealth alone, but honour, wealth, and reverence, are poured into their laps by the deluded multitude.'[10]

The sinister interests of judges are directly allied to those of both professional lawyers and *mala fide* suitors, though in different ways. Under the fee-gathering system judges and practitioners have a shared, if not identical,[11] interest that the mass of profit-making business should be as great as possible, that indigent litigants should be discouraged and that unnecessary effort should be minimized. Judges and lawyers constitute a single class or corporation, a partnership in substance, if not in form, which Bentham refers to as 'Judge and Co.'.[12] This is part of 'the regime of corporations', which includes the aristocracy and the priest-hood, powerful exclusive groups which pursue their own interests at the expense of others.[13]

The interests of Judge and Co. coincide, or rather are made to coincide, with those of *mala fide* suitors, whose interest is profit rather than justice.[14] Bentham believed that under the technical system 'a vast majority' of those prosecuted were in fact guilty and when they disputed this, 'mala fides is next to certain'.[15] Although he is less explicit on this, one can infer that in his view about 50 per cent of civil litigants know themselves to be in the wrong.[16] To be involved in litigation under the technical system almost inevitably involves becoming a party to false-hood. It stimulates unfounded claims and it encourages those who are in the wrong, in both civil and criminal proceedings, to contest their case, and generally to increase expense and delay.[17] Furthermore, the preservation of the technical system requires the corruption of the moral and intellectual faculties of all the people and this is 'among the constant studies of the man of law'.[18] There is no more effective way of blunting criticism than recruitment. Under the fee-gathering system one object is not only to increase litigation, but also to convert 'the whole body of suitors, little less than the whole body of the people, into a company of liars'[19] by rolling them 'through the mire of mendacity'.[20]

Bentham concentrates his attack on the class interests of Judge and Co. and on the technical system as a system. He allows that there may be competition and conflicts of interest within the system;[21] he even concedes that some of its defenders may be sincere, but deluded;[22] in particular, he stresses that there is little bribery and corruption among individual judges: in practise, their general interest in preserving the technical system is not incompatible with individual integrity.[23] Public opinion imposes limits on the opportunities for judges to profit directly from individual suits, through peculation, bribery or extortionate profit.[24] The sinister interest has to operate in less obvious ways. Some sacrifices have to be made to appearances and, Bentham concedes, 'it becomes necessary to them notwithstanding (to the prejudice, and *pro tanto* to the sacrifice, of these their objects) to apply a part of such monies, commonly by much the greater part, to the services for which it was designed'.[25] This distancing of the judges from too overt an interest in individual cases reduces the potential competition between them and practising lawyers. The main identity of interest lies in the maximization of the aggregate of business and in the preservation of the system as a whole.[26]

For similar reasons, although individual lawyers may be in competition with each other, they have an interest in increasing their numbers. In contrast with business partnerships, the increase in 'partners' among lawyers is a cause rather than a consequence of an increase in business.[27]

> The more neglects and the more blunders, the more business . . . . Moreover, the greater the number of professional channels through which a profitable lie can be made to flow, the more effectively is detection prevented, or at least retarded; and, by the destruction of all individual responsibility, the more effectually is all danger removed of punishment or shame . . . . So, in another branch of trade, the *hustling* trade, the greater the number of the partners, the more difficult it is to ascertain, at each given moment, in whose possession the purse or watch is to be found.[28]

Thus Bentham, having delivered his scathing attack on Judge and Co., back-pedals a little by arguing that the faults lie with the system rather than with individuals and are attributable as much to imbecility as to design. The root cause was the system of fee-gathering, which was established long ago. From this flowed not only the devices in the technical system calculated to maximize profit but also the whole paraphernalia of bad reasons which may conceal the true nature of the system from its priests as well as the public. The system, once created, can be sustained as much by self-interested, but honest, blindness and negligence as by deliberate intention to sacrifice the ends of justice. 'Between the company of dupes, and the fellowship of hypocrites, who shall draw the line?', asks Bentham, and he purports to have an open mind.[29] But on this basis, he is able to claim that his argument does not involve any allegations of bribery or even illegality on the part of the judiciary. Furthermore, the solution lies in changing the system. 'The fault lies not in the individual . . . but in the system itself . . . . Amend the system, you amend the individual. Render it his interest to pursue the ends of justice, the ends of justice will be pursued'.[30] In short, the

78 Theories of Evidence

root fault of the technical system is that it violates the principle of artificial identification of interests.

Bentham attributes the evils of the technical system to the operation of class interest rather than individual malice or corruption. However there are some constraints on the operation of the sinister interests. First, the depredations of lawyers must not be on such a scale as to destroy national wealth, the hen that lays the golden eggs of judicial profit.[31] Secondly, lawyers in their capacity as men have an interest in security and hence in combatting crime, especially crimes against property which are typically committed by people too poor to contribute to the fee-gathering system. Lawyers have little to gain as prosecutors or defenders of such criminals, therefore they have an interest in securing their conviction with a minimum of factitious vexation, expense and delay.[32] Thirdly, the power of the legislature may resist the pursuit of profit by Judge and Co., depending on its power, knowledge and skill and the degree of support from public opinion.[33] Fourthly, public opinion itself can act as a direct check, but given the extent of obfuscation of the nature of the technical system, its operation tends to be feeble and irregular.[34] Fifthly, the existence of competition between courts (the 'double-shop or rival-shop principle') is thought to operate to the advantage of all suitors; in practice, it has the effect of diminishing the probability of misdecision against plaintiffs as the courts vie with each other to attract suitors.[35]

Bentham's method of reconciling the probity of judges with his theory of the sinister operation of the partnership of Judge and Co. bears some similarity to the line taken by Edward Thompson, Douglas Hay and others in recent debates within Marxism about law as ideology.[36] Thompson has argued that it is consistent to see the rule of law as 'an unqualified human good'[37] while acknowledging the role of law both as an instrument of the interests of the ruling class and as a means of mystification and legitimation:

> The rhetoric and the rules of a society are something a great deal more than sham. In the same moment they may modify, in profound ways, the behaviour of the powerful, and mystify the powerless. They may disguise the true realities of power, but, at the same time, they may curb that power and check its intrusions.[38]

In the case of a tradition-bound, complex discipline like law, 'there will always be some men who actively believe in their own procedures and in the logic of justice'. Similarly Douglas Hay has contended that law is not merely superstructure and that legal doctrines sometimes do take on a life of their own in ways which offer genuine protections to the ruled and place inhibitions on the rulers.[39] Bentham's argument, though different in some respects, similarly emphasizes that some sacrifice of sinister interests has to be made, that a price has to be paid for legitimation and mystification and that some lawyers become the dupes of their own rhetoric.

Most of Bentham's main targets, such as the exclusion of parties as witnesses, the multiplicity of jurisdictions and other complexities of evidence and procedure have either disappeared or have been modified out of all recognition. At times he may seem to be belabouring the obvious against indefensible targets and, today, some of his most powerful arguments may seem to be among the least interesting because they are now taken for granted. Yet much of the strength of his argument rests on its simplicity and its close logical integration. And it is the more general thesis, rather than the detailed critique of eighteenth-century judicature, that requires consideration as a theory with claims to lasting significance. Accordingly, rather than summarize his critique of specific devices, I propose to pick out for inspection four of the threads which run through his argument and help to hold it together: the theme of mystification, the fallacies of sentimental liberalism, religion and the operation of the technical prejudice.

Mystification The theme of demystification, as Professor Hart has elegantly shown,[40] was as central to Bentham's thought as it has been to Marx and Engels and many of their successors. As social theories Marxism and Benthamism are rightly seen as mutually antipathetic, although there may be more affinities between them than are commonly acknowledged.[41] The ideas of mystification and, to a lesser extent of false consciousness, are one aspect of this affinity. Bentham's psychology and, in this respect, his terminology, were less sophisticated, but no one has before or since, attacked the mysteries of law with such vigour or penetration. For him, the true nature of the law, and in particular of the technical system of procedure, was hidden by a collection of masks, screens, veils, pretences, pretexts and fallacies which were all the creatures of interest, operating as often as not through folly and delusion as through the deliberate deception of others. The theme of delusion runs through his theory of fictions, his accounts of political fallacies, and his writings on religion.[42] But it received its most sustained treatment in his writings on adjective law and, in particular, in the *Rationale*.

In Book VIII Bentham surveys twenty devices of judicature which are in practice used to further the ends of the fee-gathering system rather than the ends of justice.[43] Several of these are essentially mystifying devices, which have as their purpose, or at least as their subsidiary effects, the concealment of the sinister interests which are being served. Thus the exclusion of parties from giving evidence (and from the presence of the judge at other stages) is primarily a device for increasing the business of lawyers, but it also functions to distance the parties from what is going on, so that the judges' profit, the lawyers' mistakes, the falsehoods of *mala fide* suitors and the nature of other devices are all effectively masked.[44] Similarly the use of legal fictions is to justice

80 *Theories of Evidence*

'[e]xactly as swindling is to trade'.[45] Fictions complicate the law, increase the chances of error, increase business, render proceedings incomprehensible to the jury, make the law unknowable, corrupt the minds and understanding of the people and of the legislator by accustoming them to bow down to falsehood and absurdity.[46]

Another device, the principle of nullification, is a variation on the principle of fiction:[47] the fiction treats as existing something which does not exist, for example 'the sham action' in common recoveries which enabled 'the proprietors of entailed estates to cheat their heirs';[48] under the principle of nullification, the judge causes something to be considered as not having been done or not existing, which has in fact been done or does exist, for example, on the basis of some quirk or quibble or technicality, an appellate court ordering the acquittal of a person found guilty by a jury or denying justice to a plaintiff or defendant in a civil suit because of some procedural error committed by his lawyer.[49] Under the principle of nullification, Bentham seems rather sweepingly to include all decisions not grounded on the merits. Nullification defeats the ends of justice; it also opens the way to a mystifying mode of *justification* particularly prevalent in English law: 'Under the technical system . . . a judge says, with equal facility and indifference, my decision was grounded on the merits, or my decision was not grounded on the merits.'[50] As with fictions some of the main uses of the principle of nullification are essentially to do with mystification: 'Nursing uncertainty . . . . Establishing and supporting arbitrary Power . . . . Blinding the Legislator . . . . Awe-striking, as well as blinding, the people . . . . Repelling the eye of the legislator by disgust.'[51]

Closely related to fictions is Jargon or Jargonization.[52] In most of his writings the importance of a clear, simple and precise vocabulary is one of Bentham's constant themes. The *Rationale* contains a powerful critique of lawyers' abuse of language. The object of language is to convey information; the object of lawyers' language, law jargon, is to prevent information from being conveyed or to convey false or fallacious information, 'to secure habitual ignorance, or produce occasional misconception'.[53] Jargon is pervasive in the law: Law French, Latin, other languages, dead or living; obsolete terms; undefined technical language; nonsense; fiction; ordinary language perverted, often to mean the opposite of what it seems or is generally understood to mean. Jargon supports circumlocution and surplusage in wills, pleadings, statutes and other legal documents. Jargon serves as a cover, as a bond of union between lawyers and judges and as an instrument of plunder. Through jargon the public is kept in ignorance of the law – their liability to prosecution enhanced, their dependency on lawyers increased. Jargon disgusts the legislator and deters him from keeping the law under close scrutiny: 'It converts the whole field of legislation into a thicket, impenetrable to the legislator's eye.'[55] Jargon reminds lawyers of their common interest; it conceals their mistakes and their ignorance;[56] it provides the basis for a sham science; and it secures a monopoly of judicial office for lawyers and, like other devices, it increases business. Thus profit, power and reputation are enhanced; ignorance, error and indolence are masked. Elsewhere Bentham developed a coherent and remarkably sophisticated theory of language;[57] the *Rationale* contains his most powerful polemic against its abuse.

The theme of mystification has a role in Bentham's account of other devices of the technical system: in giving opinions ('the opinion trade'), lawyers have an interest in the non-reporting of cases and in not questioning too closely their clients' versions of the facts;[58] jurisprudential law, i.e. judge-made law, is uncertain, complex and difficult to discover;[59] there is a general interest in the irrationality of the law; under the technical system many immunities are granted from the law of perjury and other sanctions against falsehood – a 'mendacity-licence';[60] the system of special pleadings serves to exclude the parties from participation and to obscure what is going on;[61] finally, there is the double-fountain principle:[62] just as jugglers can win applause by ingeniously serving either red or white wine from the same vessel at pleasure, so judges, through juggling other devices such as fiction, the principle of nullification, conflicting precedents, and through adopting liberal or literal interpretations as it suits them can decide a case at will on a technicality or on the merits:

> Praise you are sure of: all that you need consider is, which of two sorts of praise is most to your taste. Decide against the merits, on the ground of the quirk, the fiction, the jargon, you receive the joint praise of profound science and inflexible steadiness: the praise of adhering to the rule *stare decisis*. Decide in favour of the merits, disallowing the quirk, discarding the fiction, the jargon, you receive the praise of liberality; of attachment to the laws of substantial justice . . . . Exclude the witness, you bow to the name of lord Kenyon and with him pronounce the laws of evidence to be the perfection of wisdom: receive the witness, your bow points to lord Hardwicke, and with him you confess your disposition to admit lights.[63]

Just as a cocktail of truth, falsity and evasion is a more powerful instrument of deception than undiluted falsehood, so a dash of reason in 'the fountains of corruption'[64] enhances the arbitrary power of the judge, increases uncertainty and maximizes business for lawyers.

In addition to the specific devices of the technical system catalogued in Book VIII of the *Rationale*, the mystery of the law is sustained by a collection of myths, pretexts, fallacies and beliefs which, in modern parlance, could be termed an 'ideology' in the Marxist sense – a body of ideas distorted by the vested interests of a powerful class, in this case the sinister interests of Judge and Co.[65] Bentham's treatment of the

82 Theories of Evidence

operation of ideology in adjective law is less systematic than his account of the 'devices' of the technical or fee-gathering system of judicature. However, a reasonably coherent account of it can be gathered from passages scattered throughout the *Rationale* and other works.[66] It can be conveniently considered under three heads: an attack on sentimental liberalism, as exemplified by Montesquieu and, through him, Blackstone; the distorting influence of religious prejudices; and the perversion of sensibility represented by the professional or craftsman who is seduced by the technicalities of his subject.

Sentimental liberalism Halévy interprets Bentham's attack on the technical system and his advocacy of the natural system in political terms.[67] Bentham's theory of procedure 'is nothing else than Cartwright's theory transposed', that is an espousal of a radical plea for a return to a form of democratic authoritarianism in which simplicity is the guiding principle.[68] In this view, Bentham's polemic is simultaneously directed against both the conservatism of the magistracy and the popular liberal prejudices of the time. Halévy concludes that Bentham moved from aristocratic to democratic authoritarianism (as exemplified by the doctrine of the single judge) without espousing liberalism.[69]

The precise timing and the nature of the shifts in his political views have been a matter of controversy among Bentham scholars.[70] In particular, attention has been focused on the question whether Bentham underwent a late conversion to democracy under the influence of James Mill or whether there is a greater continuity in his political views than Halévy's account suggests. The period of intensive work on evidence included the years of his closest association with James Mill and both Mills were actively involved in editing the manuscripts on evidence for publication. It is not necessary to concern ourselves here with this controversy. It is, however, worth making two points: first, there is very little overtly political (as the term is used here) about the writings on evidence. Bentham's main concern was with adjective law and he wrote as a jurist; the *Rationale* touches on a wide range of philosophical, psychological and other issues, but it is a work about adjective law. There is no mention of political writers such as Cartwright and De Lolme and there are only scattered references to Montesquieu and even to Blackstone in the writings on evidence.[71] Politics are only incidental and many of his arguments are not dependent on a particular political theory. This said, however, Halévy is correct in interpreting some of Bentham's polemic as being directed against liberal fallacies and, by and large, the *Rationale* is in tune with a radical democratic authoritarianism which put a high premium on simplicity.

What, specifically, were these fallacies? At a general level there are two that Bentham regularly attacks: the notion of checks and balances and the idea that complexity and formality are essential safeguards of liberty.

Montesquieu can safely be treated as the leading protagonist of both ideas. The doctrine of separation of powers and of different organs of government acting as a check on each other belongs to the sphere of constitutional law rather than of procedure.[72] But Bentham's opposition to this doctrine is clearly exemplified in his insistence that the function of adjective law is to implement substantive laws and that it is irrational for a legislator to set up a system which is divided against itself. If the substantive law is good, then so is its enforcement. If a particular law is not consonant with utility, or is so unpopular as to have that effect, the remedy is to change the law, not to frustrate its implementation.[73] Bentham was generally opposed to the use of juries as a check on unpopular laws,[74] to the use of technicalities and the principle of nullification to mitigate or evade excessively harsh penal laws, and to the, in his view, misplaced humanitarianism which exhibited more sympathy for the criminal (or the suspect) than for his victim.[75] He acknowledged that on occasions to nullify or mitigate bad laws might be consonant with utility, but it was irrational for a legislator to design institutions to 'balance' each other. To do so is to set justice in opposition to itself.[76]

Similarly, Bentham explicitly attacked the maxim that 'The Judicial forms are the shields of liberty'.[77] In *L'Esprit des Lois*, Montesquieu had written:

> If we examine the set of forms of justice with respect to the trouble the subject undergoes in recovering his property or in obtaining satisfaction for an injury or affront, we shall find them doubtless too numerous: but if we consider them in the relation they bear to the liberty and security of every individual, we shall often find them too few; and be convinced that the trouble, expense, delays, and even the very dangers of our judiciary proceedings are the price that each subject pays for his liberty.[78]

This theme was taken up in Bentham's time by Blackstone and others and persists to this day, in various forms, as an important 'liberal' idea.

Bentham's response is scornful: 'As to the *screen* for *corruption* – the screen made out of the panegyric on *delay* and *forms*, I have seen it in use these five and fifty years: the name of the manufactory is visible on it. *Esprit des loix* [sic] the manufactory: *Montesquieu* and Co. the name of the firm: a more convenient or fashionable article was never made.'[79] Montesquieu, although 'a man of gallantry – a *bel esprit* – a fine gentleman, and a philosopher,' was first and foremost a lawyer and a judge, who could not have failed to have perceived the close connection between his rank and 'the respect entertained for the abuses by which that rank was conferred'.[80]

For Bentham, judicial forms were not shields, but screens. 'Liberty' was a logical fiction abused alike by despots, revolutionaries and the legal profession:

84 *Theories of Evidence*

'The Judicial forms are the shields of liberty' . . . . *Liberty*, indeed! What liberty? Whose liberty? What in his dictionary means *liberty*? What unless it be liberty to rulers to oppress subjects, and to lawyers to plunder suitors? Liberty, indeed! Why thus keep hovering over our heads in the region of vague generalities, but that he finds his procedure unable to stand its ground on the *terra firma* of individual and appropriate facts?[81]

In the *Rationale*, Bentham most directly attacks some liberal fallacies, specifically in considering self-disserting evidence and, in particular, the maxim: *Nemo Tenetur Seipsum Accusare*.[82] He interpreted this maxim to mean that no man is bound to answer questions the answers to which would constitute evidence against himself. At the time, in most cases the parties to a civil suit and the accused in criminal proceedings were not competent to give evidence, that is the parties were excluded and no questions could be put to them. Bentham appears mainly to be concerned with this exclusionary rule, but also treats the argument as applying to witnesses' privilege against self-incrimination and, with less force, to what would now be included under the phrase 'the right to silence' outside the courtroom.[83]

Bentham sees these obstacles to examination of witnesses and parties as being based on five fallacies, pretexts or pretences, which mask the sinister interests of criminals, *mala fide* suitors and lawyers. At least four of these arguments are still in common currency and it is worth examining them briefly. First the *nemo tenetur* maxim is treated as self-evident and not in need of justification. This, says Bentham, is begging the question, a *petitio principii*, illustrated daily in books and news-papers.[84] He would have had no difficulty in finding examples of this today in claims that 'the right to silence' and 'the privilege against self-incrimination' are 'sacred' or 'basic' or 'fundamental' rights. To exclude the evidence of those in the best position to answer them excludes the best sort of evidence, leads to greater reliance on inferior evidence (e.g. alleged hearsay confessions), and increases vexation, expense and delay. Accordingly such exclusion needs justification, it is not self-evident.

Secondly, there is 'the old woman's reason . . . 'tis hard upon a man to be obliged to criminate himself'.[85] This is misplaced sentimentality. It is like an old woman exclaiming that it is hard on a child to be subjected to the surgeon's knife in order to effect a cure. Of course it is hard, but it is the lesser of two evils. If being required to answer questions is hard, being punished is even harder. On this argument all punishment of criminals should be abolished. The weakness of the argument is inconsistency; the cause a misplaced sympathy for accused persons and criminals, whose pains are considered without reference to the pains of all past and potential future victims.[86] Such 'humanity' not only impedes the direct ends of justice; it also creates a demand for increase in the magnitude of punishments – especially the death penalty. For, according to Bentham, the biggest single factor behind the proliferation of statutes imposing the death penalty was misplaced leniency in the execution of existing laws.[87]

The third fallacy frequently advanced in favour of the exclusion of self-disserving evidence is 'the fox-hunter's reason'.[88] This introduces the sporting notion of justice: like the fox, the criminal must be given a *fair* chance to escape. But the analogy with sport is false; the end of sport is amusement; if the most efficient means of killing foxes were adopted, there would be little amusement and, in turn, few or no foxes. For Bentham, the direct end of judicature is not entertainment but rectitude of decision, for him the elimination of crime would be an excellent thing. Once again sinister interest lies behind the fallacy:

> In the mouth of the lawyer, this reason, were the nature of it to be seen to be what it is, would be consistent and in character. Every villain let loose one term, that he may bring custom the next, is a sort of bag-fox, nursed by the common hunt at Westminster . . . . To different persons, both a fox and a criminal have their use: the use of a fox is to be hunted; the use of a criminal is to be tried.[89]

The old woman cries 'hard'; the fox-hunter cries 'unfair'. If these fallacious arguments are to be influential, they must be disguised. Lawyers must be careful not to give the game away. In particular the fox-hunter's reason '[I]f let out at all, it must be let drop in the form of a loose hint, so rough and obscure, that some country gentleman or other, who has a sympathy for foxes, may catch it up, and taking it for his own, fight it up with that zeal with which genius naturally bestirs itself in support of its own inventions.'[90]

The last two pretexts are based on historical associations. The fourth, 'confounding interrogation with torture', involves another false analogy.[91] To put a person under an obligation to answer questions is not the same as extracting answers by the application of physical suffering. If extraneous witnesses are compelled to answer, why not the parties? The only difference is that the latter stand to lose the case, if their answers are untrue or evasive, in addition to the sanctions for perjury.[92]

The fifth and final pretext is '[r]eference to unpopular institutions'.[93] Because parties were subject to direct questioning in the Star Chamber, in the High Commission Court and in the Spanish Inquisition, this method is to be disallowed. But this is the fallacy of guilt by association. The Star Chamber and the High Commission Court used efficient means to bad ends; in the case of the Inquisition, direct questioning was used in conjunction with close imprisonment and torture, but its methods were essentially the same as those used in trials for serious offences in ordinary civilian procedure. Because a particular method was used in some abominable courts, it does not follow that the method itself is bad.

86   *Theories of Evidence*

Bentham's treatment of these fallacies constitutes a direct attack on some deeply held civil-libertarian ideas. In particular he challenges the notions of the 'rights' of the accused, of procedural fairness, and the idea that the interests of persons suspected of crime can be looked at in isolation from consideration of the interests of actual and potential victims of crime. His central charge is that these ideas are irrational prejudices for which no reasoned justification can be advanced. Similar charges against civil-libertarian views are made today, often with less cogency than Bentham.[94] For example, civil libertarians are regularly accused of showing more sympathy for the accused than for the victims of crime; many of the procedural 'safeguards' of the accused, the privilege against self-incrimination, and the exclusion of illegally or improperly obtained evidence in the United States, are alleged by their critics to be based on prejudice and sentiment rather than a coherent theory of procedural justice. It would not be appropriate here to enter into these contemporary controversies. In some respects Bentham's critique looks simplistic and naïve compared to much contemporary discussion on such matter as illegally-obtained evidence or the right to silence. But at a more general level it has the merits of simplicity and coherence; by taking a clearcut and extreme position he offers a direct challenge, to those who disagree, to provide a reasoned response. Later in this chapter, I shall consider the first attempts to articulate such a response by the Whig *Edinburgh Review*. A high proportion of the subsequent debates about criminal procedure and evidence can be read as dialogue between those who have accepted at least important aspects of Bentham's position and those who have sought to develop counter-arguments. Today Bentham is still, perhaps, the most important ideologue of 'law and order' and, for civil libertarians, he remains a worthy opponent.

Religion   Religion has to some extent been another ally of the technical system. The religious sanction operates both for and against correctness and completeness in testimony.[95] For although, as the story of Jephthah's daughter illustrates, the original texts of the Jewish and other religions may place a great emphasis on the duty of adherence to truth, subsequent glosses tend in the opposite direction.[96] Some religious codes give a wide licence to perjury or even encourage it; as in the case of sham miracles and other pious frauds. Sometimes religion is harnessed to serve the sinister interests of a powerful section of society. The religious sanction is often weak on its own, although it may be efficient when joined with other sanctions. In respect of evidence, religion has been an ally of the technical system in two particular respects: oaths and genealogical facts, such as births, deaths and marriages.

When Bentham went up to Oxford, he was required to subscribe to the Thirty-Nine Articles, in many of which he did not believe.[97] He felt that he had been coerced into committing perjury. This incident left a permanent scar. It strengthened his opposition to the established Church and it explains the extended attention he gave to the judicial oath. His main critique was so outspoken that it may have contributed to the delay in publication of *An Introductory View*.[98] It is not necessary to consider all its ramifications here. His central argument was that the institution of the oath was based on the false notion that the power of the Almighty can be invoked by any man, however worthless, and for whatever ends. Jesus had prohibited it ('Swear not at all'),[99] yet the Church permitted it.[100] The oath is only efficacious when backed by other sanctions, notably punishment and shame. In practice, it is unnecessary; it is so often abused or taken so lightly that it serves to corrupt moral sensibilities, as in the case of Custom House oaths and University oaths.[101] It can be used as an instrument of coercion, for instance in forcing jurors to return unanimous verdicts against their consciences. It strengthens the technical system in two important ways: first, falsehood in the form of perjury is only punished for testimony given on oath; thus both the opprobrium and the legal sanction are transferred from deception to the ceremony. Accordingly, it is 'an indispensable instrument in the organization of the system of mendacity licences'.[102] Secondly, when the ceremony of the oath is made a condition of giving evidence, the evidence of several classes of witnesses is excluded, including that of Quakers, than whom no one has a more scrupulous regard for the truth.[103] Thus, in its existing form, the judicial oath is an ineffective and unnecessary security for trustworthiness, and in practice it has been productive of several evil consequences. Bentham was not, however, opposed in principle to the use of oaths and in the *Rationale* he made detailed proposals for adapting the ceremony to serve the ends of justice.[104]

In considering preappointed evidence, Bentham argued that established religion, by emphasizing formal ceremonies rather than operative facts, had both distorted an important form of evidence and hampered the compilation of valuable statistics.[105] The Church of England had registered baptisms rather than births, marriage ceremonies rather than marriage contracts, and funerals rather than deaths, and then only of its followers. 'If this be no reproach to the church, it is at least one to the state. Does it consider all, who are born without the pale of the ruling religion, as unimportant beings, whose births, marriages or deaths do not deserve the attention of the legislature?'[106]

Here again Bentham is attacking concentration on formalities rather than on natural facts. This is part of a more general theme: not Paul, but Jesus; not the letter, but the spirit; not factitious ceremony, but ordinary facts.[107] The analogy between lawyercraft and priestcraft is close; in respect of oaths and genealogical facts their forces are combined. There is, however, one important difference: 'Near 300 years has religion had her Luther. No Luther of Jurisprudence is yet come'[108] . . . at least

88 Theories of Evidence

until Bentham.

The technical prejudice   The technical system is also sustained by professional attitudes. Interest can breed self-deception as well as fraud and lawyers can become the victims of their own fictions, fallacies and pretexts. Bentham comments on lawyers' convenient ignorance of psychology, especially of their own motives,[109] their interest-begotten prejudices,[110] and on the 'imperturbable complacency' of judges in the face of absurdity and inconsistency.[111] Furthermore, lawyers are prone to the perversion of sensibility shared by many craftsmen, sportsmen and other professionals – a tendency to become attached to technicalities as ends in themselves:[112]

> What sensation is ever produced in the breast of an angler by an impaled and writhing worm? in the breast of a butcher, by a bleeding lamb? in the breast of an hospital surgeon, by a fractured limb? in the breast of an undertaker, by the death of the father or mother of an orphan family? If a fly were to be put on the hook, in a month when a worm is the proper bait – if the lamb were to be cut up into uncustomary joints – if, in the tying up of the stump after amputation, a three-tailed instead of a five-tailed bandage were to be employed – if, in the decorations of the coffin, the armorial bearings of the deceased were to be turned topsy-turvy – if the testimony of a duke or an alderman, exposed to the temptation of a sinister interest to the value of the tenth part of a farthing, were to be admitted, and an oppressed widow or orphan family gain their rights in consequence – if the rules established in the several professions, established with reason or against reason, were to undergo violation – these are the incidents by which, in the several classes of professional men, a sensation would be produced; meaning always a sensation of the unpleasant kind.[113]

Thus, the technical system is sustained by institutionalized devices, by an ideology replete with pretexts, fallacies and myths, and by the general tendency of specialists to become obsessed with technical detail and thereby to confuse means with ends.

(e) Rectitude of decision as a value

One reason for Bentham's lasting significance as a thinker was his willingness to adopt clear and, in some respects, extreme positions: thus utility is the only criterion of good and bad in both morals and legislation; there are no non-legal rights; no binding rules of evidence can be devised that will maximize rectitude of decision. The same uncompromising clarity underlies his theory of adjective law. The direct end of evidence and procedure is to implement substantive laws deemed to be consonant with utility; there is accordingly almost no place for rules or institutions which set the system against itself, for instance the notion of the jury as a check on unpopular laws. The means of achieving this end is by establishing the truth through the rational and efficient collection, presentation and weighing of evidence. The pursuit of truth is a means to an end, but the end – the enforcement of legal rights and duties – is of primary social importance; that end can be weighed against other collateral ends, notably the avoidance of the pains of vexation, expense or delay. Where they are preponderant, judged by the principle of utility, the collateral ends prevail; but there is no doubt about the high value Bentham placed on rectitude of decision. There is no doubt either about his sharply critical attitude to unnecessary vexation, expense or delay in adjudication as he found it in the technical system.[1] To this day Bentham's theory represents the most fully developed and unequivocal form of a 'truth theory' of adjudication.[2]

Why did Bentham attach such a high priority to rectitude of decision within his general scheme? When was he prepared to allow other considerations to 'preponderate' over the pursuit of truth in litigation and why? Some light can be thrown on these questions by exploring briefly his general attitude to truth, the notion of 'vexation', and his treatment of conviction of the innocent, privilege and compromise. This will help to illustrate how Bentham's approach was intellectually consistent at a general level, yet his personal biases and attitudes coloured his judgements in respect of particular policies and institutions.

The value of truth[3] It is ironic that the proponent of the most uncompromising 'truth theory' of adjudication is sometimes presented as being amoral about truth-telling. Charles Fried, for example, contrasts the attitudes to lying of Kant and Bentham: the former held that lying is always wrong;[4] the latter 'plainly believed that lying is neither wrong nor even intrinsically bad'.[5] This is somewhat misleading. In discussing penal offences by falsehood Bentham says: 'Falsehood, take it by itself, consider it as not being accompanied by any other material circumstances, nor therefore productive of any material effects, can never, upon the principle of utility, constitute any offence at all.'[6] However, he immediately goes on to say: 'Combined with other circumstances, there is scarce any sort of pernicious effect which it may not be instrumental in producing.'[7] Fried is correct in stating that Bentham took an instrumental view of lying: falsehood is only bad because of its effects; the pursuit of truth is good as a means to an end. But on its own this does justice neither to the importance Bentham attached to truth as a social value nor to his deep emotional antipathy to all forms of falsehood.

For Bentham, truth is one of the foundations of good government in all its aspects:

90 Theories of Evidence

Veracity is one of the most important bases of human society. The due administration of justice absolutely depends upon it; whatever tends to weaken it, saps the foundations of morality, security, and happiness. The more we reflect on its importance, the more we shall be astonished that legislators have so indiscreetly multiplied the operations which tend to weaken its influence.[8]

There is a potential tension between the cool intellectualism of Bentham's instrumentalist position on truth-telling and his emotional attitude to falsehood, which amounted almost to an obsession. From the *Rationale* alone one could extract the outlines of a general theory of lying, encompassing not only its morality, but its etiology, its psychology, how to prevent and detect it and, indeed, how to lie successfully.[9] Oaths, perjury, forgery, 'mendacity licence' feature prominently in many of his writings, especially those on evidence. There is a convergence between Bentham's ideas and his emotional attitude in that he hated all forms of falsehood and he gave a very high priority to truth in the calculus of utility. Both aspects deserve comment.

When Bentham was pressured into subscribing to the Thirty-Nine Articles he considered that he was being coerced into *lying*.[10] Whether this particular incident is best interpreted as a symptom or as a cause of his general attitude, there can be little doubt about the strength and the persistence of his feelings. Some of his most virulent prose is directed at hypocrisy, fraud, swindling, quackery, and all forms of falsehood; his polemical vocabulary centres to an extraordinary degree around the themes of mendacity, deception and pretence.[11] A clear example is the ferocity, indeed the intemperance, of his attack on legal fictions as deliberate falsehoods. To cite but one passage:

Falsehood – corrupt and wilful falsehood – mendacity, in a word – the common instrument of all *wrong* – was, in the instance of all those judicatories (as any man may see, even in Blackstone,) among the notorious foundations or instruments of their power . . . *falsehood*, the irreconcilable enemy of justice – *falsehood*, under the name of *fiction* – is passed off upon the deluded people – passed off as the true friend and necessary instrument of justice![12]

This hatred of falsehood is apparent throughout the writings on evidence. Yet Bentham maintained a consistently instrumentalist rationale for placing such a high value on verity and veracity. His position can be restated as follows: the foundation of all good government is the principle of utility. This provides the ultimate test of the goodness and badness of all acts, decisions and institutions, including laws. The calculus is concretized by four principles subordinate to utility: security, subsistence, abundance and equality. The most important of these, subject always to the direct application of the principle of utility, is security:

Among these objects of the law, security is the only one which necessarily embraces the future: subsistence, abundance, equality, may be regarded for a moment only; but security implies extension in point of time, with respect to all the benefits to which it is applied. Security is therefore the principal object.[13]

'Truth is one of the first wants of man',[14] for it is a foundation of security. Reliable information is of crucial importance as a basis for forming expectations, as a ground for confidence and as a condition of ensuring that expectations are not disappointed. The implementation of law is the main way of satisfying expectations and hence of upholding security. Evidence is the basis of justice.[15] Justice under the law and rectitude of decision are thus directly linked to the principle of security and hence to utility. When there is a conflict between security and one or more of the other subordinate ends, utility determines – but in Bentham's calculation that is likely to be exceptional. If this interpretation is correct, and it is in some respects controversial, justice will normally be in harmony with utility. Thus rectitude of decision will command a very high priority indeed as a social value in utilitarian calculations.

This interpretation is borne out by Bentham's treatment of particular topics in which the pursuit of truth in adjudication competes with other social values. As we have seen, while he is deeply committed to fighting unnecessary vexation, expense and delay, he accepts that the processes of implementation of law inevitably involve some pains. A price has often to be paid for justice, but how high that price should be largely depends on what is at stake in the particular case. At a more general level, however, security requires that people should be in a position to expect to be able to vindicate their legal rights cheaply, quickly and efficiently. How high a price should we be prepared to pay as part of the design of a system directed to this end? One key lies in the concept of vexation.

Vexation Bentham took a strongly instrumentalist view of litigation. He was scathing about sporting analogies with their suggestions of the excitement of the chase or the pleasures of combat and victory or of the game being an end in itself.[16] Similarly he was dismissive of notions of procedural fairness, except in so far as they promote the true ends of procedure.[17] But he was acutely aware of the point that, generally speaking, litigation is a potentially painful and damaging process for most, if not all, participants. Hence his emphasis on the collateral ends of procedure.

The central concept in this context is 'vexation'. Unfortunately he did not subject the term to rigorous scrutiny nor explore its potential implications for a utilitarian analysis of procedure.[18] In his published writings he treated it as being almost unproblematic. There are,

92 Theories of Evidence

however, a few places, mainly in unpublished manuscripts, that suggest at least a partial recognition that it is not entirely straightforward. In one passage he states that vexation in general seems to be understood as 'neither more nor less than pain, present pain, evil actually felt as such, considered as produced by some particular and assignable cause'.[19] He also recognized that in principle 'vexation' could be interpreted to cover expense and delay, but he preferred to treat these as separate heads, because they tend to be produced by different causes and require different remedies.[20] Vexation, then, is a residual category: all the pains produced by the pursuit of the direct end or ends of procedure, other than those attributable to the specific pains of expense and delay. The collateral end of procedure is the minimization of these evils; but, government being but a choice of evils, to some extent they have to be borne as the necessary price for trying to achieve rectitude of decision.

Bentham made a quite elaborate and illuminating analysis of the sources and mischiefs of delay and complication in *Scotch Reform*[21], but his published writings contain no comparable analysis of the pecuniary costs and other vexations of litigation.[22] In *The Principles of Judicial Procedure*, he lists the principal modifications of 'juridical vexations' as (i) consumption of time; (ii) confinement in respect of place; (iii) pecuniary expense, loss or charge; and (iv) anxiety of mind, which he explicitly confines to apprehension of being subjected to one of the first three heads.[23] He implies that this list is not exhaustive, and he emphasizes that '[t]hese inconveniences, or some of them, have a mutual tendency to increase and generate each other'.[24] He also states that expense is the most 'prominent' because it can be more precisely ascertained and more exactly measured, thereby acknowledging by implication the difficulty of making precise utilitarian calculations about non-pecuniary costs in this context.[25]

Bentham's treatment of vexation is rather less systematic than one might have expected. He does not use the term consistently,[26] he hints at some of the complexities and difficulties of making a cost-benefit analysis of litigation, but he does not develop the analysis to a point when its more important implications become clear. In this respect he is vulnerable to criticism on a least two grounds. Firstly, he fails to distinguish clearly between what might be termed the direct and the consequential vexations of participating in litigation as a party, witness, juror, official or other actor. The former might include the whole range of physical and psychological discomforts of being suspected, sued, cross-examined, exposed to publicity, and so on: for many people, being involved in litigation can be a painful, even a traumatic, experience. After the event, involvement can have further bad consequences over and above the suffering of sanctions imposed by the court and the pecuniary costs. Such bad consequences may range from physical or psychological after-effects to the imposition of social or moral sanctions (such as loss of reputation of impaired personal relationships) and continuing conflict with one's opponent.[27] Litigation is not normally considered to be conducive to the restoration of harmony.[28] The Natural System of Procedure is designed at least to mitigate many of the direct, experiential vexations of procedure, but Bentham fails to take into account in any systematic way the consequential vexations, other than sanctions and expense. He can accordingly be criticized for failing to take sufficient account of some of the main deterrents to becoming involved in litigation, especially in adversary proceedings, and one of the main incentives to compromise – the restoration of harmonious relations. By placing so much emphasis on expletive justice as the direct end of procedure, Bentham ignored some of the consequences of strict enforcement of law and standing on one's rights. *Fiat iustitia, ruat coelum* is hardly a utilitarian maxim, but at times Bentham comes quite close to accepting it by implication.

A second criticism is that Bentham may have seriously underestimated both the variety of direct vexations and the gravity of some of them. In addition to his explicit mention of confinement and anxiety, there are scattered throughout his writings occasional references to pains commonly associated with litigation such as loss of privacy,[29] being brow-beaten[30] and disclosure of collateral facts.[31] Bentham was not insensitive to such matters, but he does justice neither to the extent nor to the intensity of the potentially unpleasant experiences to which litigants, witnesses, jurors and other participants are liable to be subjected. Anxiety is hardly restricted to anxiety about expense, loss of time or fear of confinement.[32] For many the experience of being suspected, of being unjustly accused or interrogated, or publicly paraded in court, or cross-examined, or subjected to judgment, to say nothing of all that is associated with the 'trouble' of being involved in a dispute, carry enormous psychological and other non-pecuniary costs.[33] Bentham seems to ignore or to dismiss these too lightly as trivial or sentimental considerations.[34]

These criticisms are not fundamental. Indeed, one of the merits of utilitarianism is that it provides a framework for systematically and flexibly analysing the costs and benefits of participating in litigation and of the consequences of such activities.[35] If Bentham is to be faulted, it is for failing to apply his own approach systematically in this sphere and for either overlooking or underestimating the significant factors that ought to form part of such a calculation. Moreover, it would not be difficult to rescue him from most of these charges. As we have seen, the Natural System of Procedure is designed to mitigate all vexations to participants as far as is consistent with the direct end of procedure; it is arguable that Bentham's theory is flexible enough to adjust to facts that he may have overlooked – to admit of fresh calculations, so to speak; in his view, the social importance of rectitude of decision justifies paying a quite heavy price for its attainment; and some of the pains of litigation – such as

94 Theories of Evidence

suspicion or disharmony – are more the occasion for, than the result of, litigating.

Even if one concedes all these points, the criticisms are not trivial. For I hope to show that there is a direct connection between these flaws in Bentham's treatment of vexation and other weak points in his analysis. In the next section, I shall link this line of criticism with his treatment of two particular topics on which he appears to be guilty of serious misjudgement: compromise and the conviction of the innocent. These link directly to the more general thesis that any theory that attributes a single primary end to the complex activity of litigation is bound to fail.[36]

Compromise Dispute settlement and the enforcement of law are sometimes posited as contrasting ends of adjudication. The former objective is concerned with restoration of harmony and the preservation of order and is directed to the future; the latter is concerned with justice and rights and is directed to the past. The contrast can be drawn too sharply, not least because a continuing sense of injustice is a source of potential conflict. Nevertheless, the distinction is a valuable one. Procedures designed to restore harmony can be very different from those concerned to vindicate rights. One difference is to be found in the treatment of compromise and reconciliation.[37]

Settlement out of court, plea-bargaining and other alternatives to third-party adjudication are a central feature of most legal systems;[38] in many societies they account for the vast majority of disputes settled; in some societies third-party adjudication is entirely absent. A characteristic of such methods of dispute settlement is that the outcomes of the processes deviate significantly from what is prescribed by the substantive law – there is little or no correspondence of rules and results:[39] the plaintiff accepts less than he claimed as his due; the accused pleads guilty to a lesser charge; instead of winner-takes-all, the risk of losing is distributed and so on.

Bentham's treatment of compromise and reconciliation suggests a certain ambivalence:[40] he had mixed feelings about Danish Courts of Reconciliation and similar experiments in France.[41] In *Scotch Reform* he says: 'Another mode of termination is by what is called a *compromise*: which, being interpreted, is *denial of justice*'.[42]

Yet in the *Principles of Judicial Procedure*, he explicitly provides that the judge should exercise a conciliative function in cases in which each side has complained of a series of supposed wrongs. One objective of this provision is to enable all dimensions of a quarrel to be dealt with together, thereby avoiding the expense and delay of multiple suits. Another objective is to effect a reconciliation. However, it seems that Bentham considers that this is best achieved by applying the law:

The increased faculty of extinguishing ill-will, *and at the same time rendering complete justice* [italics added] as between any two or any greater number of persons regarding themselves as wronged, is among the advantages possessed by the system of natural procedure, in comparison of the system of technical procedure . . .[43]

Bentham's assumption appears to be that reconciliation is best achieved by conformity to law; in the passage quoted from *Scotch Reform* his main concern was to attack compromises made under pressure of delay (or, *semble* expense); the litigant no more freely consents to give up his due than the traveller consents to surrender his money 'to the unlicenced plunderer' in order to secure his life.[44] Similarly, the use of pardon in penal cases is only justified in exceptional circumstances.[45] However, there is manuscript evidence to suggest that Bentham considered any compromise to be a denial of justice and, even where the parties freely consent, it is only justified when both parties in good faith believe that they are right or when 'the natural and inevitable' cost of litigation (as opposed to unnecessary expense) is likely to be greater than what is at stake.[46] In short, Bentham seems to give only a grudging place to compromise as the lesser of two evils in some circumstances and to make the rather dubious assumption that reconciliation will best be achieved through rectitude of decision, that is, a strict adherence to justice under the law.

Innocence   The idea that in criminal cases a party should only be found guilty by 'a very great weight of evidence' is an ancient one.[47] It has had a chequered history.[48] The expression of that idea in the ambiguous notion of the presumption of innocence and in that of the standard of proof beyond reasonable doubt was to come quite late. Both formulations were known in Bentham's time, but neither was established as part of the settled law. Some late-eighteenth-century cases had suggested that the standard of proof in capital cases was higher than in other cases, but no one formula was generally accepted until Starkie gave currency to the notion of 'moral certainty, to the exclusion of reasonable doubt' in the first edition of his treatise in 1824.[49] Nevertheless, the practice of warning juries of the need for clear and cogent evidence and the dangers of convicting the innocent were familiar ideas.

Perhaps the most common mode of expressing the notion was in terms of numerical comparisons between the relative evils of mistaken acquittals and convictions. Fortescue had stated: 'I would rather wish twentie evill doers to escape death through pitie than one man to be unjustly condemned.'[50] In the *Trial of Five Popish Lords* in 1680, Lord Stafford is quoted as saying (on his own behalf): 'it is better that a thousand persons that are guilty should escape than that one innocent person should die'.[51] A century later Blackstone stated in connection with felony, 'the law holds, that it is better that ten guilty persons escape,

96 Theories of Evidence

than that one innocent suffer'.[52] Bentham was familiar with this mode of argument, with its quasi-utilitarian associations, and he poked fun at it.[53]

Paley had criticised Blackstone's formulation in *The Principles of Moral and Political Philosophy*[54] and this in turn had provoked a response by Romilly[55] that was soon recognized as an eloquent and penetrating statement of the humanitarian view. Although he does not directly refer to this debate, Bentham was almost certainly familiar with the arguments on both sides and he may have been directly influenced by some of Paley's points. It is accordingly illuminating to set Bentham's view in the context of this debate.

Paley's criticism of Blackstone is curious. The object of the criminal law is to preserve the security of civil life through the dread of punishment. Without it there would be universal misery and confusion. The misfortune of an individual, including the death of an innocent person, 'when *occasioned by no evil intention* [italics supplied], cannot be placed in competition with this object'.[56] The courts of justice should not be deterred from carrying out their duty 'by every suspicion of danger, or by the mere possibility of confounding the innocent with the guilty . . . They ought rather to reflect that he who falls by a mistaken sentence may be considered as falling for his country, by suffering under rules by the general tendency of which the welfare of the community is maintained and upheld.'

Romilly's reply is devastating.[57] The escape of ten guilty criminals is no trivial ill, but it is less destructive of the security and happiness of the community than that one innocent man should be put to death 'with the forms and solemnities of justice'. Paley treats the misfortunes of the victim as if they were the only evil. He overlooks the disrespect and loss of confidence arising from admission that the laws cannot protect the law-abiding; that the courts may make terrible mistakes and that each wretch who goes to the scaffold may be an innocent victim. He does not take into account the comfort that such fatal errors may provide to the guilty and the sense of insecurity they may create in the population at large. When guilty men escape, the law has merely failed; when an innocent man is condemned it does a great harm; it creates the very evil it was to cure and destroys the security it was made to preserve. The idea that the innocent man is dying for his country is a false consolation. It overlooks the damage to his reputation and to his family and much else besides.[58]

Bentham seems to have been sympathetic to Paley's position but, perhaps because he was aware of Romilly's criticisms, he proceeded by indirection. He adopts or concedes some of the main humanistic points, such as that conviction of the innocent is a worse evil than acquittal of the guilty or that public confidence and security may be even more threatened by miscarriages of justice than by tender-minded acquittal, but he then proceeds to undermine them. In neither the *Rationale* nor the *Introductory View* is there any sustained discussion of the issue, and one has to glean Bentham's opinions from scattered passages in these and other works.[59]

Nevertheless it is possible to construct a coherent position along the following lines: every person counts for me; the pains of innocent victims of crime; the pains of innocent victims of judicial process; *and* the pains of guilty persons lawfully punished.[60] For infliction of pain on the guilty as well as on the innocent is an evil that needs to be justified. Echoing Paley, Bentham even suggests that the suffering of the innocent is not so great as the suffering of the guilty.[61] The infliction of punishment on guilty and innocent alike is contrary to utility unless there is preponderant inconvenience. Sometimes punishment may have to be mis-seated, that is applied to the wrong person.[62] Where it is avoidable, mis-seated punishment ought never to be employed; when it is unavoidable, it may be employed in accordance with utility.[63]

Bentham claims that the risk of pain to victims of crime is more widespread and more serious than the pains of occasional punishment of the innocent who have their consolations.[64] Nevertheless he acknowledges that there are good reasons for treating the conviction of one innocent man as a worse evil than the acquittal of one guilty man.[65] This is because, if the non-guiltiness of the convicted persons becomes a subject of popular belief, two mischiefs result: alarm, produced by apprehension of undue suffering from the like source and the pain of social sympathy.[66] In both instances, the crucial fact is public belief in his innocence.[67]

Bentham's treatment of the presumption of innocence needs to be considered against this background. In the *Principles of Judicial Procedure* he treats the presumption as an artificial device of the technical system:

> In all cases of penal procedure, the declared supposition is, that the party accused is innocent; and for this supposition, mighty is the laud bestowed upon one another by judges and law-writers. This supposition is at once contrary to fact, and belied by their own practice.
>
> The defendant is not in fact treated as if he were innocent, and it would be absurd and inconsistent to deal by him as if he were. The state he is in is a dubious one, betwixt non-delinquency and delinquency: supposing him non-delinquent, then immediately should that procedure against him drop; everything that follows is oppression and injustice.[68]

However, in the *Treatise*, in the context of discussing presumptions, the tone is decidely more moderate: 'It is necessary to set out from a fixed point: *innocence ought to be presumed*. This is not one of those fine maxims of humanity, which do more honour to the heart than to the experience of

98 Theories of Evidence

those who maintain them; it is a maxim founded on a solid basis.'[69]

That basis is the fact that the vast majority of mankind is restrained from crime by the four tutelary sanctions: the natural, the legal, the moral (opinion) and the religious. Accordingly an accusation of crime against an individual is *prima facie* improbable unless backed by evidence; the more heinous the crime the more improbable it is and the stronger the evidence needed to establish it.[70] The role of criminating circumstances is to counterbalance this general presumption of innocence. Bentham thus transforms what he treats as an artificial rule of the technical system into a general premise about prior probabilities, which provides a starting-point for analysis. This presumptive premise will vary according to the gravity of the charge, the apparent motives of the accuser and other circumstances of the particular case.[71] It does not provide the basis for formal rules about the standard and burden of proof.

In the *Treatise* Bentham seems to give more weight to the evils of conviction of the innocent[72] than he does in other passages, because he acknowledges that the alarm will tend to be greater than in the case of a 'too easy acquittal'.[73] And he concludes this passage, on what is for him, a moderate note:

> Thus, then, although a judge should have an internal presumption against the accused, he should not hesitate to act on the presumption of his innocence, and, in doubtful cases, to consider the error which acquits as more justifiable or less injurious to the good of society, than the error which condemns. In listening to the voice of humanity, he will only be following that of reason.
>
> But we must be on our guard against those sentimental exaggerations which tend to give crime impunity, under the pretext of insuring the safety of innocence. Public applause has been, so to speak, set up to auction. At first it was said to be better to save several guilty men, than to condemn a single innocent man; others, to make the maxim more striking, fixed on the number *ten*; a third made this ten a hundred, and a fourth made it a thousand. All these candidates for the prize of humanity have been outstripped by I know not how many writers, who hold, that, in no case, ought an accused person to be condemned, unless the evidence amount to mathematical or absolute certainty. According to this maxim, nobody ought to be punished, lest an innocent man be punished.[74]

Further research is needed to establish whether the hand of Dumont is to be discovered in this more moderate stance. But even in this version, not all of Romilly's points are met; nor are other objections that could be raised from a humanitarian point of view.[75] As we shall see, some of these points were taken up by Denman in his review of the *Treatise*, in an attempt to defend some of the formal safeguards for the accused, while

Bentham on evidence **99**

accepting the main thrust of Bentham's general thesis about evidence.[76]

Further clues to Bentham's own values are to be found in his treatment of other issues. He places little weight on values which constrain the uninhibited pursuit of truth. He is opposed to rules of privilege designed to protect marital harmony or confidential relationships; and he makes it quite clear that such factors should normally be given less weight than rectitude of decision.[77] He is particularly harsh on the lawyer-client privilege and gives no quarter to the claim that this may serve to increase rectitude of decision in the long term;[78] he is dismissive of the privilege against self-incrimination and the right to silence[79] and gives short shrift to many of the specific provisions that would today be subsumed under such notions as due process, natural justice and process values, except in so far as they would promote rectitude of decision.[80] For example, parties should be present and be heard because, and to the extent that, this is the best way of arriving at the truth. Bentham is tough-minded about confessions, while recognizing the unreliability of statements made under pressure;[81] he is even prepared to consider torture as an instrument of the administration of criminal justice as a last resort in certain limited cases – such as coercing an arsonist to reveal the identity of an accomplice who is still at large and who poses a continuing threat to lives and property.[82]

Two major exceptions to the priority of rectitude of decision are justified on special grounds: he was prepared to make a quite limited exception to the non-exclusion principle by giving privileged status to confessions to a Catholic priest on the grounds that compulsion would involve a preponderant vexation and that little evidence would be lost as a result.[83] He was also prepared to give quite wide, if vague, protection to secrets of state from disclosure on the grounds of preponderant harm connected with security.[84] However, it is not entirely clear how far he would in practice have been prepared to go in treating this as a ground for excluding such evidence from the tribunal as opposed to making an exception to the general principle of publicity, but allowing an appropriately constituted body to hear the evidence in private.[85]

To conclude: Bentham's treatment of the presumption of innocence, of the value to be attached to wrongful conviction and of related topics illustrates how high he placed rectitude of decision above other social values. It also shows the importance he attached to considerations of security in making such assessments. The issue is posed in terms of security against crimes and security against the errors and corruption of judicial procedure. The main reason for protecting the innocent is expressed in terms of 'alarm', that is self-regarding feelings of insecurity prompted in the public at large by fears of, and loss of confidence in, the machinery of justice. It is reasonable to treat both the arguments and the conclusions as reflecting Bentham's attitudes and scale of values rather than as a necessary consequence of a utilitarian analysis. Even a strict

100 Theories of Evidence

utilitarian could adduce different or additional arguments in favour of safeguards for the accused and against conviction of the innocent, as Romilly's criticisms of Paley illustrate. A modified utilitarian or non-utilitarian approach to the protection of the innocent from wrongful conviction would involve some other kinds of consideration.[86]

This opens up a problem of interpretation, which cannot be pursued here. How far should Bentham's views on particular issues be treated as direct applications of his general ideas, how far as particular utilitarian calculations with which a committed utilitarian might disagree on objective, rational grounds and how far as reflections of Bentham's personal biasses and attitudes? His hatred of falsehood, his attacks on the legal profession, his emphasis on security and his rather less consistent tough-mindedness towards the victims of misdecision in criminal cases[87] are examples of topics of which it is tempting to say that his judgement was clouded by his emotions. However, there is by and large a remarkable consistency both in his general thesis and his relentless application of a few simple ideas to an extraordinary range of topics. His passionate commitment to the reform of adjective law is balanced by a combination of intellectual honesty, courage and patient attention to detail. Moreover, the principle of utility and the natural system of procedure both allow some scope for modification of his recommendations in special or changed circumstances.[88]

(iv) Aftermath: *The Edinburgh Review*

The *Edinburgh Review* tended to look on Bentham with cautious admiration.[1] The Whiggish journal carried lengthy anonymous reviews of Dumont's *Traité* in 1824 and of the *Rationale* in 1828.[2] These are two contrasting studies in ambivalence. They presage the mixed reception that Bentham's theory was to receive during the next hundred years.[3]

The difference in tone of the two reviews is revealing. The first starts with adulation which is then modified by respectful dissent on a range of particular issues. The second is outspokenly critical, yet it finishes on a note of grudging admiration. Both agree on Bentham's general importance, on the exceptional interest and significance of his work on evidence and on his good fortune in having Étienne Dumont as his acolyte, collaborator and publicist. Both accept that there is a strong case for substantial changes in the law of evidence, but not to the extent of the total abolition of the rules of exclusion. But their points of disagreement with Bentham are significantly different.

The reviewer of the *Traité* has subsequently been identified as Thomas Denman, a barrister and Whig member of Parliament, who was later to become Lord Chief Justice.[4] A lifelong friend and associate of Brougham, Denman was a leading advocate of many measures for the

Bentham on evidence 101

reform of law and procedure during his time in Parliament (1817-26); but this review was written nearly twenty years before the enactment of the measure which came to be known as 'Lord Denman's Act', viz. the Evidence Act, 1843, which abolished the rule making witnesses (other than parties to the record)[5] incompetent by reasons of crime or interest. Denman was an admirer of Bentham and an energetic reformer but, as will become apparent, he was not a committed utilitarian.[6]

Denman began his review by praising both Bentham and Dumont.[7] The great value of their collaboration was to pursue truth on the basis of reason alone, 'driving hypocrisy and fraud to their hiding places', and 'boldly bidding defiance to authority'.[8] The subject of evidence and proof is both important and neglected.[9] For the most part the reviewer 'acquiesced' both in the general theory and in most of the specific proposals for reform.[10] He does not expressly dissent from the suggestion that most of the faults of the existing system can be attributed to the interests and obscurantism of the legal profession, at least in the moderate version that is presented in the *Traité*. However, the core of the review is taken up with exploring a number of points of disagreement. The first difference might be thought to be fatal to acceptance of Bentham's argument. Denman questions the analogy with the family which Bentham 'is disposed to make the foundation of his whole system'.[11] This is to revive the theory of paternal government of Sir Robert Filmer and 'the Tories of his day'.[12] The father is the protector and preserver of his children; all the powers of governance are united in him as a benevolent, authoritarian ruler. The prudent paterfamilias turns a blind eye to many of the faults of his children, punishes them sparingly and assumes the responsibility himself or tries to lay it on others: 'His object is to reclaim the wandering, his triumph is to attain that object without severity . . . . [I]n the administration of Criminal Justice the aim and object of the law is directly *contrary* to that of the father of a family.'[13] Is to detect, punish and expose offenders publicly. Denman continues:

> [Everyone] must submit, for the sake of justice to many things which interfere with their habitual comfort, their pecuniary interest, their personal liberty, – to what extent, the necessity of the case must decide. All that is unnecessary is vexatious and oppressive; *and general rules must be laid down to prevent persons in office from abusing the powers intrusted to them* [my italics].[14]

This is an explicit plea for making safeguards against abuse a matter of formal legal regulation; it is reasonable to interpret it as giving implicit support to Montesquieu's scheme of checks and balances in place of Filmer's paternalistic authoritarianism.[15] Most subsequent civil-libertarian arguments for safeguards for the accused have followed this kind of approach, whether or not they have been based on a doctrine of

102 Theories of Evidence

procedural rights or, more generally, of inalienable human rights.[16]

How far does this undermine Bentham's central thesis? The review claims that the merits of Bentham's case exist in spite of the analogy with the family:

> While then we definitely reject the 'natural model of jurisprudence', we agree with the measures proposed to be adopted, in the majority of cases. With him, we exhort the judge to aim directly at his object, and, discarding all idle technicalities, to apply his mind to the discovery of truth, with the simple wish to arrive at a rational conviction; to cast aside all useless shackles that may impede his march, and keep his eyes and ears ever open for the reception of proofs, in whatever quarter they may be obtained.[17]

Denman does not question the proposition that the probative force of evidence is not susceptible to regulation by rules and he supports the view that most relevant evidence should be admitted. But he does not accept the whole of Bentham's anti-nomian thesis. 'Some *Rules of Evidence* must . . . be laid down',[18] though not necessarily the particular set of rules favoured by the English courts. He agreed with Bentham that parties should be competent and compellable as witnesses and that interest should affect credibility, rather than competency, of witnesses. But Denman envisages a role for exclusionary and other rules, especially in criminal cases. His argument can be treated as the first important statement of a coherent civil libertarian position within the Rationalist Tradition.[19]

In advocating only selective support for Bentham's thesis, Denman drives a wedge between the notion of freeing the law from outdated, inconsistent or irrational technicalities and the non-exclusion principle. Denman was in favour of extensive reform, but he wished to preserve and strengthen the structure of rules which purport to provide safeguards for the accused. Some of these safeguards involve exclusion of evidence, for example the right to silence and involuntary confessions; others, such as the doctrines concerning the burden and standards of proof, are rules for decision in situations of uncertainty. It is in respect of rules of the latter type that Denman pinpoints what is arguably the most vulnerable aspect of Bentham's position:

> Mr Bentham's mode of treating criminals and accused persons, does not appear to us quite philosophical. In his balance, their interests and safety seem to weigh very little against his eagerness for the detection of crime, and the infliction of punishment.[20]

Accusing Bentham of surprising indifference to 'so terrible an evil' as conviction of the innocent,[21] he attacks him with an eloquence reminiscent of Romilly's critique of Paley.[22]

The next major objection to Bentham, his treatment of the lawyer-

Bentham on evidence 103

client privilege, is linked directly both to his attitude to the presumption of innocence and to his antipathy to the legal profession. Bentham had argued that privilege should attach only to communications between priest and penitent and that no other relationship, including those of husband and wife and lawyer and client, should be protected.[23] He thereby recommended the complete reversal of the existing law of privilege. The reviewer agreed in respect of priests, dissented mildly in respect of marital privilege, but took strong exception to Bentham's argument that a lawyer who respects the confidences of his guilty client thereby becomes his accomplice.[24] Bentham treated the relationship as being merely contractual:

> Why should any higher regard be paid to the engagements, with legal practitioners, into which, after the fact, these very criminals may have entered to aid their safety? . . . It is in the interest of society, that honest engagements should be observed and dishonest and hurtful engagements violated.[25]

In a succinct footnote, Dumont had commented:

> Admit this opinion of Mr. Bentham, it is said, and the accused have no longer counsel; they are surrounded by agents of justice and the police, against whom they ought to be so much the more upon their guard, as no man of a noble or elevated mind would stoop to such an employment. They are so many spies and informers placed round the accused. This is to suppress the defence entirely. The question ought to be examined in this new shape.[26]

There are further reasons, suggests Denman, to bolster Dumont's remonstrance. 'The author evidently presumes the guilt from the accusation.'[27] Nor does he give any role to the professional defender, except to usurp the role of the court by deciding whether or not his client is guilty. It is absurd to treat the relationship as one of contract or of accomplices in crime: '*We* think, however, that all such communications ought to be sacred'.[28] Later he adds: 'His proposal will be received in almost every quarter, with the exclamation he has anticipated – *Quoi! trahir! trahir son client!* Perhaps it deserves no farther reply.'[29]

This argument leads directly to acceptance of an un-Benthamite position, viz. the acceptance of the doctrine of the procedural rights of all accused persons. This the reviewer acknowledges in a passage which has often been quoted in part, but which deserves to be given in full:

> Even in the very few instances where the accused has intrusted his defender with a full confession of his crime, we hold it to be clear that he may still be lawfully defended. The guilt of which he may be conscious, and which he may have so disclosed, he has still a right to see distinctly proved upon him by legal evidence. To suborn wretches

104 *Theories of Evidence*

to the commission of perjury, or procure the absence of witnesses by bribes, is to commit a separate and execrable crime; to tamper with the purity of the judges, is still more odious: But there is no reason why any party should not, by fair and animated arguments, demonstrate the insufficiency of that testimony, on which alone a righteous judgment can be pronounced to his destruction. Human beings are never to be run down, like beasts of prey, without respect to the laws of the chase. If society must make a sacrifice of any one of its members, let it proceed according to general rules, upon known principles, and with clear proof of necessity: 'let us carve him as a feast fit for the gods, not hew him as a carcase for the hounds.' Reversing the paradox above cited from Paley, we should not despair of finding strong arguments in support of another, and maintain that it is desirable that guilty men should sometimes escape, by the operation of those general rules, which form the only security for innocence.[30]

Denman's critique of Bentham combines both utilitarian and non-utilitarian elements. On the one hand, it is suggested, Bentham, by his own test of utility, undervalues the evils of conviction of the innocent and overvalues rectitude of decision. On the other hand, a possible line of attack on utilitarianism is that it cannot satisfactorily take account of 'feelings of unmingled and salutary horror'[31] and of notions of justice and fairness which can only be adequately expressed in terms of principles independent of utility.[32] The very notions of weighing and calculation, the argument goes, are inapposite where questions of guilt and innocence are involved. What Bentham dismisses as sentimentality is, in this view, capable of being defended on the basis of non-utilitarian principles. Thus rejection of Bentham's treatment of the presumption of innocence can be based either on utilitarian, modified utilitarian or non-utilitarian grounds; the first important critic of his views on evidence invoked just such a mixture of arguments.[33]

A second point about the argument in favour of the lawyer-client privilege relates to attitudes to the legal profession. Bentham, by attacking the operation of the sinister interests and by placing a low value on lawyers' services generally, avoids the dilemma of those who, to put the matter in extreme terms, wish both to abolish the legal profession and to argue for extension of its services to all.[34] An ambivalence about the social value of legal services runs through much civil-libertarian thinking.[35] In this instance, the reviewer sidesteps the issue. He appears to acquiesce in Bentham's thesis that the technicalities of the law of evidence and many evils of procedure are attributable to the sinister interests of Judge and Co. At least he does not openly dissent from it and offers no alternative explanation for the evils he agreed should be abolished. Instead he resorts to an *ad hominem* argument and suggests that Bentham 'is obviously far from familiar with the practice of the law, and his denunciations will no more persuade mankind to do without lawyers, than some proofs of pedantry and error will annul the faculty of medicine'.[36] Bentham's argument about the causes of the technical system, although not fully expounded in the *Traité*, is a sufficiently important part of his theory to warrant a more direct response than that.

Finally, Denman's treatment of self-inculpation deserves at least a brief mention. Although different aspects of 'the right to silence' are not adequately distinguished, there can be few more eloquent defences of the notion in print. Denman accepts some of Bentham's contentions, but argues for a moderate position falling far short of the doctrine that silence implies guilt: 'Between the opposite methods of compulsive interrogation, and an indiscriminate injunction of silence, common sense suggests a middle course, which leaves the party to judge and act for himself.'[37]

Bentham's arguments are attacked on several grounds. He takes too little account of the 'overwhelming calamity' to an innocent man of the mere fact of being accused;[38] if the nerves always stood firm *and* if the accused knew all the proofs on which the suspicion is founded, then it might be difficult to refute Bentham's thesis. But the opposite is often the case; there are many situations, not all of them extreme, in which 'the ordinary badges of guilt would naturally be found in company with perfect innocence'.[39] An innocent person may not be in a position to give an adequate explanation; in a distracted state anything he says may increase suspicion. 'The discreet and candid Dumont' has pointed out that public examination of suspects has its faults: it often involves unseemly bickerings between judge and suspect, thereby degrading the dignity of justice. The balance of power is such that 'it is easy to foresee which side will have the best of the argument'.[40] Finally, Bentham's rejection of the analogy between interrogations and the *question* of the inquisition is attacked. '[T]he state of accusation is itself a state of torture . . . . [E]ven truth may be bought too dear.'[41] The maxim 'silence implies guilt' can be translated into 'We will punish the contumacy of your silence, by condemning you for a crime which we do not know you to have committed'.[42]

The Dictionary of National Biography claims that Denman's article in the *Edinburgh Review* helped to draw public attention to the need for reform of the law of evidence.[43] Both eloquent and readable, it may indeed have helped to make Bentham's critique of the existing system better known. But Denman's dissent, which concentrates on criminal evidence, amounts to much more than some judicious caveats uttered by a practical lawyer and politician, conscious of the constraints upon radical change. Rather it represents the firm rejection of important parts of Bentham's thesis on the basis of argument which contained a strong non-utilitarian element. There are many reasons why Bentham's thesis, even today, has only achieved a partial victory. One factor was that

106 *Theories of Evidence*

considerations of principle, as well as of pragmatism, from the outset affected the approach of the leading practical reformers, such as Romilly, Denman and Brougham, who responded to his ideas.[44]

Four years after the review of the *Traité des Preuves Judiciaires*, the *Edinburgh Review* published an even longer article devoted to a critique of the *Rationale*.[45] The second piece was as profoundly ambivalent as the first and even more critical. The article finishes as follows:

> As we have spoken plainly our real sentiments regarding the flaws, which strike across this great work a vein so deep and coarse that there is scarce a page together which we have read with unmixed pleasure; we are bound to state, with equal sincerity, that we should have thought it impossible for any book upon a subject, with which we had fancied ourselves well acquainted, and with which, in our idiomatic form of it at least, we had been long conversant, to have given us so many new ideas and to have so completely changed our old ones.[46]

The anonymous author was almost certainly William Empson, who was at the time Professor of General Polity and the Laws of England at the East India College, Haileybury. Empson was a frequent contributor to the *Edinburgh Review* on a wide variety of subjects and in time he became its editor.[47] An intellectual rather than a politician, a theorist of law rather than a practitioner, Empson was valued by his friends for his wide learning and balanced judgement. He was not, however, afraid of polemics. In 1843 he wrote a long, highly critical and controversial review article of Bowring's *Memoirs of Jeremy Bentham*.[48]

Although the general judgements of the two reviews are similar, there are striking differences both in tone and in the explicit grounds for criticism. Perhaps this reflects more profound differences in the attitudes of the two reviewers: Denman the follower, expressing reservations; Empson, the reluctantly admiring opponent. Even when expressing disagreement on crucial points, Denman is respectful, polite and friendly; Empson's review is polemical and angry to the point of blustering. Denman rejected the natural system,[49] but purported to accept most of Bentham's theoretical analysis and many of his recommendations. Empson seemingly accepts the natural model (subject only to a few caveats), but attacks Bentham's analysis of the causes of the technical system. He concentrates his fire on two related themes: Bentham's attack on the legal profession and the tone of his critique.

Empson's argument can be briefly restated as follows. It is true that the English law of evidence is riddled with unnecessary technicalities and is in need of wholesale reform; but Bentham spoils his case by attributing these evils to the sinister interests of lawyers and to the fee-gathering system. This is bad history and worse diplomacy. The truth of the matter is that many of the rules were originally pragmatic solutions to particular difficulties. They may now have largely outgrown their usefulness. In

Bentham on evidence 107

particular, the accumulation of technical learning concerning the weight of evidence is misplaced. 'Never did ingenuity more thoroughly overreach itself.'[50] A sensible man would accept the need 'for a clear arrangement and definition of rights and offences and a proper scale of punishments', but in respect of 'the remaining and more menial division of the law' (that of Pleading and of Evidence) he would be satisfied with 'a few simple rules, and those of instruction and caution, rather than of indispensable obligation'.[51] In short, Empson argues that Bentham is right in attacking the very idea of having rules of weight and in arguing for simplicity. But he errs in making lawyers the scapegoats (a substitute for historical analysis) and by his extreme polemical tone: 'Some doubtless will be disgusted – and more, simply fatigued, by such indiscriminate, fanatical and interminable abuse.'[52] Yet the best hope for reform lies with lawyers, for instance, Brougham, Romilly, and Mackintosh, all 'great ornaments of the law'.[53] Opposition to reform comes from politicians rather than from lawyers and, as a matter of political realism, the best that can be hoped for is evolutionary, piecemeal reform with enlightened lawyers slowly winning over public opinion.

Even in one of the best chapters of the book – on jargon – suggests Empson, Bentham spoils a good case.[54] At a few points he is neatly hoist with his own petard: 'Bentham language . . . is in this respect a match for any lawyer language upon earth';[55] the alleged hostility of all lawyers to reform is an example of 'too hasty generalization', and Bentham is guilty of arguments that he himself castigated as fallacies.[56]

There are hints in the 1828 article that Empson was more favourably disposed to the *Traité* than Denman had been. The *Rationale* is larger and much less readable than the *Traité*:

> This additional and portentous girth is obtained, for the most part, by two cognate ingredients, specially provided for our home market; an elaborate application of the pure principles of supposed Natural evidence to the practice of the English law, and corresponding copious libations in dishonour of English lawyers. We trust the first of these divisions will attract the attention it deserves, of that portion of our readers who take any interest in such subjects. If it is scarcely possible to exaggerate *its* importance, it would be no less difficult than foolish to treat the other seriously.[57]

These two reviews can fairly be said to be representative of most subsequent responses to Bentham's ideas on evidence. Much of the substance of his analysis was accepted, almost without comment. In particular, the common-sense epistemology and the rejection of the idea of trying to submit judgements of weight and credibility to formal regulation have been almost universally accepted. Some of the main exclusionary rules, such as the exclusion of parties and of various kinds of

108 Theories of Evidence

witness, have been repealed over time, though not without struggle. Few have mourned their passing. Both reviewers concentrated almost exclusively on criminal evidence and, as it were, allowed Bentham to win by default in respect to most aspects of civil evidence. Again, in England at least, the atrophying of technical rules of civil evidence has been relatively uncontroversial. Criminal evidence, on the other hand, has continued to be the main arena of disagreement.[58]

In many crucial respects the pattern of debate was established by the time of Bentham's death. He represents one extreme: the elevation of the pursuit of truth in adjudication above nearly all other competing claims of value or policy; the principle that inferior or otherwise defective evidence is better than no evidence; the evaluation of weight and credibility to be left to the discretion of the ultimate decision-maker, who is expected to proceed rationally and efficiently largely unconfined by formal rules. Abuse is to be controlled by means other than the rules of evidence.

It is characteristic of Bentham's work as a whole that it often provokes profoundly ambivalent reactions.[59] His writings on evidence are no exception. The reactions of Denman and Empson anticipate patterns of debate that have continued ever since. Denman represents one reaction of civil libertarianism rooted in a distrust of abuse of power and a refusal to accept the consequences of unmodified utilitarianism. Empson represents a different strand in a continuing debate: a more conservative view, attracted by Bentham's emphasis on security and on efficiency in implementing substantive law (two aspects of 'law and order'), but repelled by his uncompromising rationalism and his radical critique of the established order, represented in this context by 'Judge and Co.'.

The purpose of this essay has been to present a largely expository introduction to Bentham's ideas on evidence in the context of his own concerns and those of some of his predecessors and contemporaries. In the next essay we shall see how his most important successor in this field, while working broadly within the same tradition, developed a quite different kind of theory that had much greater potential appeal to practitioners. Wigmore's 'science of proof' complements Bentham's *Rationale* rather than supersedes it. In the final chapter I shall try to show how, taken together, these two contrasting theories reveal both the strengths and the limitations of the intellectual heritage to which they both belong.

3

Wigmore on proof

(i) Old Northwestern

The visitor who enters Levy Mayer Hall, the main building of the Northwestern University Law School, is immediately struck by something distinctive about its atmosphere. Dark wood panelling dominates the entrance hall and corridors; around the walls are hung nearly 2500 portraits, engravings, etchings and photographs of famous jurists, trial scenes, court buildings and legal documents from all over the world; the two largest classrooms echo, rather than copy, the debating chambers of the House of Commons and the House of Lords; a life-size replica of the Code of Hammurabi is the phallic *pièce de résistance* of a permanent exhibition of legal memorabilia in what a modern architect would call the 'circulation areas'; a framed version of the Law School song 'Old Northwestern' – more rousing than poetic – hangs in the hall. First impressions suggest an atmosphere that is homely, old-fashioned and slightly eccentric. Levy Mayer Hall is a building of character.

This distinctive character is largely due to the influence of one man, John Henry Wigmore, who was Dean of the Law School from 1901 until 1929 and who was associated with it almost continuously from 1893 until his death in 1943.[1] It was Wigmore who raised the funds for the building, argued over its design, collected its pictures and exhibits, fought to save the panelling from cuts by an economy-minded administration and built up an unrivalled collection of legal novels, plays, detective stories and other law-related literature.[2] Wigmore composed the words and music of 'Old Northwestern'; he also designed and manufactured the chimes, which until only a few years ago played the tune of the song every day at noon in Levy Mayer Hall. These pleasant eccentricities illustrate the former Dean's wide interests, his concern for detail and his distinctive style. If the song is worse than mediocre, if the mechanism of the chimes rivals Heath Robinson, if the taste in books and pictures might be kindly designated 'Catholic', such considerations do not detract from the affection and respect which persist for the memory of the man who almost single-handed transformed the institution into one of the leading law schools.

Outside Northwestern, Wigmore was best known as an educational

110 *Theories of Evidence*

innovator, as a pioneer in a number of fields such as Criminology and Air Law and, of course, as the leading Evidence scholar of his generation. But his reputation for folksiness was quite widespread. At meetings of the Association of American Law Schools, the American Bar Association and other professional groups he was almost as well known as an entertainer as he was as a scholar. He organized sing-songs (sometimes serving as accompanist to Roscoe Pound), he gave slide shows and he aired his opinions on almost everything to generally unreceptive audiences. He wrote a number of 'popular' works, which were indeed quite popular with non-academics. The best known was *A Panorama of the World's Legal Systems* which provides a Cook's tour of all Law in the style of the *National Geographic Magazine*.[3] An anthology of his occasional verse, *Lyrics of a Lawyer's Leisure*, contains items which would surely defeat even Karl Llewellyn's weaker efforts in a competition for the McGonagall Award for Legal Poetry.[4] His efforts as a publicist were not taken as seriously as he would have liked. He expressed his opinions on a wide range of subjects in the press, on the radio and in numerous speeches. His views were clearcut, forcefully expressed and not always entirely consistent.[5] He alienated liberals by his intemperate attacks on Clarence Darrow for his defence of Leopold and Loeb and on Felix Frankfurter in connection with the Sacco-Vanzetti case.[6] He also lost some friends in the legal profession for his equally outspoken criticisms of some judicial decisions and of professional attitudes. Generally his attempts to influence local and national opinion on political matters seem to have made little impact. He was revered as a scholar, popular as an entertainer, but not often taken very seriously as a reformer or leader of opinion.

Wigmore's reputation among his contemporaries is a fair reflection of his strengths and limitations. From Levy Mayer Hall one gains some sense of his energy, breadth of interest, forcefulness and folksiness. Several additional qualities contributed to the greatness of his work on evidence: a methodical approach, exceptional industry, mastery of the detail of his chosen field and great clarity of thought allied, for better or for worse, to simplicity of vision and supreme self-confidence.[7] In dealing with people he was known for his courtesy, elegance and wit. Although he was in the army for only a relatively short period during the First World War, he was thereafter known to many as 'the Colonel' – a sobriquet that could imply either affection or recognition of a military cast of mind as well as bearing.[8] He could muster, marshall and reduce to order enormous quantities of variegated material and would then parade it smartly and efficiently. Apparently untroubled by doubt or the elusiveness of reality, he said what he had to say clearly, systematically and forcefully. He was also an astute strategist, able to take a long or a broad view and to redeploy his forces in unexpected ways. He commanded both loyalty and respect. In his prime it would not have

Wigmore on proof   111

been inappropriate to call him the Supreme Commander of the Law of Evidence.

Today most of Wigmore's achievements and eccentricities are largely forgotten. He is remembered almost entirely as the leading authority on the law of evidence and the author of the great institutional treatise on the subject.[9] Few works in the history of Anglo-American legal scholarship have been so highly praised or have dominated a field so thoroughly or for so long. When the first edition was published in 1904–05, it was immediately hailed as a masterpiece. One of his teachers, Joseph Henry Beale of Harvard, while taking exception to the use of neologisms[10] and a tendency to be disrespectfully critical by one so young, nevertheless praised it in the words which have been quoted again and again by later reviewers: 'It is hardly too much to say that this is the most complete and exhaustive treatise on a single branch of our law that has ever been written.'[11]

Other reviewers of the first and later editions were at least as adulatory. In 1940, the most notable dissentient from some of Wigmore's ideas, Professor Edmund Morgan of Harvard, ended a quite critical review of the third edition with the following words: 'Not only is this the best, by far the best treatise on the Law of Evidence, it is also the best work ever produced on any comparable division of American Law.'[12] As Morgan may have ruefully noted, one of the difficulties of debating with Wigmore was that, so great was his influence, once he had perpetrated a doctrine on the basis of little or no authority, precedents would soon follow to fill the gap.[13] Great treatise writers are among those who can pull themselves up by their own bootstraps.

Great treatise writers are also particularly vulnerable to the passage of time.[14] Towards the end of his life, criticisms of the *Treatise* began to be more open and more persistent. The publication of the third edition, three years before his death, stimulated a series of criticisms that became widely accepted.[15] Until recently it has been the received wisdom among American evidence specialists that on some key theoretical issues, notably relevancy, the general theory of admissibility and the role of judge and jury, the views of James, Morgan and Thayer have prevailed over those of Wigmore.[16] However, as we shall see, Professor Peter Tillers has recently advanced a spirited defence of Wigmore, the general thrust of which is that he was less simple-minded and closer to Thayer than his critics have suggested.[17] The merits of this debate need not detain us at this stage. What is significant here is that from the early 1940s, Wigmore's general theory of evidence was widely thought to have been discredited. That is one reason why it has not attracted much attention. His treatment of particular doctrines fared rather better in the courts and on many issues his views prevailed. However, on some matters, such as the privilege against self-incrimination, his positions were rejected; on others, his analysis was overtaken by events.[18] The fact

112 Theories of Evidence

that he was not treated as having a coherent general theory made it easier for both courts and commentators to accept or reject his positions on particular issues eclectically. The decline in Wigmore's reputation and influence was further accelerated by successive efforts at codification, starting with the Model Code of Evidence, over which he entered a sharp dissent,[19] and culminating with the Federal Rules of Evidence, which since 1975 have virtually swept the board in the United States. In the circumstances, it is remarkable that the *Treatise* has survived for so long. It is still kept alive by the heroic, if uneven, efforts of dedicated editors.[20] Neither the Federal Rules of Evidence, nor *McCormick*, *Weinstein* or *Cross* have completely eclipsed it. The field is still open for someone to do to *Wigmore* what he did to *Greenleaf* and what Greenleaf did to *Starkie* and *Phillipps*.

Paradoxically, the projected demise of Wigmore's *Treatise* opens the way for a reappraisal of his significance as a theorist of evidence. For a legal scholar's general ideas tend to be less ephemeral than his particular contributions. If Wigmore deserves attention today, other than as a figure of historical interest, it is because he is still significant at the level of theory. However, one may anticipate some sceptical objections. First, the *Treatise* does not contain an explicit and coherent general theory;[21] secondly, even if an implicit theory can be reconstructed from scattered passages, some of the most important general ideas have been widely discredited; and, thirdly, there were two John Henry Wigmores: are not nearly all the general writings about evidence outside the *Treatise* the work of the composer of 'Old Northwestern' rather than of the great institutional writer?

The first two objections will be dealt with in due course.[22] The third needs to be confronted at the outset. For the two popular images of Wigmore the man are indeed reflected in contrasts between his *Treatise* and *The Principles of Judicial Proof* (hereafter *Principles*),[23] which is the subject of this essay. The former ranks as one of the most successful and influential treatises in the history of Anglo-American legal scholarship; the latter, neglected in his lifetime and almost entirely forgotten since his death, looks more like the work of an eccentric dilettante than of a revered magisterial scholar. On the surface, there is something old-fashioned and gimmicky about both the style and the substance of the *Principles*. Much of the book is taken up with lengthy extracts from famous trials, mostly murder cases; a few rather indifferent photographs of bullets and fingerprints adorn the text; elaborate charts expressed in Wigmore's own system of symbols seem almost calculated to deter the ordinary reader; as do such neologisms as autoptic proference, prospectant, concomitant, retrospectant, ratiocinative, catenate; lengthy passages are devoted to the psychology of lying and to considering whether generic human traits, such as race or sex, affect the credibility of witnesses. These passages address questions that were standard at the

Wigmore on proof 113

time; today they seem offensive as well as outdated. Wigmore's answers, although guarded, reveal him as sharing many of the prejudices of white, American, middle-class males of his day.[24] Thus some features of the *Principles*, suggest that this is at best little more than a picturesque period-piece, a combination of outdated psychology and idiosyncratic theorizing. It may lead more critical readers to conclude that Colonel Wigmore is ripe for demythologizing.[25]

One purpose of this essay is to suggest that such judgements are mistaken. Although it contains much material that is obsolete, and some that is offensive, Wigmore's *Principles* also contains the most articulate and coherent statement of the general theory underlying all his writings on evidence. In order to understand the foundations of the *Treatise* and to set it in the context of a general view of the subject as a whole it is necessary to study the *Principles*, especially its analytical aspects. There are several further reasons for undertaking a critical examination of Wigmore's general ideas and of the *Principles* in particular. Firstly, there has recently been a resurgence of interest in theoretical aspects of evidence, as exemplified by the recent debates on probabilities, the burgeoning of psychological literature related to law and by the appearance of a new edition of the first volume of Wigmore's *Treatise* by Peter Tillers in which he forcefully defends Wigmore against his critics on a number of important issues.[26] Second, the *Principles* advances a method of analysing evidence, the 'chart method', which after more than forty years of neglect may at last come into its own; this is because it provides a flexible and usable way of injecting some analytical rigour into direct teaching of some important practical skills and because it invites development and use in connection with computers. More important, however, in the present context is the claim that Wigmore's science represents the only attempt since Bentham to set out a comprehensive interdisciplinary theory of evidence and proof, which incorporates the legal, logical, psychological and scientific aspects of the subject within a single coherent framework. On this view, Wigmore built on Thayer but went much further in developing a comprehensive general theory. I shall argue that this both complements and provides illuminating contrasts with Bentham's theory and that taken together the two main theories of evidence amply illustrate the strengths and limitations of the intellectual tradition to which they belong.

In developing this thesis, I shall first look at some historical and analytical connections and contrasts between Bentham and Wigmore and hence the justification for linking Bentham's masterpiece with an unsuccessful coursebook written a century later. The next section explores the genesis and conception of the *Principles* and its relationship to the *Treatise*. The following sections deal in turn with the logical, psychological, scientific and other aspects of Wigmore's theory and his view of the relationship between the Science of Proof and the Law of

114 *Theories of Evidence*

Evidence. The essay concludes with a brief account of the reception and neglect of the *Principles*. This paves the way for a personal assessment of the contemporary significance of the contributions of Bentham and Wigmore and of the Rationalist Tradition in general.

(ii) **Bentham and Wigmore**

Almost exactly one hundred years separate the period of Bentham's main work on evidence and Wigmore's work on proof. During that period much had happened in the way of changes in the law of evidence, in the legal literature on evidence and in adjacent disciplines such as logic and psychology. There had also been many other relevant developments, not least the emergence of the police and elaborate pre-trial procedures. Bentham's onslaught on the exclusionary rules of evidence had only been partially successful. His successors had managed over a period of many years to ensure the enactment of a series of notable legislative reforms; but, from a pure Benthamite point of view, these were only half-measures, piecemeal changes which would introduce some new anomalies in place of the old ones. Codes of evidence had been drawn up by Edward Livingstone in Louisiana and Fitzjames Stephen for India, both half-hearted Benthamites in respect of evidence. The nineteenth century had seen the rise of the tradition of great treatises on evidence: *Best, Phipson, Starkie, Taylor, Wills, Burrill, Chamberlayne, Greenleaf,* and *Thayer*.[1] Even before Wigmore came on the scene, in terms of scholarly writing, evidence was one of the best served fields. In the late nineteenth century there had been a growing interest in forensic science and forensic psychology, led by Hans Gross and Hugo Muensterberg in Germany, and men like Gorphe and Bertillon in France. One of the most interesting works was by an English civil servant in India and Burma, G. F. Arnold, who was neither a lawyer nor a trained psychologist.[2] John Stuart Mill's *Principles of Logic* had opened up a new era in the study of logic, especially induction. It is difficult to establish how much, if at all, Mill had been influenced by his work on Bentham's manuscripts on evidence,[3] but there is little doubt that there is considerable continuity in the tradition that runs from Bacon through Locke, Hume, Bentham and Mill to Jevons and Sidgwick and beyond.

Wigmore was well read in this body of literature. Thayer had taught him at Harvard. As a young man he had edited the last edition of *Greenleaf on Evidence*. He had debated with Hugo Muensterberg about forensic psychology in 1909 on the basis of exhaustive canvassing of available literature on psychology.[4] He dedicated the *Principles* to Hans Gross. Wigmore based his logical analysis almost entirely on the work of Mill, Sidgwick and Jevons.

During the period spanning the publication of the first and third

Wigmore on proof 115

editions of the *Principles* there were further developments. Significant theoretical work was done by Gulson and Michael and Adler; Robert Maynard Hutchins and Donald Slesinger made some pioneering studies of the empirical basis of some rules of evidence; forensic psychology lingered in the doldrums, but forensic science, to which Wigmore himself gave a not inconsiderable stimulus, developed rapidly in the United States. By the mid-1930s a new generation of noted American evidence scholars had emerged, of whom Edmund Morgan, Charles McCormick and John Maguire were perhaps the most highly regarded. There was a rich periodical literature and from the late 1920s much debate about reform and codification of the law of evidence. There were also some notable works by practitioners, such as Wellman's *The Art of Cross-Examination*, Charles C. Moore's *Treatise on Facts* and Albert Osborn's *The Problem of Proof* and his writings on questioned documents.[5] All of these attempted to draw on and to generalize the lessons of experience of legal practice. Thus, by the time of the third edition of the *Principles* there was a rich and relatively developed literature from which to draw.[6]

Much could be made of the contrast between the respective situations and concerns of Bentham and Wigmore. For example, the differences between early-nineteenth-century England and early-twentieth-century America; between London, Bowood and Ford Abbey on the one hand and Chicago and Evanston on the other; between the conditions of litigation, the courts and the legal profession in England in 1800 and their American counterparts a century later; between the intellectual world of the philosophical radicals and that of the successors of Christopher Columbus Langdell. Bentham reacted against Blackstone; Wigmore worked in the shadow of Langdell, Holmes and the early realists. Bentham's theory of evidence was part of an extraordinarily ambitious design for a comprehensive theory of law and government based on utilitarian principles; his overriding concern was always radical reform. Wigmore's theory of proof developed outwards from the interests of a relatively orthodox pragmatic legal scholar whose special expertise was in evidence. His concerns were less single-minded. Bentham abhorred judge-made law; Wigmore considered the law reports to embody accumulated wisdom fashioned out of practical experience. Bentham was an ardent codifier; Wigmore was at most half-hearted. Bentham inclined to an inquisitorial system of procedure, strengthened by the common law practice of cross-examination; Wigmore wished to curb abuses of the adversary system, but treated its essentials as settled, especially party presentation of issues and evidence. Bentham was a committed utilitarian; Wigmore's moral views were far less clearcut. Bentham wrote from his head on what was almost a *tabula rasa*, so far at least as legal thought was concerned.[7] Wigmore gathered, sifted and imposed order on the mass of material he found in libraries. Wigmore

116 Theories of Evidence

wrote for the legal profession; Bentham wrote against it.[8]

Such contrasts could be catalogued *ad nauseam*. They are, of course, important in interpreting the writings of the two men. Yet from the point of view of the contemporary study of evidence, several fundamental similarities link Bentham's *Rationale* and Wigmore's *Principles*. First, both were working in the context of the same legal tradition, the Anglo-American system of common law. Both treated jury trials, adversary proceedings, cross-examination, the forms of action and the legacy of legal language as central features of that tradition. Neither the author of *A Panorama of the World's Legal Systems* nor the honorary citizen of France could be accused of being narrowly parochial, but their knowledge of other languages, of European literature and of foreign laws provided little more than background to their work on evidence. They were both reacting to and writing about the common law system of adjudication.

Secondly, Bentham and Wigmore both worked within broadly the same intellectual tradition. As we have seen, Anglo-American writers on evidence from Gilbert to Cross and McCormick have shared almost identical assumptions, to such an extent that one is justified in talking of a single Rationalist Tradition of evidence scholarship. The main disagreements and debates have taken place within a largely shared intellectual and ideological framework. Wigmore inherited and shared quite similar views on logic, epistemology, and to a lesser extent on science with Bentham. The conceptual framework of his theory of proof is also very close to Bentham's, although by his day the language of scholarly discourse about evidence had been extended and refined. In short, as a theorist of evidence Wigmore is a direct lineal descendant of Bentham.

Thirdly, the similarities in cast of mind and general outlook of the two men is as important as their differences. Both were, first and foremost, thinkers and writers about the law, rather than practitioners. Each had a limited firsthand experience of legal practice and an armchair interest in the law in action. Bentham was not a conventional academic lawyer, as that term is known today, but he shared many of the characteristics of that profession, without the burdens on his time of teaching and administration. Their primary concern was to introduce system, clarity, simplicity, efficiency and above all rationality into the field of evidence. Both saw the study of evidence and proof as a fit subject for scientific treatment; even more important they saw factual inquiries in adjudication as being a standard example of factual inquiries in general, the peculiar conditions and constraints of litigation being but secondary. Their common starting-point is a general theory of belief in the context of all factual inquiries.

Even in respect of rules of evidence, as we shall see, Bentham and Wigmore ended up much closer to each other than first impressions

Wigmore on proof 117

might suggest. After devoting several hundred pages to attacking all rules of evidence, Bentham sets out some guidance to judges in the form of 'instructions', which he sometimes refers to as 'rules'. Wigmore, the greatest expositor of evidence doctrine, was against having rigid rules on almost all topics; rather, he argued, the law of evidence should provide guidance in the form of rules which should be 'directory rather than mandatory' and these should only exceptionally be subject to review.[9] Both men advocated giving considerable discretion to the judge, subject to flexible guidance from the legislature. The convergence, however, was not complete. Wigmore favoured a discretion to exclude and the retention of a few strict rules of admissibility. Bentham's maxim was: exclude nothing unless it is irrelevant or superfluous or involves preponderant disutility. Moreover, Wigmore wanted to give detailed instructions to judges and practitioners on every point, drawing heavily on the traditional wisdom of the common law; Bentham, in this respect like Morgan, favoured a few simple guidelines and the scrapping of nearly all of the traditional common law 'wisdom'.[10]

Fourthly, Bentham and Wigmore both concentrate on *adjudicative decisions*, that is to say formal determinations of liability or of guilt by judges or juries in trials. They deal only peripherally, if at all, with the processing and determination of facts at other phases of legal process (such as negotiation and sentencing) and in other arenas (such as arbitrations and administrative tribunals).[11]

Finally, both men were firmly committed to the view that the overriding objective of fact-finding in adjudication is the pursuit of truth as a means of achieving rectitude of decision. 'Evidence is the basis of Justice', wrote Bentham, and Wigmore used this as the keynote quotation for his students' textbook.[12] Both recognized that the pursuit of truth had to compete with other values in particular contexts; in some respects Bentham was less prepared to compromise than Wigmore, but it is symptomatic of the latter's commitment to this view that he sought to rationalize and to justify the surviving exclusionary rules largely in terms of their tendency to promote correct decision rather than in terms of what he, perhaps somewhat slightingly, termed considerations of 'extrinsic policy'.[13] Bentham may represent an extreme on the spectrum of views about the aims of adjective law, but Wigmore was not far behind him in giving high priority to rectitude of decision.

Thus, despite important differences in their situation, in their immediate concerns and objectives, in temperament and in ideology (Bentham the radical utilitarian, Wigmore the pragmatic conservative), there are strong arguments for treating our two leading theorists as horses from the same stable. They were both writing about common law; they had remarkably similar views on logic and epistemology; they were both concerned to develop a systematic, indeed a scientific, theory of evidence and proof; and they thought that the overriding aim of such a

118 *Theories of Evidence*

theory was to maximize rationality and the pursuit of truth in adjudication.

Some of the main contrasts between Bentham and Wigmore stem from the fact that they concentrated on different standpoints. This led them to ask different questions, to adopt different criteria of relevance and of significance, and to emphasize different topics. Both were concerned with decision-making on issues of fact in trials on the basis of evidence presented to the senses of the tribunal. But each adopts a markedly different perspective. Bentham's central aim is to recommend a system of procedure designed to maximize reliability of results: this covers what evidence can be made forthcoming, what should be presented to the tribunal and how it should be evaluated. He addresses himself almost exclusively to the legislator, and only indirectly to the judge through advice to the legislator on what general instructions should be given to him. Wigmore addresses the trial lawyer directly, judges and jurors indirectly, in respect of modes of analysis designed to maximize rationality and hence reliability in analysing and deciding on evidence. He deals with legislative aspects of the rules of evidence as part of his treatment of doctrine, but this is only a secondary interest. Unlike Bentham, he did not develop a rounded theory of procedure.[14] Bentham provides a clearer and more systematic set of criteria for evaluating institutions, rules and procedures and he applies these systematically, but at a fairly high level of generality; Wigmore, on the other hand, has much more to say about the detailed problems involved in dealing with different kinds of evidence in practice.

From this point of view the main contrast between Bentham and Wigmore as theorists of evidence is that they were primarily concerned to answer different questions: Bentham's is a design theory addressed to the legislator; Wigmore's is primarily a working theory for trial lawyers and judges.[15] Naturally there is substantial overlap in their writings, for example on the logical aspects of probative processes (on which Wigmore's treatment is the more detailed); on the effect of particular factors on the reliability of evidence (e.g. witness psychology, the oath); on what principles, if any, should govern the weight to be attached to different kinds of evidence and on the role of exclusionary rules. They differed on many points of detail and even on some central matters, such as the value of retaining some exclusionary rules, the jury system, and their attitudes to the legal profession, they are in sharp disagreement. But on many shared questions, they reached substantially the same conclusions. Against this background we can now turn to consider Wigmore's *Principles* in detail.

(iii) The genesis and conception of *The Principles of Judicial Proof*

In June 1913, Wigmore published an article in the *Illinois Law Review* entitled 'The Problem of Proof'.[1] It began: 'This article aspires to propose, though in tentative form only, a *novum organum* for the study of Judicial Evidence.'[2] In it he set out in short compass a logical scheme for collating all the evidence in even the most complicated case into a single chart. The article was in fact a draft chapter of a much longer work, *The Principles of Judicial Proof*, which appeared later in the same year. A second revised edition was published in 1931 and a third edition, entitled *The Science of Judicial Proof*, appeared in 1937. The change of title from *Principles* to *Science* was done at the instance of the publishers, largely for commercial reasons, and not too much weight should be attached to it. All three editions of the work will be referred to as The *Principles* throughout.

The full title of Wigmore's work was *The Principles of Judicial Proof As Given by Logic, Psychology, and General Experience and Illustrated in Judicial Trials*.[3] This gives a fair indication of the basic conception and scope of the project: the subject is judicial proof, as contrasted with the rules of evidence; the basis is to be found in logic, especially inductive logic, in psychology, especially witness psychology, and in general experience, which includes both common-sense generalizations and developments in all fields of human knowledge, but especially in forensic science. The main arena is the courtroom in trials at first instance; the subject is an applied science which can be directly illustrated by, and used in, actual judicial trials.

The basic conception is best expressed in Wigmore's own words:

> The study of the principles of Evidence, for a lawyer, falls into two distinct parts. One is Proof in the general sense, – the part concerned with the ratiocinative process of contentious persuasion, – mind to mind, counsel to Judge or juror, each partisan seeking to move the mind of the tribunal. The other part is Admissibility, – the procedural rules devised by the law, based on litigious experience and tradition, to guard the tribunal (particularly the jury) against erroneous persuasion. Hitherto, the latter has loomed largest in our formal studies, –has, in fact, monopolized them; while the former, virtually ignored, has been left to the chances of later acquisition, casual and empiric, in the course of practice.
>
> Here we have been wrong; and in two ways:
>
> For one thing, there is, and there *must* be, a probative science – the principles of proof – independent of the artificial rules of procedure; hence, it can be and should be studied. This science, to be sure, may as yet be imperfectly formulated. But all the more need is there to begin in earnest to investigate and develop it. Furthermore, this process of

120 *Theories of Evidence*

Proof represents the objective in every judicial investigation. The procedural rules for Admissibility are merely a preliminary aid to the main activity, viz. the persuasion of the tribunal's mind to a correct conclusion by safe materials. This main process is that for which the jury are there, and on which the counsel's duty is focussed.

And for another thing, the judicial rules of Admissibility are destined to lessen in relative importance during the next period of development. Proof will assume the important place; and we must therefore prepare ourselves for this shifting of emphasis.[4]

In handling evidence, a practising lawyer has to take into account four main considerations: what he has to prove; what evidence he needs or has available to prove it; how he can get the evidence before the tribunal; and what the effect the evidence presented (for and against his case) is likely to have on the tribunal.[5] Wigmore's science is mainly concerned with the last phase. It explicitly excludes questions of materiality or admissibility and it deals only indirectly with the practical problems of gathering evidence and preparing for trials. It deals with the logic and psychology of proof in a specific context, the courtroom, at a fairly advanced stage in a legal process, although in the later editions he gave some emphasis to preparation for trial. Within this context the educational aim is to develop skill in thinking about evidence.[6]

About three-quarters of the book is taken up with elaborating a method of analysing the process involved in proving various types of probanda by different kinds of evidence. It deals in turn with different kinds of data within what is now the familiar threefold scheme of circumstantial evidence, testimonial evidence and, the awkward category, autoptic proference (the direct presentation of data to the senses of the tribunal), more commonly referred to as real evidence. Wigmore analyses each type of *probandum*, each type of evidence appropriate to it, the forms of inferences involved in reasoning from it, common pitfalls and fallacies, and the state of relevant scientific knowledge.

The combination of systematic treatment, lavish illustrative detail, and clear exposition make this part of lasting value even though large sections of it were inevitably destined to become outdated as psychology, forensic science and technology developed. However, for Wigmore's purposes these sections are to be viewed merely as preliminary.[7] The culmination of the book, set out in Part v of the third edition, is a method of analysing mixed masses of evidence in trials. He introduces it as follows:

Part v thus represents the ultimate stage, viz. the practice of the principles of Proof; namely, the *method of solving a complex mass* of evidence in contentious litigation. Nobody seems yet to have ventured to offer a method, – neither the logicians (strange to say), nor the psychologists, nor the jurists, nor the advocates. The logicians have furnished us in plenty with canons of reasoning for specific single inferences; but for a total mass of contentious evidence in judicial trials, they have offered no system. What is here put forward is a mere provisional attempt at method. One must have a working scheme. What is wanted is simple enough in purpose – namely, some method which will enable us to lift into consciousness and to state in words *the reasons why a total mass of evidence does or should persuade us to a given conclusion*, and why our conclusion would or should have been different or identical if some part of that total mass of evidence had been different. The mind *is* moved; then can we not explain *why* it is moved? If we can set down and work out a mathematical equation, why can we not set down and work out a mental probative equation?[8]

Before examining in detail Wigmore's treatment of the logical, psychological, scientific and other dimensions of his 'science', it is worth commenting briefly on his perception of the nature of this enterprise and its relationship to the *Treatise*. He unreservedly rooted his science in everyday practice in the adversary system; he saw himself as providing systematic reconstruction of what good trial lawyers do all the time. Like Bentham, he saw the theorist of evidence standing in the same relation to his audience as the grammarian stands to Monsieur Jourdan. But Wigmore's audience was actual and prospective trial lawyers, and to a lesser extent, judges and jurors, rather than Bentham's legislator. The theorist's task is to articulate and to systematize everyday practice and thereby increase the rationality and the trustworthiness of decisions on issues of fact. Like nearly all writers on evidence, Wigmore believed that the principles of reasoning of judicial proof can and should accord in their essentials with the principles of sound reasoning and practical decision-making in everyday life; that '[t]he number of *types of mental process*, in dealing with evidence, is strictly limited'[9] and that, generally speaking, the appropriate kind of inference is based on a fairly straightforward application of simple principles of induction. Similarly the main kinds of *probanda* and the main kinds of evidentiary fact can be subsumed under a quite simple scheme of classification:

Starting then with a classification based on the Probandum, we find that judicial proceedings do not range over the infinite variety of matters that face the scientist. Just as the chemist, the biologist, the astronomer, deal professionally with only a limited number of topics, so the judicial tribunal deals usually with a limited number of probanda, most of which recur constantly in the crimes and civil disputes. These probanda fall into four distinguishable groups:
I. *The Doing of a Human Act*;
II. *The Trait or Condition of a Human Being*;

122 Theories of Evidence

III. *An Event, Quality, Cause, or Condition of a Thing* (i.e. external, inanimate nature);

IV. *The Identity of a Person or Thing.*

This classification is a workable one, because the evidence applicable to the one class does not ordinarily apply to the other. Thus, there is little waste by overlapping, and the conditions of inference peculiar to each class will best reveal their common features.[10]

Within this scheme he considers each kind of evidentiary fact in relation to the form(s) of inference involved, relevant psychological and scientific findings and particular factors or difficulties typically associated with weighing the probative value of a piece of this kind of evidence. The section on Testimonial Evidence is similarly systematic, dealing successively with the logical processes involved; with generic human traits as they affect probative value of testimony; with the testimonial elements of perception, recollection and narration; then with methods of detecting testimonial error and, finally, with a comparison of testimonial and circumstantial evidence. Throughout, the main emphasis is on methods of analysis.

It is tempting to adopt Wigmore's own distinction between the Science of Proof and the Rules of Admissibility and to treat the *Principles* as dealing with the Science and the *Treatise* as dealing with the rules. However, the relationship is rather more complex than that, for both works are based on the same system of classification and a shared conceptual scheme.[11] Indeed, there is considerable overlap between the two works; substantial portions of Wigmore's text in the first edition of the *Principles* are adopted with very little change from his *Treatise*. Later editions of the *Treatise* incorporated material from the *Principles*.

In order to clarify the relationship between the two works, it is necessary to consider the genesis and scope of the *Treatise*. Thayer had taught his students that the American law of evidence needed to be systematized on the basis of a coherent theory.[12] He outlined a general thesis about the law of evidence, but he never fulfilled his ambition of writing a systematic treatise. Three of his students, Chamberlayne, McKelvey and Wigmore, took up the challenge. McKelvey wrote a successful student's textbook; Chamberlayne, who was eight years older than Wigmore, edited American editions of *Best* and *Taylor* before embarking on his four-volume *Treatise*, which he did not live to complete.[13] Like Chamberlayne, Wigmore served his apprenticeship as the editor of a leading practitioners' work, *Greenleaf on Evidence*; but here the resemblance ends. Chamberlayne was a practitioner who was committed to radical reform of the law of evidence on crypto-Benthamite lines;[14] Wigmore was an academic who followed his mentor closely both in emphasizing the historical development of the rules of evidence by the courts and in his general theory of admissibility. As Chamberlayne

Wigmore on proof 123

remarked, Wigmore wrote very much the kind of treatise that Thayer might have written.[15]

Simon Greenleaf's *A Treatise on the Law of Evidence* had been conspicuously successful since its first publication in 1842.[16] By the time Wigmore came to edit the first volume of the sixteenth edition it was showing its age. Originally designed as a students' text, it had grown uneasily into a three-volume reference work; successive editors had found it difficult to keep pace with rapid and multifarious developments in the law of evidence; the idea of a single common law of America had been undermined; and Thayer's penetrating scholarship had cast doubt on the historical accuracy and coherence of some of Greenleaf's rationalizations. Wigmore did a workmanlike job as an editor, but he was well aware of the need for a fresh start. When Little, Brown offered the opportunity, he seized it promptly and with great success.

Wigmore's *Treatise* differed from *Greenleaf* and other treatises in several important respects. The nineteenth-century Anglo-American treatises on evidence tended to cover a lot of ground. Most of them started with a theoretical statement about the nature of evidence and proof. Some leading works, such as *Greenleaf* and *Starkie*, dealt with a great deal of material that today would be treated as falling outside the law of evidence; for example, what needs to be proved in order to succeed in a prosecution for burglary or an action for debt or to establish a particular defence. Wigmore excluded such matters as belonging to substantive law, and most modern academic writers on evidence have followed his lead. Thus Wigmore only edited the first of Greenleaf's three volumes, and his own work is essentially a successor to that part of *Greenleaf*. But in some other respects Wigmore's *Treatise* ranges more widely than its predecessors.[17]

In the preface to the first edition, Wigmore laid down three main aims for the work:

> . . . first, to expound the Anglo-American law of Evidence as a system of reasoned principles and rules; secondly, to deal with the apparently warring mass of judicial precedents as the consistent product of these principles and rules; and, thirdly, to furnish all the materials for ascertaining the present state of the law in the half a hundred independent American jurisdictions.[18]

Thus the express aims went significantly beyond bare exposition of evidence doctrine. Wigmore was concerned both to systematize and to rationalize – that is to say to develop a coherent rationale at the level of principle as well as in respect of each detailed rule. He sought to reduce apparent inconsistency by treating each jurisdiction as independent and by charting variations between all the jurisdictions, 'for opposition is not inconsistency'.[19] This led him to attempt to provide a more comprehensive account of the case law than *Greenleaf* and to criticize those

124   *Theories of Evidence*

solutions which did not accord with his rationale. Wigmore's approach involved both a more detailed account of the law in the various North American jurisdictions and a more systematically critical approach than Greenleaf's. It might be said that Greenleaf, like some of his contemporaries, tried to expound a consistent body of doctrine for a single, non-existent jurisdiction (the United States), whereas Wigmore attempted to map legal doctrine in over fifty jurisdictions and to appraise different solutions by reference to a single theory of evidence. In respect of the *law* of evidence, we will argue that Wigmore adopted Thayer's theory with only minor glosses.[20] But he went further than his mentor in treating the legal rules of evidence as only one part of the subject of evidence. The *Treatise* is based on a scheme of classification and a system of concepts that integrates the law of evidence and the principles of proof within a single theoretical framework. The *Principles*, is based on exactly the same scheme of classification.

Why, then, it may be asked, did he feel it necessary to produce an entirely separate book on the subject of proof? Perhaps the key lies in the literary form and the primary audiences of the two works. The *Treatise* is presented as being a reference work for practitioners. Wigmore had gone quite far in including historical and non-legal material and in criticizing the existing rules as well as expounding them. But for the excellence of the work and its undoubted usefulness as a source of references, quotations and raw material for arguments, it would have been in danger of being dismissed by the profession as too academic. To have tried to develop his non-doctrinal analyses within the confines of the *Treatise* might have gone beyond the tolerance of its primary market, not least because he was advancing some new ideas and dealing with some highly speculative material, such as the findings of forensic psychology and novel aspiring 'sciences', such as psychometry and graphology, which had yet to be accepted by the profession. There was a further, more fundamental reason: Wigmore's 'science' was certainly intended to be practical, but mastery of the science involved developing certain skills and only to a much lesser extent acquiring information. The *Treatise* was designed to be *used* regularly as a reference work, as a resource book, and, in time, as a work of authority in its own right. The *Principles*, once mastered, has largely served its function; like the proverbial ladder, once mounted, it could be dispensed with. A less confident author than Wigmore might have written a monograph addressed to a scholarly audience, elaborating and defending his theory of proof. Wigmore boldly presented his ideas as a method to be mastered largely through practical exercises, rather than as a theory to be argued about and justified.

The *Principles* was devised as an educational work in a form that was novel for legal education: cases, materials and text. The cases were based on records of trials at first instance rather than law reports, and the

Wigmore on proof   125

materials were drawn largely from non-legal sources – writings on logic, psychology, forensic science and general literature. The first edition of the *Principles* even included extracts from Balzac, Dickens, Mark Twain and other writers of fiction. Wigmore's general theory is expounded in the text in a magisterial style which suggests that there is little scope for argument or doubt. Thus a novel literary form, the originality of both content and presentation and Wigmore's assertive self-confidence may all have combined to dissuade teachers in other law schools from adjusting their ways or even of trying out the book. Its lack of commercial success stands in sharp contrast to the *Treatise*. More significant here is the fact that the *Principles* was not perceived nor taken seriously as a work of theory. Wigmore's choice of literary form masked the nature and significance of his enterprise.

(iv) Analytical dimensions of proof

Wigmore's science rests on a number of apparently simple philosophical assumptions, which he advanced more by way of assertion than argument. 'The number of *types of mental process*, in dealing with evidence, is strictly limited.'[1] Generally speaking, the appropriate kind of inference from an evidentiary fact (*factum probans*) to a fact to be proved (*factum probandum*) involves a straightforward application of ordinary principles of inductive logic, deduction having a limited, and secondary, place.[2] Wigmore's epistemology, also adopted without fuss or argument, is a common-sense empiricism in the tradition of Locke, Bentham and John Stuart Mill.[3] He acknowledges that, typically, what is at stake are judgements of probabilities. These he assumes are generally non-mathematical, but he does not acknowledge that such judgements are philosophically problematic.[4] The main recurrent source of difficulty, in his view, arises when a *mass* of different kinds of evidence needs to be 'rationally co-ordinated' in order to arrive at a single conclusion. In short, the main difficulty relates to the complexity of particular cases rather than to fundamental questions about epistemology or about the kinds of logical processes involved.[5]

The task of analysing a mixed mass of evidence consists 'in analyzing each piece of evidence available, in classifying and placing each one in its proper place in the scheme of proof, and in making the detailed inferences from stage to stage; finally arriving at a conclusion upon the main probandum or probanda'.[6]

There are two methods of doing this: the narrative method and the chart method. 'The Narrative Method rearranges all the evidential data under some scheme of logical sequence, narrating at each point the related evidential facts, and at each fact noting the subordinate evidence on which it depends; concluding with a narrative summary.'[7] Much

126 Theories of Evidence

argument about evidence in court by counsel, and most secondary accounts of debatable *causes célèbres* (such as accounts of the Sacco-Vanzetti case and the Kennedy assassination), adopt versions of the narrative method, often in a rather more casual form than Wigmore suggests.[8] This approach is suitable for the beginner and accords with ordinary practice; it may also be better suited to giving 'holistic' presentations of a story or of 'the theory of a case' or of a 'theme';[9] but it lacks the clarity and rigour of the chart method, Wigmore's own invention, and, in his view, 'the only thorough and scientific method'.[10]

The history of the *Principles* and the author's experiences of attemping to introduce Wigmore's approach to the analysis of evidence make it clear that it is wise to anticipate resistance from readers to what follows. This can be due to a combination of one or more factors, such as distrust of novelty (conservatism); dislike of symbols (literalism); aversion to hard work (indolence) and scepticism about careful analysis (irrationalism). I have pandered to these weaknesses by trying to keep the exposition simple, by cutting out the symbols, and by relegating to an appendix a personal evaluation of the validity and the practical utility of the approach.[11] In return, the reader is asked to suspend judgement until he has read the whole chapter and to bear two points in mind: first, we are here more concerned with Wigmore's general approach to the analysis of evidence, which is an integral part of his science of proof, than with the specific heuristic technique (using symbols and charts) which he set out in the *Principles*. Secondly, few people have been attracted or persuaded by descriptions of the chart method; but, in the experience of the author, most people who have tried to master it have become convinced of its validity and of its practical value in some contexts. My own assessment is that the general approach is sound, but in need of refinement, and that the specific technique is a marvellous pedagogical device which is also a very useful practical tool of analysis, but only in some quite specific contexts.

The chart method derives its name from the fact that the ultimate product is a diagrammatic presentation of all the relations between all of the relevant evidence and the ultimate probanda in a particular case. The constituent elements are simple propositions of fact, each listed and numbered in a 'key-list of evidence'; the relations between the propositions are depicted on the chart by a system of symbols devised by the author. In order to understand this elaborate scheme we need to consider Wigmore's account of the logical processes involved, and what goes into compiling a key-list and a chart.

The narrative and chart methods both involve the adoption of 'the same logical scheme'.[12] Central to Wigmore's theory is the idea that analysis of evidence involves the study of relations between propositions. Every simple fact can be expressed as a proposition. Evidence is a relative term, signifying the relation between a proposition to be proved (*factum probandum*) and a proposition which tends to support it (*factum probans*).

Wigmore on proof 127

The same proposition can be a *factum probans* in relation to one proposition and a *factum probandum* in relation to another, for often a series or chain of inferences may be involved. To use Wigmore's example, a scrap of coat cloth is found in the hand of a murdered man (X); the scrap fits a coat found in the room of the accused (Y). The chain of inference tending to support the ultimate *probandum* that it was the accused who murdered Y might be stated as follows:

C.1 The scrap of cloth grasped fits this coat → P (C.2), the scrap came off this coat;

C.2 The scrap grasped came off this coat → P (C.3), this coat was worn by someone other than the victim at the time of the assault;

C.3 The other person wearing the coat at the time → P (C.6) was the assailant;

C.4 The coat was found in Y's room → (P) C.5 the coat belongs to Y;

C.6 Y was wearing the coat at the time of the murder → (P) it was Y who killed X.[13]

This example illustrates two points: the same proposition can be both a *factum probans* and a *factum probandum* in a series of inferences which are 'catenate', i.e. forming a chain. Such inferences upon inferences are very common in judicial trials, especially where circumstantial evidence is concerned.[14] Secondly, there is room for doubt at each stage of the reasoning: for example, the scrap may not have come off the coat; the coat may not have been worn at the time of the assault; the accused may not have been the owner; or though the owner, he may not have been the wearer; or, even if the wearer, he may have been a bystander rather than the assailant. In respect of each inference, the conclusion does not follow ncessarily from the premises and is open to question. By articulating all the steps involved in such 'common-sense' (Wigmore's term is 'subconscious') reasoning, we can spot the vulnerable points.[15] 'It is only by careful dissection of the implicit steps of inference that we can lay bare and locate the possibilities of doubt.'[16]

The main source of doubts is the possibility of challenges to the alleged *probandum*. In legal trials in the adversary system the proceeding is an antiphonal one. Proponent and opponent in turn offer evidence: looked at from the viewpoint of the proponent of an item of evidence, the matter can be put as follows:

If the potential defect of Inductive Evidence is that the fact offered as the basis of the conclusion may be open to one or more other explanations or inferences, the failure to exclude a single other rational inference would be, from the standpoint of *Proof*, a fatal defect; and yet, if only that single other inference were open, there might still be an extremely high degree of probability for the *Inference* desired. When Robinson Crusoe saw the human footprint on the sand,

128 Theories of Evidence

he could not argue inductively that the presence of another human being was absolutely proved; there was at least (for example) the possible inference of his own somnambulism. Nevertheless, the fact of the footprint was, as a basis of *Inference*, evidence of an extraordinary degree of probability. The provisional test, then, from the point of view of valuing the Inference, would be something like this: *Does the evidentiary fact point to the desired conclusion* (not as the only rational inference but) *as the inference* (or explanation) *most plausible or most natural out of the various ones that are conceivable?* Or (to state the requirement more weakly), is the desired conclusion (not the most natural, but) *a* natural or plausible one among the various conceivable ones? After all the other evidential facts have been introduced and considered, the net conclusion can be attempted. But in dealing with each separate fact, the only inquiry is a provisional one: How probable is the Probandum as the explanation of this Probans?[17]

Wigmore continues:

Thus, throughout the whole realm of evidence, circumstantial and testimonial, the theory of the inductive inference, as practically applied, is that the evidentiary fact has probative value only so far as the desired conclusion based upon it is a more probable or natural inference, and as the other inferences or explanations of the fact, if any, are less probable or natural. The degree of strength required will vary with different sorts of evidentiary facts, depending somewhat upon differing views of human experience with those facts, somewhat upon the practical availability of stronger facts. But the general spirit and mode of reasoning of the Courts substantially illustrates the dictates of scientific logic.[18]

The proponent proceeds by assertion, offering evidence tending to prove a particular *probandum*. In judicial proceedings there are three basic responses open to his opponent. He may offer an alternative *explanation* which weakens or negates the probative force of the proponent's original probative fact – for example, by adducing evidence that Y had lent his coat to Z that day, which tends to show that it was not Y who was wearing it at the time of murder; or by *negating* the proponent's evidentiary fact, for example, by showing that it was not Y's coat; or the proponent may introduce a new fact, which by a *rival* inference, tends to disprove the proponent's *probandum*; for example, evidence that Y was elsewhere at the time of the murder (alibi) or that the fingerprints of another person, T, were found on the murder weapon.[19] Finally, the proponent may add new evidence to negate a proposition put forward by his opponent, for example, by showing that Y's alibi is false or that Y had recovered the coat from Z before the time of the murder. This involves no new logical type – it involves negating or explaining

Wigmore on proof 129

away an explanation – though it may represent 'a new stage of presenting evidence'.[20]

Wigmore recognizes the great variety of types of evidence: indeed, he devotes several hundred pages to exploring them. But he maintains that the logic is essentially simple: nothing is involved other than a straightforward application of general principles of induction.[21] The basic probative processes can be succinctly stated:

> Hence, the five probative processes applicable to any piece of evidence are as follows:
>
> PA = proponent's assertion of a fact to evidence a probandum;
>
> OE = opponent's explanation of other facts taking away the value of this inference PA;
>
> OD = opponent's denial of the evidentiary fact on which the inference PA is based;
>
> OR = opponent's rival fact, adduced against the probandum, without any reference to the inference PA;
>
> PC = proponent's corroborative facts, negating the explanations OE.[22]

To give a simple example, adapted from Wigmore's textbook for students: to charge D with a homicide the prosecution offers an old quarrel (P^1), a recent threat (P^2) and blood traces on clothes (P^3). D now *explains away* the old quarrel by showing a reconciliation (OE – P^1); *explains away* the blood traces by showing a recent killing of a chicken (OE – P^3) and *denies* the fact of the threat (OD – P^2) and advances the *rival facts* of an alibi and a character of peacefulness ($OR^1 + OR^2$).[23]

A key-list for the above passage might be set out as follows:

Probandum: It was D who killed X
1. D had quarrelled with X [P1]
2. A testifies to this.
3. On the previous Saturday, D threatened to kill X [P2].
4. B testifies to this.
5. There were blood stains on D's clothes [P3].
6. C testifies to this.
7. D and X had been reconciled between the time of the quarrel and X's death.
8. E testifies to this.
9. The blood came from a chicken.
10. D killed a chicken the day before the killing of X.
11. E testifies to this.
12. D was 40 miles away at the time of the killing.
13. E testifies to this.
14. D has no previous record of violence.
15. 16 and 17 F, G, and H testify to this.

130 Theories of Evidence

18. D did not threaten X.
19. D testifies to this.
20. E's testimony is unreliable.
21. E is D's brother.
22. E has a previous conviction for perjury.

In order to picture the relations between all the propositions in a key-list it may be useful to construct a chart. This involves devising a set of symbols suitable for pictorial presentation. Wigmore devised a relatively simple set of symbols for the purpose. Experience of using the chart method in teaching suggests that these symbols are easily learned; indeed many students find it helpful to increase the number of symbols, and to use a variety of colours, in order to make further differentiations between types of relations and degrees of probative force. Wigmore was wise to keep his presentation simple, but the mere fact that he used symbols at all was probably the most important single factor in his failure to persuade either teachers or practitioners to take his method seriously. Most lawyers confronted with symbols or mathematical formulae just switch off.

Some elementary points are illustrated by this example. A key-list for even this very simple case involves more than 20 propositions. While nearly all of the propositions on the key-list have only one place on the chart, propositions 20–22 will appear at several places, because E testifies to several matters and his testimony was impeached.[24] This, of course, is a very simple example which would not ordinarily need to be subjected to elaborate analysis in order to be grasped.[25] The method was devised to help analysis of mixed *masses* of evidence in complex cases. For present purposes, this example will suffice; dealing with a complex case involves little more than the patient accumulation and arrangement of numbers of bits of analysis using the same basic techniques. A complex case will tend to have a more varied set of relations which have to be depicted by a correspondingly wider range of symbols, but the basic technique is essentially quite simple. The main requirements for mastering it are self-discipline and patience.

The main difficulty of applying elementary principles of logic to analysis of evidence in law is the amount or complexity of the evidence that is often involved in disputed cases. Even in the simple example of relating a scrap of cloth to the owner of a coat, a number of propositions and steps in reasoning was involved, but these represent only one phase in the evidence in the case as a whole and even that phase has not yet been adequately analysed. For example, no account has been given of how the conclusion was reached that the scrap of cloth fits the coat; nothing has been said about the sources of such evidence nor about the credibility of each source. Thus even in a relatively simple and straightforward case we are likely to find ourselves presented with what is potentially an ever-

Wigmore on proof 131

expanding collection of allegations and data. Of course, many cases are neither simple nor straightforward. The problem therefore arises how so to arrange the varied data in order to come to some judgement about its overall probative force for the case as a whole, while contemplating *all* the data simultaneously. Or, to put the matter in Wigmore's terms, we need 'some method which will enable us to lift into consciousness and to state in words the *reasons why a total mass of evidence does or should persuade us to a given conclusion*'.[26]

The chart method is Wigmore's solution to this problem. The object is:

[t]o perform the logical (or psychological) process of conscious juxtaposition of detailed related ideas, for the purpose of producing rationally a single final idea. Hence, to the extent that the mind is unable to juxtapose consciously a larger number of ideas, each coherent group of detailed constituent ideas must be reduced in consciousness to a single idea; until at last the mind can consciously juxtapose them with due attention to each, so as to produce its single final idea.

This requires, therefore, first, analysis, and then synthesis.[27]

To achieve this objective, a number of conditions must be satisfied 'at least to a substantial degree'.[28] The method must employ types of evidence which fit all kinds of case; it must be based on a logical system which includes all the fundamental logical processes; it must include *all* the evidence that may be presented in a given case; it must be able to show the probative relation of each evidential fact to each and all the others; it must be able to chart and distinguish alleged 'facts' and the belief or disbelief of the tribunal (or chart-maker) in the propositions; and it must be able to represent all the data at once to the consciousness – in contrast to the narrative method, which presents it sequentially; it must be 'compendious' (i.e. comprehensive), and it must use symbols which are not too complicated.[29]

The proposed method involves two steps: analysis, which involves the preparation of a key-list of all the relevant evidence expressed as simple propositions; and synthesis, in the form of a chart which depicts the relations between each item on the key-list with all other items. Each proposition on the key-list has a number; a system of symbols depicting different kinds of evidence (for example, testimonial evidence affirmatory; circumstantial evidence affirmatory; testimonial evidence negatory; a fact judicially noticed etc.) and different kinds of relation between two individual pieces of evidence (for example, tends to support, tends to negate, tends to explain, tends to corroborate, etc.).

Wigmore emphasized that what is being charted is the chart-maker's *actual state of belief* both about each relationship between a *factum probans* and its immediate *probandum* and about the overall probative force of the evidence as a whole. He explicitly rejected the idea that probative force

132 Theories of Evidence

can, at least in the present state of our knowledge, be expressed objectively in terms of laws which should be consciously obeyed in the process of weighing evidence:

> . . . there is no law (yet known) of logical thought which tells us that $(A + B + C) + (D + E)$ *must* equal X or *must* equal Not-X. We know only that our mind, reflecting upon the five evidential data, *does* come to the conclusion X or Not-X, as the case may be. All that the scheme can do for us is to make plain the entirety and details of our actual mental process.[31]

Although the final judgements are not typically based on objective criteria, the process is essentially rational:

> Hence, though we may not be able to demonstrate that we *ought* to reach that belief or disbelief, we have at least the satisfaction of having taken every precaution to reach it rationally. Our moral duty was to approximate, so far as capable, our belief to the fact. We have performed that duty to the limits of our present rational capacity. And the scheme or method, if it has enlarged that capacity, will have achieved something worth while.[32]

There is both a logical and psychological dimension to a chart. It is a rational reconstruction of what, in the chart-maker's view, *ought* to be the logical relations between the data. It does not purport to depict actual judgements of decision-makers, still less the mental processes leading to such judgements. Nevertheless, according to Wigmore, what is registered is belief, the belief of the chart-maker at the time of completing the chart. Doubts, degrees of confidence, etc., are to be expressed in the chart. It is a map both of the maker's beliefs about the relations between a collection of propositions and about his provisional conclusions. Such relations are judgements about probative force expressed in terms of 'tends to support', 'tends to negate', 'tends to explain'; the conclusions express belief or disbelief about particular propositions and their relations to each other; such beliefs are of varying strength, ranging from firm belief (however categorized), through different degrees of confidence and doubt to firm disbelief.[33]

Here one may anticipate an objection that we have already considered in relation to Bentham. Does this not, it may be objected, conflate subjective and objective criteria and logical and psychological analysis?[34] Logical relations are objective matters; beliefs are subjective. How can the two be depicted together in a single chart? Wigmore, as an optimistic rationalist, believed that reason can and should play a large part in decision-making processes. Perhaps he glossed over such problems in presenting his system, but his chart method is sufficiently flexible to be capable of being rescued from such objections. To put the matter briefly, it is for the chart-maker to specify what he is charting and what

Wigmore on proof 133

assumptions he is making. For example, a chart need not necessarily depict the chart-maker's own beliefs about propositions and relations; it could purport to *predict* the likely future judgements of some third party or to *reconstruct* an actual argument which has been used, (e.g., in a published judgement or a secondary work on a famous case) or the possible arguments that might be advanced by an opponent. So long as the chart-maker makes clear what standpoint he is adopting and what he conceives to be the nature of the relations that are being depicted, the method is available to him. Objections of the kind raised above may apply to a particular chart, but not to the chart method as such.[35]

The final chart depicts the chart-maker's belief at the time of completion. Accordingly it takes account of changes that have taken place in the maker's mind during the process of composition. Since the task of analysis and synthesis is an arduous one, which involves individuating every single item of relevant evidence and considering all significant relations between all of the items, the process typically involves reflecting on, forming and revising a large number of provisional judgements. Indeed, this may be its main value. Thus the chart method does not merely serve to depict and communicate judgements on the weight of evidence; it also offers a systematic aid to forming considered judgements. The process may be at least as valuable as the product.

The relations being charted are *relations between propositions*. The distinction between facts and propositions of fact is implicitly recognized by Wigmore, but he appears to have proceeded on the assumption that any fact can be expressed in the form of a proposition.[36] The key-list is a list of propositions; the chart maps logical relations between propositions.

One important limitation of the chart method is that it is a method for organizing and depicting the relations between the components of a given body of evidence.[37] In Wigmore's account, the components, the propositions on the key-list, are given. They are data. The method gives no guidance on how the evidence is to be identified and, beyond a general test of relevance, it provides no basis for deciding what to include in or to exclude from the key-list. In theory an almost infinite number of facts is potentially relevant in a given case and selection is inevitable; deciding how each fact is to be individuated and expressed and what level of generality is appropriate requires the exercise of both skill and judgement. The chart method gives guidance on how to *organize* a body of data, but not on how to compile the data.

Constructing a key-list is neither a mechanical nor an easy task. Considerations of economy, judgement about what is important or appropriate, and technical considerations (such as the rules of admissibility of evidence) are all involved in the process of assembling the data. In this respect the chart method is analogous to the algorithm, that is a

134 Theories of Evidence

precise set of instructions, capable of being presented in diagrammatic form, for solving a well-defined problem[38] By breaking down a complicated rule (or body of data) into a number of simple components and presenting each in turn in a particular order, it can enable the reader to find his way around a complex body of rules and locate the answer to his particular problem. But the instructions are taken as *given* and it is assumed that they are clear, well-defined and that they do provide an answer. Similarly, a Wigmorean chart can depict relations between the components of a mass of evidence, provided that all the relevant evidence (of any potentially probative value) has been collected and accurately presented in the key-list.

Finally, the chart method is a rather more flexible tool than Wigmore suggests, since it may be used to chart other matters than the chart-maker's own beliefs.[39] For example, it may be used to reconstruct arguments about evidence made by others or to predict the likely reactions of some future decision-maker. It can be used in preparing for trial, as well as in analysing past trials. Moreover, is it not necessarily restricted to forensic situations or legal evidence. It is theoretically possible for the same person to apply the chart method to a case, from the point of view of the actual arguments put forward at the trial, or from the point of view of an historian trying to analyse as detachedly as he can all the evidence available to him for whatever purpose he specifies, or even from the point of view of a logician trying to reconstruct the explicit and implicit arguments about particular *probanda* to be found in somebody else's account, even a fictitious account, such as F. Tennyson Jesse's novel about Bywaters and Thompson, *A Pin to See the Peepshow*.[40] All of these are significantly different exercises and it is vital at the outset to clarify the standpoints from which the evidence is being analysed. The common element is that every chart depicts or reconstructs a particular kind of *argument*, that is an argument about the probable truth or untruth of one or more specific allegations of fact (ultimate *probanda*).

The 'chart method' is a working theory for the practical application of ordinary principles of logic to the analysis of evidence. The best way to understand it is to study actual examples and then to try to apply it; the only way to master it is through practice. It is beyond the scope of this chapter to provide instruction in the method, but we shall return to consider further aspects of its theoretical status and practical utility in the section on general experience and in the appendix.[41] Here it is pertinent to make one observation about its reception. During his lifetime and for many years after his death, the reception of Wigmore's chart method ranged from polite scepticism to complete indifference. With a few exceptions, it was ignored by academics and practitioners alike. Recently, however, there have been signs of changes in the climate of opinion. Professor David Schum and his collaborators have used it as the starting-point for a series of notable empirical studies in the psychology of inferential reasoning.[42] Professor Terence Anderson and others have adapted it as a basis for introducing some analytical rigour into training courses in trial practice; for over ten years the author has used it in a variety of more theoretically-oriented courses; he is convinced that it is an excellent pedagogical vehicle for teaching rigorous analysis and for exploring a variety of issues in the theory of evidence. It is demanding for the student and fun to teach. Perhaps more important than any of these is the fact that, like the algorithm, the method seems to offer considerable possibilities for use in connection with new information technology. This is as yet a largely unexplored field, but it seems quite possible that Wigmore's method will come into its own in the computer age.[43]

(v) Psychology and forensic science

From an early stage Wigmore had been interested in the emerging field of criminology. In time he came to play a significant role in the development of the subject in the United States.[1] He had a working knowledge of several European languages and, by the turn of the century, he was familiar with much of the pioneering work that was being done in several European countries.[2] Criminology, in this context, was interpreted quite widely to include the psychology of crime, methods of police investigation, forensic science and the interrogation of suspects and witnesses.

Until 1908 the specific field of witness psychology had merely been one of his many interests. He had included some material on it in the first edition of the *Treatise*, but the treatment was rather cursory. His attention became more sharply focused on the subject in 1908 by the publication of a series of lectures given at Harvard by a German psychologist, Hugo Muensterberg.[3] In this book, entitled *On the Witness Stand*, Muensterberg forcefully criticized the judiciary and the legal profession for their ignorance and neglect of the findings of experimental psychology. He drew attention to methods of testing the reliability of witnesses that had been developed by Stern and others and to the 'word-association method' for testing consciousness of guilt, developed by several scholars, notably Wertheimer, Jung and Alfred Gross, on the basis of more general work by Galton and Wundt.[4] Muensterberg, *inter alia*, advocated the use of psychologists as court experts to test the veracity of witnesses. Wigmore interpreted him to be claiming that psychologists had now developed a usable method for distinguishing between true and false testimony. He was highly sceptical of Muensterberg's claims and he took strong exception both to his failure to give citations to the allegedly 'easily available data' and to his strictures on the obscurantism of the Bench and Bar. When American psychologists failed to respond, Wigmore decided to take on the task himself.[5] He went

136   *Theories of Evidence*

about it with typical thoroughness, combing the libraries in Chicago and its vicinity for all available literature.[6] His article, published in 1908, contained a bibliography of 127 works in several languages.[7]

Wigmore's article was uncharacteristically acerbic. It took the form of a mythical libel action, *Cokestone* v. *Muensterberg*, in which the psychologist was himself placed on the witness-stand and subjected to cross-examination. The result was an effective satire. The gist of Wigmore's attack was that the research findings were not 'easily accessible', that they were highly controversial and that there was a considerable body of opinion, not cited by Muensterberg, to the effect that the specific methods he had recommended were not yet sufficiently developed to be relied on by courts; furthermore some of the alleged findings of experimental psychology were not particularly new and by and large corresponded with lawyers' working assumptions in the courtroom. While the legal profession might be charged with culpable neglect of criminology, they could hardly be convicted of neglect of or indifference to methods which were not yet agreed on by scientists. Far from being obscurantist, the Bench and Bar were eager for assistance from psychology, but so far virtually nothing of use had been forthcoming.[8]

According to one commentator, this scathing attack discouraged a nascent interest in testimony among American psychologists with the result that progress was delayed for a generation.[9] This is probably an exaggeration. Robert Gault, a Professor of Psychology at Northwestern, and a close associate and a friend of Wigmore gives a different impression. In an unpublished memoir of Wigmore, written shortly after his death, he wrote:

> Dean Wigmore's publication was quite popular among professional psychologists during a period of years because it was an excellent survey of an area that, up to that time, had received practically no attention in the United States. A good many university instructors made the article available to students as required collateral reading. At least one of them [presumably Gault] was responsible for wearing out seven copies of the *Review*.[10]

Whether or not Wigmore's biting satire deterred psychologists from pursuing the subject, it did not dampen his own enthusiasm. It might be said that, having dispatched Muensterberg, he moved in to occupy the field himself. The first edition of the *Principles* contained extensive extracts from psychological literature and Wigmore's own magisterial pronouncements on the uses and limitations of psychological findings in litigation. He maintained his interest in the subject for the rest of his life and this is particularly reflected in the extensive changes made in the second edition.[11]

Robert Gault reports that Wigmore used to tease him about the

Wigmore on proof 137

inability of the psychologists to come up with anything of practical value to lawyers.[12] In a letter to another psychologist, Professor H. P. Weld of Cornell, in 1930, about *the Principles*, Wigmore wrote:

> What I have needed more than anything else is to make up my mind first how to revise Part II on Testimonial Evidence, so as to take advantage of the recent developments in psychology. I do not find that the psychologists have contributed anything except in the two narrow fields of lie detecting and of the ratio of errors in general.[13]

In the previous year he had invited Dean Robert Maynard Hutchins of Yale to collaborate with him on the new edition of the *Principles*, saying 'You are the only other teacher of Evidence who has shown any conviction and initiative in that field'.[14] Hutchins had worked for some years with a psychologist, Donald Slesinger, on a series of articles on the psychological assumptions underlying a number of particular rules of evidence.[15] Hutchins was clearly attracted by the invitation, and the two men met to discuss the possibility, but shortly afterwards he was elevated to the Presidency of the University of Chicago and wrote to say that, although he would now be living in the same city as Wigmore, 'since I am taking a job of which I am quite ignorant, I may be unable to do anything else but try to learn it'.[16] Later, in his famous *The Autobiography of an Ex-Law Student*, Hutchins wrote in a spirit of considerable disillusionment about his ventures into inter-disciplinary research at Yale and hinted that he felt that little could be expected of collaboration between lawyers and psychologists.[17]

Despite his own scepticism about what had been achieved, Wigmore remained rather more optimistic than Hutchins. He never doubted the potential relevance or worth of psychological research into forensic questions, but he recognized the enormous obstacles to progressing to the point where *positive* usable techniques for testing the reliability of testimony could be developed.[18] On the other hand he acknowledged the importance of the negative or cautionary lessons of psychology – the dangers of generalization, the many factors, apart from dishonesty, which can render the testimony of honest witnesses unreliable, and the crudity of the psychological assumptions on which some rules of evidence were based.[19]

Wigmore was well aware that there are many aspects of the operation of the human factor in legal processes and that the potential contributions of scientific psychology to the study of such processes is correspondingly varied. In the *Principles* his main concern was to explore the mental processes which culminate in statements by witnesses, the factors which increase or decrease the reliability of such statements, the extent of testimonial error and the methods available for detecting error. Accordingly, the bulk of the psychological material in the *Principles* relates to witness psychology. There are, however, a few other places

138 *Theories of Evidence*

when psychological questions are at least touched on. Wigmore followed Bentham in rejecting the idea that the credibility of different types of evidence could be made the subject of formal regulation;[20] for, as he put it, neither logic nor psychology had yet developed 'laws of necessary belief' to provide a foundation for such rules.[21] We have seen that the charts of mixed masses of evidence are charts of *belief*, but in this respect his account is based on common-sense psychology, without reference to any specific psychological literature. In dealing with certain types of *probanda* – notably character, emotion, intention, identity and habit – he considers rather cursorily the past and potential contributions of psychology.[22] In dealing with narration by witnesses he includes some material on questioning – examination and cross-examination in court and police interrogation – and on motives for confessions, but the coverage is not very systematic.[22] There is almost nothing on psychological aspects of communication, persuasion and deciding from the point of view of the decision-maker, nor on such important notions as 'prejudicial effect' and 'cognitive competence'. Less surprisingly, he does not deal with a number of other topics which have recently attracted attention, such as bargaining, negotiation and non-verbal communication.[24] The main focus of attention in the *Principles* is on the cognitive processes of one participant in legal processes, the witness, whereas today, psychologists tend to be more concerned with all relevant participants and the interactions between them.[25]

If Wigmore's focus of attention was, in this respect, rather narrow, his treatment of witness psychology was systematic. First, he explores how far generic human traits are known to affect probative value. In a chapter which violates a number of contemporary taboos he summarizes what the literature has to say on the influence of various traits – Race, Age, Sex, Mental Derangement, Character (the disposition to lie), Temperament, Emotion, Experience (the psychology of expert witnesses) – on the reliability of testimony.[26] Some of the flavour of this chapter is conveyed by Wigmore's introduction to the section on sex (i.e. gender):

> Sex.   There exist, so far, no recorded observations by women upon the testimonial peculiarities of *men*.
>
> But of observations by men upon the peculiarities of *women*, we have numerous fragmentary pronouncements and a few careful surveys. They may perhaps be summarized with the statement that, in point of *perception*, the woman as such does not differ appreciably from the man; that, in point of *recollection*, women are more apt to confuse what they have really observed with what they have imagined or wished to occur; and that, in point of *narration*, they are apt to excel in quickness and positiveness, but are apt to fall below in candor and honesty.[27]

In this chapter Wigmore draws heavily on literature which is based more on speculation and impressions than on empirical evidence. If this section seems to the modern reader to be antiquated, this is perhaps due as much to the questions that are posed as to the answers. At the turn of the century, writers like Arnold[28] and Gross seriously addressed themselves to such questions as: 'Does race affect credibility?' and 'Are women less reliable witnesses than men?', and Wigmore surveyed and anthologized what he considered to be the best discussions. In fact, his own conclusions are largely cautionary: there is no evidence that race or sex operates as a constant factor on reliability;[29] no safe generalizations can be made about the effect of age or mental derangement on testimony;[30] 'No new method has been offered for determining the degree of influence of [perception] upon the correctness of a specific assertion';[31] 'No method appears yet to have been invented for measuring an individual's recollection-capacity for specific topics';[32] 'Science tells us that the traits which affect the probative value of testimony are numerous and subtle';[33] 'The Trial Rules coincide with Science . . . in recognizing the infinite variability of Recollection and do not attempt to make any minimum requirement'[34] and so on.'

It is not necessary to examine in detail Wigmore's treatment of such topics as testimonial error, hypnotism and lie-detectors. Much of it has been overtaken by events, though the modern reader may find it sobering to note how little that is really usable in everyday practice has emerged in the last fifty years.

Wigmore's treatment of the psychological dimensions of proof did not claim to be particularly original.[35] He set out to survey the available literature, to fit the findings of psychologists into the framework of his general theory of proof and to present an assessment of the actual and potential contributions of psychology to the field.[36] His critique of Muensterberg and some particular remarks about the limited practical value of existing findings might, on their own, give a misleading impression of quite strong scepticism about the value of forensic psychology. In fact Wigmore was deeply interested in the subject, he kept up with the literature and he gave encouragement and support to a number of young researchers in the field. He was sympathetically aware of the enormous practical obstacles in the way of rapid progress of psychometry and other related aspects of applied psychological research. If his conclusions tended towards pessimism, there is little that has happened in the last 50 years of psychological research to suggest that this was unjustified.[37]

However, if Wigmore's science were to be updated in the light of developments in psychology since 1937 his general conclusions on the particular questions he posed might not need radical revision. If anything, his admonitions to caution and his recognition of the difficulties of bridging the gap between the experimental conditions of the laboratory and the complex world of the courtroom might be made

140   *Theories of Evidence*

even more emphatically. When Wigmore debated with Muensterberg the situation was much simpler than it is today. Wigmore's bibliography, which covered several languages, listed 127 items. It has been estimated that articles related to law in English language/American psychology journals has risen from just over one hundred in 1965 to over a thousand per year in the late 1970s.[38]

Scepticism about the immediate practical utility of the findings of experimental psychology to legal practice may have reinforced the gap between pure and applied research. The response of some psychologists was to turn to more manageable and more narrowly focused questions, such as the capacity to recall particular words or sounds under laboratory conditions. It is only relatively recently that psychologists have re-emerged from the laboratory in substantial numbers to consider in a sustained way the practical application of psychology to problems of evidence and proof. They have brought with them a greater concern for theory, a mass of new data and an increased sophistication about the uses and limitations of psychology in forensic and other legal contexts. For example, cognitive psychologists are now much more wary of isolating particular sub-systems, such as memory and perception, from the total complex process of cognitive functioning; at least as much attention is focused on the collection and processing of evidence before trial as on what happens in the courtroom. Not only has a much wider range of questions been opened up, but there has been a growing recognition of the inherent complexities of legal processes. Updating Wigmore's psychology would involve much more than substituting new and better-grounded answers to the same questions.[39]

Wigmore considered himself to be a progressive in regard to science. Part of the sharpness of his attack on Muensterberg is attributable to resentment at the suggestion that the legal profession was obscurantist and reactionary in its attitude to scientific advances.[40] He stressed the enormous obstacles in the way of significant breakthroughs in forensic psychology, but he was careful to emphasize that this was no reason for giving up. His attitude to psychology was pessimistic, but sympathetic and constructive.

His attitude to forensic science was even more positive. He had personally been interested in the field from an early stage in his career. The first and subsequent editions of the *Principles* were dedicated to Hans Gross, 'who did more than any other man in modern times to encourage the application of science to judicial proof'.[41] Wigmore himself played an important role in supporting the development of 'police science' at Northwestern and elsewhere in the United States.[42] Each new edition of the *Principles* attempted, *inter alia*, to synthesize and to take stock of the whole field of forensic science as it bore on judicial proof. One of the main differences between the third and earlier editions is the amount of space devoted to such topics as ballistics, fingerprinting,

Wigmore on proof 141

blood grouping, spectroscopy and advances in telecommunications. Over time, material drawn from psychology and forensic science drove out extracts from famous trials to an extent that led one reviewer, Zachariah Chafee, to comment that he found the last edition 'more instructive than the old, but less amusing'.[43] If anything, Chafee suggested, Wigmore was not sufficiently critical of some of the claims of 'scientific crime detection'.

At several places in the third edition Wigmore expressed his enthusiasm for recent developments.[44] But he was careful to make explicit his own assessments of the uses and dangers of particular findings. His treatment of graphology is a good example:

> Thus the data of graphic science make it possible to assert almost the universality of the proposition: No two persons' handwritings are normally the same, nor can they be made precisely the same by willpower. This proposition can not be stated with the same universality as in the case of finger-prints and bullet-marks. But it approaches towards a universal truth, and as such it is the basis for inferences from style of handwriting to authorship of documents.[45]

Wigmore did not theorize much about his conception of science. From what he says in the *Principles* about psychology, forensic science and the science of proof itself, one may reasonably infer that he held a simple view of science as representing a steady pushing forward of the frontiers of knowledge through the accumulation of more and better data and generalizations tested by research. Although the principle of relativity and developments in the philosophy of science were already undermining Victorian conceptions of science as progress, they do not seem to have made much of an impact on Wigmore. Much of the clarity and power of his writing depend on his bold and rather simplistic vision of the world. He recognized diversity and complexity in this world and in his subject, but he wrote as if he was superbly confident that even the most complicated subject could be classified, organized, and brought to order.

Associated with this attitude is a tendency to adopt a somewhat monolithic view of science. This is particularly apparent in his treatment of psychology. To be sure it is a young discipline, that has a long way to go, but the way forward is through research and experiment. Wigmore writes almost as if the perennial battles within psychology between Freudians and Jungians, between behaviourists and their critics, between experimentalists and others did not exist. In so far as he notes that there are differences, he seems to assume that they would be sorted out in due course and that truth would prevail. This is essentially an atheoretical, positivistic and consensualist view of science, not untypical of nineteenth-century thinkers. Such views, of course, lingered on into the twentieth century. The temper of his thought and many of his specific assumptions stand in quite sharp contrast to many of Wigmore's

142 Theories of Evidence

American contemporaries, for example, William James, Charles Beard, Thorstein Veblen, Oliver Wendell Holmes, Jerome Frank, and other apostles of the revolt against formalism.[46]

As anthologies of findings on particular matters, the sections in the *Principles* have been superceded by modern works of reference, some of which are themselves vulnerable to the charge that they adopt rather simplistic and outdated perspectives on legal processes.[47] However, these sections should not be dismissed out of hand. Problems tend to be less ephemeral than solutions and some of Wigmore's analysis of problems of proving particular kinds of probanda, such as identity,[48] are still illuminating. More important, however, is the point that Wigmore's general theoretical framework still provides by far the best model for coherently integrating and mapping connections between the logical, psychological, scientific and legal dimensions of proof. In particular, Wigmore's treatment of the logical processes typically involved in arguing about different kinds of *probanda* and evidence provides an invaluable link between daily practice and some rather abstract and difficult theoretical issues. The nature of this link is best perceived by looking closely at the nature and role of background generalizations in arguments about proof. This topic has attracted a good deal of attention in the recent debates about forensic probabilities; Wigmore dealt with it under the rather broader rubric of 'general experience'.

(vi) General experience

Introduction

V is found dead from a stab wound in the back. W, a forensic scientist, testifies that a particular knife was the murder weapon. He also testifies that there was one clear set of fingerprints on the weapon with characteristics x, y, z etc. and that M's finger patterns conform precisely to the prints. In this simple example, particular scientific findings establish the cause of death, the identity of the murder weapon and the identity of a person who had handled the weapon.[1] They all form a part of a chain of reasoning which has strong, but not necessarily conclusive, probative force despite the length of the chain. It is possible that W is lying or mistaken, or that the prints were planted, or that M's fingerprints were there innocently or that V was killed by accident or in self-defence. In short, the argument is open to attack at a number of points. Nevertheless, most people would agree there is a strong *prima facie* case against M.

How do we arrive at this judgement? The standard answer lies in the fact that several, but not all, of the links in the chain are backed up by a body of well-founded *general* scientific knowledge. In ordinary discourse

Wigmore on proof 143

we tend to gloss over the background generalizations that support such inferences. For example, we tend to move directly from the fact that M's finger patterns coincided with the prints on the knife to the conclusion that it was almost certainly or very probably M who killed V. If called on to justify such inferences and our assessments of their strength we invoke generalizations of the kind 'A finger pattern x, y, z etc. can be borne by one person only' or, more cautiously, 'Where a person's finger patterns coincide exactly with a set of clear fingerprints it is very probable indeed that the prints were that person's.' The generalization thus forms the major premise of a syllogism:

A finger pattern x, y, z etc. can be borne by one person only
M bears that finger pattern
M is that person.[2]

In this instance the major premiss is based on a well-developed body of scientific knowledge; yet it is striking that even in this context forensic scientists are very reluctant to give precise numerical estimates of the chances of more than one person in a given population having the same fingerprints.[3] It is only exceptionally that we are in a position to appeal to such scientific generalizations as a basis for making inferences from evidence. Typically we have to appeal to our own personal or vicarious experience, often referred to as 'common sense', 'general knowledge' or 'experience of the common course of events'. Some of the problems surrounding such generalizations can be illustrated by another example.

Edith Thompson was accused of inciting her lover, Frederick Bywaters, to murder her husband, Percy.[5] Edith was twenty-eight years old at the time, Freddy was only twenty. Is this discrepancy in age relevant to the *probandum* of incitement? Many people would intuitively feel that it is; counsel for the prosecution in the case, the trial judge and many commentators have all assumed it to be relevant. Yet an argument which goes: 'X was older than Y, therefore she incited Y' seems highly dubious. Can the inference be justified analytically and, if so, how?

The standard answer to this kind of question is that the *factum probans* is linked to the *factum probandum* by an implicit generalization. Common sense does suggest that there is *some* connection between age and influence in human relationships but this is too vague. What precisely is the generalization? Let us consider just two possible candidates:

(i) All older women always dominate younger men in all circumstances.

(ii) There is a tendency for the older person in an intimate relationship to be the dominant partner.

The first proposition provides the major premiss for a syllogism proving that Edith dominated Freddy. The argument is valid, but the premiss is easily falsified. There is no scientific evidence to support such a broad generalization and most people can produce counter-examples

144 *Theories of Evidence*

from their own experience to show that (i) is at the very least grossly over-generalized. Furthermore it appears to be both prejudiced and prejudicial.

At first sight, (ii) seems to meet these objections. It is not framed in sexist terms and it is more likely to be true than (i). However, it is open to some further objections. First, it is very vague – it does not even differentiate between often, sometimes and occasionally, let alone quantify the estimate of frequency; secondly, how are we to know whether it is true or not? and, thirdly, it is not universal. It therefore does not establish a *necessary* connection between the fact that Edith was older than Freddy and the allegation that she incited him to murder.

Thus (i), if it were true, would establish a very strong probative relation between the *factum probans* and the *factum probandum*; but it is not true. On the other hand, (ii) might be true, but its strength as a bridge between the *factum probans* and *factum probandum* is both weak and indeterminate. To complicate matters (i) and (ii) are by no means the only possible generalizations that might provide a link between the relative ages of Edith and Freddy and the allegation of incitement. Indeed, taken in isolation from a whole mass of other general and particular background information it is not possible to make any confident judgement about the probative value, if any, of this particular fact.

These relatively simple examples illustrate some of the questions relating to the nature and role of generalizations in evaluating and reasoning about evidence.[6] Surprisingly little detailed attention had been paid to this complex topic by theorists of evidence until recently and it is fair to say that much of the debate is still at a relatively early stage even in 1984.[7] Wigmore wrote before these modern debates; his own writings provoked a long and rather sterile controversy about logical and legal relevancy that preceded the recent, more sophisticated discussions about probabilities and proof.[8] We have already seen that Wigmore had little to say about probabilities as such; like Bentham, he is recognizable as a fairly consistent, but rather primitive, proponent of a non-mathematical (Baconian) approach.[9] The purpose of this chapter is to clarify Wigmore's positions on a number of issues rather than to explore these complex matters in depth. These include the meaning of 'general experience', its sources (whose generalizations?), the relationship between logic and general experience, the value and limits of articulating background generalizations and the difficulties involved in making such articulations. In the following chapter we shall consider his general theory of relevancy in the context of an examination of the relationship between the science of proof and the law of evidence. Finally, some further points of contact with the recent debates on probabilities will be dealt with in the Appendix.[10]

The nature and role of general experience

As the full title of the *Principles* suggests, the science of judicial proof is founded on Logic, Psychology and General Experience. What is encompassed by 'general experience' in this context? How does it provide a basis for the principles of proof? What precisely is the relationship between general experience and the logical and psychological dimensions of proof?'

Like Bentham, Wigmore subscribed to an empirical theory of knowledge in that he held that all knowledge is derived from human experience, which provides the ultimate test for the correctness or otherwise of all beliefs about matters of fact.[11] He was well aware that a high proportion of what passes for knowledge in a given society is not based on scientific laws which have satisfied criteria of authentication widely accepted within the scientific community and that many judgements on questions of fact in forensic situations have to be based on generalizations few, if any, of which would be regarded as scientific.[12]

In discussing testimonial capacity in the law of evidence, Wigmore distinguishes between 'general experience' of 'subjects of testimony . . . on which a sufficient experience is assumed to be possessed by the normal adult' and 'special experience', those on which 'a sufficient experience is possessed only by those who have followed a special occupation, trade, art, science or other appropriate activity', i.e. experts.[13] In the *Principles* 'general experience' is used rather more widely to include 'special experience' as defined above as well as the general knowledge expected of ordinary adults. Indeed, it is probably wider than that. Thus, in this context, 'general experience' encompasses both scientific findings, expert opinion and the empirical generalizations about the common course of events which ordinary people typically bring to bear on their judgements of practical affairs.

Writers on evidence have expressed such notions in varying terms. Binder and Bergman state a commonly-held view:

> A generalization is, then, a premise which rests on the general behavior of people or objects. How does one formulate generalisations? Usually, one adopts conventional wisdom about how people and objects function in everyday life. All of us, through our own personal experiences, through hearing about the personal experiences of others, and through knowledge gained from books, movies, newspapers and television, have accumulated vast storehouses of commonly-held notions about how people and objects generally behave in our society. From this storehouse one formulates a generalization about typical behavior. The generalization, in turn, becomes the premise which enables one to link specific evidence with an element one hopes to prove.[14]

Sociologists of knowledge, sceptics and relativists of various kinds

146 *Theories of Evidence*

have done much to heighten our awareness of the difficulties and dangers of accepting 'common-sense' generalizations and the like as constituting 'objective knowledge'.[15] In respect of any such generalization one should not assume too readily that there is in fact a 'cognitive consensus' on the matter. The stock of knowledge in any society varies from group to group, from individual to individual and from time to time. Even when there is a widespread consensus, what passes as 'conventional knowledge' may be untrue, speculative or otherwise defective; moreover, 'common-sense generalizations' tend not to be 'purely factual' – they often contain a strong mixture of evaluation and prejudice, as is illustrated by various kinds of social, national and racial stereotypes.[16]

Some of the conventional wisdom in writings about judicial evidence is vulnerable to attack along these lines. Is this true of Wigmore? The answer is a qualified 'yes'. He was not so naïve as to believe in a universal cognitive consensus nor to assume that 'common sense' would always be confirmed by science.[17] Although not a crude positivist, he tended to underplay the extent to which 'evaluating' evidence is in practice not solely a matter of estimating likelihoods, but also involves value judgements on the part of adjudicators.[18] There was a strong tendency, shared by many legal scholars of his time, to take a widespread consensus among reasonable men for granted.[19] Indeed, such an assumption is almost a necessary presupposition of many of the numerous magisterial pronouncements in the *Principles* on the weight to be accorded to particular kinds of inferences.[20] Similar assumptions about common sense, general experience and the common course of events are made by most writers on evidence in the Anglo-American tradition.[21] They are perhaps best characterized as representing pragmatic rather than naïve empiricism. On these matters it is fair to say that Wigmore belongs to the mainstream of the Rationalist Tradition.

What, it may be asked, is the precise relationship between logic and general experience in the science of proof? The answer to this question has already been suggested in discussing the chart method.[22] The discipline of analysing a mass of evidence into a list of propositions and then charting all the probative relations between all the propositions in the key-list forces us to make explicit all the steps in an argument and all the assumptions that have been made either explicitly or implicitly. Once articulated, these assumptions can be examined critically in respect of their truth, clarity, precision and so on. Logical analysis can help to reveal more clearly the nature and validity of an argument, but logic alone cannot test the truth of the assumptions nor tell us what weight should be given to an inference; for 'the strength of any particular inference depends on the *experience in the subject under inquiry*, not on logic. Logic only assists us in revealing our mental process'.[23]

Wigmore based his treatment of inference explicitly on the work of Mill and Sidgwick. He emphasized that the form of argument in judicial proof is typically 'inductive', with deductive logic playing a relatively minor role.[24] This has been variously interpreted. On one view, the claim that 'the form of argument is inductive' implies little more than that this is a form of 'open-system' reasoning in which the conclusions do not follow from the premisses as a matter of strict logical necessity.[25] One reason for this is that it is rarely possible in judicial proof to establish a major premiss which is both universal and true. However, Wigmore has been interpreted by some critics as having underestimated the importance of generalizations in judicial proof by failing to realize that every inference in this kind of argument is necessarily based on a generalization.[26] Michael and Adler advanced a deductive theory of proof based on Aristotelian logic and this was popularized in rather more readable form by Professors James and Trautman and used as a basis for criticizing Wigmore.[27]

In order to make some sense of this debate it is necessary to try to disentangle the views of Wigmore and his critics on a number of distinct, though related, issues. First, did Wigmore believe that every inferential step involved an appeal to a generalization? In both the *Treatise* and the *Principles* he cites Sidgwick to the effect that 'strictly speaking, all Proof, so far as really *Proof*, is deductive. That is to say, unless and until a supposed truth can be brought under the shadow of some more certain truth it is self-supporting or circular'.[28] In more than one place, he quite explicitly acknowledged that all instances of inference from evidence are capable of being expressed 'in the syllogistic or deductive form'.[29] However, he then went on to state that this 'is not the true form', for two reasons. First, in litigious argument the argument is in practice put forward in inductive form, that is to say the background generalization is left implicit and, secondly, even if this transmutation could be effected it would be useless because it would merely shift the court's attention to the major premiss of the syllogism.[30]

Taken out of context this seems difficult to reconcile with Wigmore's claim that one of the main values of the chart method of analysis is to help us to spot logical jumps and fallacies and generally to evaluate the strength of an argument through the discipline of articulating what is normally left unstated: 'Only by careful dissection of the implicit steps of inference can we lay bare and locate the possibilities of doubt'.[31]

Not only does Wigmore seem to be inconsistent, but it has been shown that he was, to say the least, rather casual in his own attempts to formulate implicit generalizations. Thus, in one notorious example, he has been shown to have been guilty of an elementary confusion. He had stated that in an argument in the form: 'A planned to kill B; therefore A probably did kill B' the implicit major premiss was: 'Man's fixed designs are probably carried out';[32] furthermore, he suggested that nothing was gained in articulating the generalization. James pointed out that not only is Wigmore's formulation very vague, but also few people would accept it

148 *Theories of Evidence*

as being true. However, there is a much more acceptable formulation, viz. 'Men having such a fixed design are more likely to kill than are men not having such a fixed design.' The conclusion that follows from this is not that A probably did kill B, but that the evidence of design increases the probability of A's guilt.[33] Wigmore was thus shown to be guilty of just the kind of sloppy thinking that his chart method was designed to counteract.[34] By articulating this particular generalization he exposed his own error.

If this were the end of the matter, this criticism would be devastating. However, Wigmore's instinctive reservations about the value of articulating generalizations may be justified by better arguments than those he advanced or his critics recognized. First, the main offending passage relates explicitly to the form in which arguments are advanced *in court*.[35] It follows a lengthy discussion of 'the practical necessities of legal controversy in general'. Now it is quite clear that it would be impractical, tedious and often unnecessary to insist on trying to articulate all, or even a significant number, of the relevant generalizations during oral argument in court,[37] just as it would only very exceptionally be appropriate to present actual key-lists and charts directly to a jury or other tribunal. The *practical* value of rigorous logical analysis lies elsewhere: in preparing for trial, in order to test the relative strength of one's own case and to spot weak points in that of one's opponent; in subjecting past arguments to critical analysis and, as a pedagogical matter, in developing analytical skill and critical perspectives in students. Articulating generalizations and constructing charts are behind-the-scenes activities to be used in contexts where rigorous logical methods are appropriate in constructing and evaluating arguments. The practical exigencies of litigation in the adversary system obviously leave relatively little scope for using them regularly 'on stage'.[38]

Tillers has suggested some more fundamental reasons that justify Wigmore's aversion to articulating background generalizations.[39] First, he suggests that Wigmore's critics tend to fall into the error of assuming that all such generalizations can be appropriately formulated in terms of relative frequency statements. Wigmore, he suggests, is exempt from charges of having made this error.[40] Secondly, he argues that one good reason for scepticism of the value of attempting to articulate all background generalizations is that in practice our intuitions often outrun our capacity for analysis;[41] related to this, the extreme sort of rationalism of the followers of Michael and Adler greatly underestimates the difficulties and dangers of attempting to extract precise, individuated propositions from the complex 'web of belief' that typically constitutes the background knowledge on which we base our judgements.[42]

Tillers' analysis raises a fascinating range of difficult theoretical issues that cannot be pursued here.[43] It provides powerful arguments against Wigmore's critics, but as a defence of Wigmore it is less convincing. By

Wigmore on proof 149

dismissing Michael and Adler's theory solely on the grounds that it was of no use to practitioners, Wigmore failed to produce clear answers to such questions as: does *every* inference involve appeal to a background generalization? and can all such generalizations be adequately formulated as estimates of relative frequency?[44] How far is it possible to articulate and analyse arguments about evidence 'atomistically' (i.e. in the form of individuated propositions) without filtering out important elements in our background knowledge of a kind that we can and often do take into account in making judgements about the probable truth of allegations of fact? Wigmore may be less vulnerable than his critics suggested, but his account of inference leaves a lot of questions unanswered.

Wigmore may also have been concerned to discourage a form of scepticism that he felt was inappropriate to the practical conduct of litigation. In order to make decisions we are forced to rely on general experience with all its imperfections. Unlike the historian and the scientist, the adjudicator has a duty to decide; all that one can hope for is that such decisions will be based on the best available grounds for making judgements of fact. To harp continually on the fallibility of common sense and the relativity of knowledge would be to open up a Pandora's box of doubts in a way that would be inimical to the smooth conduct of practical affairs and public confidence in the legal system.[45]

Another important series of questions that were not explored in depth by Wigmore relate to criteria of identifying and formulating appropriate generalizations in an argument. The problem is familiar in the context of reasoning about questions of law, but curiously is rarely discussed in relation to questions of fact.[46] At what level of generality, using what categories, is it appropriate to formulate a proposition, whether it be a statement of the facts in a particular case, the categorization of the situation in that case as a type, or the protasis of a rule potentially applicable to the case?

It is a truism that any situation, or type of situation, can be described at an almost infinite number of levels of generality using an almost infinite number of different descriptive categories. For example, when describing an accident, is it appropriate to categorize the agent of harm as John Brown's chattel, a red Buick, a 1979 Buick with a particular registration number, an automobile, a vehicle, a dangerous thing, a thing, or a mass of atoms and molecules?[47] The particular context and purpose of the inquiry may narrow the range of choice in practice, but will not eliminate all choices of levels of generality and of categories. In a common law action for negligence in which the purpose is to attribute responsibility for injuries caused in a road accident, it is relatively uncontroversial to eliminate a description in terms of a mass of atoms and molecules or in terms of John Brown's chattel. But whether it is more appropriate to categorize the alleged agent of harm as a Buick, an

150 *Theories of Evidence*

automobile, or a dangerous thing may be less clear. In most contexts, there is at least some leeway for choice and, typically, there are no clear criteria of appropriateness for evaluating particular choices.

An almost identical problem arises in arguing about evidence. Thus in the example discussed above about the respective ages of Edith and Freddy, Edith could have been variously described as a woman, a lover, an adulteress, and a milliner. The implicit generalization linking the fact of the age discrepancy with the *probandum* of incitement could have been formulated at one of a number of different levels of generality using a variety of terms for describing each of the elements in the proposition. For example, older women/persons/lovers always/usually/frequently/sometimes influence/dominate/manipulate/make demands on etc.

An interesting example is to be found in arguments (about the murder weapon) that were actually used in the same case. The charge against Edith was based on the theory that she either conspired with or incited Bywaters to kill her husband. For this purpose it was important, possibly essential, for the prosecution to prove that the attack was planned. In order to prove premeditation the prosecution sought to suggest that the weapon had been purchased for the purpose of killing Percy Thompson and, more important, that Bywaters had put it in his overcoat pocket because he intended to attack Percy. The defence claimed that Bywaters' purchase and carrying of the knife were both innocent, in that he had bought the knife a long time previously, that he had taken it abroad with him on his last voyage, that he used it for many purposes, and that he regularly carried the knife with him in his overcoat pocket.[48]

In the process of the arguments about premeditation, the weapon was variously described as an ordinary sheath knife, a hunting knife, a deadly weapon, a dagger, a stabbing weapon, and a dreadful weapon.[49] There were also some striking differences in the generalizations invoked in the context of considering this issue. Counsel for the prosecution suggested that possession of a knife of this kind is in itself suspicious;[50] in order to cast doubt on the suggestion that Bywaters had possessed the knife for some time, the prosecution suggested that if this were true it would have been a subject of jocular remarks;[51] the judge stated: . . . 'no reasonable man living in London carries a knife like that about in his pocket.'[52] Defence counsel, on the other hand, said: 'It is not a strange thing that Bywaters should purchase such a knife, a seafaring man visiting seaports in foreign countries.'[53] And, 'there are few sailors who do not possess a knife'.[54] The editor of the record in the Notable British Trials series commented on the last remark in a footnote: 'Bywaters was not a "sailor" in the technical sense. He was a clerk on board a ship, and had more use for a fountain pen than for a knife.'[55]

It should be noted that in the preceding examples not only is Bywaters variously categorized as a sailor, a seafaring man visiting foreign ports, a clerk, and a man living in London, but quite different generalizations are

Wigmore on proof 151

invoked about the purchase, possession and carrying of knives. In the actual case, the jury had the opportunity to inspect the knife itself and thus could form their own judgement on its description and on the specific issue of whether it would fit conveniently in the inside pocket of Bywaters' coat. They could also check the accuracy of the various categorizations of Bywaters; for example, it is arguable that he was both someone living in London and a seafaring man who visited foreign countries, but the jurors were hardly better placed than the modern reader for making confident judgements about the habits of sailors in respect of knives nor of the likelihood that, if someone possesses a knife of this kind for a considerable period, it would be the subject of jocular remarks.

The example of the knife in *Bywaters and Thompson* is a simple example of the room for choice in selecting and in formulating generalizations as part of an argument about a particular issue of fact. It shows how there is room for the use of emotive terms, for distortion, and for selection by emphasizing different aspects of the same situation. Moreover, it is an example of invoking commonplace generalizations, for example about the normality of carrying knives about London and of sailors possessing and carrying knives, about which the jury is expected to rely on its own version(s) of general experience in order to come to a conclusion. Clearly there is scope in this kind of context for the intrusion of bias, prejudice and sheer speculation.[56] Moreover, it is doubtful whether all the relevant background knowledge can ever be fully articulated. But, as Wigmore would no doubt have wished to emphasize, what better basis is there for making such judgements?[57]

(vii) The Science of Proof and the Rules of Evidence

In the Anglo-American tradition there have been four principal attempts to develop an explicit general theory of the law of evidence.[1] Gilbert tried to subsume all the rules of evidence under the Best Evidence Rule; Bentham argued that there should be no binding rules at all within the framework of the Natural System of Procedure; Stephen tried to seek a coherent rationale for the whole of the law of evidence in the single principle of relevancy; and Thayer treated the rules of evidence as a mixed group of exceptions to a general principle of freedom of proof; he also advanced what became widely, if misleadingly, known as 'the doctrine of logical relevancy'. Nearly all modern writers on evidence in the common law world have accepted some version of Thayer's thesis and it has more or less explicitly provided the basis for most modern attempts to codify this branch of the law, including the Federal Rules.[2]

Where does Wigmore belong in this scheme? We have seen that his *Treatise* is widely regarded as the execution of a project that Thayer had

152 Theories of Evidence

planned, but failed to complete.[3] The *Principles* went far beyond Thayer in providing an integrated framework for the systematic study of all aspects of the subject of evidence and proof, with the rules being treated as only one part of a larger whole. In this section we shall consider first how far Wigmore rejected or modified his teacher's general views on admissibility and relevancy and his own treatment of the relationship between the Science of Proof and the Law of Evidence.

Logical and legal relevancy

Wigmore's general theory of admissibility and relevancy in the law of evidence is usually associated with the first volume of the *Treatise*.[4] At the outset he states two axioms of admissibility which he explicitly attributed to Thayer, 'the great master and expounder of the history of our law of Evidence'.[5] They are (1) 'None but facts having rational probative value are admissible';[6] (2) 'All facts having rational probative value are admissible, unless some specific rule forbids.'[7] Naturally, there are differences on some particular issues and Wigmore went into much more detail and ranged more widely than his mentor; but his general theory of admissibility is essentially the same as Thayer's. At this level of generality the main modern development has been the recognition of a general discretion to exclude evidence if its prejudicial effect outweighs its probative value, 'even though no specific exclusionary rule mandates exclusion'.[8] This is best seen as a gloss on Thayer's second axiom rather than as a rejection of it.

Wigmore's 'general theory of relevancy', as outlined in sections 24–36 of the *Treatise*, has been the subject of protracted controversy.[9] One way of characterizing this debate has been to contrast the 'theory of logical relevancy' with Wigmore's 'theory of legal relevancy': the former builds on and develops Thayer's view that relevancy is a matter of logic and not of law;[10] the latter emphasizes some peculiar characteristics of legal treatments of evidence.[11] The 'theory of logical relevancy', as advanced by James, Trautman and Ball, was presented as a championing of Thayer against Wigmore;[12] in fact, at least in its most rigorous articulation, it represented what Tillers has called an 'extreme sort of rationalism'[13] which owes a great deal to Michael and Adler.[14]

It would be of limited value to pursue the ramifications of this rather arid controversy here, for at least two reasons. First, Tillers has convincingly shown that several of the main criticisms of Wigmore misinterpreted his views and exaggerated the extent and significance of his divergence from Thayer;[15] secondly, in so far as there are important differences, it is clear that it is Thayer's version of 'logical relevancy' rather than that of either Wigmore or Michael and Adler that has prevailed, at least in the United States.[15] It is, however, worth considering briefly two specific issues, the notion of 'minimal relevancy'

Wigmore on proof   153

and the role of precedents in the law of evidence, because they throw some light on Wigmore's views on the relationship between the rules of evidence and the science of proof.

Minimal relevancy

The law of evidence is a conceptual minefield. Most writers are agreed that it is important to distinguish clearly between 'materiality', 'relevance', 'admissibility' and 'weight' (or 'probative force'); but there is no agreed terminology and some issues of substance are hidden in some of the debates about words.[16] One widely-held view might be restated in simplified form as follows: 'materiality' concerns what has to be proved for the proponent to succeed (the facts in issue) and is governed by substantive law; 'relevance' denotes a direct or indirect probative relation between an evidentiary fact and a *factum probandum* ('tends to support' or 'tends to negate') and is a matter of logic; 'probative force' denotes the strength of such support or negation; it is based on 'experience', but there are few settled criteria for evaluation; questions of 'admissibility' concern the exclusion of otherwise relevant evidence and are governed by the law of evidence (including the principles governing judicial discretions to exclude).[17] In the *Principles* and some parts of the *Treatise* Wigmore seemed to subscribe to such a scheme.[18] But it has been alleged that his doctrine of 'legal relevancy' blurred these distinctions.

There are two parts to the allegation. The first relates to the criterion for determining whether an evidentiary fact is 'relevant' to a particular *probandum*. Rule 401 of the Federal rules of Evidence states: ' "Relevant evidence" means evidence having any tendency to make the existence of any fact that is of consequence to the determination of the action more probable or less probable than it would be without the evidence.' This is generally regarded as embodying the principle of 'minimal relevancy', which insists on keeping the notion of relevance *conceptually* separate from the notions of admissibility, weight and sufficiency. All that 'relevance' does is to indicate *some* connection between the evidentiary fact and at least one fact in issue. In this view there are no degrees of relevancy, but there are degrees of probative force.[19]

Wigmore is accused of sowing unnecessary confusion by purporting to distinguish between 'logical' and 'legal' relevancy.[20] In a notorious passage he stated:

The judge, in his efforts to prevent the jury from being satisfied by matters of slight value, capable of being exaggerated by prejudice and hasty reasoning, has constantly seen fit to exclude matter that does not rise to a clearly sufficient degree of value. In other words, legal relevancy denotes first of all *something more than minimum probative value*. Each single piece of evidence must have a plus value.[21]

154 *Theories of Evidence*

This notion of 'plus value' has been criticized on several grounds: (1) it conflates the notions of sufficiency and relevancy of evidence; (2) it opens the door to confusing notions of relevancy and probative force; and (3) it suggests that a judge is able to predetermine the weight of a single item of evidence outside the context of the whole corpus of evidence.[22]

Wigmore's motive for introducing the dubious notion of 'plus value' is fairly clear. The context is a discussion of the relative roles of judge and jury and the practical necessities of legal controversy;[23] he is emphasizing the point that in contested jury trials a judge has the power to exclude matter which is superfluous, trivial or prejudicial; he is accordingly called on to make preliminary judgements about what is worth considering; the result is that the jury does not have access to all of the potentially relevant data that is considered by the historian or the naturalist.[23] The proponents of 'minimal relevancy' do not deny that the judge performs this filtering role and that this involves him in the task of making some judgements of weight. What they object to is subsuming all of these matters under the notion of 'relevancy'.[24] In their view three questions need to be differentiated: (1) is there *any* connection between this item of evidence and one or more facts in issue? (relevance); (2) is the evidence nevertheless to be excluded on the ground that its probative value is too slight to be worth considering?; (3) does its prejudicial effect outweigh its probative value? In the context of disputed jury trials it is probably fair to say that it is of little or no practical consequence whether one treats this as one test or three and whether one confines the notion of relevancy to the first question or broadens it to cover the other two.[25] However, the broader usage of 'relevancy' is less precise and has little to be said in its favour. Morever, questions about relevancy arise at other stages in legal proceedings and in other arenas; in these other contexts the narrower and more precise usage assists clear thinking. Indeed, in other contexts Wigmore himself quite clearly distinguishes between relevancy and sufficiency[26] and relevancy and probative force.[27] From this point of view Wigmore's notion of 'plus value' muddies the waters by conflating analytical questions about the concept of 'relevance' and institutional questions about the respective roles of judge and jury.

The third criticism is less straightforward: under either theory it is generally agreed that judges are sometimes called on to take the probative value of particular items of evidence into account in order to determine their admissibility; to point out that this may sometimes give rise to both theoretical and practical difficulties, highlights a problem, but is hardly a criticism of Wigmore.[28]

The precedent value of decisions on relevancy Another criticism of the theory of legal relevancy relates to precedent. Stephen had tried to subsume all of the law of evidence under the principle of relevancy.

Thayer attacked this by firmly stating that relevancy is a matter of logic and not of law.[29] Wigmore quoted Thayer's statements with approval, but glossed them by arguing that there are thousands of judicial rulings which deal with pure questions of inference and probative value and that these should be studied as precedents.[30] These 'rules of relevancy' may be based on logic, but 'so long as Courts continue to declare in judicial rulings what their notions of logic are, just so long will there be rules of law that must be observed. For these rules the only appropriate place is the Law of Evidence.'[31]

Wigmore's thesis, which was seen as one aspect of his 'doctrine of legal relevancy', was severely criticized by George James on the grounds that precedent is useless in this context because every case is unique, an argument that echoes Bentham.[32] He advocated a return to Thayer's position and this was generally accepted by both commentators and the courts. It became the basis for Rule 401 of the Federal Rules of Evidence.[33]

Recently Tillers has challenged both James' interpretation of Wigmore's position and his ground for rejecting it. In Tillers' view, Wigmore was not suggesting that the law reports should be treated as a source of binding precedents on questions of relevancy; rather he saw them as repositories of judicial experience and hence as representing one special kind of source of general experience – what might be termed 'legal experience'. He argues that James' emphasis on the uniqueness of individual cases is greatly exaggerated and could be applied *pari passu* to other areas of law in which precedents are used.[34]

Tillers' interpretation has its attractions: it explains why Wigmore cited Thayer with seeming approval before going on to expound his own, apparently inconsistent, doctrine; it suggests that this aspect of the doctrine of 'legal relevancy' can be reconciled with Wigmore's rejection of the idea of rules of weight;[35] and, historically, it fits in with a view in vogue at the time that the law reports could be viewed not only as authoritative sources of law but also, as Corbin put it, as 'a mighty storehouse of facts'.[36] This helps to explain Charles C. Moore's extraordinary compendium *A Treatise on Facts*, which Wigmore himself gently criticized.[37] It is also consistent with his general respect for professional opinion based on tradition and accumulated practical experience.[38] Unfortunately, he quite explicitly talked in terms of precedents on relevance producing *rules of law* and was rightly criticized for doing so. The matter is now mainly of historical interest since it seems clear that, whatever interpretation one puts on Wigmore, it is Thayer's formulation that is generally accepted.[39]

The relationship between the Science and the Rules

Wigmore made his reputation, and a substantial amount of money, as the

156   *Theories of Evidence*

leading writer on the *law* of evidence. Yet in the first chapter of the *Principles* he states firmly that the study of the science of proof deserves to be given a higher priority than the study of 'the artificial legal rules peculiar to our Anglo-American jury system'.[40] The principles of proof should be studied before the rules; the process of proof is the most important aspect of the trial; the artificial trial rules might be abolished 'yet the principles of Proof would remain, so long as trials remain as a rational attempt to seek the truth in legal controversies'.[41] Furthermore, he implied, there had hitherto been an imbalance in the amount of attention paid to the two subjects.

Bentham established a clear distinction between questions of admissibility and questions of weight and credibility. Wigmore carried the matter further by insisting that the Science of Proof and the Rules of Evidence represent distinct fields of inquiry.[42] Yet he maintained that there was a close connection between the two. We have seen that the *Principles* and the *Treatise* were based on a shared conceptual framework and even overlapped to some extent, so that it is more accurate to treat Wigmore's principles of proof as part of an integrated theory of evidence and proof. In an appendix to the *Principles*, he summarized the relationship as follows:

1. That there *is a close relation* between the Science and the Trial Rules – analogous to the relation between the scientific principles of nutrition and digestion and the rules of diet as empirically discovered and practiced by intelligent families.
2. That the Trial Rules are, in a broad sense, *founded upon* the Science; but that the practical conditions of trials bring into play certain limiting considerations not found in the laboratory pursuit of the Science, and therefore the Rules do not and *cannot always coincide* with the principles of the Science.
3. That for this reason the principles of the Science, as a whole, cannot be expected to *replace* the Trial Rules; the Rules having their own right to exist independently.
4. But that, for the same reason, the principles of the Science may at certain points *confirm the wisdom* of the Trial Rules, and may at other points *demonstrate the unwisdom* of the Rules.[43]

The homely dietary analogy is best interpreted as an attempt at a vivid contrast between an emergent science and aspects of a traditional practical art that are likely to atrophy in large part over time as science and reason progress. The rules are in need of considerable simplification and revision, but not complete abolition.[44] But the time was not yet ripe for radical reform, according to Wigmore, for two main reasons: first, the Science has not been developed very far;[45] secondly, it would be dangerous to introduce a radical simplification of the law until practitioners and judges have been equipped with a basic knowledge of the

Wigmore on proof 157

science.[46] It is a sobering thought that in the twenty-four years between the first and third editions of the *Principles*, Wigmore made so little progress that he made identical disclaimers for his science, as being a tentative first effort.

In the appendix to the *Principles*, Wigmore accounts for the continuing need for rules of admissibility largely in terms of differences between the conditions of the laboratory and of the courtroom. The purpose of the rules is to determine whether a given piece of evidence should be considered; it is not to establish the precise probative value to be attached to each individual item or to a mixed mass of evidence in a case.[47] The historian, the naturalist or other scientist applies a single mind to the whole process of collection, sifting and evaluation of data. But, in litigation, roles are differentiated: the parties gather and present the evidence; the judge acts as a filter, ensuring that only 'appreciably useful data'[48] are submitted to the jury, whose role it is to determine finally questions of credibility and weight.

Why, asks Wigmore, should there by any need for rejecting evidential data of inferior value?[49] The answer rests primarily on four main conditions which differentiate the courtroom from the laboratory. First, a trial must be held at a fixed time and place and there is a need for immediate and final decision.[50] Secondly, 'a judicial tribunal deals with issues of fact that have become the subject of controversy between human beings moved by strong emotions and constantly tempted to gain their cause by fraud or other means of deceiving the tribunal'.[51] Accordingly the legislator must provide securities against characteristic dangers arising from the adversary nature of the proceedings. To suggest that this should be done by exclusionary rules represents an un-Benthamite solution to a problem expressed in Benthamite terms.[52] Thirdly, the laboratory is typically manned by experts; but so extensive is the reach of the law that even experienced judges are generalists; in any trial time also needs to be saved by rejecting trivial data and avoiding proliferation of issues.[53] In jury trials, ordinary inexperienced citizens are called on to assess the evidence: 'Hence the trial rules may well guard against the jurors being misled by specially plausible but weak evidence or against being perplexed and misguided by a confusion of petty data which have only trivial probative value.'[54] Finally, unlike the quiet, solitary, matter-of-fact routine of the laboratory, 'the courtroom is a place of surging emotions, distracting episodes and sensational surprises'.[55] Accordingly special safeguards are needed to prevent the emotional conditions of litigation from unduly influencing the reasoning processes of the tribunal.

This, in a nutshell form, is Wigmore's rationale for the rules of admissibility. It is elaborated and refined in the *Treatise* both in general terms and in his exhaustive consideration of the reasons for particular doctrines.[56] Even in this simplified version, Wigmore explains and

158 *Theories of Evidence*

justifies the survival of the exclusionary rules by reference to several factors. In the historical debate on the origins of the rules of evidence, it is sometimes alleged that Wigmore, like Thayer, attributed the origin and the survival of the exclusionary rules solely to the institution of the jury.[57] This is too simple. It is true that Wigmore's historical account follows Thayer's quite closely, but he is careful to emphasize the complexity of the story. In the present context, he is concerned with the rationale for the *continuation* of rules of admissibility in a system where they are taken to be 'on their best behavior', that is to say liberally and flexibly interpreted and applied in accordance with their reasons.[58] These reasons include conditions to be found in any system of adjudication, notably constraints of time, place and expense, the necessity for final decision, and the emotional conditions of most disputes. The special features of Anglo-American trials, the jury and the adversary system of procedure, are important; but they are not the only factors justifying the survival of some exclusionary rules. Thus Wigmore sees the rules of admissibility as having a continuing role to play as artificial constraints on the operation of what would otherwise be a natural system of proof based only on the science. The latter provides the main, but not the only, criterion for evaluating particular rules.

The last half of Wigmore's appendix is devoted to a succinct assessment of the wisdom and unwisdom of the main rules of evidence in the light of the science.[59] It is an illuminating and convenient précis of views about the soundness of evidence doctrines and the bearing of the science on the exclusionary rules as applied in jury trials.[60] But this account is neither as comprehensive nor as systematic as it may seem. On its own, it could give a misleading impression of the place of the science in Wigmore's general conception of a theory of evidence and proof. It is incomplete in four main respects: it concentrates on the rules of admissibility, which do not constitute the whole of the law of evidence; by focusing on the science as the basis for the rules, it does not adequately stress its significance in areas where the rules have little or no importance; it deals with jury trials and says almost nothing about non-jury trials and adjudicative decisions by other tribunals; and it gives an incomplete picture of Wigmore's attitude to the reform of the rules of evidence. In order to gain a more complete picture of his views on these matters, we need to look to some of his other writings. From these it will appear that his science is not as narrowly focused as the appendix to the *Principles* might suggest.

The scope of the Rules Wigmore's *Treatise* covers much more than the rules of admissibility. Firstly, it deals with matters of procedure governing the presentation of evidence, in particular by whom evidence is presented, to whom, and in what order.[61] Secondly, it deals with the

Wigmore on proof 159

general question of what facts-in-issue evidence needs to be presented. This refers especially to the topics of judicial notice and admissions.[62] Thirdly, the general heading of rules of auxiliary probative policy (such as burdens of proof and presumptions) includes a number of categories in addition to that of exclusionary rules: preferential, analytic [hearsay], prophylactic, simplificative, and quantitative rules.[63] The *Treatise* also deals with rules of extrinsic policy, notably those governing illegally obtained evidence and various kinds of privilege.[64] These, says Wigmore, have no relation to the principles of proof as 'they frankly exclude good evidence on other grounds of policy which are supposed to override the policy of obtaining all possible useful evidence'.[65] Finally, the *Treatise* includes, for reasons of practical convenience, the Parole Evidence Rules, although they are strictly part of substantive law rather than the law of evidence. Nevertheless, Wigmore notes, the empirical basis of these rules is supported by the science in that written contracts are less susceptible than oral to errors in perception, recollection and narration of exact words.[66]

Both in his general introduction to the *Principles* and in his discussion of the relation between the Science of Proof and the Trial Rules, Wigmore seems to treat the Law of Evidence as being co-extensive with the rules of admissibility. This is clearly inconsistent with the *Treatise*, but it is probably best treated as a case of Homer nodding, for in the appendix to the *Principles* Wigmore does in fact deal, although rather cursorily, with most of the different types of rules of evidence. Surprisingly he makes no systematic attempt to relate the Science to the law relating to burdens and standards of proof, presumptions and judicial notice. However, his views can be inferred from his treatment of these topics in the *Treatise*.[67] The first three are closely related. They are essentially rules for decision in situations of uncertainty. Their omission from the appendix may be symptomatic of a more general weakness of his theory, viz. that it does not focus squarely on *deciding* as a crucial aspect of the process of proof.[68]

The scope of the science So much for the positive aspect of the relationship between the principles of proof and the rules of evidence. There is, of course, an important negative aspect, i.e., those parts of probative processes which are not governed by formal rules. Like Bentham, Wigmore maintains that it is not the role of the law of evidence to measure and establish probative value.[69] The law does not prescribe that any preference should be given to testimonial over circumstantial evidence. He contends that in nearly all circumstances where former rules of exclusion – such as the old law of competency – have been curtailed or abolished, the changes have generally been in conformity with the Science. Appropriate modes of reasoning from evidence are

160 Theories of Evidence

governed by principles of reasoning rather than rules of law and, as we have seen, he claimed that there is little or nothing that is unique about the modes of reasoning involved in arguments about disputed questions of fact in legal processes.[70]

These are all examples of aspects of proof on which the rules are almost completely silent, but which fall within the province of the science. But that is still to understate the point. The rules of admissibility are actually or potentially important only in some cases in some areas. In such cases, the science is also important quite independently of its relationship to the rules. Wigmore specifically mentions two stages where 'the practitioner needs some acquaintance with the science of proof, viz. (a) the pre-trial gathering and analysis of his evidential data, and (b) the explanation of the probative force of those data in his argument to the jury'.[71]

Even this is an understatement: for there are other participants, for example, detectives and jurors, for whom the science is central, but the rules are of little or no *direct* practical importance.[72] Moreover, there are many disputed cases in which the rules play only a minor role. To put the matter simply, the rules of evidence are only important in some cases and at some stages of those cases; the science of proof bears on all stages of all disputed cases.

Non-jury adjudication Wigmore was, of course, well aware that the rules of evidence had primary importance in trials by jury, which even in the United States constitute a very small proportion, although an important one, of all adjudicative processes. In the *Treatise* he dealt explicitly with the application of the law of evidence to non-jury trials and to a wide variety of other proceedings.[73] He also considered waiver of the rules in jury trials and contracts made before trial to alter or to waive the jury-trial rules.[74] In his *Textbook* he summarized his perception of the overall picture as follows:

> The jury trial rules of evidence originated in jury trial, being peculiar to the historical control of the judge over the jury . . . . Hence they do not, in principle or in policy, apply as a matter of law to bind the judge or presiding officer in any other form of tribunal. But in the course of events, they have come to have an important influence in the procedure of other tribunals. The chief reason was that the study and use of the jury-trial rules led them to be looked upon and venerated by the Bar as the systematic instrument for judicial ascertainment of truth, and that in almost all other tribunals the judges and the counsel were men in whose minds the rules had been indelibly ingrained.[75]

Thus Wigmore intellectually grasped the important point that jury trials represent only one part of the total picture of all adjudicative processes, but he followed convention by treating them not only as the

Wigmore on proof 161

most important but also as the paradigm case for the study of proof in adjudication. Accordingly, it is again worth stressing the distinction between his conception of a science of proof which is broad enough to encompass a wide variety of legal processes, and his exposition, which concentrates on the jury trial.[76]

Reform of the rules of evidence

In the appendix comparing the science and the rules, Wigmore placed far more emphasis on the role of the law of evidence as a means for promoting the search for truth than on its role in constraining that search in the interest of other values and policies. He treated rules of extrinsic policy as falling outside the purview of this comparison.[77] Accordingly he excluded from consideration some of the most controversial aspects of evidence doctrine, such as illegally obtained evidence, the privilege against self-incrimination and other privileges. These were, of course, extensively discussed in the *Treatise*. In any general discussion of reform of the law of evidence, the rules of extrinsic policy are likely to command at least as much attention as other topics, such as exceptions to the hearsay rule. Accordingly, the appendix to the *Principles* does not deal with all aspects of Wigmore's views on the value and future of the rules of evidence. Another aspect of his attitude to the rules that does not emerge very clearly from the *Principles* and that provides a striking contrast to Bentham, is Wigmore's assumption that the law of evidence is *par excellence* 'lawyer's law'.[78] Wigmore was only mildly critical of surviving evidence doctrine.[79] A general simplification and the abolition of a few archaic survivals would be welcome, but on the whole there was no need for radical reform. In the introduction to his *Textbook*, he stressed the good sense and the rationality of most of the rules: '[It] is important to remember that all of the fundamental rules have some *reason* underneath. They are not arbitrary. Their aim is to get at the truth by calm and careful reasoning.'[80]

Wigmore was far more critical of abuses and misinterpretations of the rules than of the rules themselves:

> Our *judges* and our *practitioners* must *improve in spirit*, as a prerequisite for any hope of real gain to be got from better rules. In the end, the man is more important than the rule. Better rules will avail little, if the spirit of using them does not also improve . . . .
>
> ALL THE RULES IN THE WORLD WILL NOT GET US SUBSTANTIAL JUSTICE IF THE JUDGES AND THE COUNSEL HAVE NOT THE CORRECT LIVING MORAL ATTITUDE TOWARDS SUBSTANTIAL JUSTICE.[81]

Implicit in this view is the notion that legislative or judicial reform of the law of evidence is likely to be much less important in practice than changes in attitude on the part of the main users of the rules, that is to

162   *Theories of Evidence*

say, the legal profession and the judiciary. This judgement seems to have contributed to Wigmore adopting a cautious, pragmatic attitude to attempts to make sweeping changes in the law.[82]

These issues came into sharp focus shortly before his death. In 1939 the American Law Institute announced a project to prepare a Model Code of Evidence.[83] Professor Edmund Morgan was appointed Reporter, with Wigmore as Chief Consultant. At the time Wigmore was seventy-six years old, Morgan was fifteen years his junior. For many years Morgan was one of Wigmore's most persistent, if respectful, critics. He took issue with him in print on a number of topics, notably relevancy, the functions of judge and jury as to questions of fact preliminary to admissibility, presumptions, the classification of hearsay, and vicarious admissions.[84]

Sharp differences soon emerged between Wigmore and Morgan over the general approach to the A.L.I. Code project. These were made public when Wigmore dissociated himself from Tentative Draft No.1 of the proposed Code.[85] There were in fact three main views on the best strategy to adopt to the project. Judge Charles E. Clark recommended virtually the total abolition of the law of evidence;[86] Morgan and his advisers prepared a draft which involved a radical simplification and reduction of the scope of the law, but still retained a nucleus of specific rules;[87] Wigmore recommended that a detailed draft should be prepared which would contain specific confirmation or repudiation of every concrete rule adopted by a majority of jurisdictions. Although he was prepared to recommend a number of changes, he was not prepared to go nearly as far as either Morgan or Clark. In his view each rule should be 'directory, not mandatory' to the judge whose rulings would be subject to review only in extreme instances.[88] In recommending guidelines rather than rules, Wigmore moved quite close to Bentham's notion of 'cautionary instructions'.[89] However, he suggested that the guidelines should cover every detail and he offered his own 550-page Code of Evidence as the model.

The draft prepared by Morgan and his advisers proceeded on a different basis. It began by a general declaration of the Thayerite principle that all relevant evidence is admissible except as otherwise provided by a specific rule. It abolished all disqualifications and privileges of witnesses. The effect of their proposals would have been to make sweeping inroads into the existing laws. However, the surviving exceptions to the general principle of admissibility would have the status of rules and were in some cases tightly drafted in a style reminiscent of that of English statutes.[90]

Wigmore objected that the first draft represented too sharp a departure from the existing law in both style and substance and that it did not give sufficiently clear and detailed guidance to judges and practitioners.[91] Judge Clark, on the other hand, argued that Morgan's draft was

Wigmore on proof 163

too detailed and proposed that even greater discretion should be granted to the judge.[92]

At the very start of the project Wigmore had submitted six 'postulates' as the basis for a general approach to drafting.[93] They included acceptability and comprehensibility to the legal profession, that they should be concrete and comprehensive and that the rules should be 'guides, not chains – directory, not mandatory'. Morgan claimed that he and his advisers accepted all the postulates except the one requiring detailed rules rather than general principles and that the draft Rules substantially conformed to Wigmore's postulates.[94] Wigmore disagreed and set out his criticisms of the draft at length in an article in *The American Bar Association Journal*.[95]

The differences between Wigmore and Morgan were more profound and far-reaching than this public exchange reveals. Morgan's concern was to secure a radical reduction in the scope of the exclusionary rules and to leave much more to judicial discretion. The purpose of precise drafting was generally to limit the scope of mandatory rules of exclusion. The outcome would almost certainly have been that far more evidence would be admitted in practice. Wigmore wished to move in a similar direction, but very much more cautiously. This may reflect tension between his concern for rationality and his deference to the legal profession, in respect of its power as well as its experience. There may also have been an element of vested interest, for this episode is reminiscent of the clash between Williston and Llewellyn over the Uniform Commercial Code.[96] In each case the leading scholar of an earlier generation resisted changes in form and substance in his area of expertise and justified this opposition partly in terms of the established ways of thought of the practising profession. In each case the older scholar was vulnerable to charges of having a vested interest in the *status quo*, as both Williston and Wigmore were well aware. In both cases their fears were justified, for the Uniform Commercial Code and, later, the Federal Rules of Evidence accelerated the demise of their treatises.

Wigmore's view of the rules of evidence was that, by and large, they represented the accumulated wisdom of the 'trial experience of generations'; that their function was to provide *detailed* guidance to lawyers as the basis for normal routine at trial and competent preparation beforehand; that these objectives could best be served by rules that were directory, not mandatory, but which covered all points of detail and were expressed in a simple, but familiar terminology. The Bench and Bar needed to be educated in the science of proof, to be cajoled into approaching the rules in a flexible and liberal spirit and to be helped by detailed guidance. But ultimately, the test of any reform was its acceptability to the legal profession, the users of the rules. He concluded that 'this draft Evidence Code is not one that Bench and Bar could stand'.[97] The contrast between the attitudes to the legal profession of

164   *Theories of Evidence*

Bentham and Wigmore could hardly be greater.

This deference to the settled ways of thought of lawyers had disastrous consequences. Wigmore's 'Science' is significant largely because it provides a coherent alternative to traditional conceptions of the subject of evidence. In legal discourse generally, and in legal education and legal writing in particular, far more attention has been, and still is, paid to the rules of evidence than to problems and possible principles of proof. Worse than that the subject of evidence is typically treated as being co-extensive with the law of evidence; topics such as probabilities, which are not governed by legal rules, are either totally ignored or uneasily slotted into discussions of the law; books and courses on evidence are either very narrowly conceived, incoherently organized, or both. Wigmore boldly claimed that the science of proof is broader than, anterior to and of more practical importance than the rules of evidence. But instead of driving the point home by argument and example, he played it down, thereby pandering to the prejudices and inertia of his audiences and seriously underselling his theory. His idea of a science of proof is better known through the *Treatise* and his students' *Textbook of the Law of Evidence*, where, since they are primarily works of exposition, not unnaturally the science is subordinated to the rules. Even his appendix to the *Principles*, perhaps inadvertently, has the effect of weakening his thesis. The result has been that evidence doctrine has yet to be put in its proper place as just one part of the science of proof; instead, in so far as the science has not been entirely ignored, it has typically been treated as a satellite of the law of evidence. That is rather like treating England as a suburb of London.

(viii) The lead balloon

The *Principles of Judicial Proof* remained in print for over thirty years in three editions. It received warm reviews in the United States and abroad, including some by such prominent figures as Zachariah Chafee, Judge Hutcheson, Charles C. Moore and Lord Wright.[1] Wesley Newcomb Hohfeld was among those who provided a statement for promotional purposes.[2] Each edition incorporated substantial changes, which were on the whole acknowledged to be improvements. Wigmore was still collecting material for a fourth edition at the time of his death.[3] Yet, the fact remains that the *Principles* made almost no visible impact on American legal thought, on legal education or on evidence scholarship.[4] The records of Wigmore's correspondence with his publishers reveal that the work was sold almost entirely to libraries and to individuals, the main exception being students taking the author's own courses on proof. A modest flow of sales appears to have been maintained largely to practitioners, many of whom enjoyed the accounts of famous trials and skipped the analytical sections.[5] To this day there has hardly been any

Wigmore on proof 165

sustained discussion in print of Wigmore's notion of a science of proof nor of particular aspects, such as his chart method, his account of the logical processes involved, and his, often excellent, analysis of the problems of proving different kinds of fact.[6] Some reviewers made occasional critical observations, most commonly about his use of symbols, but for the most part they were content to praise the work in general terms as a contribution of both theoretical and practical significance.[7] Occasional references to the work are to be found scattered in the literature over a long period of time. More often than not they treated it as nothing more than a quaint, even bizarre, period-piece.[6] It was not unknown, but it was ignored.

Even more striking is the fact that a major book, designed as a students' work – text, cases, materials, exercises – appears hardly to have been adopted outside Northwestern. The evidence is incomplete, but the record in the Wigmore papers suggests that parts of the book were occasionally recommended in a few college courses, mainly in departments of philosophy and psychology; the author has found only one report of an adoption of the work as a course book in another law school, by Dean George Ayres of Idaho.[8] In the later correspondence with Little, Brown it is clear that, at least by the mid-1930s, it was taken for granted that the main sales would be among practitioners, with a possible untapped secondary market among non-lawyers.[9]

Wigmore himself practised what he preached. From 1913 until shortly before his death, he regularly offered a course based on the book. In the early years this was known as Evidence I, it was compulsory, and it preceded the course on the rules (Evidence II). But even at Northwestern its position in the curriculum was gradually eroded. In the period 1919–24 it appeared variously as a third-year option, as an offering in the summer programme and as a foundation course, sometimes with reduced weight. Then, from 1924, it was re-established on a regular basis as Evidence I, but only as a one-hour course, until Wigmore's retirement in 1933. Thereafter he offered it for several years in the summer session.[10] It is not quite accurate to say that Proof was a required two-hour foundation course while Wigmore was Dean, that it was given a reduced status in the curriculum when he ceased to be Dean, and that after his retirement it was relegated to the summer programme. But this is not very far from the truth. What is significant is that Wigmore seems to have been the only law teacher who used the *Principles* as a course book, except for Ayres (and Kocoureck, who once jointly taught Evidence I with Wigmore).

Thus, the *Principles* seems to have sunk like the proverbial lead balloon. It was kept in view for a number of years by the steady, if unspectacular, persistence of its progenitor. It is not uncommon for works of acknowledged academic excellence to make little or no impact on scholarship or education in their own time. It is not difficult to suggest

166 Theories of Evidence

some commonsense explanations for this particular failure: for example, the approach was novel; few law teachers could be expected to feel either competent or confident enough to teach Wigmore's science, even if they were persuaded by its rightness. The enthusiasm for new-fangled ideas, such as polygraphs, graphology and psychometry, the strange terminology and, above all, the use of symbols, all suggest the Wigmore of 'Old Northwestern' and *A Panorama of the World's Legal Systems* rather than the author of the *Treatise* and master of the law of evidence. If challenged, many American law teachers would point to the Bar examinations, almost exclusively concerned with exclusionary rules, as a major constraint on curriculum in this area. Wigmore's behaviour suggests that he never lost faith in the idea of a science of proof, but he did remarkably little to try to sell the idea. He was not himself an inspiring classroom teacher and he did not very actively try to proselytize others. The *Principles* was left to speak for itself.

In the circumstances this was not enough. There are some general factors which tend to explain the relative neglect of the study of non-doctrinal aspects of evidence, proof and fact-finding – the toughness and conservatism of the rule-centred tradition of academic law; a widespread feeling that much of what is encompassed by Wigmore's science is best left to be picked up in practice; a fear that probing beneath the surface of evidentiary processes may open a Pandora's box of doubts and difficulties; and, perhaps surprising in the context of American law schools, a certain submissiveness and lack of self-confidence on the part of law teachers.[11] A further factor was a failure to perceive the close connection between the *Treatise* and the *Principles*. Wigmore maintained to the end that the principles of proof are anterior to and more important than the rules of evidence. He thought that the rules would decrease in scope and complexity over time, but not to the extent that they would completely disappear; as they became simpler the importance of the science of proof would become more apparent. By presenting the fullest and clearest exposition of the general theory underlying most of his *Treatise* in a work that looked like a cross between a student's course book and a coffee-table anthology, Wigmore inadvertently contributed to the narrow and myopic view of evidence that he was seeking to undermine.

Such considerations may explain the failure and subsequent neglect of the *Principles*, but they do not justify it. In the final chapter, I shall suggest why, forty years after the author's death, some aspects of this unusual work are still of value. Enough has been said here to show that this is a *magnum opus* of John Henry Wigmore, one of the greatest systematic legal scholars of all time, rather than of Colonel Wigmore, the folksy American intellectual tourist with wide-ranging but simple tastes in literature, gadgets and architecture.

4

The contemporary significance of Bentham and Wigmore

There are several kinds of reasons for treating past thinkers as being worthy of attention at a given time in a particular place or places. A jurist may be considered to be significant because of his place in the history of ideas, as someone who has been thought to be original or influential or representative; or because he had some influence on historical events, as has been claimed for Bentham in connection with many reforms in the nineteenth century in England and elsewhere; or because he is still worth reading on one or other of several grounds.

The historical importance of both Bentham and Wigmore in the history of Anglo-American thought about evidence is incontestable. Commentators may dispute the extent of Bentham's 'influence' on particular reforms or whether the success of Wigmore's *Treatise* was an unmixed blessing. There cannot be much room for doubt that, apart perhaps from Thayer, they are the two leading figures – representative as well as influential – in a remarkably homogeneous and tough tradition that still dominates most contemporary thought about evidence. If the thesis is correct that what has been called the Rationalist Tradition of Evidence scholarship is based on a set of broadly-shared assumptions about adjudication and proof then, at least at the level of theory, the similarities between them are more important than the differences. The question arises whether and in what respects they still deserve attention apart from their historical importance? This chapter addresses this question in relation to each of them separately and to the current status of the Rationalist Tradition as a whole.

Why read Bentham on evidence today? How much is still worth reading? It is, of course, easy to exaggerate the contemporary significance of an eighteenth-century figure, however great his stature. There is much repetition and dead wood in the *Rationale* and Bentham's other writings on evidence, as even his contemporaries pointed out. In 1876 Fitzjames Stephen wrote that 'during the last generation or more Bentham's influence has to some extent declined, partly because some of his books are like exploded shells, buried under the ruins which they have made . . .'[1] Stephen was probably referring to such matters as the general contraction of the scope of the law of evidence, the almost total disappearance of the rules of competency (though in England the

168   *Theories of Evidence*

accused could still not testify on oath),[2] improvements in provision for what Bentham called pre-appointed evidence, and numerous other particular reforms in adjective law and judicial organization. These had tended in the general direction that Bentham had charted, although in a piecemeal fashion that he would have condemned.

Since Stephen's day, the rules of evidence have slowly continued to diminish in importance. The process has gone further in England than in the United States, especially in respect of civil litigation. The trend may continue, but it seems very unlikely that either the Natural System of Procedure or the anti-nomian thesis will be accepted as fundamental principles for the design of our systems of adjudication in the forseeable future.

At this very general level there are perhaps three main reasons for the partial failure of Bentham's prescriptions. First, pure utilitarianism was never fully accepted as the basis for law reform. Many of our existing institutions, rules and practices in adjective law reflect compromises between Benthamite utilitarianism on the one hand and a mixture of notions of due process and professional pragmatism on the other. The latter attitude is generally inimical in both spirit and substance to Bentham's uncompromising rationalism. A major factor in explaining the differences between current arrangements and practices in England and the United States is the relative strength in the two countries of such non-utilitarian ideas as procedural rights.

A second, closely-related factor, is that evidence and procedure are still generally seen as belonging to the sphere of 'lawyers' law'. In the present context this elusive term refers to areas of law in respect of which it is felt appropriate to give great weight to the practical experience and mastery of detail of practising lawyers. Stephen criticized Bentham for failing to recognize the substantial merits of the system he criticized, a system 'full of sagacity and experience' of a kind that Bentham lacked.[3] Wigmore, too, often made enlightened professional opinion an important touchstone in his assessment of particular provisions or proposals for reform. What was castigated by Bentham as interest-begotten prejudice is widely regarded by others as practical wisdom. Even in the seemingly perpetual, and often quite politicized, debates on 'balancing' the interests of accused persons against other considerations, professional ideology[4] has tended to play an important role. It has been the dominant force in other areas of adjective law that are perceived as being more 'technical'. By and large, lawyers have continued to defend the adversary process and many particular features of the technical system that Bentham attacked.

A third major factor is, of course, passage of time. In a review of the *Book of Fallacies* Sydney Smith suggested that the great mass of readers needed a middle-man between them and Mr Bentham, 'after that eminent philosopher has been washed, trimmed, shaved and forced into

The contemporary significance of Bentham and Wigmore   169

clean linen.'[5] In the 150 years since his death, some of his ideas on evidence have ceased to be interesting because they have become commonplace – for example, the distinction between weight and admissibility of evidence – some battles have been won, others have been forgotten. Economic, political, social and technological changes have produced a strikingly different context for considering issues affecting adjective law – or rather one should say contexts, for the situations in the United States and England are not the same. The conditions of litigation today in both countries are vastly different from those obtaining in 1800. Developments in philosophy, psychology, statistics, forensic science and in other relevant fields have also rendered some of Bentham's ideas of no more than historical interest.

Given all this, what is remarkable is the extent to which Bentham's central concerns and themes still have resonance today. Which ideas and how much resonance is partly a matter of opinion. All that will be attempted here is to express some general judgements on which aspects of his writings on evidence seem to the author to be still worth studying, if at all, by five classes of person: Bentham scholars; jurists; students of evidence; participants in debates on law reform and legal practitioners.

Bentham scholars have often remarked on the importance of his writings on evidence in the context of his work as a whole; but they have not given them a corresponding amount of attention. Halévy's excellent treatment of adjective law in only twenty-seven pages has yet to be bettered.[6] Bentham's work on evidence between 1803 and 1813 represents a watershed in his intellectual development: it follows the relatively fallow period of the 1890s when, it has been suggested, he experienced a midlife crisis;[7] it coincides with changes in his political views and it precedes the prolific later years during which he wrote, *inter alia*, *The Constitutional Code*, *Scotch Reform*, *The Principles of Judicial Procedure*, the later manuscripts on logic, fictions and fallacies and a number of *opera minora*. The *Rationale* was the most substantial and coherent work to be published in his lifetime; it is so closely integrated into the general fabric of his thought and it touches on such a wide range of topics that it illuminates Bentham's ideas on many issues. One purpose of the present work is to make this flawed masterpiece more accessible.

In the specialized field of evidence, Bentham's is the most comprehensive general theory of the subject. Wigmore is the main rival but, as we have seen, Bentham's thought on evidence has the great strength of being part of a general theory of procedure and adjudication which in turn belongs to a comprehensive legal and political philosophy. The connections between evidence and epistemology, logic and political theory are more clearly mapped than in any other theory of evidence. This is particularly important today precisely because the study of the subject has suffered in modern times by virtue of its artificial isolation

170 Theories of Evidence

from adjacent fields of study. This also makes it of considerable significance as a work of general, as well as applied, jurisprudence.

Another reason for his continuing significance is that Bentham was so often prepared to take unequivocal and provocative positions on perennial questions. He is the foremost and most formidable champion of a truth theory of adjudication, of freedom of proof as a basic principle, and of utility as the only ultimate test of good and bad, of right and wrong. His attack on 'the fox-hunters' argument' and other alleged fallacies of sentimental liberalism assaults some central notions that the author, for one, considers to be worth defending, but not on the basis of bad arguments. The 'Natural System' may seem to be a non-starter as a model for modern complex litigation, but it has considerable explanatory potential as an ideal type; and the general challenge it offers to all artificial technicality and formality has an abiding appeal. Bentham was not alone in his day in attacking the excessive technicality of adjective law. What made his theory unique was that he attacked all formality. The fact that nearly all reforms of evidence and procedure since his day have tended in the direction that Bentham so boldly advocated also gives pause for thought. On these and other issues he still has a role to play, as a penetrating observer, as a powerful ally or as a formidable opponent.[8]

This tendency to take clear, often extreme, positions makes Bentham's writings a potentially attractive source of arguments and quotations for participants in contemporary public debates. The attraction is double-edged, especially for those who do not agree with many of his conclusions. To some of us Bentham's treatments of, for example, the presumption of innocence, the right to silence or punishment of the innocent appear unappealing, if not horrendous. Because nearly all of his views (utilitarian miscalculations excepted) are derived from a generally consistent philosophical position and because he was both a courageous and acute thinker, his arguments often cut deep. With disconcerting frequency they tend to show up the frailty of some of the standard arguments (or 'arguments') that are advanced to support civil-libertarian views. On the other hand, there is a danger that he will be quoted selectively and out of context by those who find his tough-minded positions on such issues appealing. For supporters of such views are very often conservatives or reactionaries who are far removed from the spirit of Benthamite radicalism. They would reject many of the conclusions to which his peculiar brand of critical rationalism would lead them.

An example of this kind of misuse of Bentham is to be found in the debate on criminal evidence that took place in England in 1972–3.[9] On that occasion his criticism of the 'right to silence' *in court* was quoted in support of moves to undermine the right to remain silent during *pre-trial* interrogation by the police. Yet his argument needs to be set in the context of his espousal of the Natural System, with its inquisitorial tendencies; and publicity, Bentham's primary safeguard, is conspicu-

The contemporary significance of Bentham and Wigmore 171

ously absent from police stations. Bentham is a much more thorough-going radical than the vast majority of contemporary critics and defenders of technical 'safeguards' in criminal processes. His views on such matters need to be seen in the context of his general theory of adjective law and of the very different conditions of criminal investigation and prosecution in the early nineteenth century. Perhaps his principal relevance to contemporary debates on such topics is that he presents a sharp challenge to the theoretical foundations of many civil-libertarian positions and that, to quote Professor Hart, 'on this subject as on others . . . where Bentham fails to persuade, he still forces us to think'.[10]

To a large extent, the same factors that contribute to Bentham's continuing significance at the level of theory reduce his appeal to practising lawyers and judges. The abstract nature of his concerns, his disdain for technical detail and his tendency to extremism made his writings at least appear to be remote from everyday practical concerns, even to his contemporaries. A few introspective or masochistic lawyers might enjoy his polemics against the legal profession; his attack on jargon has a wider appeal; the stark simplicity of his account of the direct and subordinate ends of procedure gives it a powerful cutting edge as a tool of analysis and argument. The *Rationale* is a rich source of quotable epigrams, but beyond that, even with the help of a middleman, Bentham is unlikely to commend himself to many modern practitioners. But then, one may ask, which jurists do?

One exception might be Wigmore. One of the sharpest contrasts between the two subjects of this study is that while Bentham attacked the legal profession from the outside, Wigmore wrote for it, though not uncritically, from within. The *Treatise* was addressed primarily to the legal profession, the *Principles* to intending practitioners. The theories of Bentham and Wigmore complement each other because, starting from very similar premises, they address significantly different questions. In assessing Wigmore's contemporary significance it is important to bear in mind that he was concerned with the detailed practical application of some quite simple general ideas. This makes him potentially more attractive to practitioners and law students, but more vulnerable to the passage of time.

What then is the contemporary significance of Wigmore's 'science'? Perhaps its primary importance is that it constitutes the theoretical basis of his *Treatise*. Bentham was a more original and influential theorist; Thayer may have been a more profound scholar; but neither of them wrote systematic treatises. In the history of Anglo-American legal scholarship no expository work has been so highly praised as *Wigmore on Evidence* and few can have been so influential. So long as this vast work continues to be used by practitioners and scholars, the relevant parts of the *Principles of Judicial Proof* are important because they contain the

172 Theories of Evidence

clearest and most systematic statement of Wigmore's general ideas.

But, it may be asked, has not the *Treatise* outlived its usefulness? Opinions differ on this point. By the time of Wigmore's death in 1943 his *magnum opus* was beginning to show signs of age. Commentators respectfully suggested that in his later years Wigmore had not always kept up with the periodical literature and that he often seemed disinclined to rethink his views in the light of recent case law or academic criticism. The portents were that it might soon go the way of all treatises.[11] However, in the forty years since his death the work has been kept alive by its immense reputation and authority, by the dedication and skill of some outstanding editors, and by the absence of rivals, the principal exception being Weinstein's *Evidence*, first published in 1975.[12] In some respects the refurbished *Wigmore* has clearly been improved, but not surprisingly over the years it has declined in coherence and authority and has come to appear increasingly old-fashioned.

Even in his youth Wigmore's views could have been considered fairly conservative by his contemporaries. Kocoureck affectionately called him 'the last Mid-Victorian'.[13] Wigmore was not afraid to proclaim his opinions and they influenced his treatment of many topics in evidence. Given that his attitudes to women and race and crime are hardly compatible with modern liberal opinion he seems ripe for debunking on such matters. The process has begun, but it is perhaps surprising that it has not yet proceeded very far. Wigmore's solemn conclusions that there is no evidence to support the notion that gender and race have a direct bearing on credibility of witnesses, for example, hardly disguises his underlying prejudices. A recent article suggests that his treatment of corroboration in rape cases is based on a selective and biased use of the scientific sources that were available to him.[14] Despite some skilful cosmetics, *Wigmore on Evidence* deports itself in a manner which, if not mid-Victorian, is hardly later than Edwardian. The *Principles* has not had the services of modern editors.

Despite such considerations, there are some cogent reasons for suggesting that it is an error to dismiss the *Principles* as a quaint period-piece, the only significance of which is as a satellite of an ageing masterpiece that has nearly run its course. Wigmore rightly claimed that his was the first attempt in English since Bentham to deal with the principles of proof *as a whole and as a system*.[15] In 1984 it appears that the *Principles* remains the only such attempt. It is true that on particular topics there are some more refined theories. For example, Michael and Adler's account of the logic involved is more sophisticated philosophically and more detailed; the recent debate on probabilities adds new refinements and complications and raises new issues; similarly modern works on forensic psychology and forensic science not only provide new answers to old questions, but also pose questions that had not been

The contemporary significance of Bentham and Wigmore 173

confronted or even envisaged in Wigmore's time. None of these attempts to provide a general framework for a coherent theory of evidence and proof, comparable to Wigmore's. Significant advances have been made in several specialized fields, but despite ritual pleas for inter-disciplinary co-operation, the general tendency of these studies has been centrifugal, with the result that such areas as the logic and psychology of proof, forensic science and scholarly work in the law of procedure and evidence are less closely integrated today than they were in 1937.[16]

The *Principles* remains the only modern attempt to develop a basis for an approach to the study of evidence which reaches systematically beyond the rules and seeks to incorporate the non-legal elements in a coherent framework. It can be argued that Wigmore's theory is narrowly conceived in that it concentrates too much on the courtroom and on the jury trial and does not take adequate account of the variety and complexity of legal processes.[17] But this is mainly to signal a limitation; in this respect his approach was broader than most subsequent treatments of evidence. In providing a coherent framework for the integrated study of the logical, legal, psychological, scientific and common-sense aspects of proof in jury trials, Wigmore took a major step forward. That he did so with his normal clarity, system, and mastery of detail should be sufficient warrant that it is of lasting value.

As we have seen, Wigmore's 'science' complements rather than supercedes Bentham's theory of evidence. They start from very similar conceptions about adjudication and the nature of proof, but they concentrate on different standpoints. Bentham's is a design theory addressed to the legislator; Wigmore is concerned to give detailed assistance to actual and intending practitioners. Much of his analysis belongs to middle-order theorizing, that is to say it is at a less abstract level than fundamental questions of philosophy, but it is not so particular as to be dependent on the survival of particular legal doctrines in a given jurisdiction. The rules of hearsay may change or disappear in a jungle of exceptions, but the problems to which hearsay doctrine is addressed remain relatively constant.

Thus, the *Principles* is still worth studying for its detailed treatment of the probative process involved in dealing with different types of *probanda* and for its analysis of particular examples. The reading must, of course, be selective, for some of the material is outdated, but to a remarkable extent, Wigmore's accounts of such topics as proof of design, alibis and identity are still among the best available in print.

It is at this level of generality that the value of the chart method needs to be assessed. Its uses and limitations and the validity of its underlying assumptions have already been extensively canvassed.[18] But its almost total neglect during Wigmore's lifetime and the continuing scepticism of teachers of evidence and others justify restating the case for taking it seriously. The chart method is a unique attempt to develop a systematic

174   *Theories of Evidence*

and disciplined approach to the evaluation of evidence. Nearly all of the few teachers who have used it testify to its educational value. In its purest and most rigorous form, it may be too laborious and elaborate for direct application to run-of-the-mill cases. But the method rests on a solid theoretical foundation and it can be shown to represent a systematization and rational reconstruction of the general approach adopted in a looser fashion by many experienced and effective practitioners when they are analysing and arguing about evidence. Like any tool, it has its limitations, but its full potential as a usable technique for attorneys, detectives, historians and others remains largely unexplored and under-exploited, especially in the computer age.

The two most telling criticisms that have been made of Wigmore's account of the method are that he gives insufficient guidance on how to evaluate particular kinds of evidence and that he begs questions about how judgements of probability can be combined.[19] In response to the first criticism it can be pointed out that he drew on the best material that was available at the time and that this is all that one can hope to do. Scientific advances in the last forty years or so have not in most respects left us noticeably better off. The second criticism has more force. The problem of combining probabilities is one central issue in the current debate between Baconians and Pascalians.[20] There is still no consensus about the applicable criteria. Wigmore's chart method helps us to organize a mass of evidence, but is less useful in guiding us in assessing its net probative force. That signals a limitation, but hardly undermines its validity.

What explains the continuing scepticism of both teachers and practitioners in the light of such claims? In the education context, any advocate of the method has first to overcome the inertia and conservatism of most academic lawyers. Many teachers of evidence continue to cling to the absurd fallacy that the subject of evidence is co-extensive with the rules of evidence. Others, more understandably, assert that they are not competent to teach the method. This is often due more to lack of confidence than to incompetence; both are quite easily remediable. Some argue that the basic technique can easily be picked up in practice without direct instruction. *Per contra*, others claim that too much time is required to master the basic skill.[21] The author's own experience suggests very strongly that the first claim is false, but this is a personal impression that has yet to be tested by empirical research. The second argument is part of a continuing debate about the kind of priority that should be accorded to direct teaching of basic legal skills.

The initial scepticism of practitioners is more understandable. For, at first sight, Wigmore's method appears to be an over-elaborate and time-consuming way of doing what experienced trial lawyers do anyway. In this view, the benefits are only likely to outweigh the costs in complex cases in which the stakes are high. Again, experience suggests otherwise,

The contemporary significance of Bentham and Wigmore 175

but such judgements have also yet to be tested and refined by systematic research.

There is, however, a further possible reason for initial scepticism about the chart method. It may be that Wigmore's presentation of his invention obscures its real nature. His emphasis on symbols and charts and the name he gave to the method may suggest gimmickry; they also divert attention from the point that what is involved is a simple application of elementary principles of logic to the rigorous rational analysis of evidence and construction and arguments about it. It is quite possible to use this kind of analysis without resort to symbols or charts. The main lessons that Wigmore teaches are, first, that logical analysis involves exploring relations between propositions that are often not articulated in ordinary discourse and secondly, that rigorous analysis is hard work. Behind the resistance of teachers and practitioners may lie a deeper scepticism or cynicism about the idea that rigorous rationality has much to do with trial practice.[22]

The chart method is of continuing significance in another important respect. It suggests one basis for broadening the range of standard materials of law study. It is a truism of the Anglo-American tradition of legal education that undue attention is paid to the law reports at the expense of other primary and secondary sources. It is less widely recognized that records of trials and secondary accounts of *causes célèbres* have immense and largely unexploited educational potential. The chart method is one way of analysing this kind of material in a disciplined manner. There are, of course, other possible uses of such material in legal education. It is to Wigmore's lasting credit that he both perceived the potential pedagogical value of this kind of material and made a sustained effort to introduce it into the curriculum. It is an ironic comment on both practising and academic lawyers that the fate of the *Principles* was to be treated as an entertaining anthology rather than as a path-breaking educational work.

Finally, the *Principles* stands second only to Bentham's *Rationale* as an outstanding contribution to the theory of evidence and proof. It has its faults, not least that much of the basic theory is asserted or assumed rather than argued. Like any book, it is a product of its time and of its author's individual concerns; much of the detail of the psychology and forensic science now seem outdated; the logic is both simple and old-fashioned; the author's opinions are those of a confident, conservative late Victorian. But this is not a quaint period-piece. The basic philosophical ideas are solidly grounded in a central tradition of empirical philosophy which is still thriving. The underlying legal theory also belongs to a central part of the Anglo-American tradition of academic law in general and of evidence scholarship in particular. Wigmore's 'science' is based on reputable, if not uncontroversial, assumptions about inductive logic and epistemology. It is a weakness of

176 *Theories of Evidence*

his presentation that he hardly acknowledges even the possibility of differing views with regard to his basic assumptions. Nevertheless, he is in good company. His logic is essentially part of the central tradition stemming from Bacon through John Stuart Mill to contemporary writers like Jonathan Cohen. His epistemology is similarly in the same tradition and finds support in the theory of knowledge expounded by A. J. Ayer. A more developed theory of evidence and proof would need to identify and acknowledge the existence of rival theories.

Thus, viewed analytically, the central ideas of the two leading theorists of evidence and proof in the common law tradition are sufficiently similar to be treated both as comparable and as complementing each other, in that they concentrated on rather different questions. Wigmore is not a rival to Bentham, nor did he, as his most important successor, supercede him. Together both theories still provide an excellent starting-point for exploring questions that ought to be treated as central to any theory of evidence. Some of these questions have been neglected. Bentham takes clear and challenging positions on many issues of current concern. Wigmore suggests one way of fitting the logical, legal, psychological and scientific aspects of evidence and proof within a single coherent framework. Yet each theory has important limitations that make it no more than a starting-point.

The most important of these limitations are shared by nearly all leading writers about evidence in the Anglo-American tradition. Boldly stated, this rich heritage suffers from two endemic weaknesses: narrowness of focus and too great an attachment to a single philosophical tradition that can be characterized as optimistic rationalism.[23]

Narrowness of focus is illustrated by Bentham and Wigmore. Both concentrate on *adjudicative decisions*, that is to say formal determinations of liability and guilt in respect of questions of fact by judges or juries in trials. They deal only peripherally, if it all, with the processing and determination of facts at other phases of legal process (such as negotiation and sentencing) or other arenas (such as arbitration and administrative tribunals). In his *Treatise* Wigmore does deal with the rules of evidence in other tribunals, but in the *Principles* the jury trial is treated as the prototype of all trials; what happens in the courtroom is treated as the fulcrum of all legal process; almost nothing is said about the manner and the significance of the selection of issues and the preliminary processing of information at early stages in the process. This narrow focus not only leaves out a great deal, but in some contexts leads to misconceptions and distortions in respect of adjudication itself. Similarly the tendency of most secondary writing on evidence is to concentrate on events in the courtroom in jury trials. As a result one, rather atypical, kind of proceeding is taken as the paradigm for the great variety of adjudicative decisions that take place in litigation. This is further compounded by a failure to treat adjudicative decisions systematically

The contemporary significance of Bentham and Wigmore 177

and relentlessly as just one stage in that complex flow of decisions and events that we know as litigation. Thus the variety of types of litigation tends to be masked at the level of theory and one stage in the process – the decision of the trier(s) of the fact – tends to be treated in isolation from the stages which precede and succeed it. Furthermore, any theory that attributes a single direct end to so complex a matter as a system of litigation is bound to fail. In short, the Achilles heel of the Rationalist Tradition of Evidence scholarship is that it is premised on an over-simple model of adjudication and litigation. As we have argued elsewhere, one way forward is to develop a broader framework for the study of evidence, one that encompasses the processing and uses of information at all stages of different kinds of litigious process.[24]

The second weakness of the Rationalist Tradition is that it is at once uncompromisingly rationalistic and is rooted in a particular view of rationality – the characteristically optimistic rationalism of eighteenth-century post-enlightenment thought. The general tendency of Anglo-American evidence scholarship is not only optimistic, it is also remarkably unsceptical in respect of its basic assumptions. Hardly a whisper of doubt about the possibility of knowledge, about the validity of induction, or about human capacity to reason darkens the pages of Gilbert, Best or Thayer, Wigmore or Cross or other, lesser writers. Bentham's theory of fictions comes as close as any to confronting such doubts, but as we have seen, his ultimate position remains firmly rooted in common-sense empiricism. For other writers confident assertion, pragmatic question-begging, and straightforward ignoring are the characteristic responses to perennial questions raised by philosophical sceptics. This debunking, sceptical tendency is by no means confined to writings by sociologists or others about criminal process. Judge Bridlegoose, Jerome Frank, Marxist critics of the bourgeois legal order and the cautionary admonitions of forensic psychologists are all familiar features of our legal culture. The trial as a forensic lottery, as a sporting contest or as a degradation ceremony are treated almost as clichés. There is hardly a contemporary writer on legal process who does not remark on the gaps between aspiration and reality.[25]

There is thus a sharp contrast in tone between the optimistic, often bland, rationalism of specialized writings on evidence and the sceptical tendencies in much recent writing about judicial process. The contrast, however, may be more of style than of substance: for the main thrust of critical writings is directed at the design and the actual operation of a particular system and the claims that are made for it, rather than at the underlying philosophical assumptions and aspirations of the Rationalist Tradition. The principal target is complacent rather than aspirational rationalism. We have argued elsewhere that many seemingly sceptical writers about judicial process invoke standards which are identical, or similar, to those outlined in the rationalist model of adjudication and

178   Theories of Evidence

that, in law as elsewhere, genuine philosophical sceptics are rare birds.[26] In brief, they are not so far removed from aspirational, even optimistic, rationalism as the sceptical tone of some of their writings suggests. If this is correct, it suggests that the obstacles to a reintegration of the literature on evidence and on the processes which constitute the context of disputed questions of fact about particular past events may not be as great as appears on the surface. There are genuine difficulties and disagreements, but they are shared by several specialized fields of inquiry that have grown apart. Reintegration is surely needed. The Rationalist Tradition of evidence scholarship, by dint of its artifical isolation, has paradoxically produced a corpus of literature which is notable both for scholarly excellence and conceptual sophistication and for a series of recurrent controversies which even some of the leading protagonists acknowledge are 'high among the unrealities'. Evidence scholarship has a lot to offer and a lot to learn.

Appendix Wigmore's method: a personal evaluation

Wigmore was more concerned to present his method as a usable technique than to explore its theoretical foundations. If anything, he undersold it. He quite properly emphasized its limitations; more significantly, by introducing unfamiliar symbols and calling it 'the chart method' he obscured its essential nature as a fairly straightforward development and application of ordinary principles of logic to a particular kind of subject-matter. Symbols and charts may be useful devices, but they are not necessary elements in this kind of disciplined approach to the analysis of evidence.

It is not possible here to undertake a full-scale appraisal of the theoretical validity, the practical value and the potential applications of Wigmore's method.[1] But since this is one of the most original and important contributions of the *Principles*, and one that has been undervalued in the past, it is worth giving a brief personal assessment, especially in the light of the recent debates on probabilities and proof.

The first question to be asked is whether the method has a sound theoretical basis. Wigmore's general approach falls squarely within the central tradition of Anglo-American evidence scholarship, which in turn is closely connected to the discourse of lawyers and of the courts. It claims to be a systematization and refinement of the methods of analysing evidence used by experienced and effective practitioners both in preparing and presenting cases. It draws on a central tradition of inductive logic – notably the work of Mill, Sidgwick, and Jevons. The study of logic has developed and changed in the past eighty years, but not to the extent that the essential soundness of their accounts or practical reasoning and induction have been generally challenged. Wigmore's treatment of probabilities is neither very clear nor very extensive, but he is reasonably recognizable as a Baconian whose views are in general compatible with those of more sophisticated contemporary theorists of the same kind, such as Jonathan Cohen.[2] It is a weakness of Wigmore's approach that he wrote as if his were the only possible views of rationality, of induction and of probabilities and he did not even consider the possibility of alternative theories. Nevertheless, his method is solidly grounded in one intellectually respectable tradition which has been developed and refined by others; to date, no one has developed an alternative method, which is comparable in sophistication and clarity, of analysing masses of evidence.

Here it is worth considering three theoretical criticisms that may be levelled

180　*Theories of Evidence*

against the chart method:[3] (1) that Wigmore does not tell us how to assign weight to individual items of evidence; (2) that Wigmore does not tell us how to *combine* judgements about the weight of evidence and other items in a key-list; and (3) that his approach, like that of most other writers in the Rationalist Tradition, is 'atomistic' rather than 'holistic'.

The first criticism is easily disposed of. The great bulk of the *Principles* is devoted to a patient and systematic exploration of the problem of weighing different kinds of evidence in respect of different kinds of probanda. The work remains the most extensive compendium of the guidance that can be obtained from science and general experience in evaluating evidence of all kinds. It is, of course, in need of constant revision; but, as Wigmore emphasized, the progress of science in this area is painfully slow and many of the 'advances' in, for example, psychology suggest that some kinds of evidence, such as eye-witness identification evidence, are less reliable than 'common sense' suggests. If the charge is that Wigmore does not tell us how to decide which of two opposing witnesses to believe, that merely reflects the state of knowledge at the time he wrote. Science has yet to develop an infallible truth machine and, if it did, this would raise a host of problems for civil libertarians. If the complaint is that Wigmore does not set out *rules* of weight, the response is that, like most other writers on evidence, he believed that the evaluation of evidence is by and large not susceptible to regulation by formal rules.[4]

A second criticism is that Wigmore gives no guidance on how to combine judgements about the weight of evidence within a given chart. The matter has become a central focus of attention in recent debates about probabilities. A short answer is that Wigmore drops a few hints about his views, but does not address the issues directly or systematically.[5] Accordingly his account, at the very least, needs to be supplemented in the light of subsequent writings on the subject. The issues have been considerably sharpened since Wigmore's time, but it is fair to say that it is still a field with many questions and few agreed answers.

Wigmore categorized the main relations between evidentiary propositions in terms of assertion, denial, explanation and rival assertion (PA, OD, OE, OR). However, he did not provide a comparable vocabulary for differentiating the principal ways in which evidentiary propositions may be combined or accumulate or otherwise be seen as allies tending to support or to negate the same conclusion, either directly or indirectly. Accordingly, it is necessary to introduce some basic distinctions between different ways in which evidentiary propositions may be so related. The main concepts used here will be: conjunction; compound propositions; corroboration; convergence; and catenate inferences (inference upon inference) – sometimes known as 'the five Cs'.[6] Each of these notions raises difficult questions about what is involved in determining the overall probative force or weight of evidence.

Conjunction　In order to succeed in a civil or a criminal case a party may have to establish each of several facts in issue or merely to establish one of a number of facts in issue in the alternative. Thus in a standard murder case the prosecution has typically to prove the fact of death of a particular victim, that death was caused by an *actus reus*, the identity of the killer, and criminal intent. Each of these is a necessary element in the prosecution's case. On the other hand, it is sufficient for the defence to establish any one of a series of defences, such as self-

Appendix 181

defence, insanity or provocation. To put the matter formally; in a typical criminal case in order to succeed the prosecution has to establish A *and* B *and* C *and* D, each of which is a *necessary* condition, and it is *sufficient* for the defence either to show that one of these conditions has not been established beyond reasonable doubt or that E *or* F *or* G (defences) applies. Sometimes it is sufficient for a proponent to establish one of a series of alternative jointly sufficient conditions – for example, that Edith Thompson either conspired with or incited Frederick Bywaters to kill Percy Thompson.[7]

In many cases more than one fact in issue is disputed. In such cases a problem arises about the *transitivity of doubt* between facts in issue;[8] should doubts in respect of one fact in issue be conjoined with doubts about one or more other facts in issue in order to make a judgement about the case as a whole? If so, what criteria govern such combinations? Jonathan Cohen has argued that if judgements about independent[9] facts in issue are combined according to mathematical criteria (for example, by applying the multiplication rule), this would lead to results that would be both surprising and unacceptable. For example, in a civil case, suppose that a plaintiff has proved each of two independent elements to a probability of 0.6, he will lose according to Pascalian criteria, because the probability of the case as a whole will be 0.36 (0.6×0.6).[10] If there are three or more disputed facts in issue, the plaintiff will have to prove each element in his case to a much higher standard than 'the balance of probabilities'. This, Cohen suggests, is 'a rule unknown to Judges and unrespected by triers of fact' and would be unfair to plaintiffs.[11] On the other hand, 'on the inductivist (Baconian) analysis, if the plaintiff gains each of his points on the balance of probability, he can be regarded as gaining his case as a whole on that balance . . . without any constraints being thereby imposed on the number of independent points in his case nor on the level of probability at which each must be won'.[12]

It is not possible here to enter into the merits of the debate on this issue. Eggleston points out that there is no reported English or Australian case directly on the point.[13] It does not seem that Wigmore addressed the issue directly, but it is reasonable to infer that as a Baconian he would very probably have agreed with Cohen.[14]

Compound propositions   Sometimes an intermediate probandum may contain a number of elements, each of which is supported by separate evidence. For example, proposition 9 in Wigmore's analysis of *Umilian* could be analysed as follows:

i	ii	iii	iv	v	vi	vii
U believed	that J	had	Falsely	informed	the Priest	that U was	to prevent
↑	↑	↑	↑	↑	already	his
|	|	|	|	|	married	marriage
14	12	16	10	10/14	↑	↑
					|	|
					10	14

Supports
(Key-List, *Umilian*).[15]

In such instances, the question arises as to how one assesses the strength of the

182 *Theories of Evidence*

proposition as a whole. Cohen treats this as an example of conjunction;[16] but it is arguable that in legal contexts different considerations apply to assessing the strength of a case as a whole and assessing compound propositions that are intermediate probanda or evidentiary facts.

Corroboration 'At its simplest testimonial corroboration occurs when two witnesses both testify, independently of one another, to the truth of the same proposition.'[17] For example W1 testifies p (e.g. A was at place X at 6 p.m.) and W2 testifies p. What amounts to corroboration in law can be a complex question but even in the most simple case the question arises how to evaluate the combined weight of corroborative evidence and whether the same principles apply to testimonial evidence, circumstantial evidence and a combination of the two.

Convergence 'Two items of circumstantial evidence converge when both facts, independently of one another, [support the] probability of the same conclusion.'[18] For example, in *Umilian* the following intermediate *probanda* support the ultimate *probandum* 'it was U who killed J'; U had a design to kill J; U had motive to kill J; U had consciousness of guilt about J's disappearance; U knew that J was dead when others did not.

It should be noted that corroboration is sometimes used widely to include convergence and to include situations in which there is a mixture of testimonial and circumstantial evidence supporting the same *probandum*. However, we shall use it in the narrower sense. Cohen states: 'Testimonial corroboration and convergence of circumstantial evidence exhibit a common logical structure.'[19] Eggleston disagrees.[20] Wigmore did not address the issue directly, but his discussions of the chart method and of corroboration do not suggest that he saw any logical difference between the two.[21]

Catenate inferences As Wigmore indicated, it is common to have a series of inferences in the following form:

$$E1 \rightarrow E2 \rightarrow E3 \rightarrow P.$$

Here we have a chain of inferences leading to a single *probandum*, rather than a series of independent supports for the same *probandum* (corroboration and convergence). Another difference between Pascalians and Baconians relates to such inferences upon inferences. At common law, according to Cohen – though he states the principle more confidently than the authorities warrant[22] – the courts insist that in both civil and criminal cases, each tier of inference prior to the final one should rest on proof beyond reasonable doubt.[23] The inductive theory of probability supports this, because the balance of proof cannot be assumed to be transitive: there may be incommensurable supports.

> Inductive probability-functions evaluate the weight of relevant evidence, and what is relatively weighty for one type of conclusion may not be nearly so weighty for another . . . a judicial proof on the balance of probability sets out to show that the ultimately derived conclusion is probable on known facts, not

Appendix 183

to show that it is knowable from probable facts.[24]

A mathematicist analysis, however, would permit inferences on inferences to go through, even though each tier was merely proved on a balance of probability. This, according to Cohen, neither conforms to legal practice nor explains the rule.

The debate about the transitivity of doubt in respect of inferences upon inferences has been complicated by confusion as to what the law is. According to Eggleston there are three points of view to be found in the authorities:[25]

(i) The traditional doctrine that completely forbade piling inferences upon inferences. This was sharply, and largely successfully, attacked by Wigmore.

(ii) The view advanced by Lockwood J in *New York Life Insurance Co.* v. *McNeely*,[26] which is the basis of Cohen's position and which was supported by Wigmore.[27]

(iii) A more flexible view 'which regards the doctrine as no more than a warning against drawing tenuous inferences.' This is supported by Eggleston and other Pascalians.[28] Wigmore chose a rather soft target to attack and again did not really address the issue, while ending up at the same point as Jonathan Cohen.

To sum up, Wigmore did not direct very much attention to questions about combining judgements of probability. In so far as he had a clear position, he seems to have been a relatively consistent, if primitive, Baconian. His account of the chart method does not throw much light on these difficult questions. In one sense, this is an advantage: for the method can be interpreted as being independent of any standard theory of probability. With a few adjustments (e.g. in respect of convergence and corroboration) a Baconian, a Pascalian and a subjectivist may use the method to analyse and to organize their judgements about a mixed mass of evidence.

One further important line of criticism is that the whole approach is 'atomistic', that is to say it assumes that it is both possible and desirable to analyse a mass of evidence in separate, individuated items, each one of which can be expressed as a separate proposition on a numbered key-list. This is a charge that can be levelled at both Baconians and Pascalians – indeed, at almost all leading Anglo-American writers on evidence. For both methods need to treat separate items of evidence and propositions in an argument as individuated units of analysis. Thus, Bentham's method of infirmative suppositions involves looking one by one at the effect of individual suppositions on the strength of support of one or more items of evidence for a particular intermediate or ultimate *probandum*.[29] Similarly, Cohen's theory of inductive support requires ordinal ranking of relevant variables.[30] Bayes' theorem purports to provide a formula for combining independent judgements of probability.[31]

It is difficult to evaluate this line of criticism at present, for the case for a 'holistic' approach to evaluation of evidence in forensic contexts has yet to be fully argued.[32] Moreover, there are several possible different interpretations of what is involved in a holistic approach. At this stage of the debate, it would be rash to attempt to do more than offer a few preliminary observations on this kind of approach as it effects Wigmorean analysis. First, the assertion that Wigmore's approach is too 'atomistic' could be interpreted to mean that he pays insufficient attention to the role of such notions as 'theories of the case', 'stories' and 'themes'

184 *Theories of Evidence*

in the presentation of evidence. Such notions, which are commonplace in the talk of practising advocates,[33] as well as of commentators on fact-finding processes,[34] all emphasize the importance of *coherence*, as a check on reliability and as a factor in assessing plausibility. Does this story hang together? Does a particular testimonial statement or line of argument 'fit' well in some broader picture? Which of two competing versions of events, taken as a whole, seems more credible? At the very least, such questions provide workable tests of credibility and acceptability in everyday discourse, as weak forms of consistency.[35]

This limited version of 'holism' reveals some important gaps in Wigmore's overall approach to the evaluation of evidence. Yet it would not be fair to accuse him of entirely neglecting synthesis by concentrating too much on analysis. For one of the functions of the chart method is to enable both the maker and the reader of charts to view a mixed mass of evidence together as a coherent whole, 'so as to produce a single final idea'.[36] Indeed, any good Wigmorean chart-maker needs to rely on 'theories', 'themes' or 'stories' as aids to selecting and organizing significant relevant data from the mass of potentially usable material available to him.

There are, however, stronger versions of 'holism' that may be potentially subversive of the whole approach. For example, Peter Tillers, the reviser of the first volume of Wigmore's *Treatise*, enters a strong reservation about an over-articulate approach to the evaluation of evidence:

> For our own part, we are inclined to believe that the effort to state systematically and comprehensively the premises on which our inferences rest may produce serious distortions in the factfinding process, in part (but only in part) because such systematic statement obscures the complex mental processes that we actually employ and should employ to evaluate evidence. It is not true that we can say all we know, and the effort to say more than we are able to say is likely to diminish our knowledge and our ability to use it. In our daily lives, we confidently rely on innumerable premises and beliefs that we often cannot articulate or explain, but our inability to express these premises and beliefs does not necessarily make them illegitimate or unreliable. The same may be true of many beliefs relied upon in the assessment of evidence by a trier of fact in the courtroom.[37]

It is not possible, in this context, to explore the issues raised by this passage. It is, however, worth making two brief observations by way of conclusion. First, neither Tillers nor other emerging 'holists' with whose work the author is familiar go so far as to deny the validity or the value of logical or mathematical analysis 'in its proper place'. Rather, they emphasize that attempts to describe or to enumerate or to analyse almost inevitably involve an element of distortion and selection and that there is a danger that easily quantified 'hard' data will tend to be preferred to 'soft' data or that arguments expressed in mathematical terms will tend to have a stronger persuasive effect than non-mathematical arguments, whether or not this is justified.[38] Their concern is to point out the dangers and limitations of certain kinds of analysis and argument, rather than to deny them any validity or utility. Finally, 'holistic' approaches tend to find their ultimate justifications in philosophical traditions different from English empiricism. Tillers, for example, is more sympathetic to Kant and Hegel than to Mill and Ayer. Some contemporary writers on evidence have exhibited signs of sympathy

Appendix 185

for intuitionist or even sceptical approaches.[39] If 'holism' comes into its own during the coming years, the main target will not be solely or primarily Wigmore, but the foundations of the dominant tradition of Anglo-American thought about evidence.

What of the practical utility of the chart method? Perhaps the biggest single obstacle to convincing practitioners of its value is the objection that, if rigorously applied, it is too complicated and laborious to be usable in practice. In short, the costs of Wigmorean analysis outweigh its benefits. While there is clearly some truth in this view, it is based on a number of questionable assumptions and it is over-generalized. First, like any recommended procedure for tackling problems, its value is partly a matter of individual preference and aptitude. Secondly, the costs and the benefits vary according to circumstances. Facility in using the technique only comes with practice. Once mastered, the approach can be applied with as much or little rigour as seems appropriate. To dismiss the method in general terms as being too ponderous or complicated is no more sensible than claiming that meticulous attention to detail never pays dividends. For it is not essentially different from any other kinds of rigorous analysis. Where the task is worth the efforts of a Hercules[40] then this is a tool of considerable potential, but like all tools it has limitations and is open to over-use or abuse. In the absence of systematic research on its uses and limitations in respect of particular tasks, the best recommendation one can give is to say that it represents a relatively systematic rational reconstruction of what many practising lawyers do in preparing for trial and in advancing an argument[41] and that there is a significant number of converts among those who have tried it out.

In evaluating the utility of the method, it is important to distinguish between its educational value as a form of mental training and its practical value as a usable technique by trial lawyers and others. The educational justification for training in formal logic or in pure mathematics is not seriously undermined by pointing out that the ordinary conditions of living often do not permit the direct applications of such methods to many practical problems in everyday life. The conditions of the academy often permit greater purity and greater rigour than can be expected in the hurly-burly of practical affairs. But, even if judged solely in terms of practical value, a rigorous training in a method of analysis which may be too time-consuming or too demanding or too 'pure' for regular practical use, may have a gymnastic value as a mental training or may set standards of rigour or may provide a general orientation justifying academic exercises in which artificiality is the price paid for these other benefits. Law students are sometimes required to analyse appellate cases in greater detail and depth than is normally possible in practice. Similar considerations apply to Wigmorean analysis: even if the chart method in its purest form may be too laborious for everyday use by practitioners – and this is a debatable assumption – it does not necessarily undermine its value as an education exercise.

What can students be expected to learn from doing exercises in Wigmorean analysis? The author's judgement, based on using the chart method in teaching for several years, is that it is an excellent vehicle serving a number of purposes: first, it creates certain kinds of awareness, awareness that the counters in any argument, and particularly in arguments about evidence, are propositions and relations between propositions; and, awareness that in ordinary discourse, whether written or oral – including discourse presented by Wigmore's 'narrative

186   *Theories of Evidence*

method' – typically many steps in argument are glossed over or left implicit. One of Wigmore's main claims for the method is fully justified: that it brings into the open and makes explicit important steps in an argument and thereby makes it easier to judge both their soundness and their probative force. A student who has been through the process of analysing even one case in a disciplined way is made aware of how easy it is to make logical jumps, to slip in hidden premises, to get away with fallacies, to confuse evidence with inferences from evidence, to introduce irrelevant material, or by a shift of standpoint to switch ultimate *probanda*, and so on. Furthermore, the fact that students, particularly in the early stages, find doing these exercises extremely laborious drives home the lesson that analysing evidence nearly always involves hard work. A student who has spent a mere fifty or a hundred hours analysing a rather simple case more readily grasps how it is that so many thousands of hours have been spent on such exercises as congressional investigations into the Kennedy assassination (to take an extreme case) or even quite routine police investigations into a murder. Thus application of the method induces a disciplined, rational, and patient approach to evidence. Adapting Marshall Macluhan, Wigmorean analysis is a medium, the message of which is that analysis of evidence requires hard work.

Finally, Wigmore's approach forces students to take facts seriously. It forces them to prepare a list of evidential propositions: propositions that could actually be asserted from the witness stand or propositions supported by real evidence physically observed by the decider of fact during trial. It forces the student to relate this mass of evidential propositions to the ultimately controlling propositions of law in a rigorous and logically coherent manner. In law, fact-handling skills are as important in practice as rule-handling skills. Within legal education, the latter have been highly developed and perhaps over-emphasized, while the former have been neglected. Wigmore's method remains the only attempt to date to approach the analysis of evidence in a systematic and rigorous manner. Apart from the other values, this is enough to justify its use.

Acknowledgements

This book is one product of a broader project on theoretical aspects of evidence and proof in litigation. In the long period of gestation of this work I have incurred more debts than can properly be acknowledged. Among those to whom I am particularly grateful for suggestions, encouragement and help are Mohammed Abu Hareira, Terry Anderson, Jess Bell, James Burns, Ken Casebeer, Jonathan Cohen, John Dinwiddy, Richard Eggleston, Tom Ewald, Michael Graham, Jolyon Hall, Eliahu Harnon, Herbert Hart, Douglas Hay, David Holdcroft, John Jackson, Stefan Landsman, Andrew Lewis, Sally Lloyd-Bostock, Christopher McCrudden, John Miller, Gerald Postema, Stephen Presser, Fred Rosen, Jack Schlegel, David Schum, Robert Stevens, Robert Summers, Elaine Teigler, Peter Tillers, Adrian Zuckerman and members of the Bentham Project; I have also benefited from discussions at seminars in several universities and from numerous students and colleagues in Warwick, Northwestern, London and Miami. I am grateful to the Social Science Research Council, as it then was, for a Personal Research grant in 1980–1; to the Librarians of University College and of Northwestern Law School for access to the Bentham manuscripts and Wigmore papers respectively; to the University of Warwick for its enlightened policy on study leave and to the University of Warwick Law School for an atmosphere which supports and encourages attempts to explore and rethink the foundations of our heritage of legal scholarship.

I wish to thank Margaret Wright, Jean Pilgrim, Mrs A. Vandzaruk, the late Olive Heaton and the friendly word-processors at the University of Miami Law School for typing and re-typing numerous drafts, and Ken Hirschkop for preparing the index. Finally, as ever, my wife has been a necessary and sufficient condition of the whole enterprise.

Notes

Abbreviations

(For further details see the Bibliography at p. 244 below.)

BENTHAM

Works	*The Works of Jeremy Bentham*, published under the superintendance of John Bowring (1838–43, Edinburgh). Roman numerals refer to volumes and Arabic numerals to pages.
CW	*The Collected Works of Jeremy Bentham*, prepared under the supervision of the Bentham Committee, University College London (London, 1968–82, Oxford, 1983–).
UC	Bentham manuscripts, University College Library, London. Roman numerals refer to boxes and Arabic numerals to pages.
Fragment	*A Fragment on Government*, in *A Comment on the Commentaries and a Fragment on Government*, ed. Burns and Hart (*CW*, 1977).
IV	*An Introductory View of the Rationale of Judicial Evidence*, ed. James Mill, (vi *works* 1–187).
RJE	*Rationale of Judicial Evidence*, ed. J. S. Mill 1827, 5v. (reprinted vi *works* 188; id. vii).
PML	*Introduction to the Principles of Morals and Legislation*, ed. Burns and Hart (*CW*, 1970).
Treatise	*A Treatise on Judicial Evidence*, extracted from the MSS of Jeremy Bentham by E. Dumont and translated into English (London, 1825).
SNAA	*Swear Not at All*, first pub. 1817 (v *works* 187–229).
PJP	*Principles of Judicial Procedure*, with the outlines of a procedure code, ed. Richard Doane (ii *works* 1–188).
SR	*Scotch Reform*, 1st edn 1808; 2nd edn 1811 (v *works* 1–53).

WIGMORE

WP	Wigmore Papers, Northwestern University Law School, Chicago.

Notes 189

Principles	*Principles of Judicial Proof, as given by logic, psychology and general experience*, 1st edn 1913; 2nd edn 1931; 3rd edn (sub. nom. *Science of Judicial Proof*) 1937 (Boston).
Textbook	*Students' Textbook of the Law of Evidence* (Brooklyn, 1935).
Treatise	*A Treatise on the Anglo-American System of Evidence in Trials at Common Law*, 1st edn 1904–5; 2nd edn 1923; 3rd edn 1940 (revised by various editors 1943 onwards, Boston). 1 *Treatise*, s.8, 123 refers to volume one, section eight, at page 123.
Treatise (Tillers rev.)	id., volume 1, revised by P. Tillers (Boston, 1983), 2v.
Roalfe	*John Henry Wigmore*, scholar and reformer, by William R. Roalfe (biography) (Evanston, 1977).

Biographical note

Jeremy Bentham (1748–1832) was educated at Westminster School and Queen's College, Oxford. After a brief period in practice as a barrister he devoted his life to the criticism and reform of English legal, political and social institutions on the basis of the principle of utility or 'The Greatest Happiness principle'. His main, but by no means his sole, concern was with the reform of the law. He was a severe critic of the common law, of the legal profession ('Judge and Co.') and of all forms of Natural Law thinking, especially the complacent version espoused by William Blackstone. He devoted almost as much energy to constructive, often highly detailed, proposals for reform, including a series of codes, elaborate plans for a model prison (Panopticon) and for many new kinds of institutions. His writings are voluminous, but he was strangely reluctant to take personal responsibility for their publication; this task was left to his disciples, who were understandably selective, in the case of his literary executor, Sir John Bowring, unforgivably so. By no means all his important writings have been published; a recent estimate suggests that if all his extant works were to be printed they would fill between sixty-five and sixty-eight substantial volumes.

His writings on evidence belong to what might be termed the later middle period – mainly 1802–12. They succeed a relatively quiescent decade when he devoted much of his energy to the abortive Panopticon project. They coincide with his conversion to political radicalism (Dinwiddy, 1975) and they largely precede his most important writings on several subjects, including politics, logic, language, judicial organization and the constitutional code. A considerable amount of unpublished material on adjective law (evidence and procedure) survives, but by and large it adds little to the published writings in this area. There is, as yet, no full biography of Bentham, but see Everett (1931), Halévy (1955), Stephen (1900) and Mack (1962). Bowring's *Memoirs* (1843) are notoriously unreliable but contain some useful material. Bentham's reconstituted remains (the auto-icon) are preserved in a cupboard in University College, London where they may be inspected and puzzled over (Twining, 1984a).

John Henry Wigmore (1863–1943) was born in San Francisco. He attended Harvard College and Harvard Law School, where he helped to found the

190 *Theories of Evidence*

Harvard Law Review. He was taught by Ames, Gray, Langdell and, above all, James Bradley Thayer, the great evidence scholar to whom Wigmore later dedicated his *Treatise*. After a relatively short period of legal practice, combined with journalism and legal writing, Wigmore accepted a post as Professor of Anglo-American Law in Keio University in Tokyo. There he spent three very productive years, during which he wrote extensively about many subjects, including Japanese law. Not long after his return he accepted a teaching post at Northwestern, where he remained for almost fifty years continuously active until he was killed in a road accident shortly after his eightieth birthday.

Like many teachers of his generation Wigmore was used to teaching a wide range of subjects – indeed, in Japan he taught almost all of a three-year curriculum single-handed – but from an early stage evidence was one of his main interests. Even before he embarked on his first major work on the law of evidence, he had taken an active interest in the broader dimensions of the subject, including its logical aspects and the developing fields of forensic science and forensic psychology. The foundation for his reputation as an evidence scholar was laid in 1899, when he produced a revision of the first volume of the sixteenth edition of Greenleaf's *A Treatise on the Law of Evidence*. The quality of Wigmore's revision was immediately recognized by his former teacher, Thayer, by the reviewers and, most important in this instance, by the publishers, Little, Brown and Company of Boston. Shortly afterwards, the latter, feeling that Greenleaf's work had outlived its usefulness, invited him to give them first option on an entirely new treatise on evidence. He had already begun work on this some years previously. In 1904–5 the four-volume first edition of Wigmore's *Treatise on the Anglo-American System of Evidence in Trials at Common Law* was published by Little, Brown. It received prompt recognition as a major work, not only in the reviews, but also from its regular use by practitioners and, after a remarkably short time, by its acceptance as an authority in the courts.

For much of his career Wigmore was almost as renowned as an innovative teacher and administrator as he was as a scholar. As Dean for nearly thirty years, he helped to make Northwestern into one of the top law schools in the country. He was also an important leader in legal education nationally; he was influential in the development of the study of comparative law, criminology, and clinical legal education. As a scholar, in addition to evidence, he made substantial contributions to several fields, including torts, military law and air law. He played a leading role in establishing and helping to edit several important series, including *The Modern Legal Philosophy Series* (1911–22), *The Continental Legal History Series* (1912–28) and *The Modern Criminal Science Series* (1911–17). He was enormously prolific. The bibliography of his published writings includes almost 900 items, including nearly fifty original books, thirty-eight edited works and six volumes on the law of the Tokugawa shogunate. The collection of his writings at Northwestern occupies eighteen feet of shelving.

For biographical details see Roalfe (1977); Kocourek (1943); *American Dictionary of Biography*; Twining (1984d); memoirs on the centenary of his birth, 58 *Northwestern Law Review* 456ff. (1963). Roalfe's biography contains a mass of information, but is neither analytical about, nor critical of, Wigmore's ideas and achievements.

Notes to pages 1–6 191

Chapter 1: The Rationalist Tradition of evidence scholarship

1. This chapter is a revised and abbreviated version of a paper originally published in Campbell and Waller (1982) at 211–49. The general relationship between jurisprudence and theories of evidence is explored in Twining (1984).
2. General surveys of the history of the law of evidence, including writers on evidence, are to be found in Wigmore, 1 *Treatise* (Tillers rev.), s.8; W. S. Holdsworth, *HEL*, (1925), esp. I, 299–312; IX, 127–222, 365–7; XIII, 466–8, 504–10; Holdsworth (1925), 119 *et seq.*; Nokes (1967), Ch. 2. Thayer (1898) remains the classic study of many aspects of the history of evidence; see also Wright and Graham (1977), Ch. 1. For a bibliography, see Wigmore, 1 *Treatise* (Tillers rev.), s.8, n.1.
3. 'Some of the most fundamental attributes of modern Anglo-American criminal procedure for cases of serious crime emerged in England during the eighteenth century: the law of evidence, the adversary system, the privilege against self-incrimination, and the main ground rules for the relationship of judge and jury.' J. H. Langbein (1983), 2. Much of the evidence for this claim is gathered in Langbein (1978).
4. See Wright and Graham (1977), Ch. 1.
5. Buller (1772).
6. Cited by Wigmore, 1 *Treatise*, 237 (original citation not traced).
7. Gilbert (1754); see Twining (1983) and Abu Hareira (1984).
8. Id., 1.
9. Wigmore, 1 *Treatise*, s.8.
10. Evans (1803).
11. Pothier (1806).
12. Glassford (1820). Glassford's significance is interestingly discussed by Abu Hareira (1982, 1984).
13. For citations, see below at 188.
14. On Bentham's followers and critics, see below at 100ff.
15. For accounts of Best and Appleton, see Twining (1982). On Denman, see below at 100–106. On Livingston and the reform of evidence, see Wright and Graham (1977), 63ff.
16. J. F. Stephen (1879), Introduction.
17. On the decline of utilitarian analysis in English legal thought, see W. L. Morison (1978), 18–20.
18. See generally op. cit., n.1.
19. On Stephen, see Radzinowicz (1957).
20. Stephen (1879), xiii.
21. Stephen (1872).
22. Stephen (1879), xiii.
23. Thayer (1927), 210.
24. On Thayer's life, see especially *The Centennial History of the Harvard Law School, 1817–1917* (1918). A fascinating interpretation is to be found in C. Chamberlayne (1908), 758–63.
25. Thayer (1898), 527.
26. Pollock (1899).
27. Chamberlayne (1908), 760.

192 *Notes to pages 6–11*

28. See especially Morgan (1956).
29. See Thayer (1898), *passim*; (1927), 305–9.
30. Thayer (1898), 279n.
31. Id. 535.
32. Id., 314n.
33. Id., 530, discussed below at 152ff.
34. A brief account is given in J. Maguire *et al.* (1973), Preface.
35. See now Weinstein, Mansfield, Abrams and Berger (1983, 7th edn).
36. See Chamberlayne, loc. cit.
37. J. J. McKelvey (1924) on which see book review by E. M. Morgan 34 *Yale L.J.* 223 (1924–5).
38. Chamberlayne (1911), I, s.172. The work had a mixed reception. For reviews of Chamberlayne, see especially 25 *Harv. L. Rev.* 483 (1911–12); E. R. Thayer 27 *Harv. L. Rev.* 601 (1913–14); H. Shulman 23 *Yale L.J.* 384 (1913–14); D. B. Wyckoff 1 *Cornell L.Q.* 144 (1915–16).
39. On Thayer and Wigmore, see Morgan and Maguire (1937).
40. On the history of these codes, see Wright and Graham (1977), ss.5001–7; Lempert and Saltzburg (1977) at 1191–2000.
41. On Michael and Adler, see Wigmore, 1 *Treatise* (Tillers rev.), s.371. Tillers suggests that Michael and Adler were indirectly influential through writings on relevancy of Professors James, Trautman and Ball. See further below at 152.
42. Michael and Adler also wrote a series of articles that were more influential: see especially (1925), (1934); also J. Michael (1948).
43. Wigmore (1937), 6.
44. Apart from periodical literature, perhaps the most significant contributions were G. D. Nokes (1952, 1967), in my view an underrated work; Z. Cowen and P. B. Carter (1956) and Glanville Williams (1963). The paucity of scholarly writing on evidence in England is directly attributable to its relative neglect in the law curriculum in university degrees and The Law Society's examinations, which in turn is partly due to the absurd idea that evidence is essentially a 'barrister's subject'.
45. Cross (1958, 1979).
46. Preface to the first edition (1958). Stephen's *Digest* was 'extremely condensed'; Cross refers to *Phipson on Evidence*, the leading practitioners' treatise which his work partly displaced as 'the repository of evidentiary law' (ibid.).
47. Cross was familiar with at least some of Bentham's writings on evidence; he cited Gulson (1923) in two places in the first edition. The fifth edition contains a few references to recent debates on probabilities and proof. On Cross, see Honoré (1981).
48. See Cross (1979), 3–4; also Twining (1983), *passim*.
49. On the misuse of Bentham by the C.L.R.C., see Twining (1973a) and below, 170–1.
50. Despite the relative simplification of the rules and their diminishing importance, the law of evidence is sufficiently rich in both conceptual and practical problems to sustain whole courses on it: see further Twining (1984b).
51. Wright and Graham, op. cit., 13.

Notes to pages 11–20 193

52. See especially C. Perelman (1963); with L. Olbrechts-Tyteca (1971); cf Twining (1980), 13–14.
53. *People* v. *Collins* 68 Cal. 2d. 319, 438 P. 2d. 33, 1968. A select bibliography on probabilities and proof is included in Twining (1983) at 156–7.
54. Eggleston (1977, 1983); W. Barnes (1983); Finkelstein (1978).
55. Cohen (1977).
56. See bibliography, ibid., n.53.
57. Useful surveys are to be found in Tapp (1980), 165; *Annual Review of Psychology* (1976), (1982); 17 *Law and Society Review* No. 1 (1982); Lloyd-Bostock and Clifford (1983); Saks and Hastie (1978). See further below, 139–40.
58. 'The rules of evidence . . . are largely ununified and scattered, existing for disparate and sometimes conflicting reasons: they are a mixture of astonishing judicial achievements and sterile inconvenient disasters. There is a law of contract, and perhaps to some extent a law of tort, but only a group of laws of evidence.' J. D. Heydon (1975), 3.
59. See L. Fuller (1978) at 358.
60. On these two models, see further Twining (1984c).
61. Thayer (1898), 199; cf. id. (1927), 307.
62. Wright and Graham (1977), 84.
63. See Tapp (1982).
64. Preface to Stephen's *Digest* (1899 edn).

Chapter 2: Bentham on evidence

(i) INTRODUCTION

1. Cited by Bowring (1843) (x *works* 18), discussed in Mack (1962) at 49–50.
2. See below, 61–4. A long footnote on the social contract is particularly revealing: *Fragment* (*CW*), 439–41n. The marginal note reads 'History of a mind perplexed by fiction'.
3. C. K. Ogden, *Bentham's Theory of Fictions*, published in 1932, the centenary of Bentham's death. Ogden claims that James Mill, J. S. Mill, Bowring, Dumont, Halévy, the *D.N.B.* and Everett all failed to grasp the significance of the Theory of Fictions; only Sir Leslie Stephen is exempted from the charge of neglect (id., xxix–xxx). The criticism is perhaps overstated, but Ogden and Richards' seminal *The Meaning of Meaning* (1923) does establish a direct historical link between Bentham's ideas and modern 'linguistic philosophy'. Mary Mack (1962, especially Ch. 4) and H. L. A. Hart (1953) are among commentators who have followed Ogden in treating the Theory of Fictions as being both highly original and a central feature of Bentham's thought; see also Harrison (1983).
4. See especially the entries for the period 1811–16 in Long (1981).
5. Bowring states: 'Even then, the objections he felt against needless swearing were strong; and the germs of his future writings on the subject of useless oaths were present to his thoughts.' (x *works* 36). On subsequent discussions of oaths, see Greer (1971) at 148–9.
6. Jolowicz (1948).
7. x *works* 37.

194 *Notes to pages 20–23*

8. Ibid.
9. See below, 87.
10. Phillips (1750), x *works* 35; id. 77–8, discussed by Mack (1962) at 37–40; see also 4 *RJE*, 80–83n. By coincidence Mrs Phillips' memoirs were probably written in the house in Queen Square Place which his father bought in 1763 and where Bentham and James Mill lived for many years: Mack (1962), 40.
11. x *works* 35.
12. Later Bentham catalogued the mischiefs of procedure more systematically:

    '*In the penal branch,*
    1. Impunity of delinquents.
    2. Undue punishments, viz. punishment of non-delinquents, or punishment of delinquents otherwise than due.

    In the non-penal branch,
    3. Frustration of well-grounded claims.
    4. Allowance of ill-grounded claims.
    5. Expense.
    6. Vexation.
    7. Delay.
    8. Precipitation.
    9. Complication.'   (*PJP*, ii *works* 19.)
    Cf. 'The Pleader's Guide', a satire on procedure quoted by Holdsworth (XIII *HEL*), 461ff.
13. A useful survey and bibliography on the historical background in respect of criminal law and procedure is to be found in Cockburn (1977), especially Ch. 1 (J. H. Baker) and the critical bibliography by L. A. Knafla, 270ff; see generally L. Stephen (1900), I; Radzinowicz (1948), I, 4, 703–26.
14. Bentham shared with many critics the view that the technicalities of the administration of criminal justice were absurd and mischievous. Recently social historians have interpreted the situation differently; see especially Douglas Hay, 'Property, Authority and the Criminal Law' in D. Hay *et al.* (1975); Cockburn (1977).
15. Keeton and Marshall (1948), 83. Cf. 1 *RJE*, 37; L. J. Hume (1981), 167–72.
16. x *works* 78.
17. Ibid.
18. Halévy (1955), 383ff.
19. Prest remarks of an earlier period: 'there was a long-standing tradition of distinguishing the abstract perfection of the laws from the manifest imperfections of those who lived by their practice'. ('The English Bar 1550–1700' in W. Prest (1981) at 80.) See also McGowen (1983).
20. I am grateful to Dr L. J. Hume for this suggestion.
21. Several relevant manuscripts for 1780 (or thereabouts) are listed in Long's chronological index (1981). It seems that Bentham considered that his views on procedure remained constant (Letter to General Mora, Sept. 1820, UC CLXXIV; 126). I am grateful to Professor Postema for this reference.
22. For details, see Twining (1985).
23. The suggestions here can only be tentative until further research has been done into the history of Bentham's intellectual development and his

activities in the period 1800–1805. For a useful general interpretation of Bentham's main concerns, see Steintrager (1977), Introduction.

24. See below, 88ff.
25. See generally, J. H. Burns (1966).
26. L. J. Hume (1981), 165ff. Hume's 'agenda theory' is not accepted by all scholars. Further research is needed into Bentham's intellectual development and the contemporary context to determine how far he was implementing a coherent plan and how far he was reacting to current events and debates or to his own experiences in the immediately preceding years.
27. The primary and secondary sources on these activities are very extensive. For a useful survey, see Bahmueller (1981), especially Ch. 3.
28. During the period 1803–12 Bentham may have presented the image of a hermit who had retired from active participation in public life; in fact he kept in close touch with current events and, in the seclusion of his hermitage, cultivated a number of highly significant contacts and made occasional ventures into the arena. However, much of the *Rationale* seems rather divorced from contemporary debates.
29. L. Hume (1981), 165; Dinwiddy (1975).
30. Id., 166, but see n.26.
31. On the role of the judiciary and these other corporations in Bentham's ideal polity, see L. J. Hume (1981) and Rosen (1983).
32. Printed, in attenuated form, in volume v of the Bowring edition. The original manuscripts are very extensive. One connecting theme of these works is that Bentham attacks the power of the Executive and seeks to design ways and means of ensuring that the judiciary performs its constitutional role of implementing the law as an efficient and subservient agent of the legislator (L. Hume (1981), 169–71).
33. See Halévy (1955); Mack (1962).
34. 1 *RJE*, 22: cf. 1 *RJE*, 284; 3 *RJE*, 269ff. cf. Jolowicz (1962), 14–19.
35. *R*. v. *Donnellan* (Warwick Assizes, 1777) and the *Calas* case (a notorious French case, made even more famous by Voltaire's account of it) were both cases in which circumstantial evidence before or after the event formed the basis of much-criticized verdicts of guilty.
36. *IV* 6n, cf. id., 140.
37. Especially *IV* 71, 143–5, 183–7.
38. For example *IV*, 140; 2 *RJE*, 120ff.
39. On Evans, see above, 2.
40. On Bentham's epistemology, see Postema (1983), 37, discussed below at 60ff.
41. On Bentham and Beccaria, see Hart (1982), Ch. 2. On Montesquieu, see Halévy (1955), 79–80 and below, 83. Bentham was generally an admirer of Voltaire: in a letter which was probably never sent, he wrote: 'I have taken counsel of you much oftener than of our own Ld. Coke and Hale and Blackstone' (November 1776?), 1 *Correspondence*, 367 (*CW*). Bentham was then 28, Voltaire 82. Despite the context, the sentiment is genuine.
42. On Bentham and Roman Law, see Jolowicz (1948), 6–7, 16.
43. Id., 14–19.
44. Shapiro (1983).
45. See above, 2–3.

196 *Notes to pages 27–31*

46. Halévy (1955), 378.
47. Id., 381, 402–3.
48. Id., 403, citing the article in the *Edinburgh Review* (1824), discussed below.

(ii) AN OUTLINE OF THE *RATIONALE OF JUDICIAL EVIDENCE*

1. On the relationship of *The Rationale* to Bentham's other writings on evidence, see Twining (1985).
2. More detailed suggestions for reading Bentham's writings are given in Twining (1985).
3. Halévy (1955), especially 374ff., 385.
4. 1 *RJE*, 1, quoted below at 66–7.
5. Cf. *IV*, 7–10.
6. 1 *RJE*, 23.
7. See below, 66ff.
8. On the relationship of evidence to procedure, see above at 12–13.
9. Book IX 'On Exclusion of Evidence' (5 *RJE*, 1–613); Book X, 'instructions, to be delivered from the legislator to the judge, for the estimation of the probative force of evidence' (5 *RJE*, 614–739). There is also a 'Conclusion', but this is more of an afterword than a summation.
10. Book I, Chs. 1–4.
11. 1 *RJE*, 40.
12. Id., 18.
13. Id., 17.
14. For example 1 *RJE*, 17.
15. For example Montrose (1968), 297. Cf. Best (1849), Art.11. On whether Bentham was a subjectivist, see below at 60ff.
16. *Treatise* at 45–6; Mill's note in 1 *RJE*, 106–9.
17. From Πιστεύω, I believe. Even Bentham apologizes for the term: 1 *RJE*, 124n. Cf. Book V, Ch.xvi (3 *RJE*, 269ff, especially 318–20).
18. 1 *RJE*, 131.
19. i *works*, 197–219; now *CW* (1983).
20. 1 *RJE*, 191, 196.
21. Id., 274ff.
22. Id., 283–4.
23. Id., 284.
24. Ibid.
25. Id., Ch.vi. Cf. *SNAA*. See above, chapter 2, n.5.
26. Id., Ch.v.
27. Especially id., Ch.ix; cf. *Treatise*, Appendix (by Dumont).
28. Id., Ch.x.
29. Id., Ch.viii.
30. See generally id., Ch.x, especially 1 *RJE*, 585.
31. 2 *RJE*, 425. Book III, Ch.xx contains a useful 'Recapitulation'. It should be borne in mind that Bentham wrote before the development of modern procedures of police interrogation.
32. Ibid.
33. Id., 431.

Notes to pages 31–39 197

34. Id., 431–2; on spurious reasons and silence, see further below at 84–5 and 105.
35. Id. 435; *Treatise*, 115n. Pre-appointed evidence is a particularly clear example of 'constructing' facts, see further below, 87. The term 'pre-constituted evidence' is used in the *Treatise*.
36. Id., 436.
37. Id., 435; cf. UC, xlv: 543.
38. 3 *RJE*, 587.
39. Keeton and Marshall (1948), 88–9. Best cites The Births and Deaths Registration Act 1836; the Judgment Act 1836; and the Court of Probate Act, 1857 as examples of piecemeal improvements in respect of pre-appointed evidence, but states that 'there is still room for improvement'. Keeton and Marshall remark that Best's treatment of pre-appointed evidence is '[p]ure Benthamism': id., 89. See further, Rosen (1983), 116ff.
40. *IV*, 183–7.
41. Book v, chs. 1–3.
42. Below at 52ff.
43. 3 *RJE*, 7–8; cf. id., 10–11.
44. 3 *RJE*, 2.
45. 3 *RJE*, 4.
46. Ibid.
47. *Treatise*, 143.
48. 3 *RJE*, 253–7n.
49. 3 *RJE*, 248–57.
50. *Treatise*, 180; see further below at 66ff.
51. 3 *RJE*, 229–30. For further examples, see *Treatise*, 180–85, reproduced in Twining (1983), 82–4. Cf. *IV*, 50–53, 167ff.
52. On 'instructions', see below at 43 and 68–9.
53. 3 *RJE*, 393–4.
54. On the metaphor of 'a chain', see the long footnote at 3 *RJE*, 223–5; cf. Wigmore on 'catenate' inferences, below, 127–8, 182–3.
55. *Treatise*, 190, where he fails to qualify the designation of circumstantial evidence as 'inferior'.
56. 3 *RJE*, 248.
57. Below at 52ff.; the length of this section is probably due to the interest it held for James and John Mill, both non-lawyers, who edited *IV* and *RJE* respectively.
58. 3 *RJE*, 270.
59. For example Thayer (1898), 265, Appleton (1860); see further above at 3–4, and below at 167ff.
60. 3 *RJE*, 283; cf. 1 *RJE*, 124ff.
60a. 3 *RJE*, 347.
61. Id., 380.
62. Id., 383–4.
63. Id., 394.
64. Id., 403.
65. Id., 404.
66. 5 *RJE*, 1–33; cf. *Treatise*, 229.
67. Book vi, Ch.iv; 3 *RJE*, 443–9.

198 *Notes to pages 39–44*

68. Ch.vi.
69. Ch.vii.
70. Ch.viii.
71. Ch.ix.
72. Ch.x.
73. 3 *RJE*, 573–4; cf. Ch.ii.
74. Id., 585.
75. Id., 586.
76. See, generally, J. W. Chadbourn (1962).
77. 3 *RJE*, 406.
78. Id., 408.
79. Ibid.
80. Op. cit. (n.76) at 937 n.32, disagreeing with Keeton and Marshall (1948) at 86. They suggest that Bentham would have ended the exclusion of hearsay altogether. Chadbourn is correct in suggesting that some hearsay could be excluded, for the reasons stated in the text, but wrong in suggesting that this was to be embodied in a *rule* of exclusion.
81. *Treatise*, 207.
82. See further below at 68–9.
83. 3 *RJE*, 588; see further above at 31–2.
84. 3 *RJE*, 622.
85. Ch.v, 619ff.
86. At 75ff.
87. See below at 76ff.
88. See also UC LVIII: *passim*, especially 124, 190, 213, 224, 326, 418.
89. *IV*, 10–11; cf. 4 *RJE*, 429.
90. 4 *RJE*, 429.
91. Ibid.
92. *Treatise*, 229–31. On priests, see 4 *RJE*, 586–92; *IV*, 98–9 (discussed below, 103).
93. Cf. 5 *RJE*, 712–13, 3 *RJE*, 342–3. Bentham seems to underestimate the difficulties of truth-telling; see further below, 211 n.9.
94. Especially 5 *RJE*, 34ff.
95. See below, 105, 170–1.
96. Cf. J. F. Stephen (1879), introduction, cited above, 4.
97. See above, n.51.
98. 5 *RJE*, 616.
99. Id., 615.
100. Ibid.
101. Id., 624.
102. Id., 618.
103. 5 *RJE*, 625; cf. quotations collected by Empson (1828), 473–82; cf. Rosen (1983), 158–9.
104. 5 *RJE*, 621.
105. Id., 623–4.
106. Id., 635–6.
107. 5 *RJE*, 642. This passage anticipates much modern psychological analysis of the ways in which the reliability of testimony can be affected at different stages in the process. See further, 644–5. For a spirited attack on the view

Notes to pages 44–51 199

that Bentham was psychologically naive, see Mack (1962), 208ff. and (1969), 209ff.

108. 5 *RJE*, 644–5.
109. Id., 736–7.
110. Cf. the review of the *Rationale* in the *Edinburgh Review*: 'Bacon calculates that there is no passion so weak, but what has on certain occasions conquered the fear even of death; therefore the *species* of interest will furnish no conclusive inference respecting its *degree*. The number of interests just as little; one ruling passion will out-vote five weaker ones, or swallow them up if they say the word.' Empson (1828), 501.
111. 5 *RJE*, 712.
112. *IV*, 136ff., 151ff.; *Treatise*, Book VII, Ch.16. See further, below at 95–8.
113. Ibid.
114. 5 *RJE*, 728ff; see further below, 53ff.
115. *Scotch Reform* (v *works* 24–5).
116. See 'Wigmore on Proof', below at 126ff.
117. 5 *RJE*, 734.
118. Id., 739.
119. Id., 740.
120. I.e. 'the Saxon County Courts' (original note).
121. 'The Sheriff's and Borough Courts in Scotland' (original note). 5 *RJE*, 741–2.
122. Id., 742; cf. *The Book of Fallacies* (ii *works*, 398): fallacy of 'The Wisdom of our Ancestors or Chinese Argument'.
123. 5 *RJE*, 744.
124. Id., 742–3.

(iii) SELECTED THEMES IN BENTHAM'S THEORY OF EVIDENCE

(a) The Natural System

1. The principal general passages in which Bentham discusses the Natural System of Procedure are: (i) 2 *RJE*, 425–34; 4 *RJE*, 5–12, 428ff. (ii) *IV*, Ch.xi, 34 5, 135 7. (iii) *Scotch Reform* (v *works* 3 16) (iv) *Treatise*, 4ff. (v) *PJP* (ii *works* 169–78). See also v *works* 444ff. There are numerous passages on the subject in the Bentham MSS. By far the most systematic account in the published writings is in *SR*.
2. *Treatise*, 7–8.
3. 'Logically speaking, the quality of the natural system will be seen to be chiefly of the negative cast; constituted by the absence of those *devices*, which constitute so many characteristic features of the technical system.' (v *works* 8).
4. See below, 52.
5. This is a condensed version, in some places a paraphrase, of v *works* 8–14 (*SR*). The italics follow the text in the Bowring edition. Compare ii *works* 178 for a more succinct statement (*PJP*).
6. For example 1 *RJE*, 584–5; 2 id., 288.
7. 1 *RJE*, 4–5, where the whole system is condemned in general terms; cf. 1 id., 484–5, 585.
8. Bentham treated a number of particular institutions as approximating to the

200 Notes to pages 51–53

natural system, including courts martial, courts of request, local magistrates courts, Danish and French courts of reconciliation, and some courts of arbitration. His treatment of these is discussed in Postema (forthcoming), Ch.vii. In *RJE* he regularly holds up the Saxon county courts (e.g. 5 *RJE*, 741) as a model to be emulated.

9. For example 1 *RJE*, 4–5.
10. See above, 46. Cf. *Treatise*, 4–6; ii *works* 398.
11. 1 *RJE*, 20.
12. 1 *RJE*, 19.
13. Id., 18–19.
14. Id., 19.
15. See Cohen (1983) at 4ff.
16. Llewellyn (unpublished, 1950) extracts from which are printed in Twining (1973) at 497ff; see especially 503.
17. 1 *RJE*, 35. There is an echo of modes of talk associated with Natural Law in 5 *RJE*, 743, quoted above at 47. See further Hart (1982) at 29–32.
18. 1 *RJE*, 128.
19. 1 *RJE*, 131.

(b) Evaluation of evidence

1. In the *Rationale* and the *Introductory View* Bentham generally talks in terms of degrees of persuasion rather than belief. In the *Treatise* Dumont's words 'persuasion', 'croire', are each variably translated as 'persuasion' and 'belief' in a way that suggests they are synonymous. See, for example, Book I, Chs.vii and viii. Bentham tends to use belief to represent an inferior degree of persuasion to knowledge (e.g. 1 *RJE*, 91), but he is not always consistent.
2. 3 *RJE*, 3–4.
3. 3 *RJE*, 351: 'Certainty, absolute certainty, is a satisfaction which on every ground of inquiry we are continually grasping at, but which the inexorable nature of things has placed for ever out of our reach. Practical certainty, a degree of assurance sufficient for practice, is a blessing, the attainment of which, as often as it lies in our way to attain it, may be sufficient to console us under the want of any superfluous and unattainable acquisitions.'
4. The main sections are in 1 *RJE*, 58–138 (Book 1), and 3 *RJE*, 219–392 (Book 5); *IV*, 14–20, 50–56, 151–95; *Treatise*, 16–20, 38–45, 180–89, 259–96. The best discussion of Bentham's approach to probability and its relationship to his theory of fictions is Postema (1983). I am much indebted to this article and to Professor Postema for many helpful suggestions in respect of this section.
5. On the history of probability theory, see Hacking (1975).
6. See generally the bibliography in Twining (1983), 156–7.
7. Bentham says: 'In the case of immediate testimonial evidence (*setting aside the consideration of any supposed improbability of the fact stated, and any supposed imperfection in the disposition and character of the witness*) the strength of persuasion on the part of the judge will be as the strength of persuasion expressed on the part of the witness.' (1 *RJE*, 72; italics added). The words in italics do not exhaust the range of possible infirmative

Notes to pages 54–55 201

conditions. This statement must be read subject to at least the following further *caveats*:

(a) that there is no counter-evidence

(b) that the evidence is properly communicated to the judge

(c) that there is no supposed imperfection in the disposition and character of the judge – all factors that Bentham allows for elsewhere.

8. See above, 30.

9. See, for example, 1 *RJE*, 113. See further below at 70.

10. 5 *RJE*, 736.

11. 3 *RJE*, 330–32. 'General' evidence refers to the general background knowledge or belief about the ordinary course of nature on which judgments of improbability are founded.

12. This passage is constructed from a variety of sources. The nearest that Bentham comes to a general summary along these lines is in *IV* at 153–5 and the *Treatise* at 38–48, 180–83. But in each case his concern to attack binding rules gets in the way of his giving clear positive guidance.

13. 3 *RJE*, 279ff. *IV* 45–7; cf. *Treatise*, 259ff.

14. See especially *IV* 153–4; 3 *RJE*, 330ff. Bentham did not accept the maxim: 'The more atrocious the offence, the greater the force of evidence requisite to prove it.' For mischievousness, odiousness or cruelty are not, *per se*, so contrary to the general course of nature as to render them improbable (3 *RJE*, 385–92).

15. 'A fact is said to be morally improbable, when it is considered as being inconsistent with the known course of human conduct. This species of improbability is confined to such facts as have their place in the human mind.' (*IV*, 153.)

16. For example 3 *RJE*, 343–51; Bentham, however, prophetically allowed for the possibility of flight of objects through the air contrary to the law of gravity, and used it to make the point that because there is no evidence that something has happened, it does not follow that it is impossible or that it has never happened. However, without special evidence to support a claim that it has, in fact, happened, he would have treated such a claim as (*prima facie*) improbable.

17. *IV*, 153.

18. For example *IV*, 151ff; 1 *RJE*, 150–61; 5 id., 628ff.; *Treatise*, Book I, Chs. 9, 16. 'Trustworthiness' applies to testimonial, but not to circumstantial, evidence; 'Probative force' applies to both – *semble*, so does the method of infirmative suppositions, but see the distinction between general and special counter-evidence; 3 *RJE*, 330ff.

19. For example *IV*, 17–18n; cf. *Treatise*, 181–3, 3 *RJE*, 113, 221–5.

20. 3 *RJE*, 219–23. Postema puts the matter thus: 'The degree of probative force of E (Evidence) on P (Probandum) according to Bentham, is equal to the ratio expressive of practical certainty minus the probability of the infirmative supposition's actually obtaining. And where there is more than one such infirmative supposition (say, I_1, I_2, I_3 . . . I_n) conceivable, the probative force of E on P is equal to practical certainty minus the probability of (I_1 or I_2 or I_3 or . . . I_n) obtaining. The basic idea seems to be that the proper degree of persuasion of P given E for a given person can be determined by measuring the shortfall from full confidence (practical

202 Notes to pages 55–58

certainty) produced by doubts put in the way of full confidence, qualified by the seriousness of these doubts.' (1983 at p.59). There is no reason in principle when two or more infirmative suppositions are mutually compatible that they cannot be added and, as Postema notes, Bentham talks of 'the sum of their infirmative forces' (3 *RJE*, 222).

21. See above, n.3.
22. 3 *RJE*, 221–2.
23. For example 1 *RJE*, 124–7; above, 29.
24. See below, 59.
25. The phrase is that of Jonathan Cohen (1980), 91.
26. Montrose (1968), 287, 297–8.
27. Cited by Best (1st edn), s.69. Bonnier (1843), s.204, referred to the device as a 'testimoniometre' and commented: 'soumise au scalpel de l'analyse, l'intime conviction se flétrit: de même que les fleurs d'un herbier se déssèchent et perdent leurs vives couleurs'.
28. Gulson (1923).
29. Cohen (1977) at 54ff.
30. Postema (1983).
31. Best (1849), 74n. refers to it as 'his thermometer of persuasion'; Bonnier (1843) as a 'testimoniometre'. Empson (1828), 496, refers to 'the moral thermometer'. Wigmore (1937), 310–12, produced something comparable, but less carefully worked out than Bentham's (see below at 225n.33).
32. 1 *RJE*, 85ff.
33. Id., 88.
34. 88–9. It is not clear whether Bentham is here suggesting, as later writers have done, that doubts about the facts could be reflected in the level of sanctions – a factor which regularly affects outcomes in bargaining. See Coons (1964).
35. Id., 85.
36. Bentham is unfair to the English language. Gilbert produced five terms each for Degrees of Evidence and Degrees of Assurance; see further the probability table below at 61.
37. 1 *RJE*, 93–5. Bentham's specific targets are the Romanist scale as adopted by Heineccius' 'school of fraud and nonsense', and M. Jousse's proposals in respect of degrees warranting capital punishment or different degrees of torture. He discredits them on other grounds, but his principal objection is that they do not measure degrees of persuasion.
38. 1 *RJE*, 97.
39. 1 *RJE*, 71–80, cf. id., 19–21; *Treatise*, 41–6, cp. 3 *RJE*, 533–5 (hearsay).
40. Twining (1980a); Cohen (1977).
41. 1 *RJE*, 74, cf. id., 20 (note by J. S. Mill) and 3 *RJE*, 533–5.
42. See generally Eggleston (1983), Ch.1.
43. 1 *RJE*, 100; *IV*, 16.
44. *IV*, 143–5, 183–7.
45. AF. ii *works* 498.
46. This is one foundation of Bentham's anti-nomian thesis: see below, 66ff.
47. For example Glanville Williams (1979).
48. 1 *RJE*, 71–2, 83, 101–2; *Treatise*, 41 and 45–6n (Dumont).
49. *Treatise*, 41.

Notes to pages 58–64 203

50. *Treatise*, 46n, cited in full and criticized by Mill in 1 *RJE*, 106–9n.
51. Postema (1983), 43. Postema comments: 'In the latter case, accepting reasonable odds may have no rational basis and these are just the sort of cases which figure prominently in law.' Bentham is more concerned with wagers as indications of the degree of confidence of the punter than as a means of making rational arguments about subjective probabilities.
52. Discussed in Twining (1984 c.II); see further below at 177.
53. On modern theories of subjective probability see Kyburg and Smokler (1964). Elsewhere Bentham remarks: 'for though a wager is no direct proof of any fact which is the subject of it, it is, however, a proof of the real confidence of him who joins in it and a punishment for rash confidence on the part of him who loses it' (3 *RJE*, 350).
54. 53ff.
55. 1 *RJE*, 100.
56. Id., 102–3.
57. 1 *RJE*, 74; cf. *Treatise*, 209–10.
58. Id., 76.
59. *Treatise*, 42.
60. Ibid. Bentham suggests that rectitude of decision will be maximized by requiring each judge to announce his degree of persuasion rather than just voting for or against a particular outcome: for the united amount of the degree of belief of three judges may be less than that of two others. This rather surprising conclusion, which no doubt contributed to the derision poured on the thermometer of persuasion, is logically consistent with the principle *pondere non numero* – count not the number of witnesses, nor the votes of judges, but the sum total of their degrees of persuasion. Not only would the method ensure that decision turned on preponderance or strength of belief rather than on the number of voices, but this commitment would be of value in appeal and in the exercise of pardon.
61. See especially Best (1849), 68–70.
62. *Best on Evidence* (J. M. Lely, 8th edn, 1893), Preface; cf. id., 56.
63. See above, 55–6.
64. Cohen (1977).
65. *Treatise*, 45–6n, cited and discussed at 1 *RJE*, 106–9n.
66. Ibid.
67. 1 *RJE*, 108–9n.
68. For example 1 *RJE*, 79–80 suggesting, *inter alia*, 'that at no time would the number of occasions calling for it . . . be very considerable'.
69. *Treatise*, 43; cf. 1 *RJE*, 80 and 80–2n.
70. 1 *RJE*, 76.
71. However, as with the calculus of utility, how far Bentham believed literally in the possibility of calculation is an open question.
72. Table at p. 61.
73. On the use of the device as a means of calculation, see n.60 above.
74. Postema (1983), 38; this section is largely based on this valuable article.
75. viii *works* 26.
76. Postema op. cit. at 48.
77. Id., 55–6.
78. Id., 57.

204 *Notes to pages 64–68*

79. 1 *RJE*, 124.
80. *PML*, Ch.2.
81. Gilbert (1754), 1.
82. Postema (1983), 42; cf. 47.
83. Id., 40.
84. *IV*, 16; cf. 1 *RJE*, 71 where the heading of Book 1, Ch.vi is 'Degrees of persuasion and probative force, how measured'.
85. *IV*, 18n.
86. Id., 17n.
87. Postema rightly points out that for Bentham, 'probative force' is a fictitious quality connected with persuasion which is psychological fact. (citing *IV*, 46; 3 *RJE*, 308–9, 263–7). But Bentham regularly uses both terms together and suggests that they do not always coincide. This point in fact bolsters, rather than undermines, Postema's argument about Bentham's modified subjectivism.
88. *IV*, 18n.
89. The key passage in *IV*, 17–18 is not inconsistent with the notion of evidence which has a tendency to produce a higher degree of persuasion than is appropriate (e.g. evidence of prior convictions may be prejudicial) but Bentham does not address the issue directly. One might infer from his general approach that he saw this as a matter for admonitory instructions rather than regulation.
90. See below, 69.
91. For example 1 *RJE*, 85; 'In this commanding station, men are without difficulty considered as exempt from, or proof against, the action of all sinister interest; proof, at any rate, against all temptation to any such malpractice as that of misrepresenting their own opinions.'

(c) The Anti-nomian Thesis

1. 3 *RJE*, 219; cf. *Treatise*, 180, quoted above at 34.
2. See, for example, *Treatise*, 180; *IV*, 151ff; 1 *RJE*, 44; 3 *RJE*, 219ff; 4 *RJE*, 477ff. The theme is found in early manuscripts, see especially UC, LI:A; LVIII: 12.
3. 1 *RJE*, 1–2.
4. It begins: 'Of the several rules laid down in this code, there is not one that is meant to be regarded as inflexible: no one is there, from which, in case of necessity, the judge may not depart.' (ii *works* 32, *PJP*.); cf. iv *works* 322: 'In judicial procedure, every rule that is not made to bend will be sure to break, or still worse must ensue.'
5. 1 *RJE*, 44. An earlier sentence also contains a qualifier: '*Hitherto* the operation of judging of the degree of connection . . . has been an operation of the instinctive class' (ibid.).
6. *IV*, 151 (twice); cf. 3 *RJE*, 200–2 (Character).
7. For example *Treatise*, 229–30. On qualified admission of makeshift evidence in the character of indicative evidence (i.e. evidence of evidence), see 3 *RJE*, 553–7. It might be argued that the non-exclusion principle is itself a mandatory rule, but this would be misleading: the exclusion of irrelevant or superfluous evidence is *justified* rather than strictly *required* and there is no

Notes to pages 68–71 205

need for Bentham to mandate the strict exclusion of all that is irrelevant or redundant except on grounds of preponderant vexation, expense or delay. The latter test has to be applied to the circumstances of each individual case according to considerations of utility. The principle of utility is the only mandatory general principle involved.

8. See passages cited above, n.2.
9. Postema (1983) at 59.
10. Thayer (1898), 265.
11. For example Chamberlayne (1908) and (1911), *passim*.
12. Wigmore, 28 *A.B.A.J.* 23 (1942) at 26; see below, 163. Cf. Zuckerman (1983), 154–5; Fitzjames Stephen, per contra, criticized Courts Martial for their disregard of rules of evidence (L. Stephen (1895), 208–9).
13. For example, Rule 403 of the American Federal Rules of Evidence reads: 'Although relevant, evidence may be excluded if its probative value is substantially outweighed by the danger of unfair prejudice, confusion of issues, or misleading the jury, or by considerations of undue delay, waste of time, or needless presentation of cumulative evidence.' Cf. *R. v. Sang* [1979] 2 All E.R. 1222, at 1228 (per Lord Diplock) and 1231. See further below at 71–2.
14. A discretion to exclude evidence likely to be prejudicial in the particular case would not be inconsistent with the anti-nomian thesis. Nor is it necessarily incompatible with an assumption of general cognitive competence. Even an optimistic Enlightenment view that reason and truth will prevail once interest and superstition have been supplanted hardly leads to the conclusion that all triers of fact under the Natural System will be free from all propensity to place too much or too little weight on certain kinds of evidence. It is not clear how Bentham might have responded to this point. I am grateful to Professor Postema for raising the issue.
15. The most important discussions are in *IV*, 29–30, 86–116; 1 *RJE*, 110ff; 4 *RJE*, 477ff; *Treatise*, Book VII.
16. 5 *RJE* 1; cf. *Treatise*, 227.
17. 1 *RJE*, 37; 3 *RJE*, 553–7.
18. See especially *RJE*, vii, 451 *et seq.*
19. The *locus classicus* is Denman (1824) in the *Edinburgh Review*, discussed below at 102.
20. Especially 1 *RJE*, 511ff.
21. See generally L. J. Hume (1981). On distrust, see Steintrager (1977), especially 110–24.
22. For example Denman (1824) and Empson (1828) in the *Edinburgh Review*, discussed below at 100ff. On Wigmore's views on exclusion, see below at 157ff.
23. See especially Halévy (1955), 376–80.
24. Especially *IV*, 8–9; 1 *RJE*, 39ff.
25. Ibid. A corollary of this is that the weighing of probative force through the method of infirmative suppositions is relative to the circumstances of each case. see above, n.7.
26. Especially 1 *RJE*, 100ff.; *Treatise*, 40–44.
27. For example *Treatise*, 180 cited above, 34.
28. See Cohen (1983), 1ff.

206   *Notes to pages 72–77*

29. Teitelbaum *et al.* (1983).
30. *IV*, 7–12; 1 *RJE*, 3–6, 33–5; UC, LVIII: 172.
31. 2 *RJE*, 436.
32. Postema (forthcoming); some indications of the general approach are given in Postema (1977) and (1983).
33. Postema (1977), 1423.
34. See above, 41.
35. 4 *RJE*, 5ff, 428ff.
36. See generally above, 30.
37. *Scotch Reform* (v *works* 18–27).
38. Id., 17.
39. 1 *RJE*, 585.
40. 1 *RJE*, 523–4.

(d) The causes of the technical system

1. By far the longest and most coherent development of this theme is to be found in Book VIII of *RJE*. Dumont played this down in the *Treatise*. It is also given less prominence in the *Introductory View*, where Gilbert is made the chief target of attack; see however, *IV*, Chs.xxxi–ii, especially 144–5, where the main argument is stated strongly but succinctly.
2. See especially Hart (1973), Ch. 1; cf. M. Mack (1962) at 217n.
3. For example 4 *RJE*, 270–73.
4. 4 *RJE*, 13ff.
5. Ibid. See also above, 41.
6. For example 1 *RJE*, 202–6.
7. For example 4 *RJE*, 31ff.; cf. 1 *RJE*, 13–15; iv *works* 495–8.
8. 4 *RJE*, 179ff.
9. 4 *RJE*, 38–40; see citations at n.7 above.
10. 4 *RJE*, 39.
11. 1 *RJE*, 533; cf. 4 *RJE*, 21ff.
12. On the expression, which is used regularly throughout *RJE* and *IV*, see v *works* 369, in which Bentham claims to have been using the term 'some thirty or forty years probably' (*Indications Respecting Lord Eldon*, 1825).
13. Halévy (1955), 376–7.
14. 1 *RJE*, 216–17; 4 *RJE*, 270–71.
15. 2 *RJE*, 249n.
16. Bentham does allow for the possibility of litigants bringing ill-grounded suits out of ignorance, e.g. 1 *RJE*, 336–9; 2 *RJE*, 95. He places most of the blame for ill-grounded suits on lawyers.
17. *Passim.*
18. 4 *RJE*, 31.
19. Id., 34.
20. Ibid.
21. For example 4 *RJE*, 41–8.
22. 4 *RJE*, 48–54.
23. 4 *RJE*, 457ff; cf. v *works* 349–51.
24. For example 4 *RJE*, 44–5.
25. 4 *RJE*, 18–19.

Notes to pages 77–80 207

26. 4 *RJE*, 28.
27. 4 *RJE*, 25.
28. 4 *RJE*, 25–7.
29. 4 *RJE*, 51.
30. 4 *RJE*, 59.
31. 4 *RJE*, 40ff.
32. 4 *RJE*, 40–43, 1 *RJE*, 216–17.
33. 4 *RJE*, 43–4.
34. 4 *RJE*, 44–5.
35. 4 *RJE*, 45–8.
36. See especially Hay (1975), E. P. Thompson (1977 edn), 262ff.
37. Thompson (1977) at 266.
38. Id., 265.
39. Hay (1975).
40. Hart (1973).
41. See, for example, Hart (1982), 21–6; Mack (1962) at 173, 217, 297, 420–21.
42. See especially, C. K. Ogden (1932); *The Book of Fallacies*, ii *works* 375; on religion, see works cited below at 209, n.95.
43. Bentham lists only twelve devices in the text (4 *RJE*, 99–102), but the chapter headings of Book VIII extend the list to twenty as follows: 1. Exclusion of the parties from the presence of the judge. 2. Tribunals out of reach, or swallowing up the inferior courts. 3. Bandying the cause from court to court. 4. Blind fixation of times for the operations of procedure. 5. Sittings at long intervals. 6. Motion business. 7. Decision without thought, or mechanical judicature. 8. Chicaneries about notice. 9. Principle of nullification. 10. Mendacity-license. 11. Ready-written pleadings. 12. Principle of jargon, or jargonization. 13. Fiction. 14. Entanglement of jurisdictions. 15. Means of securing forthcomingness uselessly diversified. 16. Creation of needless and useless offices. 17. Sham pecuniary checks to delay, vexation and expense. 18. Double fountain principle. 19. Laudation of jurisprudential law. 20. Opinion trade.
44. 4 *RJE*, 103ff.
45. 4 *RJE*, 300. This contains the famous passage that begins:

> What you have been doing by the fiction, could you, or could you not, have done it without the fiction? If not, your fiction is a wicked lie: if yes, a foolish one.
> Such is the dilemma. Lawyer! escape from it if you can . . .

46. 4 *RJE*, 300–14.
47. 4 *RJE*, 205n.
48. 4 *RJE*, 301.
49. 4 *RJE*, 205ff.
50. 4 *RJE*, 211.
51. 4 *RJE*, 214. 'Such has been the success of hypocrisy in this line, that the deluded people have learnt to regard with sentiments of love and reverence and gratitude, instead of indignation, the treachery of those ministers of justice, who, by the help of this capital engine of iniquity, have persevered in the habit of giving aid and impunity to all sorts of malefactors.' (214–15). Cp. the argument of Hay (1975). As with many

208　*Notes to pages 80–83*

other topics, Bentham's discussion of the principle of nullification deserves more extended treatment than is possible here.

52. The main discussion is in 4 *RJE*, 287–99. See also iii *works* 209, 269ff. Bentham's ideal for language in law was 'noble simplicity' (iii *works* 209).
53. 4 *RJE*, 287.
54. 2 *RJE*, 190, 200.
55. 4 *RJE*, 292.
56. 'Nursing ignorance, jargon serves at the same time for a screen to it. It does more: over a head of ignorance it puts a mask, exhibiting a face of science. It is the dissertation upon Sanchoniathon, presented to the Vicar of Wakefield' (4 *RJE*, 295).
57. See especially *Essay on Language* (viii *works* 294); Ogden (1932); *The Book of Fallacies* (ii *works* 401), and numerous manuscripts. A full-scale study of Bentham's writings on logic and language has yet to be published, but see Postema (1983); Harrison (1983).
58. 4 *RJE*, 411ff.
59. For example 4 *RJE*, 388 – a theme repeated in many other places.
60. 4 *RJE*, 227ff.
61. 4 *RJE*, 256ff.
62. 4 *RJE*, 384ff; cf. v *works* 14, 512.
63. 4 *RJE*, 385–7; cf. id., 494.
64. 4 *RJE*, 387.
65. Here, particular ideology, in Mannheim's sense, that is a segment of an opponent's thought, conditioned by interest and context: Mannheim (1936).
66. See works cited in footnotes 72–82 below.
67. Halévy (1955), 373ff. It may be objected that the term 'sentimental liberalism' is an anachronism. The term does, however, designate the object of attack (notions of technical devices as safeguards of liberty) and the main basis of Bentham's objection (that belief in such safeguards is based on sentiment rather than reason). Halévy uses 'liberal' in the same way in this context, e.g. at 388–92. Cf. Rosen (1983), 30–31.
68. Id., 378, 390.
69. Id., 403.
70. See especially J. Dinwiddy (1975), 683. Cf. Hart (1982), 70n.
71. The main place where Montesquieu is explicitly discussed in the *Rationale* is in connection with corroboration as a 'disguised exclusion', (5 *RJE*, 468ff), but it is clear from Bentham's other writings that he regards Montesquieu as the main defender of the views discussed here. In the *Traité des Preuves Judiciaires*, Appendix iii, Dumont collected some extracts from Montesquieu's *De L'Esprit des Lois*. These were left out in the English translation (the *Treatise*).
72. See for example i *works* 558–9, iv *works* 365ff, vi *works* 288–90, and UC cxxvi: 8ff (1790) (reprinted in Mack (1962), 453–7).
73. If, however, Postema's theory of adjudication is correct, above at 206 n.32, then this passage needs to be read as subject to the *caveat* that the duty of the judge is to apply the law unless its implementation in the particular circumstances would be contrary to utility.
74. Especially *PJP*, 119ff, but see 135. Bentham's views on the role of the jury

Notes to pages 83–86 209

were complex and changed over time: see Mack (1962), 420ff; Rosen (1983), 155ff.

75. For modern discussions see Radzinowicz (1948), vol. I, 364–70; Foucault (1977), part II; see further below, 95ff.
76. v *works* 195ff, cf. i *works* 558.
77. *Three Tracts Relative to Spanish and Portuguese Affairs* (1821) (viii *works* 465ff).
78. *De L'Esprit des Lois* VI.2 (tr. Nugent 1949).
79. *Three Tracts* (viii *works* 481) – where Bentham also attacks the ideas that delay is 'a tribute due to justice' and that 'precipitation is the most dangerous rock in the way of justice', ideas he also attributes to Montesquieu.
80. Ibid.
81. viii *works* 478. The 'he' in this passage is Judge Advocate Hermosa, whose 'Panegyric on Judicial Delays' (1820) was the subject of Bentham's second tract.
82. Especially 5 *RJE*, 207ff (self-disserving evidence); cf. *IV* 106–9; *Treatise*, 240–45. This contains the famous passage that reads: 'If all the criminals of every class had assembled, and framed a system after their own wishes, is not this rule the very first which they would have established for their security? Innocence never takes advantage of it, innocence claims the right of speaking, as guilt invokes the privilege of silence.' (Id., 241).
83. The exact scope of the passage is debatable, but Bentham's primary concern is to attack all bars to questioning witnesses *coram judice*, in open court. Thus his discussion includes the incompetence of the accused to give evidence, the privilege against self-incrimination and at least part of the modern right to silence. However, the private interrogation of suspects in custody by police – the main focus of modern debates about the 'right to silence' – was not in the forefront of his mind, for police questioning, as we know it, is a late development. Bentham's views on the efficiency of direct questioning and 'silence implies guilt' need to be set against his emphasis on publicity. For modern misuse of quotations from Bentham taken out of context, see Twining (1973a).
84. 5 *RJE*, 229–30.
85. 5 *RJE*, 230–38.
86. Especially 232–3; see further below, 96.
87. 233ff; cf. 1 *RJE*, 599–602n.; id., 507–10; *Treatise*, 240ff.
88. 5 *RJE*, 238–40.
89. 5 *RJE*, 239.
90. 5 *RJE*, 239–40.
91. 5 *RJE*, 240–41.
92. Ibid.
93. 5 *RJE*, 241–50.
94. Below, 170–1.
95. The main passages in *RJE* relevant to this section are 1 *RJE*, 196–201; 230–49; 364–421. 2 *RJE*, 306; 5 *RJE*, 78–88. See further *IV*, 20–21, 28–9; *Treatise*, 34–6, 58–62, 81–7, 251–2; and *SNAA*; also v *works* 457–8. An edition of Bentham's writings on religion is currently being prepared for the *Collected Works*.

210 *Notes to pages 86–89*

96. 1 *RJE*, 232, cf. v *works* 222–3.
97. Above, 20–1.
98. See Twining (1985).
99. Matthew 5, 34 (from the Sermon on the Mount); cf. *Romeo and Juliet*, Act 2, Scene 2:
    > Do not swear at all;
    > Or, if thou wilt, swear by thy gracious self,
    > Which is the god of my idolatry.
100. *IV*, 39, quoting Article 39: 'We judge that the Christian religion does not prohibit, but that a man may swear when the magistrate requireth.'
101. Id., cf. i *works* 567; v *works* 195; vi *works* 312n.
102. *IV*, 29.
103. 5 *RJE*, 137–8, 1 *RJE*, 241, 316. In addition to Quakers, persons excommunicated, children, atheists and those who refuse the oath are excluded (5 *RJE*, 134ff).
104. Especially 1 *RJE*, 397ff.
105. Especially 2 *RJE*, 435ff, 649–63.
106. *Treatise*, 120.
107. Much of Bentham's writings on religion has yet to be published; *Not Paul, but Jesus* was published in 1823 under the pseudonym 'Gamaliel Smith'.
108. 4 *RJE*, 254n. See Hart (1982), 29.
109. 1 *RJE*, 145–7, cf. 5 *RJE*, 36: 'With minds of every class the mind of the lawyer has to deal. Of the structure of the human mind what does the lawyer know? Exactly what the grub knows of the bud it preys upon. By tradition, by a blind and rickety kind of experience, by something resembling instinct, he knows by what sophisms the minds of jurymen are poisoned; by what jargon their understandings are bewildered; how, by a name of reproach, the man who asks for the execution of the laws and the formation of good ones is painted as an enemy . . .'. Cf. 4 *RJE*, 50–51 for an even more colourful piece of invective.
110. See generally i *works* 217–18, ii *works* 477–8.
111. 2 *RJE*, 183, cf. 4 *RJE*, 48–54.
112. Halévy, (1955) at 392–3.
113. 1 *RJE*, 10–11.

(e) Rectitude of decision as a value

1. For example *IV*, 10; Delay and Complication Tables in *Scotch Reform* (v *works* 24–5); 2 *RJE*, 331–3, *et passim*.
2. The term 'truth theory', popularized by Jerome Frank (1949), Ch. 6, refers to theories that treat the establishment of the truth as the primary end of adjudication, in contrast with other theories – such as 'fight theories' or conflict-resolution theories – that postulate other or more varied ends. The contrast can be misleading, if it implies that fight theories deny any place to the pursuit of truth in legal processes. See further Twining (1984c).
3. On the meanings of 'truth' and 'true' in Bentham's thought, see Postema (forthcoming).
4. Fried (1978), Ch. 5. Fried is primarily concerned with lying and truth-

Notes to pages 89–92 211

telling as a matter of individual ethics. In most of the passages discussed in this section Bentham is more concerned with truth as a social value in the context of his science of legislation.

5. Id. at 59–60.
6. *PML*, 205 (*CW*).
7. Ibid.
8. ii *works* 210 (*Rationale of Reward*).
9. Important passages in *RJE* include 1 *RJE*, 161–3, 184–249; 2 id., 1–2, 305–7; 332–3; 3 id., 342–3; 5 id., 647–9, 693–714. See further the index under Falsehood, Mendacity and Perjury. See also *Treatise* at 157–64, 184–5, 208. On modern treatments of lying, see Bok (1978) and the references therein. On psychological aspects see Wigmore (1937), 181ff, 268ff (discussed below, 135ff.); and Yarmey (1979).
10. Above, 20–1; see especially x *works* 36.
11. The recurrent theme of lying is clearly illustrated in William Empson's collection of passages attacking lawyers, 'the favourite children of the father of lies' in (1828), 673–6, discussed below at 106ff.
12. *The Elements of the Art of Packing* (v *works* 92); cf. 4*RJE*, 313.
13. *Principles of the Civil Code* i *works* 302. Postema points out that at different periods Bentham's vocabulary shifted from 'expectation utility' to 'the disappointment-prevention principle' to a more general emphasis on security. If anything, as he grew older his emphasis on security increased, but always as a principle subordinate to utility: Postema (1977).
14. i *works* 78, extracted from Dumont's *Traité de Legislation*.
15. 5 *RJE*, 1.
16. The best known example is 'the foxhunter's reason' 5 *RJE*, 238ff. See also references above at 209, n.87.
17. For example 5 *RJE*, 230ff. In a manuscript fragment (UC, LVIII: 343) he treats 'audi alteram partem' not as a fundamental principle of justice, but as a prudential maxim justified solely in terms of its tendency to avoid misdecision. The implication is that if the judge can arrive at the truth without hearing one of the parties, whether that party is winner or loser, no injustice has been done.
18. Bentham's omission is particularly unfortunate because there has been surprisingly little systematic utilitarian (as opposed to economic) analysis of the pains and pleasures of litigation (see below, 93). It is arguable that the costs are regularly underestimated in theory and practice. Thus the only mischief of misidentification is normally seen to be wrongful conviction of the innocent, rather than the great variety of pains of being subjected to criminal process: see below, n.35, and Twining (1983a).
19. UC, LVIII: 72.1 (1805).
20. UC, LVIII: 68.1–2; id:69.1 (1805).
21. 'Delay and Complication Tables' in v *works* 24–5.
22. See, however, UC box LVIII.
23. *PJP* (ii *works* 17).
24. *Ibid*.
25. The difficulties are, of course, not confined to ascertainment and measurement. There are also profound difficulties of generalization across individuals, cultures, types of case etc.

212   *Notes to pages 92–94*

26. For example, he sometimes includes, excludes or differentiates expense and delay from vexation; sometimes he confines it to present pain during the process, sometimes he includes some (but never all) painful consequences of involvement in litigation.
27. Modern writings on contract and on dispute-settlement emphasize the importance of the distinction between continuing and one-off relationships. See for example, Macaulay (1963) and MacNeil (1974).
28. On Compromise see below. Much of the literature on traditional African modes of dispute-settlement contrasts the emphasis on restoration of harmony with the strict enforcement of rules associated with imposed Western courts. As one Minister of Justice in Tanzania put it: 'People leave the courts as enemies; they leave [traditional] arbitral proceedings as friends' Twining (1964). The contrast is, of course, too stark: see further Eisenberg (1976).
29. For example 1 *RJE*, 553ff.
30. For example 1 *RJE*, 465.
31. For example 1 *RJE*, 549. Bentham also deals with collateral facts at some length in connection with the privilege against self-incrimination.
32. See above, text at n.23.
33. For a recent discussion of the psychological and economic costs of being accused of crime, see Feeley (1979). The author concludes that in some lower courts the main punishment of defendants (whether ultimately convicted or not) occurs during the processing of their cases. Cp. Ryan (1980).
34. It is arguable that a comprehensive analysis of litigation would include the benefits as well as the costs and that Bentham underplays the pleasures and satisfactions of litigation, some of which are brought out by sporting analogies. Thus it could be argued that litigation has undoubted attractions for some participants and most spectators: for example, the fascination and excitement of the contest; the satisfactions of having 'one's day in court'; the pleasures of publicity; the opportunities for vengeance and self-vindication; and the entertainment value of trials and reports of trials. Bentham recognized a limited educational value in 'the theatre of justice' (e.g. 1 *RJE*, 557ff); he took a rather puritanical attitude to the idea of trials as a form of popular entertainment and he treated enjoyment of technicality and sporting analogies as forms of perversion (see above, 85). One has some sympathy with his conclusions, but one wonders whether they are entirely consistent with hard-nosed utilitarianism.
35. For example Posner (1977), Scott (1975), Hazard (1965), Wittman (1974), Tullock (1980).
36. See Twining (1984, 1984c) and below at 176–8.
37. While the literature on dispute settlement is vast, there have been surprisingly few general treatments of compromise in litigation; see, however, Coons (1964), and Pennock and Chapman (eds) (1979), especially the articles by Shapiro, Peczenick and Coons. There is an extensive literature on particular forms of compromise such as plea-bargaining, contractual negotiation and industrial conflict.
38. Alexander Peczenick concludes: 'Compromise and cumulation of different ideas, reasons, approaches and so on, dominate legal practice, legal

Notes to pages 94–95   213

thinking, doctrinal study of law, and legal theory' in Pennock and Chapman (1979), 188.

39. Some standard examples are collected in Twining and Miers (1982) at 22–9. See, however, Eisenberg (1976), who questions whether some cases of alleged discrepancies between rules and results have been correctly interpreted.

40. The main passages in his published writings are to be found in ii *works* 46–7; iii id. 83; v id. 35; vi id. 24n. (*IV*); 1 *RJE*, 413–17, 423–7. A full analysis of Bentham's position – and his views may have changed over time – would require consideration of a variety of other passages and in particular his treatment of pardon, nullification, equity and informers. The discussion in the text is only intended as a preliminary treatment of a large and complex subject. See further, Postema (forthcoming).

41. Bentham treats the Danish Reconciliation Courts (or Reconciliation offices) as a reaction to the technical system (1 *RJE*, 560n.) His discussion of them centres on particular aspects of their procedure (such as the absence of oaths and secrecy). He only indirectly touches on the issues surrounding termination of conflict, restoration of harmony and expletive justice as potentially competing ends. See, however, ii *works* 46–7.

42. *Scotch Reform* (v *works* 35).

43. *PJP* (ii *works* 47).

44. v *works* 35.

45. For Bentham the use of pardon within the technical system was another example of the principle of nullification, by which arbitrary power was taken by judges and others to frustrate the will of the legislator. Although he was prepared to give a strictly limited power of pardon under the Constitutional Code, he was highly critical of its use in England. Gratuitous pardon, on its own, is an evil; it frustrates justice, it condemns statute law and it involves decisions other than on the merits; historically it has been the subject of abuse and an instrument of tyranny (i *works* 520). In a few limited cases, most notably where there is a doubt about the evidence in penal cases (*IV*, 228–9), Bentham is prepared to provide for it on grounds of utility – but generally he considers justice and utility to be best furthered by strict application of the law. See i *works* 520–21; ix id. 36–7, 606–7; 4 *RJE*, 205ff (nullification). Cf. Foucault (1977), 73–103, 312–17, citing Brissot (1781), 200: 'If pardon is equitable, the law is bad; when legislation is good, pardons are only crimes against the law.' See also Hay (1975).

46. Postema (forthcoming), Ch. 7.

47. Thayer (1898), 552ff.

48. Wigmore, 9 *Treatise*, 2497, 2511; on the historical background see Thayer (1898), 551–8.

49. MacNally (1802) used the phrase 'a reasonable doubt', cited by Thayer at 559, but said little about the presumption of innocence. Most of the eighteenth- and early nineteenth-century discussions of these topics centre on capital offences, and most of Bentham's pronouncements need to be read in this context.

50. *De Laudibus legum Angliae* (1st edn 1545–6), c.27. Fortescue wrote *De Laudibus* circa 1468–71 and this is not necessarily the earliest example of this mode of expression. See Holdsworth, iii *HEL*, 620.

214 *Notes to pages 95–97*

51. Howell, VII *State Trials*, 32 Charles II at 1529.
52. IV *Commentaries* Book 4, Ch. 27, 358.
53. See below, 104 (Denman).
54. Paley (1809 edn), 310–11. Discussed by Denman (1824) at 180–81.
55. Samuel Romilly (1810), note D.
56. Paley (1809).
57. Romilly (1810) states:

> 'They ought rather', continues Paley, 'to reflect that he who falls by a mistaken sentence, may be considered as falling for his country, whilst he suffers under the operation of those rules, by the general effect and tendency of which the welfare of the community is maintained and upheld.' Nothing is more easy than thus to philosophize and act the patriot for others, and to arm ourselves with topics of consolation, and reasons for enduring with fortitude the evils to which, not ourselves, but others are exposed. I doubt, however, very much, whether this is attended with any salutary effects. Instead of endeavouring thus to extenuate and reconcile to the minds of those who sit in judgment upon their fellow-creatures so terrible a calamity as a mistake in judicature to the injury of the innocent, it would surely be a wiser part to set before their eyes all the consequences of so fatal an error in their strong but real colours. To represent to them that of all the evils which can befall a virtuous man, the very greatest is to be condemned and to suffer a public punishment as if he were guilty. To see all his hopes and expectations frustrated; all the prospects in which he is indulging, and the pursuits which he is following, for the benefit, perhaps, of those who are dearer to him than himself, brought to a sudden close; to be torn from the midst of his family; to witness the affliction they suffer; and to anticipate the still deeper affliction that awaits them: not to have even the sad consolation of being pitied; to see himself branded with public ignominy; to leave a name which will excite only horror or disgust; to think that the children he leaves behind him, must, when they recall their father's memory, hang down their heads with shame; to know that even if at some distant time it should chance that the truth should be made evident, and that justice should be done to his name, still that his blood will have been shed uselessly for mankind, that his melancholy story will serve wherever it is told, only to excite alarm in the bosoms of the best members of society, and to encourage the speculations for evading the law, in which wicked men may indulge.

> It is interesting to note that most of Romilly's arguments are consequentialist, but it is debatable whether the tone and some of the nuances can be fully accommodated within a pure utilitarian calculation. See further below at 104. This passage is reprinted in full in Howell, op. cit. n.51.

58. Romilly (1810).
59. The following reconstruction of Bentham's views is taken from scattered passages in his published works where they appear in discussions of different topics, including capital punishment, whether jury verdicts should be unanimous, the evils of the technical system of procedure, rules requiring two witnesses as disguised exclusions, and mis-seated punish-

Notes to pages 97–98 215

ments. I have tried to take account of these different contexts, but it must be acknowledged that his views on this issue are open to other possible interpretations and may have varied over time. The most sustained discussion is in the *Treatise* and this may be attributable to the influence of Dumont.

60. *PML*, Ch.vi; UC, xiv: 3, discussed Mack (1962), 244–5.

61. vii *works* 522–3; i *works* 449; ii *works* 132–4. In a revealing passage he states: 'In the penal branch, the avoiding to administer punishment when undue, is certainly an end of very high importance, and altogether necessary to be attended to with unremitting and anxious care. It cannot, however, with any propriety be stated as constituting an ultimate, a primary, a direct end of the system of procedure. Why? Because, if there were no system of procedure at all, this end would be the more completely and effectually accomplished.' *PJP* (ii *works* 20); discussed Postema (1977), 1416–18.

62. 'This supposes that the non-guiltiness of the convicted individual either is at the time, or becomes thereafter, an object of popular belief, more or less extensive and intense. For, suppose the contrary, the suffering of one who is not guilty is not greater than the suffering of one who is guilty. It even is not so great. For to support him under the affliction, the not guilty has considerations which the guilty has not.' *PJP* (ii *works* 133n). On apparent justice and real justice, see 3 *RJE*, 521n. Denman commented, with a touch of irony, on Bentham's emphasis on apparent justice: 'The danger, he says, is more apparent than real: the alarm is greater than the danger, or in other words, the real danger is not so great as the apparent. In a word he treats this as a case in which imagination takes the place of reason.' (1824), 169, at 180; discussed below at 102–3.

63. i *works* 475–6. Mis-seated punishment is distinguished from groundless punishment. In the former an offence has been committed but the punishment for that offence has been attached to the wrong person (which includes vicarious, transitive, collective and random punishment): id. 478ff. On the mischiefs of misdecision see 5 *RJE*, 715ff.

64. Id., 476.

65. Op. cit. above at n.61, 62.

66. See also *Treatise*, 148, 197–8; 5 *RJE*, 715–21 (*semble* this passage deals with both civil and criminal cases); i *works* 448–9, 558 (*Principles of Penal Law*).

67. ii *works* 133.

68. *PJP* (ii *works* 169).

69. *Treatise*, 178.

70. *Treatise*, 179.

71. *Treatise*, 179.

72. *Treatise*, 196.

73. See above, references at n.16 and 19.

74. 'But allowing that, in ordinary cases, the presumption is against the accused, it is no less true that it is proper to proceed as if the presumption were established in his favour; and, consequently, that it ought to be a maxim with the judge, that it is better to let a guilty man escape, than to condemn an innocent one; or, in other words, he ought to be much more on his guard against the injustice which condemns, than the injustice which acquits. Both are great evils, but the greater is that which produces **most**

216 Notes to pages 98–100

alarm; and, every one knows, that, in this respect, there is no comparison between the two cases. Generally speaking, a too easy acquittal excites regret and uneasiness only among men of reflection; while the condemnation of an accused, who turns out to have been innocent, spreads general dismay; all security appears to be destroyed; no defence can any longer be found, when even innocence is insufficient.' (*Treatise*, 197).

75. *Treatise*, 198. Bentham argues that while the wrongful conviction of an innocent man is unlikely to lead to similar errors, 'the almost certain effect of acquitting a thief is to produce new thefts' (*Treatise*, 197). Nevertheless he is prepared to treat the first as a greater evil because of the effect on public opinion, thereby adopting the substance, but perverting the spirit, of some of Romilly's argument.

76. See below at 100ff.

77. Especially 5 *RJE*, 327–49.

78. Especially 5 *RJE*, 302–25; *IV*, 99–100.

79. See further below, 105.

80. For example 5 *RJE*, 207ff, *IV*, 106–9; on process values see Summers (1974) and below, 104.

81. For example 3 *RJE*, 100ff.

82. This is explored in detail in W. L. and P. E. Twining (1974).

83. Especially 4 *RJE*, 586–92; *IV*, 98–9.

84. 1 *RJE* 566–8 (iv *works* 317).

85. Ibid.

86. See further below at 104.

87. See for example his expressions of outrage in respect of the *Calas* case (e.g. i *works* 448; 3 *RJE*, 55).

88. The flexibility of Bentham's position is illustrated by 4 *RJE*, 511–14.

(iv) AFTERMATH: *THE EDINBURGH REVIEW*

1. On the *Edinburgh Review*, founded in 1802, and the Benthamite *Westminster Review*, founded in 1824, see Nesbitt (1934).

2. *Edinburgh Review* XL (1824), 169–207 (T. Denman); id. XLVIII (1828), 457–520 (W. Empson). Cf. *Westminster Review* V (1826), 23–58, (P. Bingham); id. IX (1828), 198–250 (J. Roebuck). Other contemporary reviews include J. C. L. de Sismondi, *Revue Encyclopédique* XIX (1823), 170–72 (*Traité*); Pellegrino Rossi, *Thémis, ou Bibliothèque du Jurisconsulte* VIII (1826), 73–92; *The Jurist* III (1832), 1ff.: 'On the Exclusion of Evidence' (Discussion of the *Rationale*) cf. id. I (1827), 98ff. *The Law Magazine* I (1828), 185ff on 'The Constitution and Practice of the English Courts of Common Law . . .' includes a discussion of Book VIII of the *Rationale*; see also id. VI (1831), 348, at 353ff; E. Lerminier (1830), 238 (praising Dumont as well as Bentham for the *Traité*). I am indebted to Dr John Dinwiddy for help with tracing these references.

3. I have not attempted here to give a full account of the reception, and rejection, of Bentham's ideas on evidence. See, however, below at 167ff. See also Keeton and Marshall (1962); Best (1849); Phillimore (1850); J. F. Stephen (1879); L. Stephen (1900), 279–82; Cook (1981); Hart (1982), 31ff; Twining (1982), 219ff.

Notes to pages 100–106 217

4. *Wellesley Index of Victorian Periodicals* (1966). On Denman see *Dictionary of National Biography (D.N.B.)*, 808–15 (J.A.H.).
5. 6 and 7 Vict. c.85.
6. See above, n.4
7. Denman (1824), 169–70.
8. Id., 170.
9. Ibid.
10. 193.
11. 171.
12. 172.
13. 173.
14. 173–4.
15. Halévy (1955), 403; see above, 208 n.71.
16. See, for example, Summers (1974); Twining (1975); Hart (1982).
17. 174–5.
18. 175.
19. Op cit., n.16.
20. 179.
21. Ibid.
22. 179–80; it is illuminating to compare Denman's critique of Bentham with Romilly's attack on Paley (cited above, 214); both are incisive and powerful, but the arguments are not identical.
23. *Treatise*, 237ff; see above at 99.
24. 177–9.
25. *Treatise*, 247.
26. Ibid., note.
27. Denman (1824) 185; but see above, 97–8.
28. 178–9.
29. 185, echoing *Treatise*, 247.
30. 186.
31. 180.
32. See H. L. A. Hart (1968) at 11ff.
33. Cf. W. L. and P. E. Twining (1974) at 79ff.
34. Elsewhere Denman argued for a right to counsel, for example at 192.
35. See for example P. A. Thomas (ed.) (1982), *passim*.
36. 185. On Bentham's legal competence see Jolowicz (1948); *Hovill* v. *Stephenson* (1829) 130 E.R. 1152, at 1153 (Best C.J.).
37. 191.
38. 187.
39. 188.
40. 189.
41. 189; *Treatise*, 161ff.
42. 190.
43. Op. cit., n.4.
44. See Morison (1978); Midgley (1975). A comprehensive account of reforms of adjective law in the nineteenth century has yet to be written: see above, n.3.
45. *Edinburgh Review* XLVIII (1828), 457–520. For a response, see Roebuck (1828).

218 *Notes to pages 106–110*

46. 520.
47. *D.N.B.*
48. Empson (1843).
49. Above, n.17.
50. Empson (1828), 490.
51. Ibid.
52. 466.
53. 488.
54. For example 477.
55. 478.
56. For example 487. Empson could have gone further and quoted the *Book of Fallacies* on vituperative personalities (ii *works* 414ff.) against its author, for many of Bentham's points make his thesis look like a gigantic argument *ad hominem*. However, Bentham's main attack was levelled against a system which set interests of lawyers against the interests of the community rather than against lawyers as such: see above, 76–8. Empson also made a number of specific criticisms, for example, about the choice of John Mill as editor; unreadability; the moral thermometer; not taking trouble to learn the thoughts of others, and 'minor inaccuracies that could fill a pamphlet'.
57. 463–5.
58. See further Twining (1973a).
59. Twining (1984).

Chapter 3: Wigmore on proof

(i) OLD NORTHWESTERN

1. See Biographical Note above, 189–90.
2. See Roalfe (1977), especially Chs. 6 and 11.
3. Wigmore wrote several books for the general reader, including *A Kaleidoscope of Justice* (1941) and *A Panorama of the World's Legal Systems* (3 vols., 1928). The last work was ridiculed by some academics. Wigmore made the mistake of submitting both works for review to specialist legal journals. While some gave them high praise (e.g. 15 *A.B.A.J.* 576 (1929), 85 *Pa. U. L. Rev.* 656) (1929), Wigmore was accused of being uncritical, unserious and inaccurate by some commentators, several of whom were English. (See especially Plucknett in 42 *Harv. L. Rev.* 587 (1929) and A. L. Goodhart, 38 *Yale L. J.* 554 (1929)). See Roalfe at 260–62, 331. Wigmore was so offended by the tone of the reviews in the *Harvard Law Review* and the *Yale Law Journal* that he instructed his publishers not to submit any further copies of his works to those journals for review. This episode is revealing of both Wigmore's own attitudes and those of some of his contemporaries. On the one hand, Wigmore's refusal, or failure, to distinguish between the dilettante and the scholarly is entirely consistent with the combination of breadth of interest, simple-mindedness, and magisterial confidence that characterize his writings on evidence. Conversely, his critics could be convicted of intellectual snobbery and narrow-mindedness. Such an audience would hardly be likely to be receptive to the accounts of famous trials and the symbols and charts in the *Principles*. The former were too

Notes to pages 110–111 219

closely associated with the literature of popular entertainment; the latter could easily be dismissed as faddish gimmickry.

4. Wigmore (1914); see further Schwerin (1981). For those unacquainted with the work of the Scottish poet, see McGonagall (1981).

5. In general Wigmore was an ardent advocate of reform in the service of traditional values which, from the perspective of today, may appear to be an odd mixture of the reactionary and the mildly liberal. Kocourek (1943) was not far out when he called him 'the last Mid-Victorian'.

6. Roalfe, 151–2; *American D.N.B.*, Wigmore (1927); on Wigmore's writings on the Leopold-Loeb case, see Schwerin (1981), 657, 661, 666, 667, 669.

7. On Wigmore's personality, see Roalfe, *passim*, especially 104–5.

8. Id., 168.

9. The first edition was entitled: *A Treatise on the System of Evidence in Trials at Common Law, Including the Statutes and Judicial Decisions of All Jurisdictions of the United States* (1904–5). The third edition was entitled: *A Treatise on the Anglo-American System of Evidence in Trials at Common Law*. In fact, Wigmore did not attempt to keep up to date systematically with developments in England. Some practitioners' evaluations of Wigmore's work on evidence are collected in Roalfe at 79–80 and 214ff. Part of the popularity of the *Treatise* with practitioners is attributable to its convenience as a work of reference, not least because of the number of citations and the succinct statements of the facts of many cases. But Wigmore's acceptance is due to much more than his clear sense of practitioners' convenience – he would hardly have been so generally accepted as an authority had he not been perceived as having good judgment and being in tune with practitioners' attitudes. When he attacked the judiciary or the bar in general terms, he seems to have lost his audience. When he had slide-shows and sing-songs he quickly regained it.

10. Beale (1905). Some of Wigmore's terminology has been widely accepted, but not without resistance: '(w)hile "autoptic" is a good word, with pride of ancestry, though perhaps without hope of posterity, the word "proference" is a glossological illegitimate, a neological love-child of which a great law writer confesses himself to be the father.' Per Powell J. in *Morse* v. *State*, 10 Ga. App. 61, 72 (1911), cited by Roalfe, 79.

11. Beale at 478.

12. Morgan (1940), reviewing the third edition. This is perhaps the most interesting and critical of the many contemporary reviews of the *Treatise*. Maguire (1963) later quoted from the lecture notes of John Chipman Gray a passage which reveals the latter's somewhat ambivalent attitude towards his former pupil, shortly after the *Treatise* was first published:

> *Wigmore* colossal book . . .
>
> Faults *on surface* (1) *Nomenclature* – autoptic proference – Integration of Contracts.
>
> (2) *Abusive language* – attribution of motives to judges, bad grace from unexperienced person.
>
> (3) *Overelaboration* in arrangement.
>
> (4) *Prolixity* ['and *repetition*' stricken through in red ink].
>
> Irritating faults, a man volubly scolding in unfamiliar language [and] an involved style [complex red ink interlineation and 'manner and with a

220 Notes to pages 111–113

flux of words' stricken through] is not agreeable.

Faults would damn a weaker book.

Motes on the sun – greatest law book since Benjamin ['on Sales' added in red ink].

Faults shadows of virtues. (1) *Nomenclature* = desire for precision ['and to avoid confusion' stricken through]:—(2) *Abusive language* = unwillingness to swear *in verba magistri*. (3) *Elaborate scheme*, ingenious and consistent if over refined. (4) If *prolix* ['not padding' stricken through], intends successfully to enforce [?] rules and relations. Likely to influence law . . . .

Book one that must be consulted. [Part of marginal addendum in red ink.]

Maguire comments: 'a mixed portion of vinegar and honey, but the honey dominated' (at 459).

13. On Morgan's relationship with Wigmore see below, 162–3.
14. In fact, Homer nodded more frequently than his contemporaries acknowledged. A fairly common criticism of the *Treatise* from the first was that Wigmore tended to make more confident assertions than was warranted by the cases. Some reviewers of the third edition politely suggested that Wigmore had not kept up with the periodical literature as well as with the case law and that he was unwilling to change his mind once he had taken a position. After his death, commentators – and even his editors – have pointed to parts of the *Treatise* that were inaccurate or sloppily compiled, while continuing to pay tribute to the breadth of Wigmore's vision and his magisterial command of the field, see especially Morgan (1940, 1956).
15. Especially James (1941), Morgan (1940), Trautman (1952), Ball (1961).
16. See *Treatise* (Tillers rev.), especially s.37.
17. Id., especially ss.1, 8, 9 and 37, discussed below at 152ff.
18. The most important judicial developments have been the constitutional decisions on issues affecting Criminal Evidence and Procedure.
19. See below at 162–3.
20. Wigmore's principal editors have been J. W. Chadbourn, John McNaughton and Peter Tillers.
21. Apart from Volume I (especially 1, 4, 8, 9, 24–43), Wigmore's views on 'autoptic proference' (ss.1150–52), the division of functions between judge and jury (ss.2549–51a), and judicial notice (ss.2566ff) are particularly important. The most valuable general discussion is by Tillers, op. cit., especially ss.4 and 37. *Principles* does not deal fully with some much-discussed issues such as the role of precedent, conditional relevance and harmless error.
22. See below, especially 120ff and 152ff.
23. 1st edn 1913; 2nd edn 1931; 3rd edn (sub. nom. *The Science of Judicial Proof*) 1937.
24. Especially *Principles* (1937), 321ff, sections on 'generic human traits'; cf. sections in the earlier editions and in the *Treatise* on such sensitive areas as corroboration in rape, on which see Bienen (1983); cp. Roalfe at 313 n.48.
25. The process has begun. See Bienen (1983); cp. Stevens (1983) at 100 on Wigmore's plea for open admission policies for non-Americans.
26. See above, n.16 and 17.

Notes to pages 114–118   221

(ii) BENTHAM AND WIGMORE

1. See above, Chapter 1.
2. Arnold (1906, 1913).
3. See McRae (1973), preface to Mill's *System of Logic*; Twining (1985).
4. Muensterburg (1908), Wigmore (1909), discussed below at 135–6.
5. For references to the works referred to in this paragraph, see the bibliography.
6. See especially *Principles*, 5–6n; cf. 1 *Treatise* (Tillers rev.), especially footnotes to ss.4, 7 and 37 for useful surveys of the literature since 1940. Wigmore was familiar with Bentham's work, cited him occasionally but used him only sparingly. However, there is indirect influence in that he drew quite extensively on J. S. Mill (especially *Logic* – including the much-discussed method of agreement and method of difference) and on Best.
7. See above, 25ff.
8. Despite his criticisms of the legal profession, Wigmore identified with them, treated them as his main audience and in the last resort, justified the retention of the main features of the existing system in terms of their established ways of thought.
9. On Bentham's use of instructions see above, 68; on Wigmore's views see below, 161ff.
10. On Morgan, see below at 162–3.
11. This line of argument is developed in Twining (1983a) and (1984). Wigmore deals extensively with the evidence in non-jury trials, but his treatment does not fit easily with his theoretical framework which is jury-centred, and concentrates on adjudicative decisions rather than a 'total process model' of litigation. See 1 *Treatise* (Tillers rev.) ss. 4. a-m; cf. Davis (1964).

      This narrow focus omits a great deal and leaves many questions unanswered, and, in some contexts, may lead to misperceptions and distortions in respect of treatments of adjudication itself. Such criticism, however, should not be taken to imply that adjudication is a small or an unimportant part of total legal processes; it is, on the contrary, a focal point which affects in complex ways decisions taken at earlier and at later stages in the process. Moreover, adjudicative decisions provide a paradigm for other decisions at different points in the same process and in analogous processes. Much of what Bentham and Wigmore say about adjudicative decisions can, with relatively minor adjustments, be applied to other decisions. In the present context, the fact that they both mainly focus on the same stage in legal processes, although emphasizing different questions, provides an important point of connection between their theories (see further, Twining (1984)).
12. 5 *RJE*, 1; *Textbook*, frontispiece.
13. See generally 8 *Treatise* (McNaughton rev.).
14. One could, perhaps, reconstruct a theory of litigation and adjudication from Wigmore's various pronouncements, but it would not be as coherent nor as comprehensive as Bentham's. The closest approximations to general statements of Wigmore's views are to be found in *Principles* at 924ff and *Textbook*, Ch. 1.
15. 4 cf. 3, 7–8, 994 *et passim*. Wigmore treats the situation of the advocate at the

222 *Notes to page 119*

time of the closing speech as the focal point. He sees this as being analytically very close to the standpoint of the trier of fact (at 4, 341, 858–62). His exercises postulate the standpoint of the historian analysing a fixed body of data retrospectively, but he claims that the method is also usable in preparation for trial (48) and in the process of detection (994ff).

Different standpoints bred different questions. For Bentham the essential questions might be restated as follows: What are and what should be the ends of judicature? What system is most conducive to promoting these ends? Given that the natural system of procedure is the most conducive to promoting rectitude of decision in adjudication, why and in what respects is it superior to the technical system? What generalizations can be made about the psychology and logic of probative processes under the natural system? How far can exclusionary rules of evidence and rigid rules governing weight and credibility of evidence help to maximize rectitude of decision? What general observations can be made on the probative value of the main types of evidence – circumstantial, testimonial, real, preappointed, and make-shift? What are the causes of the survival of the technical system? What instructions should the legislator give to the judge under the natural system?

Wigmore concentrates on a significantly different set of questions. The science of proof is primarily concerned with three main matters: the persuasive force of different kinds of evidence presented in court to the decider; the logical and psychological nature of the probative processes involved; and the best practical method for analysing mixed masses of evidence and systematically charting the relevant logical relations. Wigmore does not stick rigidly to a single standpoint and he explores a wide range of other issues in varying degrees of detail and depth, such as the relationship between the standpoint of the detective, the historian and the trial attorney in respect of evidence; the relationship between the science and the rules of admissibility and, more in his other writings than in the *Principles*, his views on many issues concerning the future of the rules. On 'standpoint' see Twining and Hiers (1982).

(iii) THE GENESIS AND CONCEPTION OF *THE PRINCIPLES OF JUDICIAL PROOF*

1. Wigmore (1913).
2. Ibid. This remains the most succinct exposition of the Chart Method. Wigmore made a few changes in his formulation of this aspect of his 'science', especially in the third edition of the *Principles*, which also deals with theoretical issues at greater length. Wigmore's claim that his work was a *novum organum* need not be treated as pure hyperbole. For it was his aim to establish an independent science, which encompassed all aspects of judicial proof in a systematic way, separately from what he termed the artificial rules of admissibility of evidence. The relationship between the Science and the Trial Rules is close (see below, 151ff.); it is 'analogous to the relations between the scientific principles of nutrition and digestion and the rules of diet intuitively discovered and practised by intelligent families' (924). The analogy is dubious, but should not be confused with the kind of 'digestive jurisprudence' later attributed to some American Realists.
3. First edn 1913; 2nd edn 1931; 3rd edn, entitled *The Science of Judicial*

Proof, 1937. All three editions are here referred to as *Principles*; unless otherwise stated references are to the 3rd edition.

4. *Principles*, 3–4.
5. Fenning (1931–2), 403.
6. *Principles*, 7.
7. Ibid.
8. At 8, where he draws a debatable analogy between the relationship of a performing musician to the Science of Harmony and that of an advocate to the Science of Proof.
9. 7.
10. 52. Within each of these groups of probanda Wigmore shifts his basis of classification to types of evidentiary facts. The main division is between Circumstantial and Testimonial Evidence, with 'Autoptic Proference' as a special case of testimonial evidence in which the tribunal witnesses evidential data for itself. Another general sub-division of evidentiary facts, put to good use by Wigmore, is in terms of time: prospectant, concomitant and retrospectant evidence, that is to say facts before, during and after the probandum. Wigmore's scheme of classification, although not uncontroversial, was very influential on subsequent work in the field.
11. Below, 155ff. In the first edition of the *Principles* much of the theoretical exposition takes the form of explicit quotations from the *Treatise*; by the third edition, this part of his work is more fully developed in the *Principles*. For a different view of the relationship see Tillers (1983) at 1004–5n.
12. Above, 6.
13. Chamberlayne (1908), discussed ibid.
14. On Chamberlayne's career, see the introduction to his article in the *American Law Review* (1908), 755.
15. Id., 762.
16. Above, 5.
17. There were other important differences between Wigmore's *Treatise* and its immediate predecessor. It was based on an entirely new scheme of classification; it contained considerably more theoretical material – for example, long sections entitled 'General Theory and Procedure of Admissibility'; 'General Theory of Circumstantial Evidence'; 'General Theory of Testimonial Evidence'; 'Theory and History of the Hearsay Rule' as well as shorter statements of the theory of particular topics. This contrasts quite strikingly with Greenleaf's relatively short introductory section on 'The Nature and Principles of Evidence', and even more so with most modern texts which deal with such matters either cursorily or not at all. As was noted above, Wigmore excluded a great deal of material to be found in the nineteenth-century treatises, but he included quite detailed historical accounts of many topics as well as reference to non-legal material, especially in relation to witness psychology, the psychology of confessions and forensic science.
18. Preface to 1st edition. This hardly does justice to Wigmore's contributions as a theorist and historian of evidence.
19. Id., xv.
20. Below, 152ff.

224 *Notes to pages 125–129*

(iv) ANALYTICAL DIMENSIONS OF PROOF

1. *Principles*, 7.
2. Id., 22–3. On the relationship between induction and deduction Wigmore follows Sidgwick: see especially 1 *Treatise* (Tillers revision), ss.30 and 37.
3. Id., 18ff. Wigmore quoted extensively from Alfred Sidgwick's *Fallacies* (1884) and W. Stanley Jevons, *The Principles of Science* (2nd edn 1907).
4. See especially 8n, 237–9. Wigmore did not confront the difficulties and controversies of probability theory. He recognized that there was some place for mathematical calculation, for example in respect of fingerprinting and other methods of proving identity (268ff), but his account of the mathematical theory of probabilities is primitive and has been criticized, e.g. by Eggleston (1983) at 39, 239–40, 250, and Tillers in the revised edition of volume 1 of Wigmore's *Treatise* at s.37. Wigmore's account of the logic of inference can be fairly characterized as 'Baconian' (cf Cohen (1977) at 69, 281); it is a bit simplistic, but it belongs to a reputable and sophisticated tradition. See especially 1 *Treatise* (Tillers rev.), ss.21–8, 30–36, especially p. 1074.
5. For example at 7–8, 858–62.
6. 821.
7. Ibid.
8. On secondary literature about *causes célèbres* see Twining '*Anatomy of a cause célèbre*' (forthcoming). See *Principles* (1st edn) at 92 for a rather unusual example of the narrative method. Cf. 3rd edn at 825ff. (*Luetgert* and *Durrant*) – examples of Wigmore's use of the method applied to data mainly derived from newspaper reports.
9. On 'holistic' approaches, see below at 183–5. It is a fair criticism of Wigmore that he pays insufficient attention to practitioners' notions of 'theory of a case', 'theme' and 'story' as discussed, for instance, in manuals of advocacy: See Bennett and Feldman (1981), Anderson and Twining (1984); Mauet (1980), Jeans (1975), Abu Hareira (1984).
10. At 858.
11. See further Appendix A and Anderson and Twining (1984).
12. 821; cf. 8–9.
13. Adapted from Wigmore's analysis at 14.
14. 13–14. On inference upon inference see below, 182. See also 1 *Treatise* (3rd edn), s.41; cf. Bentham on 'chains', above at 33.
15. 2nd edn, p. 13; cf. 3rd edn at 858–60.
16. 15 (italics omitted). On the seeming inconsistency between Wigmore's emphasis on the value of making all steps in inference explicit and his scepticism about the value of articulating background generalizations, see below at 147–9.
17. 25. Compare Bentham's method of infirmative suppositions discussed above at 53ff and Jonathan Cohen's method of relevant variables (1977), 135ff *et passim*.
18. 27.
19. 30.
20. 45.

Notes to pages 129–132 225

21. See n.4 above. On Wigmore's use of Mill's method of agreement and method of difference as subordinate tests, see 1 *Treatise* (Tillers rev.), s.33.
22. 46, cf. the formulation at 31.
23. *Textbook* (1935) at 55. This work contains an admirably well-integrated and succinct exposition of Wigmore's theory and of the general principles of the law of evidence.
24. A key-list is a key to a chart of all the evidentiary propositions. It is a list of all the propositions in an argument, or at least all those that are considered worthy of attention. In the example in the text only particular items of evidence and their sources are listed. But as we shall see, a key-list of propositions typically includes generalizations that are explicitly or implicitly relied on, rival hypotheses and any other proposition that has a place in the argument. So more than evidence is included in the key-list. Wigmore refers to it as a key-list of evidence (848); it is more accurately designated a key-list of propositions.

    Wigmore writes as if the chart comes first: 'The key-list is thus a translation of the Chart' (ibid.); the author invariably starts by compiling a list of propositions first; Professor Anderson claims to compile his lists and charts simultaneously as part of a reflexive process. See further Anderson and Twining (1984).

    The fact that one proposition may have a role to play at several points in a complex argument (e.g. a fact casting doubt on the reliability of a witness who testifies to more than one point) is one reason for rejecting an analogy, tempting to students, between jigsaw puzzles and Wigmore charts. Another reason is that the propositions are constituted, selected and individuated in significantly different ways from jigsaws. Grasping these differences is an important first step to understanding the nature of this kind of analysis. See further below at 179ff.
25. For a simple example, see Wigmore's analysis of Ainsworth (68–70). For a slightly more elaborate example see *Umilian* (*Principles*, 872–76), discussed in Anderson and Twining (1984).
26. 8.
27. At 48; cf. the formulation at 858–9.
28. 859.
29. 859–60.
30. See further Anderson and Twining (1984); Twining (1984b); and Appendix below.
31. 860–61.
32. 862.
33. Wigmore says little about how to express strength of belief; see, however, 866; cf. Gilbert and Bentham, discussed above at 64–6.
34. Compare the discussion of Bentham's position in this respect, above, 60ff. My personal opinion is that Wigmore was arguably more of a subjectivist than Bentham, but like the latter, he was – in Postema's phrase – 'a subjectivist with a difference', that is to say that judgments that ultimately turned on evaluations that were to a large degree personal to the maker of the judgment could at least be 'objectified' to some extent by following a particular intellectual *procedure* that Wigmore categorically claimed to be 'rational'.

226 Notes to pages 133–135

35. Thus a particular chart-maker may adopt Baconian or Pascalian or subjectivist criteria of probability judgments and still use the chart method, if he accepts the assumption that it is possible to *analyse* a mass of evidence, by breaking it down into individual propositions. Indeed, a standard criticism of Wigmore is that he failed to give sufficient guidance on how to evaluate the probative force of individual relations between a *factum probans* and a *factum probandum* and that he gave no guidance on how to *combine* probability judgments; see further below at 180–3. A 'holist' may part company with Baconians and Pascalians by doubting that a mass of evidence can satisfactorily be analysed in this way without significant distortions; see further below at 183.

36. See especially 868–70. Wigmore is careful to say that '[e]ach supposed piece of evidence must be *analysed, so far as practicable and reasonably necessary*, into all *its subordinate inferences*' (at 869; italics supplied). Any working method of analysing evidence must proceed on some such assumptions.

37. From the standpoint of a detective or a lawyer preparing for trial, there is not a *given body of data* to be analysed. A trial lawyer's key-list may contain items of *potential* evidence, i.e. propositions that he would like to ensure are (or are not) presented to the trier of fact, and possible inferences therefrom. Similarly a *clue* may suggest a chain of possible inferences or may serve as a lead to further information. The underlying method of reasoning remains constant, but the value of devices such as key-lists and charts varies according to the particular task and other factors; see further, Anderson and Twining (1984).

38. On algorithms, see Twining and Miers (1982), Appendix I.

39. See above, n.37 and below, 179ff. In the later editions of the *Principles* Wigmore provided a sketch of how the chart method could be adapted to the process of detection, an inventory of clues being substituted for the key-list of evidence. From this inventory the eager detective could prepare each day a Progress chart of Indications. Wigmore claimed that experienced detectives possibly already use some such system, which accordingly would be compatible with his principles of proof. He concluded on the optimistic note that 'The Inventory of Clues will some day no doubt be recognized as a necessary apparatus.' (1003). The presentation is naive, but more sophisticated versions of this kind of approach have considerable potential in the computer age: cf. Schum and Martin (1982).

40. Jesse (1934).

41. Below, 142ff and 179ff.

42. Appendix below; Anderson and Twining (1984); Twining (1984b); Schum and Martin (1982). Possible computer applications are currently being explored by Professor Schum and others.

43. See 50 *A.B.A.J.* 510–12 (1964); Schum, op. cit., n.42.

(v) PSYCHOLOGY AND FORENSIC SCIENCE

1. He was, for example, the first president of the American Institute of Criminal Law and Criminology and one of the initiators of the *Journal of Criminal Law and Criminology*, whose second and most successful editor, the Northwestern psychologist Robert Gault, was one of his greatest

Notes to pages 135–137 227

admirers. See also Gerhard O. Mueller (1969) at 78–81. On Wigmore's 1909 initiative, Mueller comments: 'Wigmore may have had no firm idea of what had to be done, but it is clear that he knew *something* had to be done, something to awaken the sleeping scholars' (at 79).

2. *The Principles* is dedicated to Hans Gross; the bibliography in the *Principles* contains references to works by German, Austrian, French and Italian psychologists and criminologists and the Wigmore Papers at Northwestern confirm that he kept in quite close touch with developments in criminology, forensic science and psychology in Europe over a long period.
3. H. Muensterberg (1908, reprinted 1923). Muensterberg died in 1916.
4. See *Principles*, 728ff.
5. Gault (1943).
6. Id. at 4.
7. J. Wigmore, 'Professor Muensterberg and the Psychology of Testimony', 3 *Ill. L. Rev.* 399 (1909). Wigmore was not the only lawyer to criticize Muensterberg at the time: see Moore (1907) commenting on an article by Muensterberg.
8. Id.
9. Cairns (1935) at 169.
10. op. cit., n.5.
11. Apart from some up-dating the main change in respect of psychology in the 3rd edition is the addition of a section on narration by non-verbal expression (Ch.xxiv). The up-dating in respect of forensic science was much more extensive.
12. Op. cit. at 3.
13. Wigmore to Weld, 20 Jan. 1930 (Wigmore Papers, Northwestern).
14. Wigmore to Hutchins, March 1929; the correspondence continued until May (Wigmore Papers). In private Wigmore accused Hutchins of taking an extreme behaviourist position (Wigmore to John Angel, 1927, cited by J. H. Schlegel (1979) at 480, n.101). This contains an excellent account of the background to Hutchins' work.
15. For full references see bibliography. Interestingly the bibliography of the 3rd edition of the *Principles* contains no reference to Hutchins, and only two of these articles are cited in the 3rd edition of the *Treatise*.
16. Hutchins to Wigmore, 12(?) May 1929 (Wigmore papers).
17. R. M. Hutchins, 'The Autobiography of an Ex-Law Student' (*A.A.L.S.*, 1933), reprinted in Hutchins (1936) at 41–50. Speaking of Eastern law schools in the twenties, he remarked: '. . . we were thoroughly Baconian as to science and thoroughly behavioristic as to psychology' (at 41). He continued: 'The fact was that though the social scientists seemed to have a great deal of information, we could not see, and they could not teach us, how to use it. It did not seem to show us what the courts would do or whether what they had done was right. For example the law of evidence is obviously full of assumptions about how people behave. We understood that the psychologists knew how people behave. We hoped to discover whether an evidence case was "sound" by finding out whether the decision was in harmony with psychological doctrine. What we actually discovered was that psychology had dealt with very few of the points raised by the law of evidence; and that the basic psychological problem of the law of evidence –

228 Notes to pages 137–142

what will affect juries – and in what way – was one psychology had never touched at all . . .' (at 43–4).

18. For example *Principles* (3rd edn) at 693, 792.

19. Id., *passim*.

20. Above at 66ff.

21. *Principles* at 860–62. In the text, Wigmore stated that 'no system of logic has yet discovered and established such laws' (861); in a footnote he added: 'They will perhaps some day be discovered. But the methods of observation and experiment in all inductive search for psychological laws involve inevitably a lengthy study of large masses of data.' This is revealing in respect of both Wigmore's assumptions about the relationship between logic and psychology and his views on science (on which see below, 141).

22. For example character at 103ff.; emotion at 118ff.; intention at 123ff., 198ff. and 214ff.; identity at 673ff.; habit at 127ff. In some of these sections he drew heavily on Sully (1892).

23. On questioning, see 575ff., and on confessions, 616ff.

24. On non-verbal communication see, however, 633ff.

25. See, for example, Clifford and Bull (1978); Saks and Hastie (1978); Lloyd-Bostock and Clifford (1983).

26. Ch.xix, 321ff.

27. At 334, citing a number of works, most of which were published in the 1920s.

28. See Arnold (1906, 2nd edn 1915), a work by a civil servant who was neither a lawyer nor a psychologist – Wigmore cites surprisingly extensive extracts from this period piece, a revealing mixture of common sense, wide reading and open prejudice; see also Bienen (1983).

29. 321–8, 341.

30. 328, 345.

31. 766.

32. 767.

33. 938.

34. Ibid.

35. 720.

36. See above, n.22.

37. See, however, the works cited in n.25 above.

38. Tapp (1980), based on an analysis of *Psychological Abstracts*.

39. I am grateful to Dr Sally Lloyd-Bostock for comments on this section.

40. See above at 135. On Wigmore's general attitude to science see below, 141.

41. *Principles*, v.

42. See Roalfe, 60ff., 85–7; Inbau (1981).

43. Chafee (1931).

44. See especially *Principles*, preface at viii.

45. *Principles*, 298–9.

46. It may have been Wigmore's simplicity and self-confidence, as well as his comparative lack of interest in empirical social science methodology, that especially provoked Underhill Moore in his savage attack on the underlying assumptions of Wigmore and Kocourek's anthology *The Rational Basis of Legal Institutions* (Modern Legal Philosophy series, 1923). Moore's article (23 *Col. L. Rev.* 609 (1923)) is discussed at length by J. H. Schlegel (1980).

Notes to pages 142–144 229

Wigmore's divorce from the mainstream of American Legal Realism is puzzling. It may in part have been due to politico-ideological differences, but also to such factors as a lack of sympathy with the philosophy of pragmatism and his orientation to laboratory-based sciences, as well as his relative isolation in Chicago.
47. For example Walls (1974), Moenssens, Moses and Inbau (1973).
48. *Principles*, 257ff.

(vi) THE NATURE AND ROLE OF GENERAL EXPERIENCE

1. The example is adapted from *Principles*, 280–81.
2. Ibid.
3. See Eggleston (1983), 81, 163–5.
4. A standard judicial phrase, adopted by writers, is 'the common course of human affairs' or 'common experience'. See for example Sir Owen Dixon in *Martin* v. *Osborne* (1936) 55 C.L.R. 367 at 375, discussed by Eggleston (1983), 88ff. See the same writer's useful discussion of the whole topic of generalizations: (1983a) at 22ff.
5. Young (1923). This example is discussed in more detail in Anderson and Twining (1984). Bywaters and Thompson is an excellent pedagogical vehicle for exploring the uses and limitations of the chart method. It is, however, too complex to be suitable as a basis for an exercise in charting all the evidence in a case.
6. American works (e.g. Lempert and Salzburg (1977); Maguire *et al.* (1973), Tillers (1983)) frequently cite the following hypothetical example by Edmund Morgan (1961), 185–6: 'Assume that X met his death by violence; the proposition to be proved is that Y killed him; the offered item of evidence is a love letter written by Y to X's wife. The series of inferences is as follows: From Y's letter (A) to Y's love of X's wife (B), to Y's desire for the exclusive possession of X's wife (C), to Y's desire to get rid of X (D), to Y's execution of the plan by killing X (F).' This passage is often used to make some elementary points about inferences: first, that *last* step involves a *typically inarticulated major premise* of a syllogism: for example, the inference from B to C rests on some such generalization as 'A man who loves a married woman probably desires her for himself alone.' Secondly, that such generalizations are not *founded* on any solid basis of evidence; thirdly, that with each step there is a *cumulative weakening* of the strength of the 'chain' as a whole and, fourthly, that despite all this, most people would agree that A is *relevant* to F. Morgan also used it to suggest a formula for assessing the strength of the chain as a whole (a version of the multiplication rule). Tillers calls Morgan's analysis of his own example 'greatly oversimplified and almost certainly defective', pointing out that a simple application of the multiplication rule is wrong and that Morgan assumes that all background generalizations can be expressed as judgments of relative frequencies. (Tillers (1983) at 1035–6n.). These criticisms are correct; one could also add that Morgan fails to bring out difficulties discussed in the text in connection with the question: 'which generalization?' and raised in connection with 'holism' (see further, below, 183–5).
7. A good introductory discussion is Binder and Bergman (1984) at 82ff.; see

230 *Notes to pages 144–145*

also Tillers (1983), Eggleston (1983), Ch. 11 and (1983a). Eggleston suggests that generalizations may become important at three stages of a trial: in deciding questions of admissibility; in deciding whether a case to answer has been made out; and in deciding which side is to win. In fact, generalizations have a part to play in any inferential argument about a question of fact at any stage of legal process. For references to other discussions on generalizations in the probabilities debate, see the bibliography in Twining (1983), 156–7.

8. See below, 152.
9. Above, 55.
10. Below, 180–3.
11. The subject of this chapter touches on some profound and controversial philosophical issues. Rather than addressing these in detail, I have concentrated on trying to elucidate Wigmore's position. Albert Kocourek wrote of Wigmore that he had 'attempted to sound the depths of metaphysics' (as a substitute for religion), but had decided that he 'was not congenitally apt to much of that material' (*Recollections*, cited by Roalfe at 246). It might also be said that Wigmore was not congenitally apt for other kinds of speculative philosophy. In the *Treatise*, vol. 1, footnote 1 states: (5) 'Truth of a proposition: in judicial proceedings we must assume for practical purposes that the subjective phenomena of existence have an objective reality. With reference to the State's force, which the Court will put in motion, the Court's determination upon a question of fact makes that fact for practical purposes a reality.' This is about as near as Wigmore got to hinting at an underlying strain of scepticism. On most philosophical issues, he was content to base his own views on standard philosophical works, such as Sidgwick's *Fallacies* and Mill's *Logic*. He tended to be impatient of writers on judicial evidence, such as Michael and Adler (1931), who tried to dig deeper into metaphysics (see *Principles*, 5–6, n.1). He found scientific psychological writings more congenial. Wigmore's views on religion were opaque; he left the Episcopal Church when young, contracted no further formal religious affiliation, expressed some sympathy for Catholicism, carried a pocket Bible about with him and gave public support to Christian values in education and public life (see Roalfe, 244–77).
12. The term 'general experience' appears in the title of the *Principles* and is used throughout, though sparingly. Wigmore's most sustained treatment of the subject is to be found in his discussion of judicial notice in 1 *Treatise*, 531ff, but the treatment is not philosophical. The topic of the admissibility of background evidence is not pursued here; for an excellent discussion, see 1 *Treatise* (Tillers rev.), s.9 at 658ff.
13. *Textbook*, 128–9. On the relationship between general experience, judicial notice and expert evidence, see Eggleston (1983), Ch. 11. On the 'general knowledge' of the jurors going beyond judicial notice, see *Treatise*, s.2570.
14. Binder and Bergman (1984), 85. Cf. Cohen (1977) at 274–5:
    [W]hen a juryman takes up his office his mind is already adult and stocked with a vast number of commonplace generalizations about human acts, attitudes, intentions, etc., about the more familiar features of the human environment, and about the interactions between these two kinds of factor, together with an awareness of many of the kinds of

Notes to page 146 231

circumstances that are favourable or unfavourable to the application of each such generalization. Without this stock of information in everyday life, he could understand very little about his neighbours, his colleagues, his business competitors, or his wife. He would be greatly handicapped in explaining their past actions or predicting their future ones. But with this information he has the only kind of background data he needs in practice for the assessment of inductive probabilities in the jury-room. He does not need to have tacitly ingested a mass of quantitative or numerical statistics for this purpose. Nor does he need implicitly to remember some sophisticated mathematical algorithm in order to compute the probabilities from the data. The inductive probability of the proposed conclusion on the facts before the court depends just on the extent to which the facts are favourable to some commonplace generalizations that connect them to the conclusion . . .

This is discussed in Twining (1984c).

15. For example Berger and Luckmann (1967), Bennett and Feldman (1981); see further Twining (1984).

16. Bennett and Feldman (1981), Ch. 7.

17. In discussing induction, Wigmore gives a rather limited place to different perceptions of human experience: 'Thus, throughout the whole realm of evidence, circumstantial and testimonial, the theory of the inductive inference, as practically applied, is that the evidentiary fact has probative value only so far as the conclusion based upon it is a more probable or natural inference, and as the other inferences or explanations of the fact, if any, are less probable or natural. The degree of strength required would vary with different sorts of evidentiary facts, *depending somewhat upon differing views of human experience with those facts* [supplied], somewhat upon the practical availability of stronger facts. But the general spirit and mode of reasoning of the Courts substantially illustrates the dictates of scientific logic.' (*Principles*, 27; cf. id., 930.)

18. Cf. Berger and Luckmann (1967); Bennett and Feldman (1981). Much modern writing on the jury emphasizes its role in reflecting a range of *values* as well as of different versions of 'general experience', 'knowledge' and commonsense. A fairly standard view is expressed by Hans Zeisel: 'The jury system is predicated on the insight that people see and evaluate things differently' (1971 at 715). See further the collection of materials on jury size in Barnes (1983), 54ff., and most discussions of jury selection, e.g. Jeans (1975), Ch. 7.

19. A similar optimism about a general consensus among reasonable men underlies Karl Llewellyn's concept of 'situation sense': see Twining (1973), 216.

20. For example *Principles*, 935–40. Such pronouncements also involve other assumptions. In an important essay, Jonathan Cohen has argued that the common law system of adjudication and the jury system in particular are based on a premise of 'universal cognitive competence', i.e. a universal but not infallible human capacity for natural fact-finding. (J. Cohen (1983) at 9ff.) Wigmore appears to have accepted some such premise. Cohen does not make much of the common law notion of 'prejudicial evidence', which serves as an important limitation on this premise, as Wigmore clearly

232   *Notes to pages 146–148*

recognized. Tillers points out: 'The view that a trial judge may exclude probative evidence because a jury may miscalculate its worth assumes that the judge has some calculus or method for determining the "correct value of relevant evidence".' (1 *Treatise* (Tillers rev.), s.10d at 688; see further s.37.) Tillers comments: '[T]he claim that the judge has superior experience or insight is usually simply gratuitous and unsupported.' (Ibid.).

21. Professor Tillers, although more cautious than Wigmore, comes to a similar conclusion: 'Our argument there rests on the premise that it is better to confess the limits of our knowledge than to pretend to an objectivity we cannot attain. We argue, in part, that emphasis should be given to ordinary introspection and inference simply because, in most cases, we have no method of inference that can promise better results.' (1 *Treatise* (Tillers rev.), s.30 at 988n.) On Tillers' inclination towards a more 'holistic' approach, see below, 184. On scepticism, see Twining (1984c), 267–74.

22. Above, p. 127.

23. *Principles*, 53–4.

24. *Principles*, 18–23; 1 *Treatise*, ss.30–36.

25. Black (1952).

26. Wigmore was criticized by Michael and Adler (1934) at 1269–72, 1278–9, and by James (1941) at 695–9, for failing to appreciate the part played by generalizations in the process of inference. He is defended by Tillers (1 *Treatise* (Tillers rev.), s.29a at 982n and s.37), who points out that 'the main difference between Wigmore and his critics seems to center on the question of the extent to which full and systematic articulation of hypotheses (which generate inferences) is possible or useful'. My own view is that there is some force in the criticism, in that Wigmore did not carry his analysis of the role of generalizations and the difficulties surrounding them very far and that, as is illustrated by his key-lists for the *Umilian* and *Hatchett* cases (*Principles*, 874–81), he failed to appreciate the subversive force of articulating generalizations in exposing weaknesses in an argument: cf. id., 869–70.

27. Michael and Adler (1931), Trautman (1952), Ball (1961).

28. Sidgwick (1894), 212; cited in *Principles*, 19–20 and 1 *Treatise*, s.30.

29. For example 1 *Treatise*, s.30 at 417.

30. Ibid.

31. *Principles*, 15.

32. 1 *Treatise*, 416–17; cf. *Principles*, 20–22.

33. G. James (1941), 694ff; cf. Eggleston (1983), 79–80.

34. This is also illustrated by Wigmore's rather casual key-list (*Principles*, 872ff.) in *Umilian*, see further Anderson and Twining (1984).

35. Op. cit., n.32.

36. 1 *Treatise*, s.27.

37. Binder and Bergman (1984), 92–4.

38. See further below, 157 and Appendix.

39. Tillers (1983) at 1017 and 1036n. See further id., 1050ff. For a more general attack on 'atomism', see Abu Hareira (1984).

40. Tillers also doubts whether any additional clarity is gained by articulating the background generalization when it is a relative frequency statement (38n.). This surely overlooks the value of articulation in spotting fallacies, testing the strength of arguments and in revealing the difficulties of

Notes to pages 148–152 233

formulating an appropriate generalization.

41. Tillers (1983) at 1044, quoting Holmes J. in *Chicago B. and Q. Rly.* v. *Babcock*, 204 U.S. 585, 598 (1907) that 'many honest and sensible judgments . . . express an intuition of experience which outruns analysis and sums up unnamed and tangled impressions – impressions which may be beneath consciousness without losing their worth'. Much of Judge Weinstein's emphasis on judicial discretion rests on similar premises.

42. Quine and Ullian (1970).

43. Tillers (1983) at 1038n.; cf. Abu Hareira (1984).

44. For example Hempel, 'The Function of General Laws in History' (1965), Ch. 9. Jonathan Cohen puts the matter as follows: 'Any alternative to the view that each step in a forensic proof has to be licensed by one or more principles which are accepted as being universally or approximately or probably true has a hard row to hoe. The central problem it has to face is this: what is to be said if the particular proof-step is challenged? A general principle which licences the step [can] be defended by appeal to other situations, i.e. by some kind of inductive reasoning.' (Private communication to the author, 28 August 1981.) Cf. Cohen (1977), Ch. 26. On Bentham's position, see above, 54–5.

45. Cf. 1 *Treatise*, 8c; *Principles*, 925–30.

46. The *locus classicus* is perhaps Julius Stone (1964), 267–74.

47. Cf. Llewellyn (1951), 48.

48. Young (1923).

49. 'a knife with a leather sheath' (defendant at 53, cf. 140); 'hunting knife' (tool merchant at 42); 'a deadly weapon' (Shearman J., charge to the jury at 135); 'a dagger' (id., several times, at 151); 'a stabbing weapon' (ibid); 'that dreadful weapon' (Solicitor-General for the prosecution at 132).

50. At 140; cf. 132.

51. At 132.

52. At 140.

53. At 110.

54. Ibid.

55. Ibid, note.

56. See above, n.18.

57. Tillers, op. cit. at 988–91n.

(vii) THE SCIENCE OF PROOF AND THE RULES OF EVIDENCE

1. See above at Chapter 1.

2. See generally, Tillers (1983), ss.24–9a, 37, 37.5.

3. Above, 8.

4. Especially 1 *Treatise*, ss.9–16, 24–36.

5. Id., s.9 at 289.

6. Ibid., citing Thayer (1889), 156; (1898), 198, 264. Cf. Thayer's wording, cited above at 7.

7. Id., s.10 at 293, citing Thayer (1898), 265, 268. Both axioms are confirmed in Tillers' revision. On other differences between Thayer and Wigmore, see Tillers (1983), *passim*.

8. Tillers (1983), s.10a at 674. Cf. *R.* v. *Sang* [1979] 2 All E.R. 1222 (H.L.).

234 *Notes to pages 152–154*

9. See especially James (1941), Trautman (1952), Morgan (1961), Ball (1980); discussed at length by Tillers (1983) in ss.14.1, 37.1–37.5.
10. Thayer (1889), 147; (1898), 265.
11. Tillers, op. cit., n.9.
12. Op. cit. above, n.9.
13. Tillers (1983) at 1006.
14. Michael and Adler (1931), (1934), discussed by Tillers, op. cit., in s.37.3.
15. Id., s.28, 37.4; cp. Cross (1979), 22. To an Englishman, modern American discussions in this general area suffer by virtue of a tendency to lump together a variety of different kinds of questions under the single heading of 'relevancy'. For example, Wigmore's treatment of the subject includes conceptual questions about such notions as 'relevance', 'admissibility' and 'probative force' and the relations between them; institutional questions about the allocation of functions between judge and jury in contested jury trials; questions about the status and role of precedents in deciding evidentiary issues; philosophical questions about the criteria for assessing the validity and cogency of different kinds of arguments about evidence; and pragmatic questions about sensible ways of promoting simplicity and intelligibility in court proceedings. From the standpoint of the advocate and the judge in jury trials many of these issues are intimately related in practice. However, to an outsider it seems that debate in this area would have been much less confused if some of the issues had been rather more carefully differentiated. One of the great strengths of the *Principles* is that it treats questions about weighing evidence and assessing probabilities independently of rules of admissibility and the peculiar conditions and problems of contested jury trials.
16. One example of a common confusion is between different meanings of the word 'probability' and what are appropriate criteria for forming or appraising particular probability judgments in given contexts.
17. The best discussion is still that of Montrose (1968).
18. See especially 1 *Treatise*, ss.2, 12, 29, 29a.
19. The most rigorous exposition of this view is by Michael and Adler (1931), Chs.iv and v, especially at 90 and 101; cf. Trautman (1952). Cp. Cross (1979), 22, who insists that '[r]elevancy is a matter of degree'.
20. Especially 1 *Treatise*, ss.28, 29a. Wigmore did not coin the term 'legal relevancy', see below, n.31. For two recent English discussions on relevance see Holdcroft (1983) and Zuckerman (1983).
21. Id., at 409–10.
22. For references to the main discussions see above, n.9 and Tillers (1983), s.37.1.
23. Id. at 409.
24. See Tillers at 974n; cf. n.15 above.
25. Ibid. Tillers states: 'We doubt that the "analytic rigor" demanded of us by the modern approach to relevancy makes much of a difference.' Tillers is here adopting the standpoint of a judge in a jury trial and, in this context, he may be right. But in preparing for trial, in constructing and evaluating arguments and in exploring the theoretical assumptions of discourse about evidence, clarity of thought and analytical rigour are important.
26. *Relevancy and Sufficiency*. Wigmore is sometimes accused of failing to

distinguish between relevancy and sufficiency of evidence (e.g. Trautman (1952)). This is based on a passage in which he suggests that some courts adopt a test of relevancy which excludes evidence that does not satisfy some standard of preponderance of evidence. The offending passage in the third edition reads: 'Does the evidentiary fact point to the desired conclusion (not as the only rational hypothesis, but) as the hypothesis (or explanation) more plausible or more natural out of the various ones conceivable?' (s.32.) This seems to suggest that if there are several possible explanations for a hypothesis only the most probable one can be admitted as relevant. For instance, in the Robinson Crusoe example, if alternative explanations for the presence of a footprint to the hypothesis of there being another human on the island were (a) Crusoe's own somnambulism or (b) it was not a human footprint, a judge would have to admit only (a) or (b) (and, *semble*, evidence in support of (a) or (b)) as relevant. If Wigmore meant this, it is clearly an error. But Tillers demonstrates that at worst Wigmore was guilty of inconsistency. In the same passage he immediately adds a weaker test; in s.12 he explicitly distinguishes between sufficiency and relevancy; and throughout the *Principles* (e.g. in his charts of *Umilian* and *Hatchett*) he clearly did not fall into the error of thinking that *each* item of evidence must meet some standard of proof. He would thus surely have agreed with the famous dictum 'a brick is not a wall' (McCormick (1954), s.152). See generally Wigmore, 1 (Tillers rev.), s.28, n.1 and 2; s32n. at 993–4. See further n.15 above.

27. Tillers, ibid.
28. Id., s.14.1.
29. Thayer (1889), (1898), *passim*, especially 264–6, 448ff, 485, 516–18.
30. 1 *Treatise*, s.12.
31. Id. at 298. Wigmore cites the following dictum from *State* v. *Lapage* (1876) 57 N.H. 588, per Cushing C.J.:

> Although undoubtedly the relevancy of testimony is originally a matter of logic and commonsense, still there are many instances in which the evidence of particular facts as bearing upon particular issues has been so often the subject of discussion in courts of law, and so often ruled upon, that the united logic of a great many judges and lawyers may be said to furnish evidence of the sense common to a great many individuals, and, therefore, the best evidence of what may be properly called common-sense, and thus to acquire the authority of law. It is for this reason that the subject of the relevancy of testimony has become, to so great an extent, a matter of precedent and authority, and that we may with entire propriety speak of its legal relevancy.

This is discussed by James (1941) at 694–5.
32. Ibid.
33. Weinstein and Berger (1979), 401; Tillers (1983) at 692.
34. Tillers, ibid., and s.37. See also Tillers' perceptive account of the seeming inconsistency between Wigmore's belief in the importance of precedent and his warnings against 'undue servitude to the bondage of precedent' (id. 751–7n.); there is no necessary inconsistency: see below, n.37.
35. *Principles*, 3–5, 924–5; 1 *Treatise*, s.26. See below, n.69.

236 *Notes to pages 155–158*

36. See for example Corbin (1914), discussed in Twining (1973) at 31–3.
37. Moore (1908), reviewed by Wigmore (1908), where he explicitly denies Moore's claim that there are 'rules of law which determine the weight or credibility of a piece of evidence which has been duly admitted to consideration'. This is perhaps the clearest passage in which Wigmore acknowledges the value of the law reports as sources of 'experience', but warns against misuse of them as the source of technical, binding rules on questions of probative value and, perhaps, relevance.
38. Below at 163–4.
39. Tillers (1983), s.12.
40. p.5.
41. Ibid.
42. Id. at 924; the appendix is at 923–46. Cf. 1 *Treatise*, ss.3a, 8a, 8b, 8c; *Textbook*, Ch. 1.
43. At 925; cf 1 *Treatise*, s.8c.
44. For example at 4. In the *Treatise* (3rd edn, 8c at 259), Wigmore stated: 'A *complete abolition* of the rules in the future is at least arguable not merely in theory, but in realizable fact . . . . But to *abolish* the bulk of the rules *now*, in the ordinary courts would be a *futile* attempt . . . . You cannot by fiat legislate away the brain-coils of one hundred thousand lawyers and judges.' However, a few pages later, in arguing that 'Our system of Evidence is *sound on the whole*' (id. at 262), Wigmore argues that most of the rules grew out of experience of human nature in trials: 'That human nature is represented in the witnesses, the counsel and the jurors. All three in their weaknesses have been kept in mind by the law of Evidence. The multifold untrustworthiness of witnesses; the constant partisan zeal, the lurking chicanery, the needless unpreparedness of counsel; the crude reasoning, the strong irrational emotions, the testimonial inexperience, of jurors . . . *that human* nature, in the same factors, *will always be with us*.' In short Wigmore envisaged a permanent role for the law of evidence in promoting truth 'by guarding the jury from the overweening effect of certain kinds of evidence' (250) and the three controlling policies of evidence of undue prejudice, of unfair surprise and of confusion of issues (272).
45. *Principles* at 6–7, 791–2, 924ff.
46. 1 *Treatise*, s.8a, 8c,; *Textbook*, Ch. 1; cf. 28 *A.B.A.J.* 23 (1942).
47. 924. Cf. 1 *Treatise*, s.26; 7 id., s.2034.
48. 925.
49. Ibid.
50. Wigmore draws heavily on Stephen, Best and Gulson in the ensuing analysis. Cf. 1 *Treatise*, s.27.
51. 928.
52. See above, 70–1.
53. 929–30.
54. 930.
55. Ibid.
56. See now 1 *Treatise*, (Tillers rev.), ss.8b and c.
57. For example E. M. Morgan (1940) at 791 (in respect of hearsay). For references to recent historical discussions of the history and origins of the rules, see 1 *Treatise* (Tillers' rev.) at 26–7n, 606n.

Notes to pages 158–161 237

58. *Principles*, 932; cf. 1 *Treatise*, s.10.
59. *Principles*, 936–7. The discussion of the bearing of the Science on Hearsay is particularly interesting (942).
60. 923–46.
61. 1 *Treatise*, s.3.
62. Ibid.
63. *Treatise*, vols. 4–7.
64. *Treatise*, vol. 8.
65. *Principles*, 945.
66. 946.
67. See especially ss.2483–97, 2565. On judicial notice see above, 230 n.30, 31.
68. See below, 176–7.
69. 'The rules of Admissibility have nothing to say concerning the weight of evidence when once admitted. The relative weight of circumstantial and testimonial evidence, therefore, does not present itself in this place.' (1 *Treatise*, s.26; cf s.2034, 3 *Ill L. Rev.* 477.) In Wigmore's view, questions of weight fall almost exclusively within the domain of the science. He cites Bentham in this context.
70. Above, 125; cf. 1 *Treatise*, s.26.
71. *Textbook*, 13; cf. 1 *Treatise*, s.1.
72. On the detective's point of view, see *Principles*, Appendix v.
73. 1 *Treatise*, ss.4–6. This point has been expanded and strengthened in the recent revision of the volume, but the reviser acknowledges that '[t]he discussion of the use of evidentiary rules in these disparate proceedings does not purport to be comprehensive'. He continues: 'Wigmore understood that the problem of the use of rules of evidence in various non-jury proceedings is a matter of theoretical and practical significance . . . . He generally strongly emphasized the connection between the rules of evidence and trial by jury . . . . Wigmore, however, may have been groping towards a broader view of the law of evidence.' The crucial point is surely that such a broader view of the *subject* of evidence and proof in the common law world today would treat jury trials as exceptional, rather than as paradigms of all types of proceeding. See further, Twining (1984).
74. Especially ss.7a, 17, 18.
75. *Textbook*, 13; cf. id., 16–19.
76. The 'disparate proceedings' dealt with in the *Treatise* include a number of administrative and other proceedings that might be considered to fall outside the scope of 'adjudication'.
77. 'The Rules of Extrinsic Policy (privileges of silence, of various sorts) have no relation to the scientific principles of proof. They frankly exclude good evidence on other grounds of policy which are supposed to override the policy of obtaining all useful evidence.' (*Principles* at 945.) This is surely over-simple.
78. Wigmore emphasizes that the rules are largely judge-made, artificial deviations from a system of free proof. He saw the main weaknesses of the system lying not so much in the substance of the rules (although some needed changing) as in the attitudes of lawyers and judges, and their tendency to abuse them. The crucial points of difference from Bentham are the ideas that the common law of evidence by and large does promote

238 *Notes to pages 161–163*

rectitude of decision and that the ultimate test of any reform of this branch of the law is its acceptability to the legal profession (see below, n.93). See further Wigmore's restatement of his views in 'Jury Trial Rules of Evidence in the Next Century', Reppy (1937).

79. On the failure of the Federal Rules to integrate the rules and the science, see 1 *Treatise* (Tillers rev.) at 450ff.
80. *Textbook*, 5; cf 1 *Treatise*, s.8.
81. 1 *Treatise*, 8c.
82. See Roalfe (1977) *passim*.
83. 25 *A.B.A.J.* 380 (1939).
84. See especially E. M. Morgan (1940); (1944); (1956) at 36ff, 49–53, 60. Other differences between Wigmore and Morgan are explored by Tillers in 1 *Treatise* (Tillers rev.), *passim*, especially at 718ff (conditional relevancy) and 1113ff (inference upon inference). Other major points of difference involve judicial notice and presumptions.
85. Relations may, however, have cooled during the period of the Model Code when Wigmore was at loggerheads with the A.L.I. as well as with Morgan.
86. 26 *A.B.A.J.* 476 (1940); 28 *A.B.A.J.* 23 (1942). For accounts of the code project, including the disagreements and difficulties, see A.L.I. *Model Code of Evidence* (1942), Introduction; C. A. Wright and K. W. Graham, 21 *Federal Practice and Procedure*, ss.5001–6 (1977). A useful overview of attempts to codify the law of evidence in the United States is to be found in R. Lempert and S. Saltzburg (1977), at 1191–1200. The differences between Wigmore and Morgan are in some ways analogous to the differences between Samuel Williston and Karl Llewellyn over the Uniform Commercial Code, discussed in Twining (1973) at 286–91.
87. 26 *A.B.A.J.* 476 (1940); See also Clark in 24 *J. Am. Judic. Soc.* 121–2 (1940). On the background to Clark's views, see J. H. Schlegel (1979) at 495ff.
88. 26 *A.B.A.J.* at 477.
89. See above at 68–9.
90. 28 *A.B.A.J.* 25; cf. A.L.I. *Model Code of Evidence* (1942), Introduction (discussions by William Draper Lewis and Edmund Morgan).
91. 26 *A.B.A.J.* 476–7 (1940); 28 *A.B.A.J.* 23 (1942).
92. 26 *A.B.A.J.* 476; see further n.87 above.
93. Id., 476–7. The postulates were: (1) the object should not be a restatement but to formulate the best rule that the Bench and Bar will probably accept and use; (2) the rules should constitute a complete code; (3) the code should avoid terms that are complex, novel and unfamiliar to Bench and Bar; (4) the code should be concrete rather than abstract and the rules should be 'only *guides*, not *chains*, – *directory*, not *mandatory* – and therefore to forbid the review of the Trial Court's rulings, except in extreme instances'; (5) all repeals of existing rules should be expressly stated in the code; (6) comments should be reserved for interpretation and should not supplement the text. (1940), 476–7.
94. 26 *A.B.A.J.* 455 (1940); Morgan's statement seems somewhat disingenuous, for the differences between him and Wigmore were far-reaching, as

Notes to pages 163–164 239

Wigmore made clear in his article in 28 *A.B.A.J.* 23 (1942). In fact the Model Code of Evidence was never adopted by any jurisdiction, although it had some influence, both negative and positive, on later exercises in codification. (S. Saltzburg and K. Redden (1982), 2–4). Professor Tillers comments that it 'undoubtedly foundered not only because of substantive objections to the proposed Code, but also, it seems, because of the conservatism of the legal profession, which seems disinclined to effect or is incapable of effecting any such radical reconstruction of judicial factfinding processes . . . . If the Federal Rules of Evidence are any measure, it seems clear that the experts in evidence have lost their capacity or willingness even to consider any fundamental revisions of factfinding procedures in order to more adequately, fairly, humanely and efficiently meet the demands of this society for procedural justice.' 1 *Treatise* (Tillers rev.) at 458.) Cf. Lempert and Saltzburg, op. cit., at 1193ff; Wright and Graham, (1977) at s.5005, pp. 85ff. See further Morgan (1961).

95. 28 *A.B.A.J.* at 28 (1942).
96. Twining (1973) at 287–90.
97. Op. cit., n.56.

(viii) THE LEAD BALLOON

1. Research in standard bibliographical sources and in the Wigmore Papers at Northwestern Law School revealed the following: at least five reviews of the 1913 edition; sixteen reviews of the 1931 edition; and twelve reviews of the 1937 edition. Of these the most interesting are by Charles C. Moore, 20 *Case and Comment* 432 (1913); E. R. Thayer, 27 *Harv. L. Rev.* 692 (1914); G. M. Whipple, 5 *J. Crim. Law and Criminology* (1914); E. M. Morgan, 31 *Col. L. Rev.* 1229 (1931); Joseph J. Hutcheson, 17 *A.B.A.J.* 817–19 (1931); Z. Chafee, 80 *U. Pa. L. Rev.* 319 (1931); W. Seagle, 24 *J. Crim. Law and Criminology* 621 (1933); Charles Morse, 9 *Can. Bar. Rev.* 455 (1931), also 15 *Can. Bar. Rev.* 824 (1937); Thomas E. Atkinson and Raymond M. Wheeler, 30 *Michigan L. Rev.* 1352 (1932); Lyman Wilson, 17 *Cornell L.Q.* 529 (1931–2), also 23 *Cornell L.Q.* 509 (1937–8); W. G. Hale, 26 *Ill. L. Rev.* 711 (1932); K. Fenning, 20 *Georgetown L.J.* 403 (1931–2); P. Bruton, 38 *W. Va. L.Q.* 98 (1931); H. M'Kechnie, 47 *Scottish Law Rev.* 294 (1931); Lord Justice Wright (as he then was) 24 *A.B.A.J.* 478 (1938); Patrick Browne, 54 *L.Q.R.* 592 (1938); W. Clark, 26 *Georgetown L.J.* 1092 (1938); M. Ladd, 23 *Iowa L.R.* 440 (1938); C. McCormick, 32 *Ill. L. Rev.* 767 (1937–8); W. H. Wicker, 15 *Tenn. L. Rev.* 404 (1938). There were several notices in European journals which were generally favourable without being analytical. Certain general patterns emerge from the reviews: almost all are favourable; some are very enthusiastic; several praise Wigmore's originality and persistence; the main dissents relate to the value of charts and symbols and his treatment of psychological aspects; remarkably little is said about its potential use in the classroom, and it is notable that hardly anyone recommended it for adoption in law schools.
2. Wigmore Papers, Northwestern. The same source reveals that Wigmore also received some encouragement from such well-known figures as

240 *Notes to pages 164–172*

Huntington Cairns (Wigmore to Little Brown, 28 April 1932); Arthur T. Vanderbilt, (see also 1933 *Am. L.S. Rev.* at 908); and Dean Ayres, who tried out the book as a course book at Michigan on at least one or two occasions. What is more striking is the lack of expressions of interest outside the often rather stilted praise of the reviews. There are a few enquiries and requests for permission to use extracts in the surviving correspondence, but apart from numerous exchanges with Little Brown, the rest is silence.

3. Wigmore Papers, Northwestern.
4. The three main exceptions known to me are: (a) the research of David Schum and Ann Martin, on which see especially Schum and Martin, (1982); (b) Professor Terence Anderson and, more recently, Professor Tom Ewald have made regular use of Wigmore's chart method in teaching at the University of Miami; (c) the author, who has used parts of the *Principles*, including the chart method, in teaching in several law schools in the United Kingdom and the United States.
5. Correspondence with Little Brown, Wigmore Papers, PLB.
6. Apart from the reviews the main exceptions are Roalfe, Schum (especially 1982) and Anderson and Twining (1984).
7. See n.1 above.
8. See n.2 above.
9. Correspondence with Little Brown. Huntington Cairns wrote to Wigmore saying that he had heard that the *Principles* was 'extensively used' in philosophy departments, specifically mentioning Johns Hopkins and Brown. (Wigmore to Little Brown, 28 April 1932. Wigmore Papers).
10. Northwestern Law School Bulletins.
11. See further Twining (1984b).

Chapter 4: The contemporary significance of Bentham and Wigmore

1. J. F. Stephen (1876), Introduction, p. xxii.
2. A series of statutes passed after 1872 made the accused a competent witness in respect of specific charges, but it was not until the Criminal Evidence Act, 1898 that this was transformed into a general principle, which was still subject to a few exceptions.
3. Stephen (1876) at xxii–xxiii.
4. 'Ideology' is here used in the neutral sense of 'the manner of thinking characteristic of a class or an individual' (O.E.D.). Bentham, like Marx, saw professional ideology as mystifications masking sinister class interests.
5. Sydney Smith (1825), 367.
6. Halévy (1955), 376–403.
7. David Lieberman, 'Jeremy Bentham's midlife crisis' (unpublished paper, University College London, 1983).
8. The theme of Bentham as a worthy opponent is developed in Twining (1984a).
9. See Twining (1973a).
10. Hart (1982), 21, 39.
11. See, however, Maguire (1963) at 460.
12. Weinstein and Berger (1975).

Notes to pages 172–181 241

13. Cited in American D.N.B.; the source is probably an unpublished manuscript by Kocourek entitled 'Recollections of a Great Scholar and Superb Gentleman', which I failed to trace in the Wigmore Papers at Northwestern.
14. Bienen (1983).
15. *Principles* (3rd edn), 5.
16. See generally, Twining (1984).
17. Id.
18. Above at 125ff, and below at 179ff. See further Anderson and Twining (1984).
19. See Appendix.
20. See above at 11.
21. See generally Twining (1984b).
22. Id.
23. See above, 12ff.
24. Twining (1983a) and (1984).
25. See further Twining (1984c).
26. Id.

Appendix – Wigmore's method: a Personal Evaluation

1. This is a condensed version of a longer appraisal in Anderson and Twining (1984).
2. Cohen (1977) and (1980); for a bibliography see Twining (1983) at 156–7.
3. There has been no sustained critique of the Chart Method in print. The three lines of criticism discussed in the text are those that have been most commonly advanced to me by colleagues and students in private discussions. I am particularly indebted to M. Abu Hareira, Terry Anderson, Sir Richard Eggleston, John Jackson, and Peter Tillers for clarifying some of these issues.
4. See above at 237n.
5. *Principles*, 46, discussed above.
6. Anderson and Twining, op. cit., Some of this terminology has been borrowed from Cohen (1977). Most of the relations are illustrated by Wigmore's own chart of *Commonwealth* v. *Umilian*, *Principles* at 872ff.
7. Discussed above at 143ff; see generally Young (1923); Twining 'Anatomy of a Cause Célèbre' (forthcoming).
8. Schum and Martin (1982); Abu Hareira (1984).
9. Cohen (1977), Ch. 4. In many cases separate facts in issue are not independent: for example, the probandum that it was X who caused Y's death is not independent of the probanda that Y is dead and that his death was caused by a human act. Cf. id., 61ff.
10. Id., 58–60. Cohen sensibly concentrates on civil cases; however, the question does arise, both in theory and in practice, whether seemingly trivial or minor doubts relevant to different facts in issue can be combined to constitute a reasonable doubt.
11. Id., 59.
12. Id., 267.

242 *Notes to pages 181–185*

13. Eggleston (1983), 35–7. Eggleston analyses the interesting case of *Morrison* v. *Jenkins* (1949) 60 C.L.R. 626 (the 'Whose Baby?' case), but treats it as an example of a chain of inferences. A Wigmore chart would show that the structure of the argument was more complex than that.
14. For example 1 *Treatise*, s.2498.
15. See above at n.6.
16. Cohen (1977), 60.
17. Id. at 94.
18. Ibid.
19. Id., 93.
20. Eggleston (1980), 678, 679. See also Eggleston (1983), Chs. 12 and 14.
21. For example *Principles*, 43.
22. Cohen (1977), 69–70, criticized by Eggleston (1983) at 261.
23. Cohen, Ch. 6.
24. Id., 269.
25. Eggleston (1983), 39.
26. 79 Pac. 2d. 948 (1938).
27. 1 *Treatise*, 438.
28. Eggleston (1983), 39ff. There are difficulties with both the Pascalian and the Baconian solutions to the problem of catenate inferences. Neither seems to reflect actual practice, which may operate in a more differentiated way, insofar as it is consistent, than any general formula can catch. The Baconian notion of 'cascaded inferences' seems to exclude consideration of many items of evidence that are in practice treated as having probative force: the application of the multiplication rule or of a version of Bayes theorem seems to make doubt too transitive, especially to 'holists' and intuitionists, for one difficulty with both Baconian and Pascalian criteria is that both appear to involve treating individual items of evidence in isolation from other items. These issues are explored sensitively by Schum (1982) and Tillers without producing conclusive answers.
29. See above at 54ff.
30. Op. cit., Ch. 13.
31. See Eggleston at 82–4, Appendix I, *et passim*; Schum (1982), and Tillers in Wigmore 1 *Treatise* (Tillers rev.) at 1011ff.
32. The subject is currently being explored by Abu Hareira (1984). For brief discussions see Wigmore, 1 *Treatise* (Tillers rev.), s.37; Schum (1982).
33. See, for example, Jeans (1975); Mauet (1980).
34. For example Bennett and Feldman (1981).
35. On coherence, see MacCormick (1978) at 106–8, 119ff. *et passim*.
36. *Principles*, 859.
37. Wigmore, 1A *Treatise* (Tillers rev.), 986n.; discussed at length, id., s.37.
38. On the argument about hard data, see L. Tribe (1971). Tribe is not necessarily a 'holist' in the sense used in the text.
39. See the discussion of the ideas of Judge Weinstein, Charles Nesson and others in Wigmore, 1 *Treatise* (Tillers rev.), s.37.1, especially at 1006ff.
40. Dworkin (1977), Ch. 4. Both Wigmore and Dworkin are proponents of a rationalist work ethic. Serious analysis involves hard work, but hard work has its rewards.

41. See generally Anderson and Twining (1984); Schum and Martin (1982).

Bibliography

(*Note:* For more comprehensive listings of works by and about Bentham and Wigmore, see *The Bentham Newsletter* (1978–ꞏ) and K. Schwerin, 'John Henry Wigmore: an Annotated Bibliography', 75 *Northwestern L. Rev.* Supplement (1981). Evanston.)
(Unless otherwise indicated the dates refer to the year of first full publication.)

Bentham

1776 *A Fragment on Government* (ed. J. H. Burns and H. L. A. Hart). London, *CW*, 1977 (abbreviated as *Fragment*).

1789 *Introduction to the Principles of Morals and Legislation* (eds. H. L. A. Hart and J. H. Burns). 1st edn, London, *CW*, 1970 (PML).

1790 *Draught of a Code for the Organization of the Judicial Establishment in France.* iv. *works* 285–406.

1791 *Essay on Political Tactics* (revised edn). London, ii *works* 299–373.

1808 *Scotch Reform.* London, v *works* 1–53; 2nd edn, 1811 (a considerable portion of this work survives unpublished in UC) (*SR*).

1813 *Swear Not At All*: containing an exposure of the inutility and mischievousness, as well as antichristianity, of the ceremony of an oath. London, v *works* 187–229. (SNAA).

1817 *A Table of the Springs of Action* (ed. Amnon Goldworth). London, *CW*, 1983.

1821 *The Elements of the Art of Packing*, as applied to special juries, particularly in cases of libel law. London, v *works* 61–186 (written 1809).

1821a *Three Tracts relative to Spanish and Portuguese affairs*; with a continual eye to English ones. *London,* viii *works* 463–85.

1823 *Traité des preuves judiciaires*, Ouvrage extrait de MSS de M. Jeremie Bentham, jurisconsulte anglais, par Et. Dumont. 2 vols, Paris. (*Traité*).

1824 *The Book of Fallacies* (ed. Bingham). London, ii *works* 375–487; reprinted sub. nom. *The Handbook of Political Fallacies* (ed. H. Larrabee), New York, 1962.

1825 *A Treatise on Judicial Evidence* (anon. trs. of Dumont's *Traité des preuves judiciaires*). London (*Treatise*).

1827 *Rationale of Judicial Evidence*, specially applied to English practice (ed. J. S. Mill). 5 vols, London, vi *works* 188ff; vii *works*, whole volume (1-end). (*RJE*).

Bibliography 245

1830 *Equity Dispatch Court Proposal*. London. Longer version, iii *works* 297–317.
1830a *Constitutional Code*, vol 1; extended version (ed. Richard Doane), London, ix *works* 1–662. Vol. 1, extensively revised (eds. F. Rosen and J. H. Burns), Oxford, *CW*, 1983.
1832 *Lord Brougham Displayed*. London, v *works* 549–612.
1837 *Principles of Judicial Procedure* (ed. Richard Doane). ii *works* 1–188 (*PJP*).
1837–43 *An Introductory View of the Rationale of Evidence for the use of Non-lawyers as well as Lawyers* (ed. James Mill, *circa* 1810). First published in vi *works* 1–187 (*IV*).
    Anarchical Fallacies; being an examination of the declarations of rights issued during the French Revolution, omitted from *The Book of Fallacies* and first printed in English in ii *works* 489–534 (*AF*).
1932 *Bentham's Theory of Fictions* (*see* Ogden (1932), below).
1973 *Bentham on Torture* (two hitherto unpublished mss. on torture; *see* W. L. and P. E. Twining (1973), below).

Wigmore

1892 *Materials for the Study of Private Law in Old Japan* (ed. and trs.). 4 vols, Tokyo.
1899 S. Greenleaf, *A Treatise on the Law of Evidence*, vol. 1 (16th edn ed. J. Wigmore), Boston.
1904–5 *A Treatise on the system of Evidence in Trials at Common Law*. Boston.
1909 'Professor Muensterberg and the Psychology of Testimony', 3 *Ill. L. Rev.* 399.
1913 'The Problem of Proof', 8 *Ill. L. Rev.* 77.
1913a *The Principles of Judicial Proof as given by Logic, Psychology and General Experience and Illustrated in Judicial Trials*. Boston.
1914 *Lyrics of a Lawyer's Leisure*. Chicago.
1923 *The Rational Basis of Legal Institutions* (eds. Wigmore and Kocourek). Cambridge, Mass.
1923a *A Treatise on the Anglo-American System of Evidence in Trials at Common Law* (2nd edn). Boston.
1927 'The Sacco-Vanzetti Verdict'. Boston Transcript, 25 April.
1927a 'The Sacco-Vanzetti Verdict — A Reply' (to Frankfurter). Boston Transcript, 10 May.
1928 *A Panorama of the World's Legal Systems*. 3 vols, Washington.
1931 *The Principles of Judicial Proof* (2nd edn). Boston.
1935 *A Students' Textbook of the Law of Evidence*. Brooklyn.
1936 *A Panorama of the World's Legal Systems* (revised edn). Washington.
1937 *The Science of Judicial Proof* (3rd edn of *Principles*). Boston.
1937a 'Jury-trial Rules of Evidence in the Next Century', in 1 *Law: A Century of Progress 1835–1935* 347 (ed. Reppy). New York.
1940 *A Treatise on the Anglo-American System of Evidence in Trials at Common Law* (3rd revised edn). Boston.
1941 *A Kaleidoscope of Justice*. Washington.
1942 'The American Law Institute Code of Evidence: a Dissent', 28 *A.B.A.J.*

246 *Theories of Evidence*

23.
1977– *Law and Justice in Tokugawa Japan*. Tokyo.
1983 1 *Treatise* (P. Tillers rev.). Boston.

General

Abu Hareira, M. A. (1982) 'James Glassford and the Holistic Approach to Judicial Fact-finding'. Unpublished paper, Warwick.
(1984) 'A Holistic Approach to the Analysis and Examination of Evidence in Anglo-American Judicial Trials'. Unpublished thesis, Warwick.
American Law Institute (1939) 'American Law Institute Undertakes Code of Evidence', 25 *A.B.A.J.* 380.
(1942) *Model Code of Evidence*. Philadelphia.
Anderson, Terence and William Twining (1984) *Analysis of Evidence*. Tentative edn, Miami.
Appleton, John (1860) *The Rules of Evidence Stated and Discussed*. Philadelphia.
Archbold, J. F. (1822) *A Summary of the Law Relative to Pleading and Evidence in Criminal Cases*. London (40th edn, ed. S. Mitchell, 1979).
Arnold, G. F. (1913) *Psychology Applied to Legal Evidence* (2nd edn). Calcutta. (1st edn 1906).
Atiyah, P. S. (1980) *Accidents, Compensation and the Law* (3rd edn). London.

Bahmueller, C. (1981) *The National Charity Company*. Berkeley, California.
Bain, Alexander (1882) *James Mill. A Biography*. London.
Ball, V. (1961) 'The Moment of Truth; Probability Theory and Standards of Proof', 14 *Vand. L. Rev.* 807.
Barnes, David W. (1983) *Statistics as Proof*. Boston.
Bathurst, J. (1761) *The Theory of Evidence*. Dublin (later incorporated in Buller, q.v.).
Beale, J. H. (1905) Review of Wigmore's *Treatise* (1st edn), 18 *Harv. L. Rev.* 478.
Bennett, W. Lance and Martha Feldman (1981) *Reconstructing Social Reality in the Courtroom*. London.
Bentham, J., see separate bibliography.
Berger, Peter and Thomas Luckmann (1967) *The Social Construction of Reality*. London.
Best, William M. (1844) *A Treatise on Presumptions of Law and Fact*. London.
(1849) *A Treatise on the Principles of the Law of Evidence*. London (8th English edn, ed. J. M. Lely, 1893).
Bienen, Leigh G. (1983) 'A Question of Credibility: John Henry Wigmore's Use of Scientific Authority in section 924a of the Treatise on Evidence', 19 *Calif. Western L. Rev.* 235.
Binder, David and Paul Bergman (1984) *Fact Investigation*. St Paul.
Black, Max (1952) *Critical Thinking*. Englewood Cliffs, N.J.
Blackstone, William (1765–9) *Commentaries on the Laws of England* (1st edn). 4 vols, Oxford.
Bok, Sissela (1978) *Lying*. New York and London.
Bonnier, E. (1843) *Traité theorique et pratique des preuves* (2nd edn 1852). 2 vols

Paris.

Bowring, Sir John (1843) *Memoirs of Bentham* (in x *works* 1).

Brougham, Henry (1871) *Life and Times of Henry, Lord Brougham*. 3 vols, London.

Buller, Sir Francis (1772) *An Introduction to the Law Relative to Trials at Nisi Prius*. London (see Bathurst).

Burns J. H. (1966) 'Bentham and the French Revolution', 16 *Transactions of the R. Hist. Soc.* (5th series) 95.

Burrill, Alexander M. (1856) *A Treatise on the Nature, Principles and Rules of Circumstantial Evidence, especially of the Presumptive Kind, in Criminal Cases*. New York.

Cairns, Huntington (1935) *Law and the Social Sciences*. London.

Campbell, Enid and Louis Waller, eds. (1982) *Well and Truly Tried*. Monash, Melbourne.

Centennial History of the Harvard Law School, 1817–1917. (1918) Cambridge, Mass.

Chadbourn, J. W. (1962) 'Bentham and the Hearsay Rule – a Benthamic View of Rule 63(4)c of the Uniform Rules of Evidence', 75 *Harv. L. Rev.* 932.

Chafee, Z. (1931) Review of Wigmore's *Principles*, 80 *U. Pa. L. Rev.* 319.

Chamberlayne, Charles F. (1908) 'The Modern Law of Evidence and its Purpose', 42 *American L. Rev.* 757.

(1911–16) *A Treatise on the Modern Law of Evidence*. 5 vols, Albany, N.Y.

Christian, Edward (1819) *A Vindication of the Criminal Law and the Administration of Public Justice in England*. London.

Clark, Charles (1940) 'Dissatisfaction with Piecemeal Reform', 24 *Jo. Am. Judic. Soc.* 121.

Clifford, Brian R. and Ray Bull (1978) *The Psychology of Person Identification*. London.

Cockburn, J. S., ed. (1977) *Crime in England, 1550–1800*. London.

Cocks, R. (1983) *Foundations of the Modern Bar*. London.

Cohen, L. Jonathan (1977) *The Probable and the Provable*. Oxford.

(1980) 'The Logic of Proof', (1980) *Crim. L. Rev.* 91.

(1983) 'Freedom of Proof', in Twining, ed. (1983), 1.

Cook, Charles M. (1981) *The American Codification Movement: a Study in Antebellum Reform*. Westport, Conn.

Coons, Jack (1964) 'Approaches to Court-induced Compromise – the Uses of Doubt and Reason', 58 *Northwestern L. Rev.* 750.

Corbin, A. L. (1914) 'The Law and the Judges', *Yale Rev.* 234.

Cowen, Zelman and Peter Carter (1956) *Essays in the Law of Evidence*. Oxford.

Criminal Law Revision Committee (1972) *Eleventh Report: Evidence (General)*. Cmnd. 4991. London. (CLRC Report).

Cross, Sir Rupert (1979) *Evidence* (5th edn). London (1st edn 1958).

Cullison, Alan (1969) 'Identification by Probabilities and Trial by Arithmetic', 6 *Houston L. Rev.* 471.

Damaska, M. (1973) 'Evidentiary Barriers to Conviction and Two Models of Criminal Procedure', 121 *U.Pa. L. Rev.* 506.

Davis, K. C. (1964) 'An Approach to Rules of Evidence for Non-jury Cases', 50

248 *Theories of Evidence*

A.B.A.J. 723.

Denman, Thomas (1824) Review of Dumont's *Traité des Preuves Judiciaires*, 40 *Edinburgh Review* 169–207.

Dinwiddy, J. R. (1975) 'Bentham's Transition to Political Radicalism', 36 *Jo. Hist. Ideas* 683.

Dworkin, Ronald (1977) *Taking Rights Seriously*. London.

(1981) 'Principle, Policy, Procedure', in *Crime, Proof and Punishment, Essays in honour of Sir Rupert Cross*. London.

Eekelaar, John (1984) *Family Law and Social Policy* (2nd edn). London.

Eggleston, Sir Richard (1983) *Evidence, Proof and Probability* (2nd edn). London (1st edn 1977).

(1983a) 'Generalizations and Experts', in Twining, ed. (1983), 22.

Ehrenzweig, Albert (1971) *Psychoanalytic Jurisprudence*. Leiden.

Eisenberg, M. (1976) 'Private Ordering Through Negotiation', 89 *Harv. L. Rev.* 637.

Empson, William (1828) Review of Bentham's *Rationale of Judicial Evidence*, 48 *Edinburgh Rev.* 457–520.

(1843) Review of Bowring's *Memoirs of Jeremy Bentham*, 78 *Edinburgh Rev.* 460–516.

Esmein, A. (1913) *History of Continental Criminal Procedure* (trs. Simpson). Boston.

Evans, Sir W. D. (1803) *A General View of the Decisions of Lord Mansfield in Civil Cases*. 2 vols, London.

(1806) *Notes on Pothier on Obligations*. London (see Pothier).

Everett, Charles W. (1931) *The Education of Jeremy Bentham*. New York.

Feeley, M. (1979) 'Pleading Guilty in Lower Courts', 13 *Law and Soc. Rev.* 461.

Fenning, K. (1931–32) Review of Wigmore's *Principles* (2nd edn). 20 *Georgetown Law Jo.* 1092.

Finkelstein M. O. (1978) *Quantitative Methods in Law*. New York and London.

Fortescue, Sir J. (1545–46) *De Laudibus Legum Angliae*. London (ed. S. B. Chrimes, 1942, Cambridge).

Frank, Jerome (1970) *Courts on Trial* (ed. E. Cahn). New York (1st edn 1949).

Fried, Charles (1978) *Right and Wrong*. Cambridge, Mass.

Fuller, Lon (1978) 'The Forms and Limits of Adjudication', 92 *Harv. L. Rev.* 353.

Gault, Robert H. and Delton T. Howard (1925) *Outline of General Psychology*.

(1943) 'Memories', Wigmore Papers. Northwestern University, Chicago.

Gilbert, Sir Jeffrey (1754) *The Law of Evidence*. Dublin (3rd. edn 1769, London).

Glassford, James (1820) *An Essay on the Principles of Evidence and Their Application to Subjects of Judicial Inquiry*. Edinburgh and London.

Gobbi, Claire and William Twining (1981) *Adjective Law* (Report to Executive Committee of the Bentham Project). Unpublished, London.

Gorphe, F. (1927). *La Critique du Temoignage*. Paris.

Grasserie, R. de la (1912) *De la Preuve au civil et au criminel en droit français et dans les legislations étrangères*. Paris.

Greenleaf, Simon (1843) *A Treatise on the Law of Evidence*. Boston.
  (1899) 16th edn, ed. J. H. Wigmore (vol 1), J. Harriman (vols 2 and 3). Boston.
Greer D. S. (1971) 'Anything but the Truth', 11 *Brit. Jo. Crim.* 131.
Gross, Hans (1879, trs. Kallen 1911) *Criminal Psychology*. London.
Gulson, J. R. (1923) *Philosophy of Proof* (2nd edn). London (1st edn 1905).

Hacking, Ian (1975) *The Emergence of Probability*. Cambridge.
Hale, Sir M. (1682) *Pleas of the Crown*. London.
Halévy, Elie (1928) *The Growth of Philosophic Radicalism* (trs. Mary Morris). London; id. (1955), preface A. D. Lindsay. Boston.
Harrison, Ross (1983) *Bentham*. London.
Hart, H. L. A. (1953) 'Definition and Theory in Jurisprudence', Inaugural Lecture, Oxford.
  (1960) 'Bentham', British Academy Lecture. London.
  (1961) *The Concept of Law*.Oxford.
  (1968) *Punishment and Responsibility*. Oxford.
  (1973) 'Bentham and the Demystification of the Law', 36 *M.L.R.* 2, reprinted in Hart (1982), Ch. 1.
  (1982) *Essays on Bentham*. Oxford.
  (1983) *Essays in Jurisprudence and Philosophy*. Oxford.
Hay, Douglas (1975) 'Property, Authority and the Criminal Law', in Hay *et al.* (1975).
Hay, Douglas *et al.* (1975) *Albion's Fatal Tree*. London.
Hawkins, W. (1776) *A Treatise of the Pleas of the Crown*. London.
Hazard, G. (1965) 'Rationing Justice', 8 *Jo. Law and Ecs.* 1.
Helvetius (1759) *De l'Esprit or Essays on the Mind and its several Faculties*. London.
Hempel, Carl (1965) *Aspects of Scientific Explanation*. New York.
Heydon, J. D. (1975) *Cases and Materials on the Law of Evidence*. London.
Himmelfarb, Gertrude (1968) *Victorian Minds*. London.
Holdcroft, David (1983) 'Relevance in Legal Proof', in Twining, ed. (1983).
Holdsworth, Sir W. S. (1903–38) *A History of English Law* (misc. editions). 17 vols, London (*HEL*).
  (1925) *Sources and Literature of English Law*. Oxford.
Honoré, A. M. (1981) 'Alfred Rupert Neale Cross, 1912–80', in *Crime, Proof and Punishment*. London.
Hume, David (1888) *A Treatise on Human Nature* (ed. A Selby-Bigge). Oxford.
Hume, L. J. (1981) *Bentham and Bureaucracy*. Cambridge.
Hutchins, Robert M. (1933) 'Autobiography of an Ex-Law Student', *A.A.L.S.* Reprinted in Hutchins (1936).
  (1936) *No Friendly Voice*. Chicago.
Hutchins, Robert M. and Donald Slesinger (1928) 'Some Observations on the Law of Evidence – Memory', 28 *Col. L. Rev.* 432.
  (1928a) 'Some Observations on the Law of Evidence – the Competency of Witnesses', 37 *Yale L.J.* 1017.
  (1929) 'Some Observations on the Law of Evidence – State of Mind to Prove an Act', 38 *Yale L.J.* 283.
  (1929a) 'Some Observations on the Law of Evidence – State of Mind in

250 *Theories of Evidence*

Issue', 29 *Col. L. Rev.* 147.
  (1929b) 'Some Observations on the Law of Evidence – Consciousness of Guilt', 77 *U. Pa. L. Rev.* 725.
  (1929c) 'Some Observations on the Law of Evidence – Family Relations', 13 *Minn. L. Rev.*675.

Inbau, Fred E. (1981) 'John Henry Wigmore and Scientific Evidence', 75 *Northwestern L. Rev. Supp.* 8.

James, George (1941) 'Relevance, Probability and Law', 29 *Calif. L. Rev.* 689.
James, M. H. (ed.) (1974), *Bentham and Legal Theory* (reprinted from the Northern Ireland Legal Quarterly xxiv (1973)). Belfast.
Jeans, James (1975) *Trial Advocacy*. St Paul.
Jesse, F. Tennyson (1934) *A Pin to See the Peepshow*. London.
Jevons, W. Stanley (1877) *The Principles of Science; A Treatise on Logic and Scientific Method* (Reprinted 1907), London.
Jolowicz, H. F. (1948) 'Was Bentham a Lawyer?' in Keeton and Schwarzenberger, eds (1948), 1.
Jones, Burr W. (1896) *The Law of Evidence in Civil Cases* (1st edn). San Francisco. (5th edn 1958; supp. 1968).

Kamenka, E. *et al.*, eds. (1978) *Law and Society*. London.
Keeton, George W. and Georg Schwarzenberger, eds. (1948) *Jeremy Bentham and the Law*. London.
Keeton, George and Roy Marshall (1948) 'Bentham's Influence on the Law of Evidence', in Keeton and Schwarzenberger, eds. (1948).
Kocourek, Albert (1943) 'Recollections of a Great Scholar and Superb Gentleman', Unpublished. Wigmore Papers, Northwestern.
Kyburg, H. and H. Smokler (1964) *Studies in Subjective Probability*. New York.

Langbein, John H. (1974) *Prosecuting Crime in the Renaissance: England, Germany, France*. Cambridge, Mass.
  (1978) 'The Criminal Trial Before the Lawyers', 45 *U. Chi. L. Rev.* 263.
  (1983) 'Shaping the Eighteenth Century Trial: a View from the Ryder Sources', 50 *U. Chi. L. Rev.* 1.
Lempert, Richard and Stephen Saltzburg (1977) *A Modern Approach to Evidence*. (2nd edn 1982). St Paul.
Lerminier, E. (1830) *Introduction Générale à l'Histoire du Droit*. Brussels.
Letwin, S. R. (1965) *The Pursuit of Certainty*. Cambridge.
Livingston, Edward (1833) *Introductory Report to the Code of Evidence*. New Orleans.
  (1873) *Works* (ed. S. P. Chase). 2 vols, New York.
Llewellyn, Karl N. (1950) 'Law in Our Society: a Horse Sense View of the Institution of Law'. Unpublished course materials, Chicago. (Extracts are printed in Twining (1973)).
  (1951) *Bramble Bush* (2nd edn). New York (1st edn 1930).
Lloyd-Bostock, Sally M. (1981) 'Psychology and the Law', 8 *Brit. Jo. L. Soc.* 1.
Lloyd-Bostock, Sally M. and Brian Clifford, eds. (1983) *Evaluating Witness Evidence*. Chichester.

Bibliography 251

Locke, J. *An Essay Concerning Human Understanding* (ed. P. H. Nidditch, 1975, Oxford).
Long, Douglas (1981) *The Manuscripts of Jeremy Bentham, a Chronological Index* (Bentham Project). London.
Lyons, David (1973) *In the Interest of the Governed*. Oxford.

Macaulay, S. (1963) 'Non-contractual Relations in Business', 28 *Am. Soc. Rev.* 55.
McCormick, Charles T. (1972) *Handbook of the Law of Evidence* (ed. Cleary *et al.*). St Paul (1st edn 1954).
MacCormick, D. N. (1978) *Legal Reasoning and Legal Theory*. Oxford.
   (1984) 'Coherence in Legal Justification', in W. Krawietz *et al.*, eds. *Theorie der Normen*.Berlin.
McKelvey, John J. (1897) *Handbook of the Law of Evidence*. St Paul (3rd edn 1924; 5th edn 1944).
MacNally T. (1802) *Treatise on Evidence in Criminal Cases*. Dublin.
MacNeil, Ian (1974) 'The Many Futures of Contract', 47 *Calif. L. Rev.* 691.
Mack, Mary P. (1962) *Jeremy Bentham, An Odyssey of Ideas 1748–1792*. London.
   ed. (1969) *A Bentham Reader*. New York.
McRae, R. F. (1973) *Introduction to J. S. Mill's System of Logic*. Toronto.
McGonagall, William (1981) *Poetic Gems*. London.
McGowen, R. (1983) 'The Image of Justice and the Reform of the Criminal Law in Early Nineteenth Century England', 32 *Buffalo L. Rev.* 89.
Maguire, John M. (1947) *Evidence: Common Sense and Common Law*. Chicago.
   (1963) 'Wigmore – Two Centuries', 58 *Northwestern L. Rev.* 456.
Maguire, John M. *et al.* (1973) *Cases and Materials on Evidence*. Mineola, New York (successor to Morgan and Maguire, q.v.).
Mannheim, Karl, (1936) *Ideology and Utopia*. London.
Manning, D. (1968) *The Mind of Jeremy Bentham*. London.
Mauet, Thomas A. (1980) *Fundamentals of Trial Technique*. Boston.
Michael, Jerome (1948) *Elements of Legal Controversy*. New York.
Michael, Jerome and Mortimer Adler (1925) 'Real Proof', 5 *Vand. L. Rev.* 344.
   (1931) *The Nature of Judicial Proof*: an Enquiry into the Logical, Legal and Empirical Aspects of the Law of Evidence (Tentative edition, privately printed). New York.
   (1934) 'The Trial of an Issue of Fact', 34 *Col. L. Rev.* 1224.
Midgley, T. S. (1975) 'The Role of Legal History', 2 *Brit. Jo. Law and Soc.* 153.
Mill, John Stuart (1873) *Autobiography*. London (1924 edn, ed. H. Laski, London).
   (1973) *A System of Logic, Ratiocinative and Inductive* (*Collected Works*, ed. J. M. Robson *et al.*) Toronto (1st edn, 1843, London).
Millar, Robert W. (1952) *Civil Procedure of the Trial Court in Historical Perspective*. New York.
Moenkmoeller, O. (1930) *Psychologie und Psychopathologie der Aussage*. Heidelberg.
Moenssens, André, Ray E. Moses and Fred Inbau (1973) *Scientific Evidence in Criminal Cases*. Mineola, New York.
Montesquieu, Charles Louis de Secondat, Baron de (1823) *De L'Esprit des Lois* (trs. Nugent). 2 vols, London.

252 Theories of Evidence

Montrose, James L. (1968) *Precedent in English Law and Other Essays* (ed. Hanbury). Shannon.

Moore, Charles C. (1907) 'Yellow Psychology', 11 *Law Notes* 125.

(1908) *A Treatise on Facts; or the weight and value of evidence*. Long Island, New York.

Moore, W. Underhill (1923) 'Rational Basis of Legal Institutions', 23 *Col. L. Rev.* 609.

Morgan, Edmund M. *et al.* (1927) *The Law of Evidence*; some proposals for its reform. New Haven.

Morgan, Edmund M. (1939) (*see* American Law Institute) 25 *A.B.A.J.* 380.

(1940) Review of Wigmore's *Treatise*, 20 *Boston U. L. Rev.* 776–93.

(1944) 'Judicial Notice', 57 *Harv. L. Rev.* 269.

(1956) *Some Problems of Proof under the Anglo-American System of Litigation*. New York.

(1961) 'Some Practical Difficulties Impeding Reform of the Law of Evidence', 14 *Vanderbilt L. Rev.* 725.

Morgan, Edmund and John M. Maguire (1934) *Cases on Evidence*. Mineola, New York. (later edns. 1942, 1951, 1957, 1965; *see also* Maguire et al.)

(1937) 'Looking Backward and Forward at Evidence', 50 *Harv. L. Rev.* 909.

Morison, W. L. (1978) 'Frames of Reference for Legal Ideals', in Kamenka *et al.* (1978).

Mueller, Gerhard O. (1969) *Crime, Law and the Scholars*. London.

Muensterberg, Hugo (1908) *On the Witness Stand, Essays on Psychology and Crime* (reprinted 1923). New York.

Napley, Sir David (1983) *The Technique of Persuasion* (3rd edn). London.

Nesbitt, George L. (1934) *Benthamite Reviewing*. New York.

Nokes, G. D. (1967) *An Introduction to Evidence* (4th edn). London (1st edn 1952).

O'Barr, W. (1982) *Linguistic Evidence*. London and New York.

Ogden, C. K. (1932) *Bentham's Theory of Fictions*. London.

Ogden, C. K. and I. A. Richards (1923) *The Meaning of Meaning*. London.

Osborn, Albert S. (1926) *The Problem of Proof*. Newark, N.J.

(1929) *Questioned Documents*. Albany, N.Y.

(1937) *The Mind of the Juror as Judge of the Facts*. Albany, N.Y.

Paley, Archdeacon W. (1809) *Principles of Moral and Political Philosophy*. London (1st edn 1785).

Parekh, B., ed. (1974) *Jeremy Bentham, Ten Critical Essays*. London.

Peake, Thomas (1801) *A Compendium of the Law of Evidence*. London (reprinted 1979).

Peczenik, Alexander (1979) 'Cumulation and Compromise of Reasons in the Law', in Pennock and Chapman (1979), 176.

Pennock, J. Roland and John W. Chapman, eds. (1979) *Compromise in Ethics, Law and Politics* (Nomos xxi). New York.

Perelman, Ch. (1963) *The Idea of Justice and the Problem of Argument* (trs. Petri). London.

Bibliography 253

Perelman, Ch. and L. Olbrechts-Tyteca (1971) *The New Rhetoric*. Notre Dame.

Phillimore, John G. (1850) *The history and Principles of the law of evidence, as illustrated by our social progress*. London.

Phillipps, Samuel M. (1814) *A Treatise on the Law of Evidence*. London (9th edn 1843).

Phillips, Teresa Constantia (1750) *An Apology for the Conduct of Mrs T. C. Phillips*. 3 vols, London.

Phipson, S. L. (1892) *The Law of Evidence*. London (13th edn 1982).

Plamenatz, J. (1958) *The English Utilitarians* (2nd edn). Oxford.

Plucknett, T. F. T. (1929) *A Concise History of the Common Law*. London (5th edn 1956).

Pollock, F. (1899) Review of Thayer (1898), 15 *L.Q.R.* 86.

Posner, Richard (1977) *Economic Analysis of Law* (2nd edn). Boston.

Postema, Gerald (1977) 'The Principle of Utility and the Theory of Procedure: Bentham's Theory of Adjudication', 11 *Georgia L. Rev.* 1393.

(1983) 'Facts, Fictions and Law: Bentham on the Foundations of Evidence', in Twining, ed. (1983), 37.

(forthcoming) Bentham and the Common Law Tradition. Oxford.

Pothier, R. J. (1761) *Traité des Obligations*. Paris.

(1806) *A Treatise on the Law of Obligations, or Contracts* (trs. Evans). London (*see also* W. D. Evans).

Pound, Roscoe (1943) 'John Henry Wigmore', 56 *Harv. L. Rev.* 938.

Prest, W., ed. (1981) *Lawyers in Early Modern Europe and America*. London.

Quine, W. V. and J. S. Ullian (1970) *The Web of Belief*. New York.

Quintillianus, Marcus Fabius (80–90 A.D.) *De Institutione Oratoria*.

Rabelais, F. (1542–52) *Gargantua and Pantagruel* (trs. T. Urquhart, 1913). London.

Radzinowicz, Sir Leon (1948–63) *A History of English Criminal Law and its Administration from 1750*. 4 vols, London.

(1957) *Sir James Fitzjames Stephen*. London.

Ram, James (1861) *A Treatise on Facts as Subjects of Enquiry by a Jury*. London.

Rawls, John (1972) *A Theory of Justice*. Cambridge, Mass. and Oxford.

Reppy A., ed. (1937) *Law: A Century of Progress*. 3 vols, New York.

Roalfe, William R. (1977) *John Henry Wigmore, Scholar and Reformer*. Evanston.

Roebuck, J. A. (1828) 'Bentham's Rationale of Judicial Evidence', 9 *Westminster Rev*. 198–250.

Romilly, Sir Samuel (1786) *Observations on a Late Publication, Entitled Thoughts on Executive Justice*. London.

(1810) *Observations on the Criminal Law of England*. London.

Roscoe, Henry (1827) *A Digest of the Law of Evidence on the Trial of Actions at Nisi Prius*. London.

(1835) *A Digest of the Law of Evidence in Criminal Cases*. London (16th edn 1952).

Rosen, Fred (1983) *Jeremy Bentham and Representative Democracy*. Oxford.

Royal Commission on Criminal Procedure (Philips, 1981). Cmnd. 8092. London.

Ryan J. P. (1981) 'Adjudication and Sentencing in the Misdemeanour Court:

254 Theories of Evidence

The Outcome is the Punishment', 15 *Law and Soc. Rev.* 79.

Saks M. J. and R. Hastie (1978) *Social Psychology in Court*. New York.

Saltzburg, Stephen A. and Kenneth Redden (1982) *Federal Rules of Evidence Manual* (3rd edn). Charlottesville.

Schlegel, John H. (1979) 'American Legal Realism and Empirical Social Science: From the Yale Experience', 28 *Buffalo L. Rev.* 459.
(1980) 'American Legal Realism and Empirical Social Science: The Singular Case of Underhill Moore', 29 *Buffalo L. Rev.* 195.

Schum, David (1979) 'A Review of the Case against Blaise Pascal and Others', 77 *Michigan L. Rev.* 446.

Schum, David and Ann Martin (1982) 'Formal and Empirical Research on Cascaded Inference in Jurisprudence: A Summary', 17 *Law and Soc. Rev.* 105.

Scott, Kenneth (1975) 'Two Models of Civil Process', 27 *Stanford L. Rev.* 937.

Shapiro, Barbara (1983) *Probability and Certainty in Seventeenth Century England*. Princeton.

Sidgwick, H. (1883) *Fallacies; a view of logic from the practical side*. London.

Simpson, A. W. B., ed. (1984) *A Biographical Dictionary of the Common Law*. London.

Smith, Sydney (1825) Review of the *Book of Fallacies*, 42 *Edin.Rev.* 367.

Starkie, Thomas (1824) *Law of Evidence and Digest of Proofs in Civil and Criminal Proceedings*. London. (4th edn 1853).

Steintrager, James (1977) *Bentham*. London.

Stenning, Anders (1975) *Bevisvärde*. Uppsala.

Stephen, Sir James Fitzjames (1872) *The Indian Evidence Act*, with an Introduction on the Principles of Judicial Evidence. Calcutta.
(1879) *A Digest of the Law of Evidence*. London (12th edn 1948).
(1890) *A General View of the Criminal Law of England* (2nd edn). London.

Stephen, Sir Leslie (1895) *Life of Sir James Fitzjames Stephen*. London.
(1900) *The English Utilitarians*. 3 vols, London.

Stevens, R. B. (1983) *Law School*. Chapel Hill and London.

Stone, Julius (1964) *Legal System and Lawyers' Reasonings*. London.

Sully, James (1892) *The Human Mind*. London.

Summers, R. S. (1974) 'Evaluating and Improving Legal Processes – A Plea for Process Values', 60 *Cornell L. Rev.* 1.
(1984) *Lon Fuller*. London and Stanford.

Swift, Chief Justice Zephaniah (1810) *A Digest of the Law of Evidence in Civil and Criminal Cases* (reprinted 1972). Conn.

Tapp, June (1980) 'Psychological and Policy Perspectives on the Law: Reflections on a Decade', 36 *Jo. Social Issues* 165.

Taylor, J. Pitt (1848) *Treatise on the Law of Evidence*. London (12th edn 1931).

Teitelbaum, L. E., G. Sutton-Barbere and P. Johnson (1983) 'Evaluating the Prejudicial Effect of Evidence', *Wisc. L. Rev.* 1147.

Thayer, James B. (1889) 'Presumptions and the Law of Evidence', 3 *Harv. L. Rev.* 141.
(1892) *Select Cases on Evidence at the Common Law*. Cambridge, Mass. (3rd edn 1925; *see also* Morgan and Maguire).

Bibliography 255

(1898) *A Preliminary Treatise on Evidence at Common Law.* (reprinted 1969). Boston.

(1927) *Legal Essays.* Cambridge, Mass.

Thomas, P. A., ed. (1982) *Law in the Balance.* Oxford.

Thompson, E. P. (1973) *Whigs and Hunters* (Revised edn 1977). London.

Tillers, Peter (1983), *see* Wigmore bibliography.

Trankell, Arne (1972) *Reliability of Evidence.* Stockholm.

ed. (1982) *Reconstructing the Past.* Stockholm.

Trautman, H. (1952) 'Logical or Legal Relevancy – A Conflict in Theory', 5 *Vand. L. Rev.* 385.

Tribe, H. Laurence (1971) 'Trial by Mathematics: Precision and Ritual in Legal Process', 84 *Harv. L. Rev.* 1329.

Tullock, G. (1980) *Trials on Trial.* New York.

Twining, William L. (1964) *The Place of Customary Law in The National Legal Systems of East Africa.* Chicago.

(1973) *Karl Llewellyn and the Realist Movement.* London (reprinted 1985).

(1973a) 'The Way of the Baffled Medic', 12 *J.S.P.T.L.* (N.S.) 348.

(1975) 'The Contemporary Significance of Bentham's Anarchical Fallacies', 61 *A.R.S.P.* 325.

(1980) 'Goodbye to Lewis Eliot. The Academic Lawyer as Scholar', 15 *J.S.P.T.L.* (N.S.) 2.

(1980a) 'Debating Probabilities', 2 *Liverpool Law Rev.* 51.

(1982) 'The Rationalist Tradition of Evidence Scholarship', in Campbell and Waller (1982), 211.

ed. (1983) *Facts in Law.* Weisbaden.

(1983a) 'Identification and Misidentification: Redefining the Problem', in Lloyd-Bostock and Clifford (1983).

(1984) 'Evidence and Legal Theory', Inaugural Lecture, University College, London. 47 *M.L.R.* 261.

(1984a) 'Why Bentham?', *The Bentham Newsletter* No.8, 34.

(1984b) 'Taking Facts Seriously', 34 *Jo. Leg. Ed.* 22.

(1984c) 'Some Scepticism About Some Scepticisms', 11 *Brit. Jo. Law and Society* I, 137; II, 285.

(1984d) 'John Henry Wigmore', in Simpson (1984).

(1985) 'Bentham on Evidence: the Modern Reader', *Bentham Newsletter*, forthcoming.

(1985a) 'Anatomy of a Cause Célèbre: the Evidence in Bywaters and Thompson'. Unpublished lecture, London.

Twining, William and David Miers (1982) *How To Do Things With Rules* (2nd edn). London.

Twining, W. L. and P. E. Twining (1974) 'Bentham on Torture' (including 2 Bentham mss), in James (1974), 39.

Voltaire (1772) 'Essai sur les Probabilités en fait de Justice', *Oeuvres complètes* xxviii (1879). Paris.

Walls, H. J. (1974) *Forensic Science.* London.

Weinstein, Jack B. (1966) 'Some Difficulties in Devising Rules for Determining Truth in Judicial Trials', 66 *Col. L. Rev.* 223.

Weinstein, Jack B. and Margaret A. Berger (1975–) *Weinstein's Evidence,*

256   Theories of Evidence

Commentary on Rules of Evidence for the United States Courts and for State Courts. 7 vols, New York.

Wellesley Index to Victorian Periodicals 1824–1900 (1966). Toronto and London.

Wellman, Francis L. (1903) *The Art of Cross-examination*. New York (4th edn 1936).

Whipple, Guy M., ed. (1910) *Manual of Mental and Physical Tests*. Baltimore.

Wigmore, J. H., see separate bibliography.

Wigmore, J. H. and A. Kocourek, eds. (1923) *The Rational Basis of Legal Institutions*. Cambridge, Mass.

Williams, Glanville (1963) *Proof of Guilt* (3rd edn). London.
(1979) 'The Mathematics of Proof', (1979) *Criminal Law Rev*. 297 and 320.

Wills, W. (1838) *An Essay on the Rationale of Circumstantial Evidence*. London. (later edns: *An Essay on the Principles of Circumstantial Evidence*.)

Wittman, D. (1974) 'Two Views of Procedure', 3 *Jo. Leg. Studies* 249.

Wright, Charles A. and K. Graham (1977) *Federal Practice and Procedure* (vol. 21). St Paul.

Wright, Lord (1938) Review of Wigmore's *Science of Judicial Proof*, 24 *A.B.A.J.* 478.

Yarmey, A. D. (1979) *The Psychology of Eyewitness Testimony*. New York.

Young, Filson, ed. (1923) *The Trial of Frederick Bywaters and Edith Thompson*. London.

Zeisel, Hans (1971) 'And then there were None: The Diminution of the Federal Jury', 38 *U. Chi. L. Rev.* 710.

Zuckerman, Adrian (1983) 'Relevance in Legal Proceedings', in Twining, ed. (1983), 145.

Index

abundance, principle of, 90
accomplices, 103
act-utilitarianism, 73
adjective law, 19, 21, 23, 51, 169; aims of, 117; ideology in, 81–8; reform of, 100, 167–8; and substantive law, 72–3, 83, 88–9
adjudication: assumptions about, 14–15; Bentham's theory of, 47–8; concentration on, 116, 118, 176–7, 221 n.11; rationalist model of, 15–17, 117; non-jury, 117, 160–1, 176, 221 n.11
Adler, Mortimer, 115, 147, 148–9, 152, 172, 230 n.11
administration, principle of, 8
admissions, 159
adversary system, 115, 116; and exclusionary rules, 158; and inference, 127–9
alibi evidence, 37–8
American Bar Association Journal, The, 163
American Law Institute, 162
Ames, James B., 7
analysis and synthesis, 131, 133, 184
analytic rules, 159
Anderson, Terence, 135, 240 n.4
anti-nomian thesis, 8, 66–75, 102, 168
Appleton, John, 3, 4
Arnold, G. F., 114, 139
artificial identification of interests, principle of, 77–8
assertion, 129, 180
atomism, 3, 149, 180, 183–4
atrocity, 33
Austin, John, 4
authentication of evidence, 40–1
autoptic proference, *see* real evidence
auxiliary probative policy, rules of, 159
Ayer, A. J., 18, 176, 184
Ayres, George, 165, 240 n.2

Bacon, Francis, 16, 26, 114, 176
Ball, V., 152

Bathurst, J., 2
Bayes' theorem, 183, 242 n.28
Beale, Joseph Henry, 111
Beard, Charles, 141–2
Beccaria, Cesare, 26
belief: nature of, 20, 138, 200 n.1; and probative force, 131–3
Bentham, Jeremy: on abuse of power, 20–1; on adjudication, 47–8; attention to procedure, 23–5; biography, 189; compared with Wigmore, 17, 18, 108, 113, 115–18, 161, 163–4; consistency of, 24–5, 51–2; and *Edinburgh Review*, 100–7; editing of works by, 39–40, 82, 218 n.56; epistemology of, 19–20, 26, 29, 145; influence of, 3–4, 6, 167–71; and the legislator, 24–5, 121, 173; on the Natural System, 51–2; origins of views, 19–22; personal biases of, 89; political views of, 82; on probability, 144, 183; and psychology, 18, 25, 26, 29–30, 79 198–9; and reform, 3–4, 24–5, 100–1, 114, 115, 167–8; and scholarship, 2–3, 17–18; sources for, 25–7; and subjectivism, 29, 55–6, 58–64; on substantive law, 72–3, 75; on technicality, 21–2, 41–4, 66–70, 71–5, 138, 170, 194 n.14; values of, 99–100; alluded to, 121, 144, 145, 155, 156
WORKS: *The Book of Fallacies*, 168, 218 n.56; *Constitutional Code*, 23, 25, 169; *Court of Lords Delegates*, 23, 25; *The Elements of the Art of Packing*, 25; *An Essay on Political Tactics*, 23; *An Introduction to the Principles of Morals and Legislation*, 25, 29–30; *An Introductory View of the Rationale of Evidence*, 43, 45, 64, 87, 97; *Judicial Establishment in France*, 23; *Principles of Judicial Procedure*, 23, 92, 94, 97, 169; *Rationale of Judicial Evidence*, 3, 4, 17, 24, 25, 27–47, 66–9, 79–82, 84, 87, 90, 97, 100, 106–7, 108, 116, 167, 169, 171, 175, 195 n.28; *Scotch Reform*,

258   Index

23, 25, 45, 48–51, 74, 92, 94, 95, 169; *The Table of the Springs of Action*, 25, 29–30; *Traité des preuves judiciaires*, 100, 107; *Treatise on Judicial Evidence*, 3, 43, 45, 97–8

Bergman, Paul, 145

Bertillon, Alphonse, 114

Best, William, 3, 4, 59, 177, 221 n.6; *A Treatise on Presumptions of Law and Fact*, 59, 114, 122

best evidence rule, 1–2, 12, 151

Binder, David, 145

Blackstone, William, 82, 83, 95, 96, 115

Bonnier, E., 55–6

Bowring, Sir John, 193 n.3; *Memoirs of Jeremy Bentham*, 106

Brougham, Henry, 3, 4, 100, 106, 107

Buller, Sir Francis, 2; *An Introduction to the Law Relative to Trials at Nisi Prius*, 1, 3, 26

burdens of proof, 6, 67, 98, 102, 159

Burke, Edmund, 1

Burrill, Alexander M.: *A Treatise on the Nature, Principles and Rules of Circumstantial Evidence*, 114

Bywaters and Thompson, 134, 143–4, 150–1, 181, 233 n.49

Cairns, Huntington, 240 n.2

California Evidence Code (1965–7), 9

Cartwright, Major J., 27, 82

casually written documents, 38, 40

catenate inferences, *see* evidentiary chain

Chadbourn, J. W., 40

Chafee, Zechariah, 7, 9, 141, 164

Chamberlayne, Charles, 7, 12, 122–3; *A Treatise on the Modern Law of Evidence*, 8, 114

chart method, 45, 113, 119, 125–35, 146, 148, 165, 173–5, 179–86

checks and balances, 82–3, 101

circumstantial evidence, 32–8, 65, 120, 127, 159

Civil Evidence Acts (1968, 1972), 10

civil-libertarianism, 86, 101–2, 104, 108, 170–1

Clark, Charles E., 162–3

codes of evidence, 9, 114

codification, 1, 12, 112, 115

cognitive competence, 231 n.20

cognitive consensus, 146

Cohen, Jonathan, 12–13, 56, 57, 176, 178, 181, 182, 183, 231 n.20, 233 n.44

coherence, 184

common sense: as basis of external

securities, 30–1; and the Natural System, 48, 52; *see also* general experience

competency, rules of, 1, 4, 67, 101, 102, 159, 167–8

compound propositions, 181–2

compromise, 93, 94–5

computers, 113, 135, 212

confessions, 32, 102, 138

conjunction, 180–1, 182

convergence, 182

corroboration, 129, 180, 182

counter-evidence, 37, 54–5, 65; *see also* infirmative suppositions

courtroom, conditions of, 119, 120, 139–40, 157, 173, 176

Criminal Law Revision Committee, 10

criminals, 84

criminology, 135

Cross, Sir Rupert, 13, 116, 177; *Evidence*, 10, 112

cross-examination, 31, 48, 51, 115, 116, 138; and deception, 45; as security for makeshift evidence, 38–9, 40

Darrow, Clarence, 110

decision, grounds of, 49

deduction, 14, 25, 147

democratic authoritarianism, 82

denial, 129, 180

Denman, Thomas, 3, 4, 98–9, 215 n.62; review of Bentham's *Traité*, 100–6, 108

Descartes, René, 57

detection, 226 n.39

Dictionary of National Biography, The, 105, 193 n.3

direct evidence, *see* testimonial evidence

dispute settlement, 94, 212 n.27

doctrine of chances, 57–8

double-fountain principle, 51, 81

Dumont, Étienne, 3, 29, 35, 58, 59, 98, 103, 193 n.3, 200 n.1, 206 n.1; *Traité des preuves judiciares*, 100, 107

Dworkin, R., 242 n.40

Edinburgh Review, 13, 86, 100, 105, 106

education, legal, 165, 174, 185–6

Eggleston, Sir Richard, 181, 182, 183, 229–30 n.7

empiricism, 16, 18, 52, 125, 146, 176

Empson, William, 3, 211 n.11; review of Bentham, 106–8

enforcement of law, 23

Engels, Frederick, 79

English legal system, 51

Index 259

epistemology, *see under* knowledge
equality, principle of, 90
Evans, William David, 2, 3, 26
Everett, Charles, 193 n.3
evidence: concept of, defined, 126; as
  data, 133–4; in human activity, 51–2;
  kinds of, 120, 129, 131
evidence, rules of: and judicial proof,
  119–20, 124; psychological assumptions
  of, 137; and science of proof, 113–14,
  156–7, 158–61, 164, 166; scope of, 3, 6,
  7, 12, 162–3, 168
evidence, study of: Bentham's knowledge
  of, 26; and general theory, 113, 116,
  122–5, 151–2, 169–70, 172–3, 175–6;
  history of, 1–13, 114–15; homogeneity
  of, 13–18, 116; narrowness of, 176–7;
  rationalism of, 177–8; and Wigmore's
  Principles, 164–6, 171–3
Evidence Act (1843), 101
evidentiary chain, 35, 127, 142, 182–3,
  229 n.6, 242 n.28
evidentiary facts, 29, 121–2, 153
Ewald, T., 240 n.4
exclusionary rules: critique of, by
  Bentham, 28, 41–4, 67, 68–71, 72; and
  evidence curriculum, 166; as false
  security, 30; general theory of, 111;
  and judicial discretion, 69, 154; and
  jury, 6, 157, 158; and makeshift
  evidence, 39, 40; as mystification, 79,
  84, 86; need for, 100, 157–8, 160; as
  promoting rectitude of decision, 117;
  reform of, 107–8, 114; and relevancy,
  152, 153
expectations, 91
expense and delay, 92
experience: and artificial rules, 70, 71–2,
  155; as source of knowledge, 19–20, 26,
  29, 52, 145; as test of relevance, 68; *see
  also* general experience
explanation, 129, 180
expletive justice, 14, 93

factum probandum, 29, 32, 131, 142; and
  inferences, 33, 35, 126–9, 143–4;
  intermediate, 181–2, 183; and
  psychology, 138; and relevance, 68, 153
factum probans, 29, 32, 131; and
  inferences, 33, 35, 126–9, 143–4; and
  relevance, 68
fallacies, 46, 51, 79, 82–6, 170, 209 n.87,
  218 n.56
falsity and falsehood, 42, 101; confused
  with deception, 39; and oaths, 87; and

utility, 89–90; *see also* lying
Federal Rules of Evidence (1975), 9, 10–
  11, 112, 151–2, 155, 163
fee-gathering system, 41, 74, 75, 76, 77,
  79, 106
fictions, theory of: and common sense,
  52, 177; and delusion, 79; and ghosts,
  18, 19–20, 37; and probability, 60–3;
  and the technical system, 50
Filmer, Sir Robert, 27, 101
forensic psychology, 114, 115, 124, 139,
  140–1
forensic science, 114, 115, 119, 135,
  140–1
formality and liberty, 82–4
Fortescue, Sir J., 95
forthcomingness: of evidence, 47, 50,
  118; of witnesses, 28, 50, 74
'fox-hunter's reason', 85, 170, 212 n.34
Frank, Jerome, 17, 141–2, 177, 210 n.2
Frankfurter, Felix, 110
freedom of proof, rules of evidence as
  exceptions to, 12–13, 151, 170, 237
  n.78
free proof, 3, 12, 71
French Revolution, stimulus of, 23
Freud, Sigmund, 18
Fried, Charles, 89

Gaius, 26
Galton, H. B., 135
Gault, Robert, 136–7
genealogical facts, 86, 87
general evidence, 201 n.11
general experience, 14, 119, 144–6, 149,
  151; precedent as, 155
generalizations, 14, 119, 142–51
general scientific knowledge, 142–3
Gilbert, Lord Chief Baron, 12, 13, 16, 27,
  32, 56, 57, 116, 151, 177, 202 n.36, 206
  n.1; *The Law of Evidence*, 1, 2, 3, 4–5,
  64
Glassford, William, 2–3, 26
Gorphe, F., 114
graphology, 141, 166
Gray, John Chipman, 7, 219–20 n.12
Greenleaf, Simon, 112, 123, 124, 223
  n.17; *A Treatise on the Law of Evidence*,
  5, 112, 114, 122, 123
Gross, Alfred, 135
Gross, Hans, 114, 139, 140, 227 n.2
Gulson, J. R., 56, 115

Hale, Sir M., 26
Halévy, Elie, 27, 82, 169, 193 n.3

260 *Index*

harmony, social, 93, 94
Hart, H. L. A., 79, 171
Hartley, David, 18, 26
Hastings, Warren, 1
Haward, Lionel, 12
Hay, Douglas, 78
hearsay: admissibility of, 40; as makeshift evidence, 38, 39; rule concerning, 1, 161, 173
Hegel, G. W. F., 184
Heineccius, 26, 202 n.37
Hermosa, Judge Advocate, 209 n.81
Hohfeld, Wesley Newcomb, 164
holistic approach to evaluation of evidence, 3, 183–5, 226 n.35
Holmes, Oliver Wendell Jr., 7, 115, 141–2
humanitarianism, 96, 98
Hume, David, 26, 29, 64, 114
Hume, L. J., 24
Hutcheson, Judge J. C., 164
Hutchins, Robert Maynard, 115, 137, 227 n.17

ideology, 70, 81–8, 168
illegally-obtained evidence, 161
impossibility, 29, 35–8; *per se* and *si alia*, 38
improbability, 29, 35–8
Indian Evidence Act (1872), 4
indicative evidence, 39, 204 n.7
indolence, 75–6
induction, 16, 177, 231 n.17; and inference, 121, 129, 147; and probabilistic reasoning, 11–12, 14, 15, 56, 182
inferences: from circumstantial evidence, 33, 34, 35; and generalizations, 142–4, 146–9; inductive, 121, 125, 127–9; and precedent, 155; psychology of, 134–5; and rationality, 14; special, 33, 34; *see also* evidentiary chain
infirmative suppositions, 53–5, 58, 183, 201–2 n.20; *see also* counter-evidence
innocence, presumption of, 1, 95–8, 100, 102–4, 170
innocent, conviction of the, 70, 95–100, 102–5, 214–16
instructions: and authentication, 41; cautionary, 68, 71, 162; and makeshift evidence, 39, 40; as preferable to rules, 43–4, 67, 68, 117, 204 n.89; on weighing of evidence, 47
interests: and mystification, 79–82, 85, 88; sinister, of legal profession, 75–9,

84, 101, 104–5, 106–7; of suspects, 86; of witnesses, 42–3, 44, 101, 102
interrogation, 85, 115; faults of, 105; as security against incorrectness, 40; study of, 135, 138; and testimonial evidence, 31

James, George, 111, 147–8, 152, 155
James, William, 141–2
jargon and jargonozation, 50, 80–1, 107
Jesse, F. Tennyson: *A Pin To See the Peepshow*, 134
Jevons, W. Stanley, 114
Jousse, M., 202 n.37
Judge and Co., 28, 74, 108; defined, 76; and ideology, 81–2; and technical rules, 41, 50, 70–1, 76–9, 81, 104
judge-made law, 2, 3, 50, 81; and practical experience, 4, 115; and retroactivity, 72–3, 74–5; and technicality, 21–2, 75–6
judges: degree of persuasion, 65–6; discretionary powers of, 7, 69, 70, 74–5, 117, 163; errors of, 46; and ideology, 81–2; interests of, 28, 75–81, 88; and relevancy, 154; as responsible for decisions, 28, 48, 108; role of, 53, 111, 157, 220 n.21; and rules of evidence, 161–4; and securities against misdecision, 54
judicial notice, 159, 220 n.21
judicial organization, 27, 42, 168
judicial proof: and general experience, 145; and induction, 147; as a subject, 119–25, 172–3; *see also* science of proof
Jung, Carl, 18, 135
jury: as check on unpopular laws, 83; as constraint on reason, 7; and exclusionary rules, 6, 157, 158; and relevancy, 154; role of, 111, 220 n.21; *see also* adjudication
justice: and legal establishment, 41, 75, 79; pre-Norman, 46–7; and principle of security, 91
justification, 80
Justinian, 26

Kant, Immanuel, 89, 184
Keeton, George, 22
key-list, 127, 129–30, 131, 133–4, 146, 183
knowledge: assumptions about, 13–14; basis in experience, 19–20, 26, 29; theory of, 13–14, 107, 116, 125, 145, 175–6
Kocoureck, Albert, 165, 172, 230 n.11

Index 261

Langdell, Christopher Columbus, 7, 115
language: and fictions, 62–3; as
  instrument of knowledge, 19–20; legal
  abuse of, 80–1; ordinary, and
  adjudication, 50; ordinary, and
  measurement of persuasion, 57; *see
  also* jargon and jargonization
law and order, 86, 108
law as ideology, 78–9
Law Reform Committee, 10
law reports, 2, 115, 155
lawyers: abuse of language by, 80–1;
  handling of evidence by, 120; interests
  of, 76, 77, 78–9, 84, 85, 88, 106–7; and
  maximization of rationality, 118, 121,
  161; and technical devices, 80–1
legal experience, 4, 115, 155
legal fictions, 79–80
legal profession: Bentham's condemnation
  of, 3, 28, 100, 102–3, 104–5, 106–7,
  108, 116; and psychology, 135, 136–7,
  140, 211 n.109; and technical system,
  28, 41–2, 161–4, 168
legislator, tasks of, 24–5, 121, 173; and
  adjudication, 28–9, 46, 48, 51; and
  circumstantial evidence, 34; and formal
  rules, 67, 157; and instructions
  regarding evidence, 68, 117, 118; and
  judicial profit, 78; and legal
  mystification, 80; and makeshift
  evidence, 38; and maximizing
  trustworthiness, 30, 47; and pre-
  appointed evidence, 31–2; and
  separation of powers, 83
Lely, J. M., 59
liberty, safeguards of, 83–4
litigation: conditions of, 169; cost-benefit
  analysis of, 92–4; and scepticism, 149;
  and study of evidence, 176–7
Livingstone, Edward, 114
Llewellyn, Karl, 52, 110, 163, 231 n.19
Locke, John, 1, 5, 18, 26, 29, 52, 114,
  124; and improbability, 36–7; and
  persuasion, 64; and rationality, 16
Lockwood, J., 183
logic: application to analysis of evidence,
  134, 175; inductive, 14, 119, 125, 175,
  179; in proof, 120, 130–1, 146–7; as
  test of relevance, 68, 153; Wigmore's
  views on, 114, 116
logical processes: and direct
  circumstantial distinction, 33; in
  judicial proof, 118, 125, 126–34, 142,
  164–5

Lolme, J. C. de, 27, 82
lying, 28, 30, 39, 42, 45, 89–90; and fee-
  gathering system, 76; and
  mystification, 79, 81; *see also* falsity and
  falsehood

McCormick, Charles T., 9, 13, 112, 115,
  116
McKelvey, John, 7, 8, 122
Mackintosh, Sir James, 107
MacLuhan, Marshall, 186
Maguire, John, 7, 115; *Cases and
  Materials on Evidence*, 7–8
makeshift evidence, 39–40
mala fide suitors, 75, 76, 84
Mansfield, Lord, 2, 26
Marshall, James, 12
Marshall, Roy, 22
Martin, Ann, 240 n.4
Marx, Karl, 75, 79
materiality, 6, 153
mendacity-licence, 20, 49, 81, 87
Michael, Jerome, 115, 147, 148–9, 152,
  172, 230 n.11; *The Nature of Judicial
  Proof*, 9
Mill, James, 82, 193 n.3
Mill, John Stuart: on Bentham, 29, 45,
  59, 193 n.3, 218 n.56; empiricism of, 5,
  16, 18, 125, 146, 176, 184; *Principles of
  Logic*, 114, 221 n.6, 230 n.11; on
  thermometer of persuasion, 60; and
  utilitarianism, 4
Model Code of Evidence (1942), 9, 112,
  162–3
Montesquieu, C. L. de S., Baron de, 26,
  82, 83, 101; *L'Esprit des Lois*, 83
Montrose, James L., 55
Moore, Charles C., 164; *Treatise on Facts*,
  115, 155
Moore, Underhill, 228 n.46
Morgan, Edmund, 6, 7, 9, 111, 115, 117,
  162–3, 229 n.6; *Cases on Evidence*, 7
motives and sanctions, theory of, 30
Muensterberg, Hugo, 114, 135, 139, 140;
  On the Witness Stand, 135
mystification, 75, 76, 78–88

narrative method, 125–6, 131, 185–6
National Geographic Magazine, 110
natural reason, 7
Natural System of Procedure, 28–9, 47–
  52, 100, 168, 170; as absence of
  technical rules, 42, 48, 67; and judicial
  power, 74; as mitigating vexations, 93;
  and probative force, 66; reviews of,

262 *Index*

106; securities of, 53–4; and utility, 46
nemo tenetur maxim, 84
non-exclusion principle, 28, 47, 67–71, 72, 100, 102, 117; exceptions to, 99
non-jury trials, *see* adjudication
'nonsense pisteutics', 29, 64
nullification, principle of, 49, 80, 83

oaths, 20, 74, 86–7
official records, *see* pre-appointed evidence
Ogden, C. K., 19, 20; *The Meaning of Meaning*, 193 n.3
'old woman's reason', 84–5
ontological fictions, 63
'opinion trade, the', 81
orality of proceedings, 31, 48, 51
Osborn, Albert: *The Problem of Proof*, 115

Paley, Archdeacon, 26, 97, 100, 102; *The Principles of Moral and Political Philosophy*, 96
Panopticon, 24
pardon, 95, 213 n.45
Parole Evidence Rule, 159
Peake, Thomas, 2, 12; *A Compendium of the Law of Evidence*, 3, 26
Peczenick, Alexander, 212 n.38
People v. *Collins*, 10
Perelman, Chaim, 11
perjury, 20–1, 38–9, 86–7
persuasion, 29, 52; and circumstantial evidence, 35; degrees of, 53–66
Phillipps, Samuel M., 2, 3, 5; *A Treatise on the Law of Evidence*, 112
Phillips, T. C.: *An Apology for the Conduct of Mrs T. C. Phillips*, 21
Phipson, S. L.: *The Law of Evidence*, 114
pleadings, abuse of, 49
plus value, 153–4
Pollock, F., 4, 6
Postema, Gerald, 56, 60–2, 64, 73, 211 n.13
Pothier, R. J.: *Traité des Obligations*, 2, 26
Pound, Roscoe, 110
power, abuse of, 20–1, 37
practitioners: and Bentham, 171; and chart method, 174–5, 179, 185; and *Cross*, 10; and *Greenleaf*, 5; and Wigmore's *Principles*, 164, 165, 171, 173; and Wigmore's *Treatise*, 124, 171; *see also* lawyers
pre-appointed evidence, 31–2, 167–8; creation of, 39, 72–3, 87

precedents: and impossible facts, 37; and law of evidence, 1; and relevancy, 154–5
preferential rules, 159
prejudicial effect, 69, 152, 154, 231 n.20
presumptions, 67, 159
principal facts, *see factum probandum*
principles, search for, 1–2, 4–5, 12–13, 18
privilege(s), 99, 159, 162; against self-incrimination, 1, 43, 84, 86, 99, 111, 161; lawyer-client, 99, 102–5; marital, 99, 103; priest-penitent, 42, 99, 103; state secrets, 99; *see also* silence
probabilities: combining, 174, 180–3, 224 n.4, 242 n.28; and degrees of persuasion, 56–66; and inference, 14, 125; mathematical, 11, 14–15, 55–60, 181, 183, 184, 224 n.4; non-mathematical (Baconian), 11–12, 125, 144, 179, 181, 182–3; as ontological fiction, 63; and subjectivism, 55–6; and truth, 13, 53
probative force or value, 153; in adversary system, 128–9; assessment of, 43–4, 53–66, 122, 131–2, 138–9, 174; and atomism, 3; and general experience, 142, 144; and precedent, 155; and prejudicial effect, 152, 154; in *Rationale*, 29; and rules of weight, 71; and technical rules, 102; *see also* weighing of evidence
probative processes, 129, 173
procedural rights, 70, 72, 86, 91, 98–9, 100, 101–2, 103–4, 168
procedure: complexities of, and interests, 79; collateral ends of, 89, 91, 92; direct ends of, 23, 27, 47–8, 88, 91, 92, 93–5; importance of, 23–5, 118; in presentation of evidence, 158; mischiefs of, 194; systems of, 28
prophylactic rules, 159
propositions: evidence as, 131, 133, 186; relations between, 126–9, 131, 133, 175, 180–3
psychological facts, 38
psychology, 9, 12, 114, 120, 139–42; and chart method, 132–3, 134–5; of interaction in legal processes, 138; and persuasion, 29, 64; witness, 12, 119, 135–9, 198–9 n.107
psychometry, 139, 166
publicity, 28, 30, 31, 51; as security, 48, 70, 74, 170–1; and state secrets, 99
public opinion, 76–7, 78
punishment: mis-seated, 215 n.63; as

Index 263

security against falsehood, 40, 74, 87; and utility, 84–5, 97

quantitative rules, 159
quantum, rules of, 67, 71

Rabelais, François, 58
rationalism: aspirational, 17, 177, 178; complacent, 17, 47, 177, 178; optimistic, 17, 47, 132, 176, 177
rationality, 14, 16, 26, 177
real evidence, 33, 120, 220 n.21
rectitude of decision: as end of procedure, 47–8, 73, 117; and non-exclusion principle, 28, 70; and reconciliation, 95; as social value, 14, 15, 27, 91, 93–4, 99; and utility, 73, 89, 91, 104; and vexation, 45, 92
reforms: and Bentham, 3–4, 24–5, 100–1, 114, 115, 167–8; and Denman, 105–6; and legal profession, 107; and Wigmore, 156–7, 161–4
Reid, Thomas, 3
relative frequency statements, 148, 149
relevancy: defined, 29, 153–4, 234 n.15, 234 n.26; legal, 152–3, 154–5; logical, 6–7, 152–3, 155; minimal, 152–4; principle of, 5, 12, 14, 151, 154; and utility, 68, 69; Wigmore on, 111
religion, 86–8
remedies, 42
retroactivity, 72–3, 75
rhetoric, new, 11
rights, vindication of, 23, 94
rival assertion, 129, 180
rival-shop principle, 78
Roman Law, 26
Romilly, Sir Samuel, 96, 98, 100, 102, 106, 107, 214 n.57
Royal Commission on Criminal Procedure, 10
rule-scepticism, 66; see also anti-nomian thesis

sanctions: and mendacity, 20–1, 28, 40; tutelary, against crime, 98
Sacco-Vanzetti case, 110, 126
scepticism, 177–8
Schum, David, 134–5, 240 n.4
science: and commonsense, 146; views of, 116, 140–2, 156
Science of Legislation, 23
science of proof, 9, 141, 145; and chart method, 126; contemporary significance of, 164–6, 171–3; as

distinct from rules of evidence, 113–14, 124, 156–7, 158–61, 166; and everyday legal practice, 121
securities: exclusionary rules as, 70; internal and external, 30–1; and judicial power, 74; and legislation, 47; and makeshift evidence, 38–9, 40; against misdecision, 54; in natural system, 49, 53–4; publicity and simplicity as, 48; for trustworthiness of witnesses, 87
security, principle of, 73, 90–1, 99, 100, 108
security of community, 96
sentimental liberalism, 70, 82–6, 170, 208 n.67
shame, 74, 87
Sidgwick, H., 18, 114, 146; *Fallacies*, 230 n.11
silence, 32; rights to, 84, 99, 102, 105, 170, 209 n.83; see also privilege against self-incrimination
simplicity, 27; and democratic authoritarianism, 82; and formal rules, 71, 107; as security, 48
simplificative rules, 159
Slesinger, Donald, 115, 137
Smith, Sydney, 168
social value(s): conflict of, 14, 27, 91–2, 93–100, 117; of legal services, 104; truth as, 14, 16, 90–1
special experience, 145
special pleadings, 81
Stafford, Lord, 95
standards of proof, 13, 14, 45, 67, 95, 98, 102
standpoint, 25, 41, 118, 221–2 n.15, 226 n.37
Starkie, Thomas, 2, 3, 95; *Law of Evidence*, 5, 112, 114, 123
statistical frequency, 58
Stephen, Sir James Fitzjames, 4, 6, 7, 167–8; and codification, 12, 18, 114; *A Digest of the Law of Evidence*, 4; and relevance, 12, 151, 154
Stern, W., 135
Stewart, Dugald, 3
subjectivism, 55–6, 58–66, 132–3, 225 n.34, 226 n.35
subsistence, principle of, 90
substantive law, 72–3, 75, 88–9
sufficiency, 153, 154, 234–5 n.26
Sully, James: *The Human Mind*, 18
superfluous evidence, 68, 69
symbols, use of, 126, 130, 131, 165, 166, 179

264 Index

Taylor, J. P.: *Treatise on the Law of Evidence*, 5, 114, 122
technical prejudice, the, 88
technical rules, 41–4; and anti-nomian thesis, 66–75, 102; as artificial, 28–9; and circumstantial evidence, 34, 36; in nineteenth century, 21–2; practical value of, 3, 4, 106–7; reform of, 107–8; and weighing of evidence, 66–9, 71–2, 107
Technical System of Procedure, 48–51; Bentham's views on, 21–2, 28, 41–3; causes of, 75–82, 88, 104–5, 106–7, 168; devices of, 207 n.43; as ideal type, 51; and presumption of innocence, 97; and probative force, 66; and religion, 86
testimonial evidence, 29–31, 120, 122, 159; and arguments of impossibility, 37–8; belief in, 29, 33; evaluation of, and psychology, 135, 137–9; probative force of, 33, 65; self-serving, 45; shape of, 48; weighing of, 43, 44, 53–5
Thayer, James Bradley, 5–9, 12, 13, 111, 151, 158, 167; on *Greenleaf*, 123; and rationality, 16, 177; and relevancy, 151, 155; and search for principles, 18; students of, 122; and Wigmore, 112, 113, 124, 151–2; *A Preliminary Treatise on Evidence at the Common Law*, 6, 7, 114; *Select Cases on Evidence at the Common Law*, 7
thermometer of persuasion, 56–60
Thompson, Edward, 78
Tillers, Peter, 111, 112, 148, 152, 155, 184, 231–2 n.20, 232 n.21
torture, 85, 99
Trankell, Arne, 12
transitivity of doubt, 181, 183
Trautman, H., 147, 152
trials: as arena of judicial proof, 119; jury, 116, 160–1, 173, 176; in Wigmore's *Principles*, 124–5
trustworthiness: causes of, 29–30, 44, 118; and formal rules, 40–1; of kinds of evidence, 35; maximization of, 30–1; and probative force, 65; suspicion of, 53–4, 55
truth: correspondence theory of, 13, 16; value of, 89–91, 99, 108, 117, 170

ultimate principal facts, 52–3
uncertainty, situations of, 44–5, 159, 200
Uniform Rules of Evidence (1953), 9

United States, study of evidence in, 5–9, 10, 11
unoriginal evidence, 38, 40
utilitarianism: and common sense, 52; critique of, 104, 105; erosion of support for, 4, 168; and litigation, 93; recent invocation of, 10; and reform, 115
utility, principle of: and conflict of ends, 27, 45, 99–100, 104, 170; and exclusion of evidence, 68, 70; and judges, 25; and natural system, 46; and nullification, 83; and punishment, 97; and substantive law, 73–4, 88–9; and truth, 89, 90–1; and vexation, 92–3

Vanderbilt, Arthur T., 240 n.2
Veblen, Thorstein, 141–2
vexation, 14, 27, 48, 91–4, 211 n.18; direct and consequential, 92–3; and non-exclusion principle, 28; and rectitude of decision, 45–6, 89
Voltaire, 26

wagering analogy, 58–9, 203 n.51–3
weighing of evidence, 52–5; instructions for, 42, 47; legislation for, 28–9; without rules, 48, 66–9, 71–2, 108, 180; *see also under* probative force or value
weight, rules of, 34, 67, 69, 71–2, 107, 155, 180, 236 n.37
Weinstein, Jack B.: *Weinstein's Evidence*, 112, 172
Weld, H. P., 137
Wellman, Francis L.: *The Art of Cross-Examination*, 115
Wertheimer (psychologist), 135
Wigmore, John Henry: biography, 189–90; compared with Bentham, 17, 18, 108, 113, 115–18, 161, 163–4; epistemology of, 116, 145, 175–6; on exclusionary rules, 69, 70; influence of, 111–12, 122–4, 134–5, 171–6; and legal profession, 161–4, 168; personal qualities, 109–11; and philosophy, 230 n.11; and probabilities, 179, 224 n.4; and psychology, 114, 124, 139, 140–1; on role of law of evidence, 159; on science, 141–2; and Thayer, 6, 7, 8, 9, 151–2; alluded to, 2, 10, 13, 16, 32, 169
WORKS: *Lyrics of a Lawyer's Leisure*, 110; *A Panorama of the World's Legal Systems*, 110, 116, 166, 218 n.3; *The*

Principles of Judicial Proof, 112–13,
114, 116, 118, 119–22, 124–5, 126,
137–8, 140, 142, 145, 146, 147, 152,
153, 156, 158, 159, 161, 171–3, 175,
176, 179, 180; impact of, 164–6; 'The
Problem of Proof', 119; *A Student's
Textbook on the Law of Evidence*, 160,
161, 164, 169; *A Treatise on the System
of Evidence in Trials at Common Law*,
113, 121, 125, 135, 147, 151–2, 153,
156, 157, 158–9, 160, 161, 164, 166,
167, 176, 184; genesis of, 8, 122–4;
reception of, 111–12, 171–2,
219 n.9–12, 220 n.14
will: and judgement, 37; and rules, 67
Williston, Samuel, 7, 163
Wills, W.: *An Essay on the Rationale of
Circumstantial Evidence*, 114
Wright, Lord, 164
Wundt, Wilhelm, 135

Zeisel, Hans, 231 n.18